THE
REWARDS
OF
Prayer

—— *5 Books in 1* ——

THE REWARDS

OF

Prayer

—— *5 Books in 1* ——

R. A. TORREY

WHITAKER
HOUSE

Unless otherwise indicated, all Scripture quotations are taken from the King James Version (KJV) of the Holy Bible. Scripture quotations marked (RV) are taken from the Revised Version of the Holy Bible. Scripture quotations marked (NKJV) are taken from the *New King James Version*, © 1979, 1980, 1982, 1984 by Thomas Nelson, Inc. Used by permission. All rights reserved. Scripture quotations marked (NIV) are from the *Holy Bible, New International Version*®, NIV®, © 1973, 1978, 1984 by the International Bible Society. Used by permission. All rights reserved. Scripture quotations marked (NAS) are from the *New American Standard Bible*®, NAS®, © 1960, 1962, 1968, 1971, 1973, 1975, 1977 by The Lockman Foundation. Used by permission. (www.Lockman.org).

THE REWARDS OF PRAYER

5 Books in 1
(previously published under the title: *Prayer and Faith*)

ISBN: 978-1-60374-509-3
Printed in the United States of America
© 2002, 2012 by Whitaker House

Whitaker House
1030 Hunt Valley Circle
New Kensington, PA 15068
www.whitakerhouse.com

Library of Congress Cataloging-in-Publication Data

Torrey, R. A. (Reuben Archer), 1856-1928.
 [Prayer and faith]
 The rewards of prayer / by R.A. Torrey.
   p. cm.
 Summary: "In this collection of five of Torrey's teachings on Christian living, the author reveals how to prevail in prayer and be effective in soulwinning, as you come to an intimate understanding of God and His Word"--Provided by publisher.
 Originally published: Prayer and faith. c2002.
 ISBN 978-1-60374-509-3 (trade pbk.)
 1. Christian life--Congregational authors. I. Title.
 BV4501.3.T67 2012
 248.3'2--dc23
                    2012022372

2 3 4 5 6 7 8 9 10 11 🔳 20 19 18 17 16 15 14 13

Contents

Your Life in God

Contents

Introduction

New Christians need a book that will outline basic principles of their faith so they will enjoy complete success in their new life. Since I could not find such a book, I wrote one myself. This book aims to tell the new convert just what he needs to know most. I hope that pastors, evangelists, and other Christian workers will find it a good book to give young converts. I hope it will also prove helpful to many who have been Christians for a long time but have not made the headway they desire in their Christian life.

1
Beginning Right

Beginning the Christian life with a solid, correct foundation influences the success of the remainder of a Christian's life. However, if someone has started life with Jesus, yet is unsure of his foundation, it is simple for him to strengthen it with solid Christian principles.

Receive Jesus as Savior

We are told the right beginning for the Christian life in John 1:12, *"But as many as received him, to them gave he power to become the sons of God, even to them that believe on his name."* The right way to begin the Christian life is by receiving Jesus Christ. He immediately gives power to become a child of God to anyone who receives Him.

If the reader of this book was the most wicked man on earth, and then he received Jesus Christ, that very instant he would become a child of God. God promises this in the most unqualified way in the verse quoted above. No one can become a child of God any other way. No man, no matter how carefully he has been raised, no matter how well he has been sheltered from the vices and evils of this world, is a child of God until he receives Jesus Christ. We are *"children of God by faith in Christ Jesus"* (Gal. 3:26) and in no other way.

What does it mean to receive Jesus Christ? It means to accept Christ as all God offers Him to be for everybody. Jesus Christ is God's gift. *"For God so loved the world, that he gave his only begotten Son, that whosoever believeth in him should not perish, but have everlasting life"* (John 3:16).

Some accept this wondrous gift of God. Everyone who does accept this gift becomes a child of God. Many others refuse this wondrous gift of God, and everyone who refuses this gift perishes. They condemn themselves. *"He that believeth on him is not condemned: but he that believeth not is condemned already, because he hath not believed in the name of the only begotten Son of God"* (John 3:18).

Jesus Is Our Sin-Bearer

What does God offer His Son to be to us?

First of all, God offers Jesus to us to be our Sin-Bearer. We all have sinned. There is not a man or woman, a boy or girl, who has not sinned. *"Even the righteousness of God which is by faith of Jesus Christ unto all and upon all them that believe: for there is no difference: for all have sinned, and come short of the glory of God"* (Rom. 3:22–23). If any of us say that we have not sinned, we are deceiving ourselves and giving the lie to God. *"If we say that we have no sin, we deceive ourselves, and the truth is not in us....If we say that we have not sinned, we make him a liar, and his word is not in us"* (1 John 1:8, 10). Each of us must bear our own sin, or someone else must bear it in our place. If we were to bear our own sins, it would mean we must be banished forever from the presence of God, for God is holy. *"God is light, and in him is no darkness at all"* (1 John 1:5).

But God Himself has provided another to take responsibility for our sins so that we do not need to bear them ourselves. This Sin-Bearer is God's own Son, Jesus Christ, *"For he hath made him to be sin for us, who knew no sin; that we might be made the righteousness of God in him"* (2 Cor. 5:21).

When Jesus Christ died upon the cross of Calvary, He redeemed us from the curse of the law by being made a curse in our stead. *"Christ hath redeemed us from the curse of the law, being made a curse for us: for it is written, Cursed is every one that hangeth on a tree"* (Gal. 3:13). To receive Christ, then, is to believe this testimony of God about His Son, to believe that Jesus Christ did bear our sins in His own body on the cross. *"Who his own self bare our sins in his own body on the tree, that we, being dead to sins, should live unto righteousness: by whose stripes ye were healed"* (1 Pet. 2:24).

We know we can trust God to forgive all our sins because Jesus Christ has borne them in our place.

"All we like sheep have gone astray; we have turned every one to his own way; and the LORD hath laid on him the iniquity of us all" (Isa. 53:6). Our own good works—past, present, or future—have nothing to do with the forgiveness of our sins. Our sins are forgiven, not because of any good works we do, but because of the atoning work of Christ on the cross of Calvary in our place. If we rest in this atoning work, we will do good works. But our good works will be the outcome of our being saved and our believing on Christ as our Sin-Bearer. Our good works will not be the ground of our salvation, but the result of our salvation and the proof of it.

We must be very careful not to believe in our good works as the basis of salvation. We are not forgiven because of Christ's death *and our good works;* we are forgiven solely and entirely because of Christ's death. To see this clearly is the right beginning of the true Christian life.

Our Deliverer from Sin

God offers Jesus to us as our Deliverer from the power of sin. Jesus not only died, He rose again. Today He is a living Savior. He has all power in heaven and on earth. *"And Jesus came and spake unto them, saying, All power is given unto me in heaven and in earth"* (Matt. 28:18). He has the power to keep the weakest sinner from falling. *"Now unto him that is able to keep you from falling, and to present you faultless before the presence of his glory with exceeding joy"* (Jude 24). He is able to save not only from the worst but also elevate to the highest all who come unto the Father through Him. *"Wherefore he is able also to save them to the uttermost that come unto God by him, seeing he ever liveth to make intercession for them"* (Heb. 7:25). *"If the Son therefore shall make you free, ye shall be free indeed"* (John 8:36).

To receive Jesus is to believe what God tells us in His Word about Him: to believe that He did rise from the dead; to believe that He now lives; to believe that He has the power to keep us from falling; and to believe that He has the power to keep us from sin day by day. Then, we must trust Him to do what He has said.

This is the secret of daily victory over sin. If we try to fight sin with our own strength, we are bound to fail. If we look up to the risen Christ to keep us every day and every hour, He will keep us. Through the crucified Christ, we get deliverance from the guilt of sin, our sins are all blotted out, and we are free from all condemnation. But it is through the risen Christ that we get daily victory over the power of sin.

Some receive Christ as Sin-Bearer and thus find pardon, but they do not get beyond that. Thus their life is one of daily failure. Others receive Him as their risen Savior also, and they experience victory over sin. To begin right, we must take Him not only as our Sin-Bearer, and thus find pardon; we must also take Him as our risen Savior, and our daily Deliverer from the power of sin.

Jesus Is Lord

God offers Jesus to us, not only as our Sin-Bearer and our Deliverer from the power of sin, but He also offers Him to us as our Lord and King. We read in Acts 2:36, *"Therefore let all the house of Israel know assuredly, that God hath made that same Jesus, whom ye have crucified, both Lord and Christ."* Lord means divine Master, and Christ means anointed King.

To receive Jesus is to take Him as our divine Master, as the One to whom we yield the absolute confidence of our intellects. Believe He is the One in whose Word we can believe absolutely, the One in whom we will believe though many of the wisest men may question or deny the truth of His teachings. Because He is our King, we gladly yield absolute control of our lives to Him, so that the question from this time on is: What would my King Jesus have me do? A correct beginning involves an unconditional surrender to the lordship and kingship of Jesus.

The failure to realize that Jesus is Lord and King, as well as Savior, has led to many a false start in the Christian life. We begin with Him as our Savior, our Sin-Bearer, and our Deliverer from the power of sin. We must not end with Him merely as Savior; we must know Him as Lord and King. There is nothing more important in a right beginning of Christian life than an unconditional surrender, both of thoughts and conduct, to Jesus. Say from your heart and say it again and again, "All for Jesus."

Surrender Your Life to Jesus

Many fail because they shrink back from this entire surrender. They wish to serve Jesus with half their heart, part of themselves, and part of their possessions. To hold back anything from Jesus means a wretched life of stumbling and failure.

The life of entire surrender is a joyous life all along the way. If you have never done it before, go alone with God today, get down on your knees, and say, "All for Jesus," and mean it. Say it very earnestly; say it from the bottom of your heart. Stay there until you realize what it means and what you are doing. It is a wondrous step forward when one really takes it.

If you have taken it already, take it again, and take it often. It always has fresh meaning and brings fresh blessing. In this absolute surrender is found the key to all truth. *"If any man will do his will, he shall know of the doctrine, whether it be of God, or whether I speak of myself"* (John 7:17). In this absolute surrender is found the secret of power in prayer. (See 1 John 3:22.) In this absolute surrender is found the supreme condition of receiving the Holy Spirit. *"And we are his witnesses of these things; and so is also the Holy Ghost, whom God hath given to them that obey him"* (Acts 5:32).

Taking Christ as your Lord and King involves obedience to His will as far as you know it in each small detail of life. There are those who tell us they have taken Christ as their Lord and King who at the same time are disobeying Him daily. They disobey Him in business, domestic life, social life, and personal conduct. These people are deceiving themselves. You have not taken Jesus as your Lord and King if you are not striving to obey Him in everything each day. He Himself says, *"Why call ye me, Lord, Lord, and do not the things which I say?"* (Luke 6:46).

Beginning Right

To sum it all up, the right way to begin the Christian life is to accept Jesus Christ as your Sin-Bearer. Trust God to forgive your sins because Jesus Christ died in your place. You must accept Him as your risen Savior who lives to make intercession for you and who has complete power to keep you. Trust Him to keep you from day to day, and accept Him as your Lord and King to whom you surrender absolute control of your thoughts and life.

This is the right beginning, the only right beginning of the Christian life. If you have made this beginning, all that follows will be comparatively easy. If you have not made this beginning, make it now.

2
Confessing Christ

Once you have begun the Christian life correctly by taking the proper attitude toward Christ in a private transaction between Himself and yourself, your next step is to make an open confession of the relationship that now exists between you and Jesus Christ. Jesus says in Matthew 10:32, *"Whosoever therefore shall confess me before men, him will I confess also before my Father which is in heaven."* He demands a public confession. He demands it for your sake. This is the path of blessing.

Many attempt to be disciples of Jesus without telling the world. No one has ever succeeded in that attempt. To be a secret disciple means to be no disciple at all. If one really has received Christ, he cannot keep it to himself. *"For out of the abundance of the heart the mouth speaketh"* (Matt. 12:34).

Are You a Closet Christian?

The public confession of Christ is so important that Paul put it first in his statement of the conditions of salvation. He said, *"That if thou shalt **confess with thy mouth** the Lord Jesus, and shalt believe in thine heart that God hath raised him from the dead, thou shalt be saved. For with the heart man believeth unto righteousness; and with the mouth confession is made unto salvation"* (Rom. 10:9–10, emphasis added).

The life of confession is the life of full salvation. Indeed, the life of confession is the life of the only real salvation. When we confess Christ before men on earth, He acknowledges us before the Father in heaven. Then the Father gives us the Holy Spirit as the seal of our salvation.

Confessing Christ

It is not enough that we confess Christ just once—for example, when we are confirmed, unite with the church, or come forward in a revival meeting. We should confess Christ constantly. We should not be ashamed of our Lord and King. In our home, church, work, and play, we should let others know where we stand. Of course, we should not parade our Christianity or our piety, but we should leave no one in doubt whether we belong to Christ. We should let it be seen that we honor Him as our Lord and King.

Backsliding

The failure to confess Christ is one of the most frequent causes of backsliding. Christians get into new relationships where they are not known as Christians and where they are tempted to conceal the fact. They yield to the temptation and soon find themselves drifting.

The more you make of Jesus Christ, the more He will make of you. It will save you from many temptations if the fact is clear that you are one who acknowledges Christ as Lord in all things.

3
Assurance of Salvation

I f one is to have the fullest measure of joy and power in Christian service, one must know that his sins are forgiven, that he is a child of God, and that he has eternal life. It is the believer's privilege to *know* he has eternal life. John said in 1 John 5:13, *"These things have I written unto you that believe on the name of the Son of God; **that ye may know** that ye have eternal life, and that ye may believe on the name of the Son of God"* (emphasis added.) John wrote this first epistle for the express purpose that anyone who believes on the name of the Son of God *will know* he has eternal life.

Eternal Life for His Children

There are those who tell us no one can know he has eternal life until he is dead and has been before the judgment seat of God. But God Himself tells us we may know. To deny the possibility of the believer's knowledge that he has eternal life is to say that the first epistle of John was written in vain, and it is to insult the Holy Spirit who is its real author.

Again Paul told us in Acts 13:39, *"And by him* [that is, by Christ] *all that believe **are justified** from all things"* (emphasis added). So everyone who believes in Jesus can know that he is justified from all things. He knows it because the Word of God says so. John told us in John 1:12, *"But **as many as received him** [Jesus Christ], to them gave he power to become the sons of God, even to them that believe on his name"* (emphasis added).

Assurance of Salvation

Here is a definite and unmistakable declaration that everyone who receives Jesus becomes a child of God. Therefore, every believer in Jesus may know that he is a child of God. He may know it on the surest of all grounds—the Word of God asserts that he is a child of God.

Faith in Fact, Not Feeling

But how can any individual know he has eternal life? He can know it on the very best authority, through the testimony of God Himself as given in the Bible. The testimony of Scripture is the testimony of God. What the Scriptures say is absolutely true. What the Scriptures say, God says. Now in John 3:36 the Scriptures say, *"He that believeth on the Son **hath** everlasting life"* (emphasis added). We know whether we believe on the Son or not. We know whether we have that real faith in Christ that leads us to receive Him. If we have this faith in Christ, we have God's own written testimony that we have eternal life, our sins are forgiven, and we are the children of God. We may feel forgiven, or we may not feel forgiven, but that does not matter. It is not a question of what we feel but of what God says. God's Word is always to be believed.

Our own feelings are often to be doubted. There are many who doubt their sins are forgiven, who doubt they have everlasting life, who doubt they are saved. They can have doubts because they do not feel forgiven or feel that they have everlasting life or feel that they are saved. Not feeling forgiven is no reason to doubt.

Suppose you were sentenced to prison and your friends secured a pardon for you. The legal document announcing your pardon would be brought to you. You would read it and know you were pardoned because the legal document said so. But the news would be so good and so sudden that you would be dazed by it. You would not realize you were pardoned. Someone could come to you and say, "Are you pardoned?" What would you reply? You might say, "Yes, I am pardoned." Then he might ask, "Do you feel pardoned?" You may reply, "No, I do not feel pardoned. It is so sudden, so wonderful that I cannot comprehend it."

Then he would say to you, "But how can you know that you are pardoned if you do not feel it?" You would hold out the document and say, "This says so." The time would come, after you read the document over and over again and believed it, when you would not only know you were pardoned, but you would feel it.

The Bible is God's authoritative document declaring that everyone who believes in Jesus is justified. It declares that everyone who believes on the Son has everlasting life. It declares that everyone who receives Jesus is a child of God. If anyone asks you if all your sins are forgiven, reply, "Yes, I know they are because God says so." If anyone asks you if you know you are a child of God, reply, "Yes, I know I am a child of God because God says so." If they ask you if you have everlasting life, reply, "Yes, I know I have everlasting life because God says so."

God says, *Every one which seeth the Son, and believeth on him, may have everlasting life* (John 6:40). Then you can say, "I know I believe on the Son, and therefore I know I have eternal life— because God says so." You may not feel it yet, but if you keep meditating on God's statement and believe what God says, the time will come when you will feel it.

God Is Not a Liar

If one who believes on the Son of God doubts he has eternal life, he makes God a liar.

> *He that believeth on the Son of God hath the witness in himself: he that believeth not God hath made him a liar; because he believeth not the record that God gave of his Son. And this is the record, that God hath given to us eternal life, and this life is in his Son. He that hath the Son hath life; and he that hath not the Son of God hath not life.* (1 John 5:10–12)

Anyone who does not believe God's testimony—that He has given us eternal life, His Son, and that he who has the Son has the life—makes God a liar.

Assurance of Salvation

It is sometimes said, "It is presumptuous for anyone to say that he knows he is saved or to say he knows he has eternal life." But is it presumptuous to believe God? Is it not rather presumptuous not to believe God, to claim God is a liar? When you believe on the Son of God and yet doubt that you have eternal life, you make God a liar.

When Jesus said to the woman who was a sinner, *"Thy sins are forgiven"* (Luke 7:48), was it presumptuous for her to go out and say, "I know my sins are forgiven"? Would it not have been presumptuous for her to have doubted for a moment that all her sins were forgiven? Jesus said that they were forgiven. For her to doubt it would have been for her to give the lie to Jesus. Is it then any more presumptuous for the believer today to say, "All my sins are forgiven; I have eternal life," when God says in His written testimony to everyone who believes, "You are justified from all things" (Acts 13:39), "You have eternal life" (John 3:36; 1 John 5:13)?

Be very sure first of all that you really do believe on the name of the Son of God, that you really have received Jesus. If you are sure of this, then never doubt for a moment that all your sins are forgiven. Never doubt for a moment that you are a child of God. Never doubt for a moment that you have everlasting life.

Your Sins Are Forgiven

If Satan comes and whispers, "Your sins are not forgiven," point Satan to the Word of God and say, "God says my sins are forgiven, and I know they are." If Satan whispers, "Well, perhaps you don't believe on Him," then say, "Well, if I never did before, I will now." And then go out rejoicing, knowing your sins are forgiven, knowing you are a child of God, and knowing you have everlasting life.

There are, without a doubt, many who say they know they have eternal life who really do not believe on the name of the Son of God. This is not true assurance. It has no sure foundation in the Word of God, which does not lie. If we wish to get assurance of salvation, we must first become saved.

Your Life in God

The reason many do not have the assurance they are saved is they are *not* saved. They need *salvation* before they need *assurance*. But if you have received Jesus in the way described in the first chapter, *you are saved,* you are a child of God, and your sins are forgiven. Believe it. Know it. Rejoice in it.

Having settled the question, let it remain settled. Never doubt it. You may make mistakes; you may stumble; you may fall. Even if you do, if you have really received Jesus, you know that your sins are forgiven. You can rise from your fall and go forward in the glad assurance that there is nothing between you and God.

4
Receiving the Holy Spirit

When the apostle Paul came to Ephesus, he found a small group of Christians. There was something about these disciples that struck Paul unfavorably. We are not told what it was. It may be that he did not find in them that overflowing joy one learns to expect in all Christians who have really entered into the fullness of blessing there is for them in Christ. It may be that Paul was troubled by the fact that there were so few of them. He may have thought that if these disciples were what they ought to be, there would certainly be more by this time.

The Holy Spirit Is Available

Whatever struck Paul as unfavorable, he went right to the root of the difficulty at once by asking them, *"Have ye received the Holy Ghost since ye believed?"* (Acts 19:2). It came out at once that they had not received the Holy Spirit; in fact, they did not know the Holy Spirit was available to them.

Then Paul told them the Holy Spirit had been given. He also showed them what they had to do to receive the Holy Spirit. Before that gathering was over, the Holy Spirit came upon them. From that day on there was a different state of affairs in Ephesus. A great revival began at once so that the whole city was shaken, *"So mightily grew the word of God and prevailed"* (Acts 19:20).

Paul's question to these young disciples in Ephesus should be put to young disciples everywhere, *"Have ye received the Holy Ghost?"* Receiving the Holy Spirit is the great secret of joyfulness in our own hearts, victory over sin, power in prayer, and effective service.

Your Life in God

The Spirit Dwells in Every Christian

Everyone who has truly received Jesus has the Holy Spirit dwelling in him in some sense. In many believers, though the Holy Spirit dwells within, He is back in some hidden sanctuary of their being, not a part of their consciousness. It is something quite different, something far better, to receive the Holy Spirit in the sense that Paul meant in his question. To receive the Holy Spirit in such a way that one knows without a doubt that he has received Him is to become conscious of the joy with which He fills our hearts. This joy is different from any joy we have ever known in the world. We can receive the Holy Spirit in such fullness that He rules our lives and produces within us, in ever-increasing measure, the fruit of the Spirit. *"The fruit of the Spirit is love, joy, peace, longsuffering, gentleness, goodness, faith, meekness, temperance"* (Gal. 5:22–23).

Paul wanted all Christians to receive the Holy Spirit in such a sense that we are conscious of His drawing our hearts out in prayer in a way that is not of ourselves. He wanted us to receive the Holy Spirit in such a way that we are conscious of His help when we witness for Christ. We are conscious of His aid when we speak to others individually and try to lead them to accept Christ and when we teach a Sunday school class, speak in public, or do any other work for the Master. Have you received the Holy Spirit? If you have not, this is how you may.

Steps for Holy Spirit Filling

1. First of all, in order to receive the Holy Spirit, one must acknowledge the death of Christ on the cross for us as the only and all-sufficient ground upon which God pardons all our sins.

2. In order to receive the Holy Spirit, we must put away every known sin. We must go to our heavenly Father and ask Him to search us through and through, bringing to light anything in our outward life or inward life that is wrong in His sight. If He does bring anything to mind that is displeasing to Him, we should put

it away, no matter how dear it is to us. There must be a complete renunciation of all sin in order to receive the Holy Spirit.

3. Third, in order to receive the Holy Spirit, we must openly confess Christ before the world. The Holy Spirit is not given to those who are trying to be disciples in secret, but to those who obey Christ and publicly confess Him before the world. *"Whosoever shall confess me before men"* (Luke 12:8).

4. Fourth, in order to receive the Holy Spirit, there must be absolute surrender of our lives to God. You must go to Him and say, "Heavenly Father, here I am. You have bought me with a price. I am Your property. I renounce all claim to do my own will, all claim to govern my own life, all claim to have my own way. I give myself up unreservedly to You—all I am and all I have. Send me where You want, use me as You like, do with me what You want—I am Yours."

If we hold anything back from God, no matter how small it may seem, that spoils everything. But if we surrender all to God, then God will give all He has to us. There are some who shrink from this absolute surrender to God, but absolute surrender to God is simply absolute surrender to infinite love. It is surrender to the Father—the Father whose love is not only wiser than any earthly father's, but more tender than any earthly mother's.

5. In order to receive the Holy Spirit there should be definite asking for the Holy Spirit. Our Lord Jesus says in Luke 11:13, *"If ye then, being evil, know how to give good gifts unto your children: how much more shall your heavenly Father give the Holy Spirit to them that ask him?"* Just ask God to give you the Holy Spirit and expect Him to do it. He says He will.

6. Finally, in order to receive the Holy Spirit, there must be faith. Simply take God at His Word. No matter how positive any promise of God's Word may be, we enjoy it personally only when we believe. Our Lord Jesus says, *"What things soever ye desire, when ye pray, believe that ye receive them, and ye shall have them"* (Mark 11:24).

When you pray for the Holy Spirit, you have prayed for something according to God's will. Therefore, you know that your prayer is heard and that you have what you asked of Him.

"And this is the confidence that we have in him, that, if we ask any thing according to his will, he heareth us: and if we know that he hear us, whatsoever we ask, we know that we have the petitions that we desired of him" (1 John 5:14–15). You may feel no different, but do not look at your feelings, but at God's promise. Believe the prayer is heard, believe that God has given you the Holy Spirit, and you will then have in actual experience what you have received in simple faith—on the bare promise of God's Word.

Give the Spirit Control

It is good to kneel down alone and look up to Jesus, putting into His hands anew the entire control of your life. Ask Him to take control of your thoughts, imaginations, affections, desires, ambitions, choices, purposes, words, and actions. In other words, ask Him to take control of everything. Then expect Him to do it. The whole secret of victory in the Christian life is letting the Holy Spirit, who dwells within you, have undisputed right-of-way in the entire conduct of your life.

5
Looking to Jesus

If we are to run with patience the race that is set before us, we must always keep looking to Jesus.

> *Wherefore seeing we also are compassed about with so great a cloud of witnesses, let us lay aside every weight, and the sin which doth so easily beset us, and let us run with patience the race that is set before us, looking unto Jesus the author and finisher of our faith; who for the joy that was set before him endured the cross, despising the shame, and is set down at the right hand of the throne of God. For consider him that endured such contradiction of sinners against himself, lest ye be wearied and faint in your minds.*
> (Heb. 12:1–3)

One of the simplest, yet mightiest, secrets of abiding joy and victory is to never lose sight of Jesus.

Focus on Jesus, Not Your Sins

First of all, we must keep looking at Jesus as the reason for our acceptance before God. Over and over again, Satan will attempt to discourage us by recalling our sins and failures. He tries to convince us that we are neither children of God nor saved. If he succeeds in getting us to keep looking at and brooding over our sins, he will soon coax us to become discouraged. Discouragement means failure.

But if we keep looking at what God sees—the death of Jesus Christ in our place that completely atoned for every sin we ever committed—we will never be discouraged because of the greatness

27

of our sins. We will see that, while our sins are very great, they all have been erased. Every time Satan brings up one of our sins, we will see that Jesus Christ has redeemed us from its curse by being made a curse in our place. *"Christ hath redeemed us from the curse of the law, being made a curse for us: for it is written, Cursed is every one that hangeth on a tree"* (Gal. 3:13).

We will see that *"he hath made him to be sin for us, who knew no sin; that we might be made the righteousness of God in him"* (2 Cor. 5:21). In short, whenever Satan taunts us about our sins, we will know they have been washed away forever. *"Who his own self bare our sins in his own body on the tree, that we, being dead to sins, should live unto righteousness: by whose stripes ye were healed"* (1 Pet. 2:24).

If you are troubled right now about any sin you have ever committed, either past or present, just look at Jesus on the cross. Believe what God tells you about Him, that this sin that troubles you was laid upon Him (Isa. 53:6). Thank God that the sin is all settled. Be full of gratitude to Jesus who bore it in your place, and do not worry about your sins anymore.

It is an act of base ingratitude toward God to brood over sins that He in His infinite love has cancelled. Keep looking at Christ on the cross and always walk in the sunlight of God's favor. This favor has been purchased for you at a high cost. Gratitude demands that you always believe in Jesus' gift and walk in the light of it.

Jesus Keeps Us Every Day

Second, we must keep looking at Jesus as our risen Savior, who has all power in heaven and on earth and is able to keep us every day and every hour. Are you tempted to do some wrong at this moment? If you are, remember that Jesus rose from the dead. Remember that at this moment He is living at the right hand of God in glory. Remember He has all power in heaven and on earth, and He can give you victory right now.

Believe what God tells you in His Word, that Jesus has power to save you this moment *"to the uttermost"* (Heb. 7.25). Believe He has power to give you victory over this sin that now attacks you. Ask Him to give you victory and expect Him to do it. In this way, by looking to the risen Christ for victory, you will have victory over sin every day, every hour, every minute. *"Remember that Jesus Christ…was raised from the dead"* (2 Tim. 2:8).

God called every one of us to a victorious life. The secret of this victorious life is always looking to the risen Christ for victory. Through looking to Christ's sacrifice, we obtain pardon and enjoy peace. By looking to the risen Christ, we obtain present victory over the power of sin.

If you have lost sight of the risen Christ and have yielded to temptation, confess your sin and know that it is forgiven because God says so. *"If we confess our sins, he is faithful and just to forgive us our sins, and to cleanse us from all unrighteousness"* (1 John 1:9). Look to Jesus, the Risen One, to give you victory now; then keep looking to Him.

Jesus Is Our Example

Third, we must keep looking to Jesus as the One whom we should follow in our daily conduct. Our Lord Jesus says to us, His disciples today, as He said to His early disciples, *"Follow me"* (Matt. 9:9). The whole secret of true Christian conduct can be summed up in these two words: "Follow Me." *"He that saith he abideth in him ought himself also so to walk, **even as he walked**"* (1 John 2:6, emphasis added).

One of the most common causes of failure in Christian life is found in the attempt to follow a good man whom we greatly admire. No man or woman, no matter how good, can be safely followed. If we follow any man or woman, we are bound to go astray. There has been only one absolutely perfect Man on this earth—the man Christ Jesus. If we try to follow any other man, we are more sure to imitate his faults than his virtues. Look to Jesus, and only Jesus, as your guide.

If you are ever perplexed as to what to do, simply ask, "What would Jesus do?" Ask God through His Holy Spirit to show you what Jesus would do. Study your Bible to find out what Jesus did do, and follow His example. Even though no one else seems to be following Jesus, be sure you follow Him.

Do not spend your time or thought criticizing others because they do not follow Jesus. See that you follow Him yourself. When you are wasting your time criticizing others for not following Jesus, Jesus is always saying to you, *"What is that to thee? follow* **thou** *me"* (John 21:22, emphasis added). The question for you is not what following Jesus may involve for other people. The question is, "What does following Jesus mean for you?"

This is the life of a disciple—the life of simply following Jesus. Many perplexing questions will come to you, but the most perplexing question will soon become crystal clear if you determine with all your heart to follow Jesus in everything. Satan will always be ready to whisper to you, "Such and such a good man does it." But all you need to do is answer, "It does not matter to me what this or that man does." The only question should be, "What would Jesus do?"

There is wonderful freedom in this life of simply following Jesus. This path is straight and clear. But the path of the one who tries to shape his conduct by observing the conduct of others is full of twists, turns, and pitfalls. Keep looking at Jesus. Follow on with trust wherever He leads. *"The path of the just is as the shining light, that shineth more and more unto the perfect day"* (Prov. 4:18). He is the Light of the World. Anyone who follows Him will not walk in darkness, but will have the light of life all along the way (John 8:12).

6
Church Membership

No Christian can have real success in the Christian life without the fellowship of other believers. The church is a divine institution, built by Jesus Christ Himself. It is the one institution that endures. Other institutions come and go. They do their work for their day and disappear. But the church will continue to the end. *"The gates of hell shall not prevail against it"* (Matt. 16:18). The church is made up of men and women, imperfect men and women; consequently it is an imperfect institution. Nonetheless, it is of divine origin, and God loves it. Every believer should realize that he belongs to it, openly take his place in it, and shoulder his responsibilities regarding it.

The church consists of all believers who are united to Jesus Christ by a living faith in Him. In its outward organization today, it is divided into many sects and local congregations. In spite of these divisions, the church is one. It has one Lord, Jesus Christ. It has one faith, faith in Him as Savior, divine Lord, and only King. All believe in one baptism, the baptism in one Spirit into one body. *"For by one Spirit are we all baptized into one body, whether we be Jews or Gentiles, whether we be bond or free; and have been all made to drink into one Spirit"* (1 Cor. 12:13). *"There is one body, and one Spirit, even as ye are called in one hope of your calling; one Lord, one faith, one baptism"* (Eph. 4:4–5).

Join a Body of Believers

But each individual Christian needs the fellowship of individual fellow believers. The outward expression of this fellowship

31

is membership in some organized body of believers. If we remain aloof from all organized churches, hoping to have a broader fellowship with all believers belonging to all churches, we deceive ourselves. We will miss the helpfulness that comes from intimate union with a local congregation.

I have known many well-meaning people who have neglected membership in any specific organization. I have never known a person to do this whose spiritual life has not suffered. On the Day of Pentecost the three thousand who were converted were baptized at once and were added to the church. *"They continued stedfastly in the apostles' doctrine and fellowship, and in breaking of bread, and in prayers"* (Acts 2:42). Their example is the one to follow. If you have really received Jesus Christ, as soon as possible find a group of people who have also received Him and unite yourself with them.

There Is No Perfect Church

In many communities there may be no choice of churches, because there is only one. In other communities, one will be faced with the question, "Which body of believers should I join?" Do not waste your time looking for a perfect church. There is no perfect church. A church in which you are the only member is the most imperfect church of all. I would rather belong to the most faulty Christian body of believers I ever knew than not belong to any church group at all.

The local churches in Paul's day were very imperfect institutions. Read the epistles to the Corinthians and see how imperfect the church in Corinth was. See how much evil was in it. Yet Paul never dreamed of advising any believer in Corinth to get out of this imperfect church. He did tell them to come out of heathenism and to come out from fellowship with infidels.

Be ye not unequally yoked together with unbelievers: for what fellowship hath righteousness with unrighteousness? and what communion hath light with darkness? and what concord hath Christ with Belial? or what part hath he that believeth with an infidel?

and what agreement hath the temple of God with idols? for ye are the temple of the living God; as God hath said, I will dwell in them, and walk in them; and I will be their God, and they shall be my people. Wherefore come out from among them, and be ye separate, saith the Lord, and touch not the unclean thing; and I will receive you, and will be a Father unto you, and ye shall be my sons and daughters, saith the Lord Almighty. (2 Cor. 6:14–18)

He never advised coming out of the imperfect church in Corinth. Though he told the Corinthian church to separate from membership certain persons whose lives were wrong, he never advised anyone to leave the body because these people were not yet separated. *"But now I have written unto you not to keep company, if any man that is called a brother be a fornicator, or covetous, or an idolater, or a railer, or a drunkard, or an extortioner; with such an one no not to eat"* (1 Cor. 5:11).

Guidelines for Finding a Church

Since you cannot find a perfect church, find the best church possible. Unite with a church where they believe in the Bible and where they preach the Bible. Avoid the churches where words, whether open or veiled, are spoken that have a tendency to undermine your faith in the Bible as a reliable revelation from God Himself. The Bible is the all-sufficient rule of faith and practice.

Unite with a church where there is a spirit of prayer, where the prayer meetings are well maintained. Unite with a church that has an active interest in the salvation of the lost, where young Christians are looked after and helped, where the minister and the people have a love for the poor and the destitute. Consider a church that regards its mission in this world to be the same as the mission of Christ, *"to seek and to save that which was lost"* (Luke 19:10).

As to denominational differences, other things being equal, unite with that denomination whose ideas of doctrine, government, and ordinances are most closely related to your own. It is better to join a living church of another denomination than to unite with a dead church of your own. We live in a day when denominational differences are becoming less and less important. Often they have no practical value whatever. One can often feel more at home in a church of another denomination than in a church of his own denomination. The things that divide the denominations are insignificant compared with the great fundamental truths, purposes, and faith that unite them.

If you cannot find a church that agrees with the pattern set forth above, find a church that comes nearest to it. Go into that church, and by prayer and work try to bring that church, as nearly as you can, to be what a church of Christ should be. Do not waste your strength in criticism against either the church or minister. Focus on what is good in the church and in the minister, and do your best to strengthen it. Keep a firm but unobtrusive distance from what is wrong while seeking to correct it.

Do not be discouraged if you cannot correct problems in a day, a week, a month, or a year. Patient love, prayer, and effort will show in time. Withdrawing by yourself, complaining, and grumbling will do no good. Grumbling will simply make you and the truths for which you stand repulsive.

7
Bible Study

There is nothing more important for the development of a Christian's spiritual life than regular, systematic Bible study. It is as true in the spiritual life as in the physical life that health depends on what we eat and how much we eat. *"Man shall not live by bread alone"* (Matt. 4:4). The soul's proper food is found in one book, the Bible.

Of course, a true minister of the Gospel will feed us the Word of God, but that is not enough. He feeds us only one or two days in the week, and we need to be fed every day. Furthermore, do not depend on being fed by others. We must learn to feed ourselves. If we study the Bible for ourselves as we should study it, we will be, in large measure, independent of human teachers. We will always be safe from spiritual harm, even if we are so unfortunate as to have a man who is ignorant of God's truth for our minister. We live in a day in which false doctrine is everywhere, and the only Christian who is safe from being led into error is the one who studies his Bible for himself, daily.

The Word Keeps Us Safe

The apostle Paul warned the elders of the church in Ephesus that the time was soon coming when vicious wolves would join them and not spare the flock. They would speak perverse things of their own creation, trying to draw disciples away from Jesus. But Paul told them how to be safe even in such perilous times as these. He said, *"I commend you to God, and to the word of his grace,*

*which is able to build you up, and to give you an inheritance among all
them which are sanctified"* (Acts 20:32).

Through meditation on the Word of God's grace, they would
be safe even in the midst of flourishing error on the part of leaders in the church.

> *For I know this, that after my departing shall grievous wolves enter
> in among you, not sparing the flock. Also of your own selves shall
> men arise, speaking perverse things, to draw away disciples after
> them. Therefore watch, and remember, that by the space of three
> years I ceased not to warn every one night and day with tears.*
> (Acts 20:29–31)

Writing later to the bishop of the church in Ephesus, Paul
said, *"But evil men and seducers shall wax worse and worse, deceiving,
and being deceived"* (2 Tim. 3:13). But he went on to tell Timothy
how he and his fellow believers could remain safe even in the
times of increasing peril that were coming. This could be done
through the study of the Holy Scriptures, which gives readers
wisdom, drawing them to salvation.

> *But continue thou in the things which thou hast learned and hast
> been assured of, knowing of whom thou hast learned them; and that
> from a child thou hast known the holy scriptures, which are able
> to make thee wise unto salvation through faith which is in Christ
> Jesus.* (2 Tim. 3:14–15)

Bible Study Brings Success

"All scripture," he added, *"is given by inspiration of God, and
is profitable for doctrine, for reproof, for correction, for instruction in
righteousness: that the man of God may be perfect, thoroughly furnished
unto all good works"* (2 Tim. 3:16–17). Through the study of the
Bible, one will be sound in doctrine and led to see his sins and to
put them away. He will find discipline in the righteous life and
be equipped for all good works. Our spiritual health, growth,
strength, victory over sin, soundness in doctrine, joy, and peace
in Christ come from study of God's Word. Cleansing from inward

and outward sin and fitness for service depend on daily study of the Bible.

The one who neglects his Bible is bound to be a failure in the Christian life. The one who studies his Bible in the right spirit and by a constant method is bound to make a success of the Christian life. This brings us face-to-face with the question, "What is the right way to study the Bible?"

How to Study Your Bible

First of all, we should study it daily. *"These were more noble than those in Thessalonica, in that they received the word with all readiness of mind, and searched the scriptures daily, whether those things were so"* (Acts 17:11). This is of prime importance. No matter how solid the methods of Bible study or how much time one may put into Bible study now and then, the best results can be secured only when one never lets a single day go by without earnest Bible study. This is the only safe course. Any day that is allowed to pass without faithful Bible study is a day that opens our hearts and lives to error and sin. I have been a Christian for more than a quarter of a century, and yet today I would not dare allow even a single day to pass without listening to God's voice as He speaks through the pages of His Book.

It is with this responsibility that many fall away. They grow careless and let a day pass, or even several days, without spending time alone with God or letting Him speak to them through His Word. Mr. Moody once wisely said, "In prayer we talk to God. In Bible study, God talks to us, and we had better let God do most of the talking."

A regular time should be set aside each day for Bible study. I do not think it is wise, as a rule, to say that we will study so many chapters a day, because that leads to undue haste, skimming, and thoughtlessness. But it is good to set apart a certain length of time each day for Bible study. Some can give more time to Bible study than others, but no one should devote less than fifteen minutes a day.

I set a short time span so that no one will be discouraged in the beginning. If a young Christian planned to spend an hour or two a day in Bible study, there is a strong probability that he would not keep the resolution and would become discouraged. Nevertheless, I know of many very busy people who have taken the first hour of every day for years for Bible study. Some have even given two hours a day.

The late Earl Cairns, Lord Chancellor of England, was one of the busiest men of his day. Lady Cairns told me that no matter how late at night he reached home, he always woke up at the same early hour for prayer and Bible study. She said, "We would sometimes get home from Parliament at two o'clock in the morning, but Lord Cairns would always arise at the same early hour to pray and study the Bible." Lord Cairns is reported as saying, "If I have had any success in life, I attribute it to the habit of giving the first two hours of each day to Bible study and prayer."

It is important that one choose the right time for this study. Whenever possible, the best time for study is immediately after waking up in the morning. The worst time is the last thing at night. Of course, it is good to spend a little time just before we go to bed reading the Bible so that God's voice will be the last voice we hear. The bulk of our Bible study should be done when our minds are clearest and strongest. Whatever time is set apart for Bible study should be kept sacredly for that purpose.

We should study the Bible systematically. A lot of time is frittered away in random study of the Bible. The same amount of time put into systematic study would yield far greater results. Have a definite place where you study, and have a definite plan of study. A good way for a young Christian to begin the study of the Bible is to read the gospel of John. When you have read it through once, read it again until you have gone over the gospel five times. Then read the gospel of Luke five times in the same way. Then read the Acts of the Apostles five times. Then read the following epistles five times each: 1 Thessalonians, 1 John, Romans, and Ephesians.

By this time you will be ready to take up a more thorough method of Bible study. A profitable method is to begin at Genesis and read the Bible through chapter by chapter. Read each chapter through several times, and then answer the following questions on each chapter:

1) What is the main subject of the chapter? State the principal contents of the chapter in a single phrase or sentence.

2) What is the truth most clearly taught and most emphasized in the chapter?

3) What is the best lesson?

4) What is the best verse?

5) Who are the principal people mentioned?

6) What does the chapter teach about Jesus Christ?

Go through the entire Bible in this way.

Another, and more thorough, method of Bible study will yield excellent results when applied to some of the more important chapters of the Bible. However, it cannot be applied to every chapter in the Bible. It is as follows:

1) Read the chapter for today's study five times, reading it out loud at least once. Each new reading will bring out a new point.

2) Divide the chapter into its natural divisions, and find headings that describe the contents of each division. For example, suppose the chapter studied is 1 John 5. You might divide it this way: first division, verses 1–3, *The Believer's Noble Parentage;* second division, verses 4–5, *The Believer's Glorious Victory;* third division, verses 6–10, *The Believer's Sure Ground of Faith.* Continue through each division this way.

3) Note the important differences between the King James Version and the Revised Version.

4) Write down the most important facts of the chapter in their proper order.

5) Make a note of the people mentioned in the chapter and any light shed on their character.

6) Note the principal lessons of the chapter. It is helpful to classify these. For instance, lessons about God, lessons about Christ, lessons about the Holy Spirit, etc.

7) Find the central truth of the chapter.

8) Find the key verse of the chapter if there is one.

9) Find the best verse in the chapter. Mark it and memorize it.

10) Write down any new truth you have learned from the chapter.

11) Write down any truth you already know that has come to you with new power.

12) Write down what definite thing you have resolved to do as a result of studying this chapter.

A beneficial order of study for you might be all of the chapters in Matthew, Mark, Luke, John, and Acts; the first eight chapters of Romans; 1 Corinthians 12, 13, and 15; the first six chapters of 2 Corinthians; then all the chapters in Galatians, Ephesians, Philippians, 1 Thessalonians, and 1 John. Sometimes you can refresh your study by alternating methods.

Another profitable method of Bible study is *the topical method*. This was D. L. Moody's favorite method. Take such topics as: the Holy Spirit, prayer, the blood of Christ, sin, judgment, grace, justification, the new birth, sanctification, faith, repentance, the character of Christ, the resurrection of Christ, the ascension of Christ, the second coming of Christ, assurance, love of God, love (for God, for Christ, for Christians, for all men), heaven, and hell. Get a Bible concordance and study each one of these topics.

We should *study the Bible comprehensively*—the whole Bible. Many Bible readers make the mistake of confining all their reading to certain portions of the Bible that they enjoy. This way they get no knowledge of the Bible as a whole. They miss altogether many of the most important phases of Bible truth. Go through the Bible again and again—a certain portion each day from the Old Testament and a portion from the New Testament. Read carefully at least one Psalm every day.

It is also beneficial to read a whole book of the Bible through at a single sitting. This lets you see the whole picture. Of course, a few books of the Bible would take one or two hours. But most books can be read in a few minutes. The shorter books of the Bible should be read through again and again at a single sitting.

Study the Bible attentively. Do not hurry. One of the worst faults in Bible study is haste. We benefit from Bible study only by learning its truth. It has no magic power. It is better to read one verse attentively than to read a dozen chapters thoughtlessly. Sometimes you will read a verse that grabs you. Don't hurry on. Stop and think about that verse.

As you read, mark in your Bible what impresses you most. One does not need an elaborate marking system; simply highlight what impresses you. Think about what you mark. God affirms that the man who meditates on God's law day and night is blessed. *"But his delight is in the law of the LORD; and in his law doth he meditate day and night"* (Ps. 1:2).

It is amazing how a verse of Scripture will open one's mind to its exact meaning. Memorize the passages that impress you most. *"Thy word have I hid in mine heart, that I might not sin against thee"* (Ps. 119:11). When you memorize a passage of Scripture, memorize its location as well as the words. A busy but spiritually-minded man who was hurrying to catch a train once said to me, "Tell me in a word how to study my Bible." I replied, "Thoughtfully."

Study your Bible comparatively. In other words, compare Scripture with Scripture. The best commentary on the Bible is the Bible itself. Wherever you find a difficult passage in the Bible, there is always another passage that explains its meaning. The best book to use in this comparison is *The Treasury of Scripture Knowledge.* This book gives a large number of references on every verse in the Bible. You may want to take a particular book of the Bible and go through that book verse by verse. Look up and study every reference given in *The Treasury of Scripture Knowledge* dealing with that book. This is a very fruitful method of Bible study. You will also gain by studying the Bible by chapters and looking up the references on the more important verses in each chapter. One will gain a better understanding of passages of Scripture by looking up the references given in *The Treasury of Scripture Knowledge.*

Study your Bible and believe it. The apostle Paul, in writing to the Christians in Thessalonica, said, *"For this cause also thank we God without ceasing, because, when ye received the word of God which ye heard of us, ye received it not as the word of men, but as it is in truth, the word of God, which effectually worketh also in you that believe"* (1 Thess. 2:13). Happy is the one who receives the Word of God as these believers in Thessalonica received it, as the Word of God. In such a person it is especially effective. The Bible is the Word of God, and we get the most out of any book by acknowledging it for what it really is.

It is often said that we should study the Bible just as we study any other book. That principle contains a truth, but it also contains a great error. The Bible, like other books, has the same laws of grammatical and literary construction. But the Bible is a unique book. It is what no other book is, the Word of God. This can be easily proven to any impartial man. The Bible should be studied, then, specifically as the Word of God. This involves five things.

It involves a greater eagerness and more careful, candid study to find out exactly what the Bible teaches. It is important to know the mind of man. It is absolutely essential to know the mind of God. The place to discover the mind of God is the Bible because it is here that God reveals His mind.

It requires a prompt and unquestioning acceptance of, and submission to, its teachings when definitely ascertained. These teachings may appear unreasonable or impossible. Nevertheless, we should accept them. If this book is the Word of God, it is foolish to submit its teachings to the criticism of our finite reasoning.

A little boy who discredits his wise father's statements simply because to his infant mind they appear unreasonable is not thinking wisely but foolishly. Even the greatest of human thinkers is only an infant compared with God. To discredit God's statements found in His Word because they appear unreasonable to our infantile minds shows our shallow thinking. When we are once satisfied that the Bible is the Word of God, its clear teachings must be the end of all controversy and discussion for us.

Correct Bible study includes absolute reliance on all its promises in all their length, breadth, depth, and height. The one who studies the Bible as the Word of God will say of any promise, no matter how vast and beyond belief it appears, "God who cannot lie has promised this, so I will claim it for myself."

Mark the promise you claim. Each day look for some new promise from your infinite Father. He has put *"his riches in glory"* (Phil. 4:19) at your disposal. I know of no better way to grow rich spiritually than to search daily for promises; and when you find them, take them for yourself.

You must also study God's Word in obedience. *"But be ye doers of the word, and not hearers only, deceiving your own selves"* (James 1:22). Nothing goes farther to help one understand the Bible than resolving to obey it. Jesus said, *"If any man will do his will, he shall know of the doctrine"* (John 7:17). The surrendered will means a clear eye. If our eye is pure (that is, our will is absolutely surrendered to God), our whole body will be full of light. But if our eye is evil (that is, if we are trying to serve two masters and are not absolutely surrendered to one Master, God), our whole body will be full of darkness.

> *The light of the body is the eye: if therefore thine eye be single* [pure], *thy whole body shall be full of light. But if thine eye be evil, thy whole body shall be full of darkness. If therefore the light that is in thee be darkness, how great is that darkness! No man can serve two masters: for either he will hate the one, and love the other; or else he will hold to the one, and despise the other. Ye cannot serve God and mammon.* (Matt. 6:22–24)

Many passages that look obscure to you now would become as clear as day if you were willing to obey everything the Bible teaches.

Blessing Comes through Obedience

Each commandment discovered in the Bible that is really intended as a commandment to us should be obeyed instantly. It is remarkable how soon one loses his thirst for the Bible and how soon the mind becomes obscured to its teachings when one disobeys the Bible at any point. I have often known people who loved their Bibles, were useful in God's service, and had clear views of the truth. Then they came to a command in the Bible that they were unwilling to obey. Some sacrifice was demanded that they were unwilling to make. As a result, their love for the Bible rapidly waned, their faith in the Bible weakened, and soon they drifted farther and farther away from clear views of the truth.

Nothing clears the mind like obedience; nothing darkens the mind like disobedience. To obey a truth you see prepares you to see other truths. To disobey a truth you see darkens your mind to all truths.

Cultivate prompt, exact, unquestioning, joyous obedience to every command that clearly applies to you. Be on the lookout for new orders from your King. Blessing lies in the direction of obedience to them. God's commands are guideposts that mark the road to present success and eternal glory.

Personal Companionship with God

Studying the Bible as the Word of God involves studying it as His own voice speaking directly to you. When you open the Bible to study, realize that you have come into the very presence of God and that He is going to speak to you. Realize that it is God who is talking to you as if you were looking at Him face-to-face. Say to yourself, "God is now going to speak to me." Nothing gives more freshness and gladness to Bible study than the realization that as you read, God is actually talking to you.

Bible study then becomes personal companionship with God Himself. What a wonderful privilege Mary had one day, sitting at the feet of Jesus and listening to His voice. If we will study the Bible as the Word of God and as if we were in God's presence, then we will enjoy the privilege of sitting at the feet of Jesus and having Him talk to us every day.

This approach makes what would otherwise be a mere mechanical performance of a duty become a wonderfully joyous privilege. One can say as he opens the Bible, "Now God my Father is going to speak to me." Reading the Bible on our knees helps us to realize we are in God's presence. The Bible became in some measure a new book to me when I took to reading it on my knees.

Bible Study

Study the Bible prayerfully. God, the author of the Bible, is willing to act as interpreter of it. He does so when you ask Him. The one who prays the psalmist's prayer with sincerity and faith, *"Open thou mine eyes, that I may behold wondrous things out of thy law"* (Ps. 119:18), will have his eyes opened to new beauties and wonders in the Word.

Be very definite about this. Each time you open the Bible for study, even though it is only for a few minutes, ask God to give you an open and discerning eye. Expect Him to do it. Every time you come to a difficult passage in the Bible, lay it before God, ask for an explanation, and expect it.

The Holy Spirit as Teacher

How often we think as we puzzle over hard passages, "Oh, if I only had some great Bible teacher here to explain this to me!" God is always present. He understands the Bible better than any human teacher. Take your difficulty to Him, and ask Him to explain it. Jesus said, *"When he, the Spirit of truth, is come, he will guide you into all truth"* (John 16:13). It is the privilege of the humblest believer in Christ to have the Holy Spirit for his guide in his study of the Word.

I have known many very humble people, people with almost no education, who got more out of their Bible study than many great theological teachers. This happened because they learned it was their privilege to have the Holy Spirit for their Bible study teacher. Commentaries on the Bible are usually valuable. But one will learn more from the Bible by having the Holy Spirit for his teacher than from all the commentaries ever published.

Use spare time for Bible study. Time is lost in almost every man's life while waiting for meals, riding planes, going from place to place, and so forth. Carry a pocket Bible with you, and use these golden moments to listen to the voice of God.

Store Scripture in your mind and heart. It will keep you from sin (see Psalm 119:11) and false doctrine. (See Acts 20:29–30, 32; and 2 Timothy 3:13–15.) *"And thy word was unto me the joy and rejoicing of mine heart"* (Jer. 15:16). *"For he will speak peace unto his*

45

people" (Ps. 85:8). It will give you victory over the evil one (see 1 John 2:14), and it will give you power in prayer. *"If ye abide in me, and my words abide in you, ye shall ask what ye will, and it shall be done unto you"* (John 15:7). The Word will make you wiser than the aged and your enemies. *"Thou through thy commandments hast made me wiser than mine enemies: for they are ever with me....I understand more than the ancients, because I keep thy precepts....The entrance of thy words giveth light; it giveth understanding unto the simple"* (Ps. 119:98, 100, 130). It will make you *"thoroughly furnished unto all good works"* (2 Tim. 3:17). Try it.

Do not memorize at random, but memorize Scripture in a connected way. Memorize texts on various subjects. Memorize by chapter and verse so that you will know where to put your finger on the text if anyone disputes it. You should have a good Bible for your study.

8
Difficulties in the Bible

Sooner or later every young Christian comes across passages in the Bible that are hard to understand and difficult to believe. To many young Christians, these perplexities become a serious hindrance in the development of their Christian life. For days, weeks, and months, faith suffers a partial or total eclipse. At this point wise counsel is needed. We have no desire to conceal the fact that these difficulties exist. We desire instead to frankly face and consider them. What should we do concerning these paradoxes that every thoughtful student of the Bible will sooner or later encounter?

Expect Difficulties

The first thing we have to say about these difficulties is that, from the very nature of the situation, difficulties are to be expected. Some people are surprised and staggered because there are difficulties in the Bible. I would be more surprised and staggered if there were not. What is the Bible? It is a revelation of the mind, will, character, and being of the infinitely great, perfectly wise, and absolutely holy God.

To whom is this revelation made? To men and women like you and me—finite beings. It comes to men who are imperfect in intellectual development, in knowledge, in character, and, consequently, in spiritual discernment.

Because of our weakness, there must be difficulties in such a revelation. When the finite tries to understand the infinite, there is bound to be difficulty. When the ignorant contemplate the speech of One perfect in knowledge, there will be many things that are hard to understand. Some things will also appear absurd to immature and inaccurate minds. When sinful beings listen to the demands of the absolutely holy Being, they are bound to be staggered at some of His demands. When they consider His works, they are bound to be staggered. These will necessarily appear too severe, stern, and harsh.

It is plain that there must be difficulties for us in such a revelation as the Bible is proven to be. If someone were to hand me a book that was as simple as the multiplication table and say, "This is the Word of God, in which He has revealed His whole will and wisdom," I would shake my head and say, "I cannot believe it. That is too easy to be a perfect revelation of infinite wisdom." There must be in any complete revelation of God's mind, will, character, and being things that are difficult for a beginner to understand. Even the wisest and best of us are only beginners.

The Bible Is God's Revelation

The second thing about these difficulties is that a difficulty in a doctrine, or a grave objection to a doctrine, does not in any way prove the doctrine to be untrue. Many thoughtless people imagine it does. If they come across some difficulty in believing the divine origin and absolute inerrancy and infallibility of the Bible, they immediately conclude that the doctrine is disproved. That is very illogical.

Stop a moment and think. Be reasonable and fair. There is scarcely a doctrine in modern science that has not had some great difficulty gaining acceptance. When the Copernican theory, now so universally accepted, was first proclaimed, it encountered a very serious dilemma. If this theory were true, the planet Venus had to have phases like the moon. But no phases could be discovered using the best telescope then in existence. The positive argument for the theory was so strong, however, that it was accepted in spite of this apparently unanswerable objection. When a more powerful telescope was made, it was discovered that Venus had phases after all.

Difficulties in the Bible

The whole problem arose, as all those in the Bible arise, from man's ignorance of some of the facts in the case. According to the commonsense logic recognized in many departments of science, if the positive proof of a theory is conclusive, it is believed by rational men in spite of any number of discrepancies in minor details. The positive proof that the Bible is the Word of God is absolutely conclusive: it is an absolutely trustworthy revelation from God Himself of Himself, His purposes, and His will, of man's duty and destiny, of spiritual and eternal realities.

Therefore, every rational man and woman must believe it despite minor discrepancies. He who gives up a well-attested truth because there are some facts that he cannot reconcile with that truth is a shallow thinker. He who gives up the divine origin and inerrancy of the Bible because there are some supposed facts that he cannot reconcile with that doctrine is a very shallow Bible scholar.

The Bible Is Logical and Unified

There are many more difficulties in a doctrine that believes the Bible to be of human origin and hence fallible, than the doctrine that the Bible is of divine origin, hence altogether trustworthy. A man may bring you some apparent error and say, "How do you explain this if the Bible is the Word of God?" Perhaps you may not be able to answer him satisfactorily.

Then he thinks he has you, but not at all. Turn to him and ask him, "How do you account for the fulfilled prophecies of the Bible, if it is of human origin? How do you account for the marvelous unity of the Bible? How do you account for its inexhaustible depth? How do you account for its unique power in lifting men up to God? How do you account for the history of the Book, its victory over all men's attacks, etc."

For every insignificant objection he can bring to your view, you can bring many deeply significant objections to his view. No impartial man will have any difficulty in deciding between the two views. The discrepancies that must confront one who denies the Bible is of divine origin and authority are far more numerous than those that confront people who do believe it is of divine origin.

We Do Not Know Everything

Do not think that because you cannot solve a difficulty you can prove that the difficulty cannot be solved. The fact that you cannot answer an objection does not prove at all that it cannot be answered. It is strange how often we overlook this very evident fact. There are many who, when they see something in the Bible that does not conform to their truth, give it little thought and promptly jump to the conclusion that a solution is impossible. Then they throw away their faith in the reliability of the Bible and its divine origin. A little more modesty in beings so limited in knowledge, as we all are, would have led them to say, "Though I see no possible solution to this difficulty, someone a little wiser than I might easily find one."

If we would only bear in mind that we do not know everything and that there are a great many things that we cannot solve now but could easily solve if we only knew a little more. Above all, we should never forget that there may be a very easy solution through infinite wisdom that to our finite wisdom—or ignorance—appears absolutely insoluble.

What would we think of a beginner in algebra who, having tried without success for half an hour to solve a difficult problem, declared that there was no possible solution to the problem because he could not find one? A man with a lot of experience and ability once left his work and came a long distance to see me. He discovered what seemed to him to be a flat contradiction in the Bible. It defied all attempts at reconciliation. But in a few moments he saw a very simple and satisfactory solution to the difficulty.

A Beautiful and Wondrous Book

The seeming defects in the Book are exceedingly insignificant when compared with its many, marvelous wonders. It certainly reveals great perversity of both mind and heart that men spend so much time focusing on the insignificant points that they consider defects in the Bible. How sad it is that they never recognize the incomparable beauties and wonders that adorn almost every page.

What would we think of any man who, in studying some great masterpiece of art, concentrated his entire attention on what looked to him like a flyspeck in the corner? A large proportion of what is vaunted as "critical study of the Bible" is a laborious and scholarly investigation of supposed flyspecks and an entire neglect of the countless glories of the Book.

Are You a Superficial Reader?

The puzzles and paradoxes in the Bible have far more weight with superficial readers than with students who read it in depth. Take a man who is totally ignorant of the real contents and meaning of the Bible and devotes his whole strength to discovering apparent inconsistencies in it. To such superficial Bible students, these difficulties seem to have immense importance; but to the one who has learned to meditate on the Word of God day and night, they have little weight.

That mighty man of God, George Müller, who carefully studied the Bible from beginning to end more than a hundred times, was not disturbed by any discrepancies he encountered. His example can encourage the student who is reading it through carefully for the first or second time and finds many things that perplex him.

The difficulties in the Bible rapidly disappear upon careful and prayerful study. There are many things in the Bible that once puzzled us that have been perfectly cleared up and no longer present any difficulty at all! Is it not reasonable to suppose that the difficulties that still remain will also disappear on further study?

Profitable Approach to Discrepancies

How shall we deal with the difficulties that we do find in the Bible?

First of all, *honestly*. Whenever you find a difficulty in the Bible, frankly acknowledge it. If you cannot give a good, honest explanation, do not attempt as yet to give any at all.

Humbly. Recognize the limitations of your own mind and knowledge, and do not imagine there is no solution just because you have not found one. There is, in all probability, a very simple solution. You will find it someday.

With determination. Make up your mind that you will find the solution, if possible, through necessary study and hard thinking. The difficulties in the Bible are your heavenly Father's challenge to you to set your brain to work.

Fearlessly. Do not be frightened when you find a difficulty, no matter how unanswerable it appears at first glance. Thousands have found such difficulties before you. They were seen hundreds of years ago, and still the Bible stands. You are not likely to discover any difficulty that was not discovered and probably settled long before you were born, though you do not know just where to find the solution.

The Bible, which has stood eighteen centuries of rigid examination and constant, intense assault, will not fail because of any discoveries you make or any attacks of modern infidels. All modern attacks on the Bible simply revamp old objections that have been disposed of a hundred times in the past. These old objections will prove no more effective in their new clothes than they did in the cast-off garments of the past.

Patiently. Do not be discouraged because you do not solve every problem in a day. If some difficulty defies your best effort, lay it aside for a while. Very likely when you come back to it, it will have disappeared, and you will wonder how you were ever perplexed by it. I often have to smile when I remember how I was perplexed in the past over questions that are now clear as day.

Scripturally. If you find a difficulty in one part of the Bible, look for other Scriptures to shed light on it and dissolve it. Nothing explains Scripture like Scripture. Never let apparently obscure passages of Scripture darken the light that comes from clear passages. Rather, let the light that comes from the clear passage illuminate the darkness that seems to surround the obscure passage.

Prayerfully. It is wonderful how difficulties dissolve when one looks at them on his knees. One great reason some modern scholars have learned to be destructive critics is that they have forgotten how to pray.

9
Prayer

The one who wishes to succeed in the Christian life must lead a life of prayer. Much of the failure in Christian living today, and in Christian work, results from neglect of prayer. Very few Christians spend as much time in prayer as they should. The apostle James told believers in his day that the secret behind the poverty and powerlessness of their lives and service was neglect of prayer. *"Ye have not,"* said God through the apostle James, *"because ye ask not"* (James 4:2). So it is today. "Why is it," many Christians are asking, "that I make such poor headway in my Christian life? Why do I have so little victory over sin? Why do I accomplish so little by my effort?" God answers, *"Ye have not, because ye ask not."*

Decide on a Life of Prayer

It is easy enough to lead a life of prayer if one only decides to live it. Set apart some time each day for prayer. The habit of David and Daniel is a good one, three times a day. *"Evening, and morning, and at noon,"* said David, *"will I pray, and cry aloud: and he shall hear my voice"* (Ps. 55:17). Of Daniel we read,

> *Now when Daniel knew that the writing was signed, he went into his house; and his windows being open in his chamber toward Jerusalem, he kneeled upon his knees three times a day, and prayed, and gave thanks before his God, as he did aforetime.* (Dan. 6:10)

Prayer

Of course, one can pray while walking down the street, riding in the car, or sitting at his desk. And one should learn to lift his heart to God right in the busiest moments of his life. But we also need set times of prayer, times when we go alone with God and talk to our Father in the secret place. *"But thou, when thou prayest, enter into thy closet, and when thou hast shut thy door, pray to thy Father which is in secret; and thy Father which seeth in secret shall reward thee openly"* (Matt. 6:6). God is in the secret place. He will meet with us there and listen to our petitions.

Prayer is a wonderful privilege. It is an audience with the King. It is talking to our Father. How strange it is that people would ask the question, "How much time should I spend in prayer?" When a person is summoned to an audience with his king, he never asks, "How much time must I spend with the king?" His question is rather, "How much time will the king give me?" Any true child of God who realizes that prayer is an audience with the King of Kings will never ask, "How much time must I spend in prayer?" Instead, he will ask, "How much time may I spend in prayer, considering other duties and privileges?"

Prepare with Prayer

Begin the day with thanksgiving and prayer. Offer thanksgiving for the definite mercies of the past and prayer for the definite needs of the present day. Think of the temptations that you are likely to meet during the day. Ask God to show you these temptations, and ask for strength from God for victory over them before they come. Many fail in the battle because they wait until the hour of battle to ask for aid. Others succeed because they have gained victory on their knees long before the battle arrived.

Jesus conquered the awful battles of Pilate's judgment hall and the cross because He prayed the previous night. He anticipated the battle the night before and gained the victory through prayer. He told His disciples to do the same. He instructed them, *"Pray that ye enter not into temptation"* (Luke 22:40), but they slept when they should have prayed. And when the hour of temptation came, they fell. Anticipate your battles, fight them on your knees before temptation comes, and you will always have victory. At the very start of the day, secure counsel and strength from God Himself for the duties of the day.

Prayer Saves Time

Never let the rush of business crowd out prayer. The more work that must be accomplished in any day, the more time must be spent in prayer and preparation for that work. You will not lose time by praying; you will save time. Prayer is the greatest time-saver known to man. The more work crowds you, the more you must take time for prayer.

Stop in the middle of the bustle and temptation of the day for thanksgiving and prayer. A few minutes spent alone with God at noon will go far to keep you calm despite the worries and anxieties of modern life.

Close the day with thanksgiving and prayer. Review all the blessings of the day, and thank God in detail for them. Nothing further increases faith in God and His Word than a calm review at the close of each day of what God has done for you that day. Nothing goes further toward bringing new and larger blessings from God than intelligent thanksgiving for blessings already granted.

Close Your Day with a Clean Slate

As the last thing you do each day, ask God to show you anything that has been displeasing in His sight. Then wait quietly before Him, and give God an opportunity to speak to you. Listen. Do not be in a hurry. If God shows you anything in the day that has been displeasing in His sight, confess it fully and frankly as to a holy and loving Father. Believe that God forgives it all, because He says He does. *"If we confess our sins, he is faithful and just to forgive us our sins, and to cleanse us from all unrighteousness"* (1 John 1:9).

Thus, at the close of each day, all your accounts with God will be settled. You can sleep in the joyful awareness that there is not a cloud between you and God. You can rise the next day to begin life anew with a clean balance sheet.

Do this and you can never backslide for more than twenty-four hours. Indeed, you will not backslide at all. It is very hard to straighten out accounts in business that have been allowed to become disordered over a prolonged period. No bank ever closes its business day until its balance sheet is absolutely correct. No Christian should close a single day until his accounts with God for that day have been perfectly adjusted.

Prayer for Specific Blessings

There should be special prayer in special temptation—when we see the temptation approaching. If you possibly can, immediately find a place to be alone somewhere with God, then fight your battle out. Keep looking to God. *"Pray without ceasing"* (1 Thess. 5:17). It is not necessary to always be on your knees, but the heart should be on its knees all the time. We should often be on our knees, or our faces, literally.

This prayer life is a joyous life, free from worry and care. *"Be careful for nothing; but in every thing by prayer and supplication with thanksgiving let your requests be made known unto God. And the peace of God, which passeth all understanding, shall keep your hearts and minds through Christ Jesus"* (Phil. 4:6–7).

There are three things for which one who desires to succeed in the Christian life must especially pray. The first is wisdom. *"If any of you lack wisdom* [and we all do], *let him ask of God"* (James 1:5). The second is strength. *"But they that wait upon the LORD shall renew their strength"* (Isa. 40:31). The third is the Holy Spirit. *"Your heavenly Father* [shall] *give the Holy Spirit to them that ask him"* (Luke 11:13).

Even if you have received the Holy Spirit, you should constantly pray for a new blessing of the Holy Spirit and definitely expect to receive it. We need to be in contact with the Spirit, ready for every new emergency of Christian life and Christian service. The apostle Peter was baptized and filled with the Holy Spirit on Pentecost.

> And when the day of Pentecost was fully come, they were all with one accord in one place. And suddenly there came a sound from heaven as of a rushing mighty wind, and it filled all the house where they were sitting. And there appeared unto them cloven tongues like as of fire, and it sat upon each of them. And they were all filled with the Holy Ghost, and began to speak with other tongues, as the Spirit gave them utterance. (Acts 2:1–4)

After his baptism, the Holy Spirit continued to work through Peter as recorded in Acts 4:8, 31: *"Then Peter, filled with the Holy Ghost, said unto them, Ye rulers of the people, and elders of Israel…And when they had prayed, the place was shaken where they were assembled together; and they were all filled with the Holy Ghost, and they spake the word of God with boldness."*

There are many Christians in the world who had a very definite baptism of the Holy Spirit. They experienced great joy and were wonderfully used. But many have tried ever since to continue with only the power of that baptism received years ago. Today their lives are comparatively joyless and powerless. We constantly need to obtain new supplies of oil for our lamps. We secure these new supplies of oil by asking for them.

Do Not Neglect Fellowship

It is not enough that we have our times of secret prayer alone with God. We also need fellowship with others in prayer. If there is a prayer meeting in your church, attend it regularly. Attend it for your own sake and for the sake of the church. If it is a prayer meeting only in name and not in fact, use your influence quietly and constantly (not obstrusively) to make it a real prayer meeting. Attend the prayer meeting regularly for that purpose. Refuse all social engagements for that night.

A major-general in the United States Army once took command of the forces in a new district. A reception was arranged for him on a certain night of the week. When he was informed of this public reception, he replied that he could not attend since it was the evening of his prayer meeting. Everything had to take second place on that night to his prayer meeting. That general proved he was a man who could be depended upon. Christ's church in America owes more to him than to almost any other officer in the United States Army.

Ministers learn to depend on their prayer meeting members. The prayer meeting is the most important meeting in the church. If your church has no prayer meeting, use your influence to start one. It does not take many members to make a good prayer meeting. You can start with two but aim for many members.

It is wise to have a little group of Christian friends with whom you meet every week simply for prayer. There has been nothing more important in my own spiritual development in recent years than a little prayer meeting of less than a dozen friends who have met every Saturday night for years. We met, and together we waited on God. If my life has been of any use to the Master, I attribute it largely to that prayer meeting. Happy is the young Christian who has a little band of friends who regularly meet together for prayer.

10
Working for Christ

One of the important conditions of growth and strength in the Christian life is work. No man can keep up his physical strength without exercise, and no man can keep up his spiritual strength without spiritual exercise—in other words, without working for the Master. The working Christian is a happy Christian. The working Christian is a strong Christian. Some Christians never backslide because they are too busy with their Master's business. Many professing Christians do backslide because they are too idle to do anything but backslide.

Ask, and Be Fruitful

Jesus said to the first disciples, *"Follow me, and I will make you fishers of men"* (Matt. 4:19). Anyone who is not a fisher of men is not following Christ. Bearing fruit by bringing others to the Savior is the purpose for which Jesus has chosen us, and it is one of the most important conditions for power in prayer. Jesus said in John 15:16, *"Ye have not chosen me, but I have chosen you, and ordained you,* ***that ye should go and bring forth fruit****, and that your fruit should remain:* ***that whatsoever ye shall ask of the Father in my name, he may give it you"*** (emphasis added). These words of Jesus are very plain. They tell us that the believer who is bearing fruit is the one who can pray in the name of Christ and receive what he asks in that name.

In the same chapter Jesus tells us that bearing fruit in His strength is the condition of fullness of joy. He says, *"These things have I spoken unto you* [that is, things about living in Him and bearing fruit in His strength], *that my joy might remain in you, and that your joy might be full"* (John 15:11). Our experience more than adequately proves the truth of these words of our Master. Those who are full of activity in winning others to Christ are those who are full of joy in Christ Himself.

If you wish to be a happy Christian, a strong Christian, a Christian who is mighty in prayer, begin now to work for Jesus. Never let a day pass without doing some definite work for Him. But how can a young Christian work for Him? How can a young Christian bear fruit? The answer is very simple and very easy to follow.

You can bear fruit for your Master by going to others and telling them what your Savior has done for you, by urging them to accept this same Savior, and by showing them how. There is no other work in the world that is so easy to do, so joyous, and so fruitful. The youngest Christian can do personal work. Of course, he cannot do it as well as he will after he has had more practice. The way to learn to do it is by doing it.

You Can Start Immediately

I have known thousands of Christians all around the world who have begun to work for Christ, and bring others to Christ, the same day they were converted. How often young men and women, yes, and old men and women, too, have come to me and said, "I accepted Jesus Christ last night as my Savior, my Lord, and my King. Tonight I led a friend to Christ." The next day they would come and tell me of someone else they led to Christ.

There are many books that tell how to do personal work. However, one does not need to wait and read a book on the subject before beginning. One of the greatest and most common mistakes that is made is frittering one's life away preparing to get ready to get ready. Some never do get ready. The way to get ready for Christian work is to begin at once. Make up your mind that you will encourage at least one person to accept Christ every day.

Success Despite Mistakes

Early in his Christian life, D. L. Moody made a resolution that he would never let a day pass without speaking to at least one person about Christ. One night he was returning home late from his work. As he neared home, it occurred to him that he had not spoken to anyone about Jesus that day. He said to himself, "It is too late now. I will not get an opportunity. Here will be one day gone without my speaking to anyone about Christ."

Then, just ahead of him, he saw a man standing under a lamppost. He said, "Here is my last opportunity." The man was a stranger, though he knew of Mr. Moody. Mr. Moody hurried up to him and asked, "Are you a Christian?"

The man replied, "That is none of your business. If you were not a preacher, I would knock you into the gutter."

But Mr. Moody spoke a few Christian words to him and passed on.

The next day this man called on one of Mr. Moody's business friends in Chicago in great indignation. He said, "That man Moody of yours is doing more harm than good. He has zeal without knowledge. He came up to me last night, a perfect stranger, and asked me if I was a Christian. He insulted me. I told him if he had not been a preacher I would have knocked him into the gutter."

Mr. Moody's friend called him in and said, "Moody, you are doing more harm than good. You have zeal without knowledge. You insulted a friend of mine on the street last night." Mr. Moody left somewhat crestfallen, feeling that perhaps he was doing more harm than good, that perhaps he did have zeal without knowledge.

Some weeks after, however, late at night, there was a loud pounding on his door. Mr. Moody got out of bed and rushed to the door, thinking his house was on fire. That same man stood at the door. He said, "Mr. Moody, I have not had a night's rest since you spoke to me that night under the lamppost. I have come here for you to tell me what to do to be saved." That night Mr. Moody had the joy of leading that man to Christ.

Working for Christ

Better to Have Zeal

It is better to have zeal without knowledge than to have knowledge without zeal. It is better yet to have zeal with knowledge, and anyone may have this. The way to acquire knowledge is through experience, and the way to gain experience is by doing the work. The man who is so afraid of making blunders that he never does anything also never learns anything. The man who goes ahead and does his best, willing to risk the blunders, is the man who learns to avoid blunders in the future.

Some of the most gifted men I have ever known have never really accomplished anything because they were so afraid of making blunders. Some of the most useful men I have ever known were men who started out as the least promising, but who had a real love for souls and worked to win them in a blundering way. Eventually they learned by experience to do things well.

Do not be discouraged by your blunders. Pitch in and keep plugging away. Every honest mistake is a stepping-stone to future success. Every day, try to lead someone to Christ. Of course, you will not always succeed, but the work will still do you good. Years later, you will often find that, where you thought you made the greatest mistakes, you accomplished the best results. The man who becomes angriest at you will often finally be the man who is most grateful to you. Be patient and hope on. Never be discouraged.

Make a prayer list. Pray alone with God. Write down at the top of a sheet of paper, "God helping me, I promise to pray daily and to work persistently for the conversion of the following people." Then kneel down and ask God to show you who to put on that list. Do not make the list so long that your prayer and work become mechanical and superficial.

Prayer Lists and Tracts

After you have made the list, keep your covenant and really pray for them daily. Watch for opportunities to speak to them—use these opportunities. You may have to wait a long time for your opportunities with some of them, and you may have to speak often, but never give up. I prayed about fifteen years for a man, one of the most discouraging men I had ever met. But I finally saw that man converted, and I saw him become a preacher of the Gospel. Many others were later converted through his preaching.

Learn to use tracts. Procure a few good tracts that will meet the needs of different kinds of people. Then hand these tracts out to the people whose needs they are adapted to meet. Follow your tracts up with prayer and personal effort.

Work for Your Pastor

Go to your pastor and ask him if there is some work he would like to have you do for him in the church. Be a person on whom your pastor can depend. We live in a day in which there are many kinds of work going on outside the church. Many of these ministries are good, and you should take part in them as much as you can. Never forget, however, that your first duty is to the church where you are a member.

Be a person your pastor can count on. It may be that your pastor may not want to use you, but at least give him the chance of refusing you. If he does refuse you, don't be discouraged, but find work somewhere else. There is plenty to do and few to do it. It is as true today as it was in the days of our Savior, *"The harvest truly is plenteous, but the labourers are few"* (Matt. 9:37). *"Pray ye therefore the Lord of the harvest, that he will send forth labourers into his harvest"* (v. 38), and pray that He will send you.

The right kind of men are needed in the ministry. The right kind of men and women are also needed for foreign mission work. You may not be the right kind of man or woman for foreign missionary work, but there is still work for you that is just as important as the work of the minister or the missionary. Be sure you fill your place and fill it well.

11

Foreign Missions

In order to have the most success in the Christian life, one must be interested in foreign missions. The last command of our Lord before leaving this earth was, *"Go ye therefore, and teach all nations, baptizing them in the name of the Father, and of the Son, and of the Holy Ghost: teaching them to observe all things whatsoever I have commanded you: and, lo, I am with you alway, even unto the end of the world"* (Matt. 28:19–20). Here is a command and a promise. It is one of the sweetest promises in the Bible.

The enjoyment of the promise is conditioned on obedience to the command. Our Lord commands all His disciples to go and make disciples of all nations. This command was not given to the apostles alone, but to every member of Christ's church in all ages. If we go, then Christ will be with us even until the end of the age. If we do not go, we have no right to count on His companionship. Are you going? How can we go?

There are three ways we can go. We must employ at least two of these ways if we are to enjoy the wonderful privilege of daily personal companionship with Jesus Christ.

You May Be God's Missionary

First, many of us can go personally. Many of us should go. God does not call each of us to go as foreign missionaries, but He does call many of us to go who are *not* responding to the call. Every Christian should offer himself for the foreign field and leave the responsibility of choosing or refusing him to the all-wise One, God Himself. No Christian has a right to stay home until he has offered himself definitely to God for the foreign field.

If you have not already done it, do it today. Spend time alone with God and say, "Heavenly Father, here I am, Your property, purchased by the precious blood of Jesus. I belong to You. If You want me in the foreign field, make it clear to me, and I will go." Then keep watching for God's leading. God's leading is a clear leading. *"God is light, and in him is no darkness at all"* (1 John 1:5). If you are really willing to be led, He will make His will for you clear as day.

Until He does make it obvious, do not worry that perhaps you are staying at home when you should go to the foreign field. If He wants you, He will make it clear in His own way and time.

If He does make it clear, then prepare to go step-by-step as He leads you. When His hour comes, go, no matter what it costs. If He does not make it clear that you should go yourself, stay home and do your duty at home. There are other important possibilities for you.

Go through Your Gifts

We all can and should go to the foreign field with our gifts. There are many who would like to go to the foreign field personally, but whom God providentially prevents. These people are still going via the missionaries they support or help to support. It is possible for you to preach the Gospel in the most remote corners of the earth by supporting or helping to support a foreign missionary or a native worker.

Many who read this book are financially able to support a foreign missionary. If you are able to do so, do it. If you are not able to support a foreign missionary, you may be able to support a native helper—do it. You may be able to support one missionary in Japan, another in China, another in India, another in Africa, and another somewhere else—do it.

Giving Is a Privilege

Oh, the joy of preaching the Gospel in lands we will never see with our own eyes! How few in the church today realize their privilege of preaching the Gospel and saving men, women, and children in distant lands by sending substitute missionaries to them—that is, by sending someone who goes for you, where you cannot go yourself.

They could not go if it were not for your gifts. You may be able to give only a small amount to foreign missions, but every bit counts. Many insignificant streams together make a mighty river. If you cannot be a river, at least be a stream.

Learn to give largely. The generous giver is the happy Christian. *"The liberal soul shall be made fat"* (Prov. 11:25). *"He which soweth sparingly shall reap also sparingly; and he which soweth bountifully shall reap also bountifully....And God is able to make all grace abound toward you; that ye, always having all sufficiency in all things, may abound to every good work"* (2 Cor. 9:6, 8).

Generosity Equals Success

Success and growth in the Christian life depend on only a little more than liberal giving. The stingy Christian cannot be a growing Christian. It is wonderful how a Christian begins to grow when he begins to give. Power in prayer depends on liberal giving. One of the most wonderful statements about prayer and its answers is 1 John 3:22. John said, *"And whatsoever we ask, we receive of him, because we keep his commandments, and do those things that are pleasing in his sight."* He received because he kept God's commandments and did those things that pleased God.

The immediate context shows that the special commandments he was keeping were the commandments about giving. He told us in the twenty-first verse that when our hearts cannot condemn us about our stingy giving, then we can have confidence in our prayers to God.

God's answers to our prayers come in through the same door our gifts go out to others. Some of us open the door such a little bit by our small giving that God is not able to pass in to us any large answers to prayer. One of the most remarkable promises in the Bible is found in Philippians 4:19, *"But my God shall supply* [the *Revised Standard Version* says *"fill full"*] *all your need according to his riches in glory by Christ Jesus."* This promise, however, was made to believers who distinguished themselves by the size and frequency of their giving. (Refer to verses 14–18.)

Of course, we should not confine our giving to foreign missions. We should give to the work of the home church as well as to rescue work in our large cities. We should do good for all men as we have opportunity, especially to those who are fellow Christians. *"As we have therefore opportunity, let us do good unto all men, especially unto them who are of the household of faith"* (Gal. 6:10). Foreign missions should receive a large part of our gifts.

Give systematically. Set aside a fixed proportion of all the money or goods you receive for Jesus. Be exact and honest about your giving. Don't use that part of your income for yourself under any circumstances.

The Christian is not under law, and there is no law binding the Christian to give a tenth of his income. But as a matter of free choice, a tenth is a good proportion to begin with. Don't let it be less than a tenth. God required the tithe from the Israelites, and Christians should give the same or more than what God required in the law. After you have given your tenth, you will soon learn the joy of giving offerings over and above your tenth.

Participate through Prayer

There is another way in which we can be a part of the foreign field. That is by our prayers. We all can go this way. Any hour of the day or night you can reach any corner of the earth by your prayers. I go to Japan, China, Australia, New Zealand, India, Africa, and to other parts of the world every day by my prayers. Prayer really makes things happen.

Do not make prayer an excuse for not going personally if God asks you. And do not make prayer an excuse for small giving. There is no power in that kind of prayer. If you are ready to go yourself, God willing, and if you are actually going by your gifts as God gives you ability, then you can go dynamically with your prayers also.

Foreign Missions

Missionaries Need Prayer

The greatest need in the work of Jesus Christ today is prayer. The greatest need of foreign missions today is prayer. Foreign missions are successful, but they are not as successful as they could be. They could be more successful if Christians at home, as well as abroad, were living up to their full potential in prayer.

Be specific in your prayers for foreign missions. Pray first of all that God will send forth laborers into His harvest—the right sort of laborers. There are many men and women in the foreign field who should not be there. There was not enough prayer about it. More foreign missionaries are greatly needed, but only more of the right kind of missionaries. Pray to God daily, believing He will send forth laborers into His harvest field.

Pray for the laborers who are already in the field. No group of men and women need our prayers more than foreign missionaries. No group of men and women are objects of more bitter hatred from Satan than they. Satan delights in attacking the reputation and character of the brave men and women who are at the battlefront for Christ. No one is subjected to as many subtle and awful temptations as foreign missionaries.

We owe it to them to support them with our prayers. Do not merely pray for foreign missionaries in general. Have a few special missionaries whose work you study so that you can pray intelligently for them.

Pray for the native converts. We Christians at home think we have difficulties, trials, temptations, and persecutions, but the burdens we have are nothing compared to what the converts in heathen lands bear. The obstacles are often enormous, and the discouragements crushing. Christ alone can make them stand, but He works in answer to the prayers of His people.

Pray often, pray earnestly, pray intensely, and pray with faith for native converts. We learn from missionary literature how God has wonderfully answered prayer for native converts. It is best to be specific in your prayers for converts and have a specific geographic area about whose needs you keep yourself informed.

Pray for the converts in that area. Do not have so many that you become confused and mechanical.

Pray for conversions in the foreign field. Pray for revivals in specific places. The last few years have been years of special prayer for special revival in foreign fields. From every corner of the earth, news has come of how God is amazingly answering these prayers. But the great things that God is beginning to do are small in comparison with what He will do if there is more prayer.

12
Companions

Our companions have a great influence on our character. The friendships we form create an intellectual, moral, and spiritual atmosphere where we are constantly breathing. Our spiritual health is helped or hindered by this atmosphere. Every young Christian should have a few wisely chosen, intimate friends with whom he can talk freely.

Choosing Your Friends

Search for a few people around your own age with whom you can associate intimately. Be sure that they are spiritual people in the best sense. Be sure they are people who love to study the Bible, who love to talk about spiritual themes, who know how to pray and do pray, and who are really working to bring others to Christ.

Do not feel at all uneasy about the fact that some Christian people are more compatible with you than others. God has made us that way. Some are attracted to certain people and some to others, and it proves nothing against the others or against you. Cultivate the friendship of those whose friendship you find helpful to your own spiritual life.

On the other hand, avoid the companionships that you find spiritually and morally harmful. Of course, we are not to withdraw ourselves totally from unconverted people or even worldly people. We are often to cultivate the acquaintance of unspiritual people, and even corrupt people, in order to win them for Christ. But we must always be on our guard with such friendships, lifting them up so they do not drag us down.

If you find, in spite of your best efforts, that a particular friendship is harming your spiritual life, then give it up. Some people are surrounded with such an atmosphere of unbelief, cynicism, criticism, impurity, greed, or other evils that it is impossible to remain without being contaminated. In such a case, the path of wisdom is plain; stop associating with those people to any large extent. Stop associating with them at all except where there is some possibility of helping them.

Books Are Influential

But there are other companionships that mold our lives in addition to the companionships of living people. The books we read are our companions. They exert a tremendous influence for good or evil. There is nothing that will help us more than a good book, and nothing that will hurt us more than a bad book. Among the most helpful books are the biographies of good men. Read again and again about the lives of such good and truly great men as Wesley, Finney, and Moody. We live in a day in which there are many good biographies. Read them.

Well-written histories are good companions. No study is more practical and instructive than the study of history. It is not only instructive but spiritually helpful if we watch to see the hand of God in history. We can see His inevitable triumph of right, and the inevitable punishment of wrong, in individuals and nations.

Some fiction is helpful, but here one needs to really be on guard. The majority of modern fiction is wicked and very morally harmful. Fiction that is not absolutely bad often promotes false views of life and prepares one more for a fantasy life rather than for reality. The habitual novel reader ruins his powers of keen and nimble thinking.

Fiction is so fascinating that it always tends to drive out other reading that is more helpful mentally and morally. We should be on our guard, even when reading good literature, that the good does not crowd out the best; in other words, that the best of man's literature does not replace the very best—God's Word. God's Book, the Bible, must always have the first place.

Companions

Pictures Can Shape a Life

There is another kind of companionship that has a tremendous influence over our lives. That is the companionship of pictures. The pictures we see every day of our lives, and the pictures we see only occasionally, have a tremendous power in shaping our lives.

A mother had two dearly loved sons. It was her dream and ambition that these sons would enter the ministry, but both of them went to sea. She could not understand why until a friend called her attention to the picture of a magnificent ship in full sail, which hung in the dining room. Every day of their lives, her boys saw that picture and had been thrilled by it. An unconquerable love and longing for the sea was created. This picture strongly influenced their lives.

How many masterpieces with worldly suggestions have sent young people on their road to ruin? Many of our art collections are so polluted with indecent pictures that it is not safe for a young man or woman to view them. The evil thoughts they suggest may only be for a moment, yet Satan will know how to bring that picture back again and again to bring harm. Do not look, even for a moment, at any picture that taints your imagination with evil suggestions—no matter how art critics praise it. Avoid, as you would poison, every painting, engraving, etching, and photograph that leaves a spot of impurity in your mind. Feast your soul on pictures that make you holier, kinder, more sympathetic, and tenderer.

13
Activities and Entertainment

Young people need recreation. Our Savior does not frown on wholesome recreation. He was interested in the games of children when He was here on earth. He watched the children at play (see Matthew 21:16–19), and He watches the children at play today. He delights in their play when it is wholesome and elevating.

In the stress and strain of modern life, older people also need recreation if they are to do their very best work. But there are pastimes that are wholesome, and there are amusements that are wicked. It is impossible to discuss amusements one by one, and it is unnecessary. A few principles are enough.

Guidelines for Choosing Recreation

Do not indulge in any form of amusement about whose propriety you have any doubts. When you are in doubt, always give God the benefit of the doubt. There are plenty of distractions that are not at all questionable. *"He that doubteth is damned...for whatsoever is not of faith is sin"* (Rom. 14:23). Many young Christians will say, "I am not sure that this is wrong." Are you sure it is right? If not, leave it alone.

Do not indulge in any amusement that you cannot engage in to the glory of God. *"Whether therefore ye eat, or drink, or whatsoever ye do, do all to the glory of God"* (1 Cor. 10:31). Whenever you are in doubt as to whether you should engage in an activity, ask yourself, "Can I do this to the glory of God?"

Activities and Entertainment

Do not engage in any activity that will hurt your influence with anybody. There are amusements that are perhaps all right in themselves, but in which we cannot engage without losing our influence with someone. Every true Christian wishes that his life would show everyone the best. There is so much to be done and so few to do it that every Christian desires every last ounce of power for good that he can have with everybody.

If a particular entertainment will injure your influence for good with anyone, the price is too great. Do not engage in it. Whether justly or unjustly, the world discounts the testimony of those Christians who indulge in certain forms of worldly amusements. We cannot afford to have our witness reduced.

Do not engage in any activity that you cannot make a matter of prayer, asking God's blessing. Pray before your play, just as you would pray before your work.

Do not go anyplace where you cannot take Christ with you and where you do not think Christ would feel at home. Christ went to happy places when He was here on earth. He went to the marriage feast in Cana and contributed to the joy of the occasion. *"And the third day there was a marriage in Cana of Galilee; and the mother of Jesus was there: and both Jesus was called, and his disciples, to the marriage"* (John 2:1–2). But there are many modern places where Christ would not be comfortable. Would the atmosphere of the modern theater be agreeable to that Holy One whom we call Lord? If not, don't go.

Don't engage in any activity that you would not like to be found enjoying if the Lord should come. He may come at any moment. Blessed is that individual who, when He comes, will be watching and ready, glad to receive to Him immediately. *"And ye yourselves like unto men that wait for their lord, when he will return from the wedding; that when he cometh and knocketh, they may open unto him immediately....Be ye therefore ready also: for the Son of man cometh at an hour when ye think not"* (Luke 12:36, 40).

I have a friend who was walking down the street one day thinking about the return of the Lord. As he thought, he was smoking a cigar. The thought occurred to him, "Would you like to meet Christ now with that cigar in your mouth?" He answered honestly, "No, I would not." He threw that cigar away and never lit another.

Do not engage in any activity, no matter how harmless it would be for yourself, that might harm someone else. Someone may be influenced to maintain or even start a harmful habit because our innocent activity was their inspiration.

For most of us the recreation that is most helpful demands considerable physical energy. These activities take us into the open air, leave us refreshed in body and invigorated in mind. Physical exercise, but not overexertion, is one of the great safeguards of the moral conduct of young people. There is little pleasure gained in watching others play the most vigorous game of football, but there is real health for the body and soul in physical exercise.

14

Persecution

One of the discouragements that meets every true Christian before he has gone very far in the Christian life is persecution. God tells us in His Word that *"all that will live godly in Christ Jesus shall suffer persecution"* (2 Tim. 3:12). Sooner or later everyone who surrenders absolutely to God and seeks to follow Jesus Christ in everything will find this verse is true.

We live in a God-hating world and a compromising age. The world's hatred of God today may be veiled. It often does not express itself the same way it expressed itself in Palestine during the days of Jesus Christ. Nevertheless, the world hates God today as much as it ever did. It also hates anyone who is loyal to Christ. It may not imprison or kill him, but in some way it will persecute him.

Do Not Be Discouraged When Persecuted

Persecution is inevitable for a loyal follower of Jesus Christ. Many young Christians, when they meet with persecution, are surprised and discouraged. Many fall away. Many seem to run well for a few days, but, like those of whom Jesus spoke, they *"have no root in themselves, and so endure but for a time: afterward, when affliction or persecution ariseth for the word's sake, immediately they are offended"* (Mark 4:17). I have seen many apparently promising Christian lives end this way. But if persecution is received correctly, it is no longer a hindrance to the Christian life but a help.

Do not be discouraged when you are persecuted. No matter how fierce and hard the persecution, be thankful for it. Jesus said,

> *Blessed are they which are persecuted for righteousness' sake: for theirs is the kingdom of heaven. Blessed are ye, when men shall revile you, and persecute you, and shall say all manner of evil against you falsely, for my sake. Rejoice, and be exceeding glad: for great is your reward in heaven: for so persecuted they the prophets which were before you.* (Matt. 5:10–12)

It is a great privilege to be persecuted for Jesus. Peter found this out and wrote to the Christians of his day:

> *Beloved, think it not strange concerning the fiery trial which is to try you, as though some strange thing happened unto you: but rejoice, inasmuch as ye are partakers of Christ's sufferings; that, when his glory shall be revealed, ye may be glad also with exceeding joy. If ye be reproached for the name of Christ, happy are ye; for the spirit of glory and of God resteth upon you: on their part he is evil spoken of, but on your part he is glorified.* (1 Pet. 4:12–14)

A Bad Disposition Can Cause Persecution

Be very sure that the persecution is really for Christ's sake and not because of your own stubbornness, fault, or eccentricity. There are many who bring the displeasure of others on themselves because they are stubborn and cranky. They then flatter themselves that they are being persecuted for Christ's sake and for righteousness' sake.

Be considerate of the opinions of others, and be considerate of the conduct of others. Be sure that you do not push your opinions on others in an unjustifiable way. Do not make your conscience a rule of life for other people. But never yield one inch of principle. Stand firmly behind what you believe. Do it in love, but do it at any cost.

Persecution

Return Persecution with Love

If when you are standing for conviction and principle you are disliked, slandered, and treated with all manner of unkindness because of it, do not be sad, but rejoice. Do not speak evil of those who speak evil of you, *"because Christ also suffered for us, leaving us an example, that ye should follow his steps:...Who, when he was reviled, reviled not again; when he suffered, he threatened not; but committed himself to him that judgeth righteously"* (1 Pet. 2:21, 23).

At this point many Christians make their mistake. They stand loyally for the truth, but receive the persecution that comes for the truth with harshness. They grow bitter and start condemning everyone but themselves. There is no blessing in bearing persecution that way.

Persecution should be tolerated lovingly and serenely. Do not talk about your own persecution. Rejoice in it. Thank God for it and go on obeying Him. Do not forget to love and pray for those people who persecute you. *"But I say unto you, Love your enemies, bless them that curse you, do good to them that hate you, and pray for them which despitefully use you, and persecute you"* (Matt. 5:44).

Remember Your Reward

Anytime the persecution seems more than you can bear, remember how great the reward is. *"If we suffer, we shall also reign with him: if we deny him, he also will deny us"* (2 Tim. 2:12). Everyone must enter into the kingdom of God through pain and trouble. *"Confirming the souls of the disciples, and exhorting them to continue in the faith, and that we must through much tribulation enter into the kingdom of God"* (Acts 14:22). But do not turn away from Jesus for this reason.

Always remember, however fiercely the fire of persecution may burn, *"the sufferings of this present time are not worthy to be compared with the glory which shall be revealed in us"* (Rom. 8:18). Remember, too, that your *"light affliction, which is but for a moment, worketh for us a far more exceeding and eternal weight of glory"* (2 Cor. 4:17). Keep looking, *"not at the things which are seen, but at the things which are not seen: for the things which are seen are temporal; but the things which are not seen are eternal"* (2 Cor. 4:18.)

When the apostles were persecuted, even suffering imprisonment and whippings, *"they departed from the presence of the council* [that had ordered their terrible punishment], *rejoicing that they were counted worthy to suffer shame for his name. And daily in the temple, and in every house, they ceased not to teach and preach Jesus Christ"* (Acts 5:41–42).

Never More than We Can Bear

The time may come when you think you are being persecuted more than others, but you do not know what others have to endure. Even if it is that you are being persecuted more than anyone else, you should not complain. It is more fitting to humbly thank God that He has given you such an honor.

Keep your eyes fixed on

> *Jesus the author and finisher of our faith; who for the joy that was set before him endured the cross, despising the shame, and is set down at the right hand of the throne of God. For consider him that endured such contradiction of sinners against himself, lest ye be wearied and faint in your minds.* (Heb. 12:2–3)

I was once talking with an old man who became saved when he was still a slave. His cruel master flogged him again and again for his loyalty to Christ, but he said to me, "I simply thought of my Savior dying on the cross in my place, and I rejoiced to suffer persecution for Him."

15
Guidance

I have met many people who are trying to lead a Christian life, but they are troubled over the question of guidance. They desire to do God's will in all things, but it puzzles them to know that the will of God is possible in every situation. When anyone starts out with determination to obey God in everything and be led by the Holy Spirit, Satan tries to confuse that person from knowing the will of God.

Satan often suggests something is the will of God, and it is not at all. When the believer does not follow the false suggestion, Satan says, "You disobeyed God." Because of this, many conscientious young Christians fall into a morbid and unhappy state of mind, fearing they have disobeyed God and lost His favor. This is one of the most frequent devices the devil uses to keep Christians from being cheerful.

Knowing the Will of God

How can we know the will of God?

First, let me say that a healthy Christian life is not governed by a lot of rules about what one is permitted to eat, drink, do, and not do. A life governed by a lot of rules is a life of bondage. One will sooner or later break some of these man-made rules and feel self-condemnation. Paul told us in Romans 8:15, *"Ye have not received the spirit of bondage again to fear; but ye have received the Spirit of adoption, whereby we cry, Abba, Father."*

The true Christian life is a life of a trusting, glad, fear-free child; not led by rules, but by the personal guidance of the Holy Spirit who dwells within. *"As many as are led by the Spirit of God, they are the sons of God"* (Rom. 8:14). If you have received Jesus Christ, the Holy Spirit dwells within you and is ready to lead you at every turn of life.

A life governed by a multitude of rules is a life of bondage and anxiety. A life surrendered to the control of the Holy Spirit is a life of joy, peace, and freedom. There is no anxiety in such a life; there is no fear in the presence of God. We trust God and rejoice in His presence just as a child trusts his earthly father and rejoices in his presence. If we make a mistake, we can tell Him all about it as trustfully as a child and know that He forgives and restores us instantly to His full favor. *"If we confess our sins, he is faithful and just to forgive us our sins, and to cleanse us from all unrighteousness"* (1 John 1:9).

Five Points in Seeking Wisdom

But how can we detect the Holy Spirit's guidance so that we may obey Him and have God's favor at every turn of life? This question is answered in James 1:5–7,

> *If any of you lack wisdom, let him ask of God, that giveth to all men liberally, and upbraideth not; and it shall be given him. But let him ask in faith, nothing wavering. For he that wavereth is like a wave of the sea driven with the wind and tossed. For let not that man think that he shall receive any thing of the Lord.*

The principle is simple. It includes five points.

Recognize your ignorance and inability to guide your own life—you lack wisdom.

Surrender your will to God and really desire to be led by Him.

Have definite prayer time with Him for guidance.

Have confident expectation that God will guide you. "Ask in faith, doubting nothing."

Follow step-by-step as He guides.

Guidance

God Guides One Step at a Time

God may show you only a step at a time. That is enough. All you need to know is the next step. It is here that many make a mistake. They wish God to show them the whole way before they take the first step.

A university student once came to me with a question about guidance. He said, "I cannot find the will of God. I have been praying, but God does not show me His will." This was in July.

"What are you seeking to know in the will of God?"

"What I should do next summer."

I replied, "Do you know what you should do tomorrow?"

"Yes."

"Do you know what you should do next autumn?"

"Yes, finish my degree. But what I want to know is what I should do when my university course is over."

He was soon led to see that all he needed to know for the present was what God had already shown him. When he did that, God would show him the next step.

Do not worry about what you ought to do next week. Do what God shows you to do for today. Next week will take care of itself. Indeed, tomorrow will take care of itself. Obey the Spirit of God for today. *"Take therefore no thought for the morrow: for the morrow shall take thought for the things of itself. Sufficient unto the day is the evil thereof"* (Matt. 6:34). It is enough to live a day at a time if we do our very best for that day.

God Gives Clear Guidance

God's guidance is clear guidance, *"God is light, and in him is no darkness at all"* (1 John 1:5). Do not be anxious about obscure leadings. Do not let your soul be ruffled by the thought, "Perhaps this obscure leading is what God wants me to do." Obscure leadings are not divine leadings. God's path is as clear as day. Satan's path is full of obscurity, uncertainty, anxiety, and questioning.

If a leading comes and you are not quite sure whether it is the will of God, simply pray to your heavenly Father and say,

"Heavenly Father, I desire to know Your will. I will do Your will if You will make it clear. But You are light, and in You is no darkness at all. If this is Your will, make it crystal clear, and I will do it." Then wait quietly for God and do not act until He makes it clear. But the moment He makes it clear, act at once.

You Need a Surrendered Will

The whole secret of guidance is an absolutely surrendered will, a will that is given up to God and ready to obey Him at any cost. Many of our uncertainties about God's guidance are simply caused by our unwillingness to follow God's guiding. We are tempted to say, "I cannot find out what God's will is." The real trouble is that we have found His will, but, because it is something we do not wish to do, we are trying to make ourselves think God wants us to do something else.

God Does Not Contradict His Word

All supposed leadings of God should be tested by the Word of God. The Bible is God's revealed will. Any leading that contradicts the plain teaching of the Bible is certainly not the leading of the Holy Spirit. The Holy Spirit does not contradict Himself.

A man once came to me and said that God was leading him to marry a certain woman. He said she was a very devoted Christian woman, and they were greatly drawn to one another. They felt that God was leading them to be married.

But I said to the man, "You already have a wife."

"Yes," he said, "but we have never lived happily, and we have not lived together for years."

"But," I replied, "that does not alter the situation. God in His Word has told us distinctly the duty of the husband to his wife and how wrong it is in His sight for a husband to divorce his wife and marry another."

"Yes," said the man, "but the Holy Spirit is leading us to one another."

Guidance

I indignantly replied, "Whatever spirit is leading you to marry one another is certainly not the Holy Spirit but the spirit of the evil one. The Holy Spirit never leads anyone to disobey the Word of God."

Search the Scriptures

In seeking to know the guidance of the Spirit, always search the Scriptures; study them prayerfully. Do not make a book of magic out of the Bible. Do not ask God to show you His will, then open your Bible at random and put your finger on some text, taking it out of context and pretending you have seen the will of God. This is an irreverent and improper use of Scripture. You may open your Bible at just the right place to find the right guidance. But if you do receive real guidance, it will not be by some fanciful interpretation of the passage you find. It will be by taking the passage in its context and interpreting it to mean just what it says as seen in its context.

All sorts of mischief has arisen from using the Bible in this perverse way. I knew an earnest Christian woman who was concerned about the predictions made by a false prophetess. The prophetess claimed Chicago would be destroyed on a certain day. She opened her Bible at random. It opened to the twelfth chapter of Ezekiel, *"Son of man, eat thy bread with quaking, and drink thy water with trembling and with carefulness....And the cities that are inhabited shall be laid waste, and the land shall be desolate"* (Ezek. 12:18, 20).

This seemed to fit the situation exactly, and the woman was considerably affected. But if the verses were studied in context, it would have been evident at once that God was not speaking about Chicago, and the verses were not applicable to Chicago. This was not an intelligent study of the Word of God and, therefore, led to a false conclusion.

Free from Anxiety and Worry

To sum up, lead a life that is not governed by rules but by the personal guidance of the Holy Spirit. Surrender your will totally to God. Whenever you are in doubt about His guidance, ask Him to show you His will, expect Him to do it, then follow step-by-step as He leads. Test all leadings by the plain and simple teachings of the Bible. Live without anxiety and worry that perhaps in an unguarded moment you have not done the right thing.

After you have done what you think God has led you to do, do not always go back wondering whether or not you did His will. You will become morbid if you do. If you really wished to do God's will, sought His guidance, and did what you thought He guided you to do, you may rest assured you did the right thing, no matter what the outcome has been.

Satan is determined to keep us from being happy, cheerful Christians—if he can. God, on the other hand, wishes us to be happy, cheerful, bright Christians every day and every hour. He does not wish us to brood, but to rejoice. *"Rejoice in the Lord alway: and again I say, Rejoice"* (Phil. 4:4).

An exemplary Christian man came to me one Monday morning, dejected over his apparent work failures of the preceding day. "I made wretched work of teaching my Sunday school class yesterday."

"Did you honestly seek wisdom from God before you went to your class?" I asked.

"I did."

"Did you expect to receive it?"

"I did."

"Then," I reassured him, "in the face of God's promise, what right have you to doubt that God gave you wisdom?" (See James 1:5–7.)

His gloom disappeared. He looked up with a smile and said, "I had no right to doubt." Let us learn to trust God.

Let us remember that, if we surrender to Him, He is more willing to guide us than we are to be guided. Let us trust that He does guide us at every step even though our actions may not bring the results we expect. Never worry, but trust God. This way we will be happy, peaceful, strong, and useful at every turn of life.

How to Bring Them to Christ

Contents

1
You Can Be a Soulwinner

Certain requirements must be fulfilled for real success in leading lost souls to Christ. Fortunately these are few and simple, and anyone can meet them.

The one who desires real success in bringing others to Christ must himself be a thoroughly converted person. Jesus said to Peter, *"When thou art converted, strengthen thy brethren"* (Luke 22:32). Peter was in no position to help his fellow Christians until he himself, after his cowardly denial, had turned again to his Lord with his whole heart.

If we desire to bring others to Christ, we must turn away from all sin, worldliness, and selfishness with our whole heart, yielding to Jesus the absolute lordship over our thoughts, purposes, and actions. If we are seeking to have our own way and not letting Him have His way in our lives, our power will be crippled and souls that might have been saved may be lost. This principle can be applied to the numerous questions that every young Christian asks as to whether he should do this or that. Each individual can find answers for himself if Christ's honor and not his own pleasure is uppermost in his mind.

Loving Others into the Kingdom

The one who desires real success in bringing others to Christ must truly love others and long for their salvation. If we have no love for other souls, our efforts will be mechanical and powerless. We may know how to approach men and what to say to them, but there will be no power in what we say. It will not touch the heart.

But if, like Paul, we have "great heaviness and unceasing pain in our hearts" (see Romans 9:2) for the unsaved, there will be an earnestness in our tone and manner that will impress even the most disinterested. Furthermore, if we have a love for souls, we will be watching constantly for opportunities to speak with the unsaved. We will find opportunities on the street, in the store, in the home, on buses and trains, and everywhere that would otherwise have entirely escaped our notice.

But how does one acquire a love for souls? Like every other grace of Christian character, a love for souls is the work of the Holy Spirit. If we are conscious that we do not have the love for souls that we should have, the first thing to do is to go to God and humbly confess this lack in our lives. We can ask Him by His Holy Spirit to supply what we need and expect Him to do it. (See 1 John 5:14–15; Philippians 4:19.) Jesus Christ had an intense love for souls. (See Matthew 23:37; Luke 19:10.) Intimate and constant companionship with Him will impart to our lives this grace that was so prominent in Him.

Feelings are the outcome of thoughts. If we desire any given feeling to develop in our lives, we should dwell on thoughts that produce that feeling. If any saved person will concentrate long enough on the peril and misery of any man separated from Christ, he will realize the worth of his soul in God's sight because of the death of God's Son to save him. An intense desire for that man's salvation is almost certain to follow. Reflection on our own ruined, unhappy condition without Christ and on the great sacrifice He made to save us is sure to fill our hearts with a desire to bring others to the Savior we have found.

Using the Word and Prayer

The one who desires to have real success in bringing men to Christ must have a working knowledge of the Bible. The Word of God is *"the sword of the Spirit"* (Eph. 6:17) that God uses to convict of sin, to reveal Christ, and to regenerate men. If we wish to work together with God, the Bible is the instrument we must rely on and use in bringing men to Christ. We must know how to use the

Bible to show men their need of a Savior, to show them Jesus as the Savior they need, to show them how to make this Savior their own Savior, and to meet the difficulties that stand in the way of their accepting Christ. A large part of the following pages will be devoted to imparting this knowledge.

The one who desires to have real success in bringing men to Christ must pray frequently. Solid work in soulwinning must be accompanied by prayer at every step. We must first ask God to lead us to the right persons to approach. God does not intend that we speak to everyone we meet. If we try to do this, we will waste much valuable time speaking to those whom we cannot help—time we might have used speaking to those for whom we could have done much good. God alone knows the one to whom He intends us to speak. We must ask Him to point him or her out to us and expect Him to do it. (See Acts 8:27–29.)

We must ask God to show us what to say to those to whom He leads us. We will need God's guidance to know which Bible passage to use in each case. Every experienced worker will testify to the many instances in which God has led him to use some text of Scripture that he would not otherwise have used but which proved to be just the one needed.

We must also ask God to give power to what He has given us to say. We need not only a message from God, but also power from God to send the message home. Most workers have to learn this lesson by experience. They sit down beside an unsaved man, reasoning, pleading, and citing texts from the Word of God, but the man does not accept Christ. At last it dawns on them that they are trying to convert the man in their own strength. When they lift an earnest and humble prayer to God for His strength, God hears. In a short time this "very difficult case" is rejoicing in Christ.

We must then ask God to carry on the work after our part of it has come to an end. After having done our whole duty in any given instance—whatever may have been our apparent success-ful or unsuccessful work—we should definitely commit the case to God in prayer. If there is anything the average worker in this hurrying age needs to have impressed on him, it is the necessity of more prayer. By praying more, we will not work any less, but we will accomplish much more.

The one who desires to have real success in bringing men to Christ must be "baptized with the Holy Spirit." *"Ye shall receive power, after that the Holy Ghost is come upon you"* (Acts 1:8). Jesus said this to His disciples after giving them the Great Commission to go out and bring men to Himself. The supreme condition of soulwinning power is the same today, *"after that the Holy Ghost is come upon you."* A later chapter will be devoted to a study of the baptism in the Holy Spirit and how any Christian can obtain it.

2
Taking the First Step

When God leads us to believe that He wants us to make an effort to lead someone to Christ, the first question that confronts us is, "How will I begin?" Regardless of who the person is, it is comparatively easy. Ask him whether he is a Christian, or ask some other direct and simple question that will inevitably lead to a conversation along this line. Even if the person is a total stranger, it is not difficult. The person can be engaged in conversation on some general topic or on something suggested by passing events and soon be brought around to the great subject of spiritual things. Christ's conversation with the woman of Samaria in the fourth chapter of John is an excellent illustration of this.

Many times, even with strangers, it is best to bring up the subject at once. Ask them if they are Christians, if they are saved, or some similar question. If this is done courteously and earnestly, it will frequently make even disinterested people start thinking, and it may result in their conversion. It is astonishing how often one who undertakes this work in humble dependence upon God and under His direction finds the way prepared and how seldom he receives any rebuff.

One day I met a man on one of the most crowded streets of Chicago. As I passed him, the impulse came to speak to him about the Savior. Stopping a moment and asking God to show me if the impulse was from Him, I turned around and followed the man. I overtook him in the middle of the street, laid my hand on his shoulder, and said, "My friend, are you a Christian?"

He was startled and said, "That's a strange question to ask a man."

I said, "I know it, and I do not ask that question of every stranger; but God put it into my heart to ask it of you."

He then told me that his cousin was a minister and had been urging this very matter upon him. He said he was a prosperous businessman but had been drinking excessively. After further conversation we separated, but later I discovered the man had accepted Christ as his Savior.

It is often best to win a person's confidence and friendship before bringing up the subject. It is good to select someone first and then plan to win him to Christ. Cultivate his acquaintance, be kind to him, and when the right moment arrives, ask him the great question. An old man in Chicago was won to Christ in this way by a young woman who found him sick and alone. She called day after day and showed him many kindnesses. After a time, she spoke to him of the Savior and had the joy of seeing him accept Christ.

A wisely chosen tract placed in the hand of the one with whom you wish to speak will often lead easily and naturally to the subject. One day I was riding on a train and praying that God would use me to lead someone to His Son. A young daughter of a minister with whom I had had some conversation on this subject came in with a friend and took the seat in front of me. I took out a little bundle of tracts, selected one that seemed appropriate, handed it to her, and asked her to read it. As she read, I prayed. When she had finished, I leaned over and asked her what she thought about it. She was deeply moved, and I asked her if she would accept Christ right there, which she did. As she left the train, she thanked me heartily for what I had done for her.

You will often meet someone whose face tells the story of unhappiness or discontent. In such a case, it is easy to ask the person if he is happy. If he answers, "No," you can say, "I can tell you about Someone who will make you happy if you will only receive Him." Skill in beginning a conversation will come with practice. You may be rather awkward about it at first, but it will become easier.

Taking the First Step

Introducing Him to Jesus

Once the subject is opened, the first thing to find out is where the person stands. Then you will know how to treat his case wisely. The following chapters describe different types of individuals you are likely to meet. To ascertain these "types," simply ask questions such as: "Are you a Christian?" "Are you saved?" "Do you know that your sins are forgiven?" "Do you have eternal life?" "Are you confessing Christ openly before the world?" "Are you a friend of Jesus?" "Have you been born again?"

These questions can be answered untruthfully either through ignorance or a desire to mislead you. You can, nevertheless, still learn a great deal from how the question is answered. A man's face will often reveal what his words try to conceal. Anyone who studies faces will soon be able to tell in many instances their exact state regardless of anything they may say.

Above all, be open to the leading of the Holy Spirit. If we only look to Him to do it, the Holy Spirit will often reveal the man's position and the exact Scripture he needs.

When we have learned where the person stands, the next thing to do is to lead him to accept Jesus Christ as his personal Savior and Master. We must always bear in mind that the primary purpose of our work is not to get people to join a church, to give up their bad habits, or to do anything other than to accept Jesus Christ as their Savior. He is the One who bore their sins in His own body on the tree, and through Him they can have immediate and entire forgiveness. He is to become their Master to whom they surrender absolutely the guidance of their thoughts, feelings, purposes, and actions.

After leading anyone to accept Christ, the next step will be to show him from God's Word that he has forgiveness of sin and eternal life. Acts 10:43, Acts 13:39, John 3:36, and John 5:24 give proof of this. Next, show him how to make a success of the Christian life that he has entered. How to do this will be explained later.

How to Bring Them to Christ

Each person is to be led to accept Christ through use of the Word of God. In the chapters that immediately follow, we will try to show what specific portions of the Word to use in certain cases and how to use them.

3
Dealing with the Indifferent

Frequent contact is made with indifferent or careless people. There are several ways of dealing with them. One is to show them their need of a Savior. A good verse to use for this purpose is Romans 3:23. Get the person to read the verse, *"For all have sinned, and come short of the glory of God."* Ask him, "Who has sinned?" Then ask him what it is that he has done, and pursue it until he plainly says: "I have sinned and come short of the glory of God." This is likely to make him realize his need of a Savior.

Another good verse to use is Isaiah 53:6: *"All we like sheep have gone astray; we have turned every one to his own way; and the LORD hath laid on him the iniquity of us all."* After the verse has been read, ask him who has gone astray. By a series of questions, bring him to the point where he will say, "I have gone astray." Then ask him what kind of a sheep is one that "has gone astray" and hold him to it until he says, "A lost sheep." "What are you, then?" should be your next question. His only answer can be: "Lost." Ask him what the Lord has done with his sin, and help him to see the truth of the verse—God has laid his sin on Jesus Christ. Now he is in a position for you to ask him the direct question: "Will you accept this Savior upon whom the Lord has laid your sin?"

Recognize the Problem

In dealing with the indifferent, I use Matthew 22:37–38: *"Jesus said unto him, Thou shalt love the Lord thy God with all thy heart, and with all thy soul, and with all thy mind. This is the first and great commandment."* Before having the person read the verse, it is good to ask him, "Do you know that you have committed the greatest sin that a man can commit?" In all probability he will answer, "No, I have not." Then ask him what he thinks the greatest sin a man can commit is. When he has answered, say to him, "Now let us see what God considers the greatest sin." Read the verses and ask him, "What is the first and greatest of the commandments?" Then ask him, "What, then, is the greatest sin?" He will soon answer that the violation of the first and greatest of the commandments must be the greatest sin. Ask him if he has kept the commandment. When he confesses—as sooner or later he must—that he has not, ask him of what he is guilty in the sight of God. Hold him to that point until he admits that he is guilty of committing the greatest sin that a man can commit.

I was dealing with a very bright young man who evidently had no deep sense of sin or of his need of a Savior. When I asked if he was a Christian, he said promptly that he always had been. But there was something in his manner that showed he had no clear understanding of what it meant to be a Christian. I asked if he had been born again, and he did not even understand what I was talking about. I then asked if he knew that he had committed the greatest sin a man could possibly commit.

He at once answered, "No, I never did in my life." I asked what he considered to be the greatest sin. He replied, "Murder."

Opening my Bible to Matthew 22:37–38, I asked him to read the verses. I then asked him, "If this is the first and greatest commandment, what is the greatest sin?"

He answered, "I suppose the breaking of that commandment."

I then asked if he had always kept that commandment, if he had always loved God with all his heart, with all his soul, and with all his mind, and if he had always put God first in everything. He replied that he had not.

I then asked him, "Of what, then, are you guilty?"

The Spirit of God convicted him, and with great earnestness, he replied, "I have committed the greatest sin that a man can commit, but I never saw it before in my life."

Personalize the Message

Another verse that can be used with effect is John 8:34. After the man has read the verse, *"Whosoever committeth sin is the servant of sin,"* ask him, "What is one who commits sin?" Then ask him if he commits sin. Ask him the direct question, "What are you, then?" Hold him to it until he says, "The servant of sin." Ask him if he desires to be delivered from that awful bondage. Hold him to this point until he sees his need of Jesus Christ as a deliverer from the slavery of sin.

The Holy Spirit has used Isaiah 57:21 for the salvation of many people who have been indifferent to the claims of the Gospel. After the verse, *"There is no peace, saith my God, to the wicked,"* has been read slowly, thoughtfully, and earnestly, ask him, "Do you have peace?"

One night a rebellious young man was going out of one of our tent meetings in Chicago. As he passed by me, I took him by the hand and said to him, "You need the Savior." He wanted to know why I thought so. I replied, "Because you have no peace."

He said, "Yes, I have."

"No, you have not," I replied with conviction. He asked me how I knew that. I told him God said so, and I quoted the above passage. He tried to laugh it off and say the verse was not true in his case. He became angry and went out of the tent in a rage. But the next night, I saw him kneeling with one of our workers in prayer.

When he arose from his knees, the worker came over and said that the man wished to speak with me. As I approached him, he held out his hand and said, "I want to beg your pardon for what I said last night. What you said was true. I did not have peace." I asked him if he had now accepted the Savior. He said he had.

Point to the Penalties

Galatians 3:10 is a verse we frequently use in our work in dealing with indifference. Allow the one with whom you are speaking to read the verse,

For as many as are of the works of the law are under the curse: for it is written, Cursed is every one that continueth not in all things which are written in the book of the law to do them.

Then ask him the question, "What is everyone who does not keep the law?"

When he answers, "Cursed," ask him if he has continued in *"all things which are written in the book of the law to do them."* When he replies, "No, I have not," ask him the direct question, "What are you, then?" Hold him to that point until he says, "I am under the curse." In many cases, he will be ready at once to be led to the thirteenth verse of the same chapter, which shows how he may be saved from that curse.

Romans 6:23 can often be used with good effect. *"For the wages of sin is death."* Ask, "What are the wages of sin?" Then, "Who earns those wages?" Then, "Are you a sinner? What wages have you earned? Do you wish to take your wages?"

John 3:36 is a verse that can be used in a similar way. *"He that believeth on the Son hath everlasting life: and he that believeth not the Son shall not see life; but the wrath of God abideth on him."* Ask the question, "Upon whom is it that the wrath of God abides?" Then, "Do you believe on the Son? What, then, abides upon you?" Finally, ask the decisive question, "Are you willing to go away with the wrath of God abiding upon you?"

Second Thessalonians 1:7–9, John 8:24, and Revelation 14:10–11; 20:15; and 21:8 set forth in a most impressive way the awful consequences of sin. If these verses are used, they should be read with deep earnestness to reveal the severity of their truth.

His Suffering—Our Salvation

Another way to rouse a person from his indifference is to show him what Jesus has done for him. I have found Isaiah 53:5–6 more effective for this purpose than any other passage in the Bible.

A lady had asked for prayer for her daughter, a young woman about twenty years of age. At the close of the service, I stepped up to the daughter and asked her if she would accept Jesus Christ as her Savior at once.

She stamped her foot in anger and said, "My mother should have known better than to do that. She knows it will only make me worse."

I asked her if she would sit down for a few minutes. As soon as we were seated, I opened my Bible to this passage and began to read,

> *But he was wounded for our transgressions, he was bruised for our iniquities: the chastisement of our peace was upon him; and with his stripes we are healed. All we like sheep have gone astray; we have turned every one to his own way; and the LORD hath laid on him the iniquity of us all.* (Isa. 53:5–6)

I made no comment on the verses whatever, but the Spirit of God touched her heart, and tears began to roll down the cheeks of the young woman. She became a Christian that same day.

It is a good idea in using these verses to get the inquirer to change the pronoun from the plural to the singular wherever possible. "He was wounded for my transgressions; He was bruised for my iniquities," and so forth.

John 3:16 can be used in a similar way. I was talking one night to someone who was apparently indifferent and hardened. She told me the story of her sin with seemingly little sense of shame. When I urged her to accept Christ, she simply refused. I put a Bible in her hands and asked her to read this verse. She began to read, *"God so loved the world, that he gave his only begotten Son...."* Before she had finished reading the verse, she broke into tears, softened by the thought of God's wondrous love for her.

First Peter 2:24 is a verse of similar character. *"Who his own self bare our sins in his own body on the tree, that we, being dead to sins, should live unto righteousness: by whose stripes ye were healed."* Ask the inquirer whose sins Jesus bore in His own body on the tree, pursuing it until he says, "My sins." First Peter 1:18–19, Luke 22:44, and Matthew 27:46 are useful to bring out in detail what Christ has suffered for us.

Still another way to challenge indifferent people is to show them that they are guilty of this one sin: the sin of rejecting Jesus Christ. Hebrews 10:28–29 is very effective for this purpose.

He that despised Moses' law died without mercy under two or three witnesses: of how much sorer punishment, suppose ye, shall he be thought worthy, who hath trodden under foot the Son of God, and hath counted the blood of the covenant, wherewith he was sancti-fied, an unholy thing, and hath done despite unto the Spirit of grace?

John 3:18–20, John 16:8–9, and Acts 2:36 can also be used.

Many times you will meet someone who is not willing to sit down and let you deal with him in this way. In that case, the only thing to do is to look to God for guidance and power and read him a verse such as Hebrews 10:28–29, Romans 6:23, John 3:36, or Isaiah 57:21. Pray for the Spirit of God to carry the truth home to his heart. A passing comment of this kind has often resulted in the salvation of a soul. The passages given above can be wisely used with one who is not completely indifferent or careless but who does not have a sufficiently deep sense of sin or a desire to accept the Gospel.

4

Dealing with the Openhearted

Many people are ready to be saved but simply do not know how. It is not difficult to lead these people to Christ. Perhaps no other passage in the Bible is more used for this purpose than Isaiah 53:6. It makes the way of salvation very plain. Read the first part of the verse to the inquirer, *"All we like sheep have gone astray; we have turned every one to his own way."* Then ask, "Is that true of you?" When he has thought it over and said, "Yes," then say to him, "Now let us see what God has done with your sins." Read the remainder of the verse, *"And the LORD hath laid on him the iniquity of us all."* Ask him, "What, then, is necessary for you to do to be saved?" He can be led to see that all that is necessary for him to do is to accept the Sin-Bearer whom God has provided.

Some years ago, I noticed a white-haired man in a meeting who did not stand up to acknowledge that he was a Christian. At the close of the service, I walked over to him and said, "Are you a Christian?" He said he was not. I was sure he was interested, so I asked him the direct question, "Would you become a Christian tonight if I would show you the way?" He replied that he would.

I opened my Bible to Isaiah 53:6 and read the first part of the verse, *"All we like sheep have gone astray; we have turned every one to his own way."*

I then said to him, "Is that true of you?" and he answered, "Yes."

"Now," I said, "let us read the rest of the verse, *'And the Lord hath laid on him the iniquity of us all.'* What has the Lord done with your sins?"

He thought a moment and said, "He has laid them on Christ."

"What, then," I said, "is all that you have to do to be saved?"

He replied promptly, "Accept Him."

"Well," I said, "will you accept Him tonight?"

He said, "I will."

"Let us kneel down and tell God so." We knelt down, and I led in prayer. He followed in a simple way, telling God that he was a sinner, but that he believed that God had laid his sins on Jesus Christ.

He then asked God for Christ's sake to forgive his sins.

When he had finished, I asked him if he thought that God had heard his prayer and that his sins were forgiven. He said, "Yes." I then asked him if he would begin to lead a Christian life at once, set up the family altar, and openly confess Christ before the world. He replied that he would. Some months later, I met his pastor and found that he had gone to his home in a distant city, set up the family altar, and united with the church. Apparently all that this man was waiting for was for someone to make the way of salvation plain to him.

Knowing and Doing

Two things must be known, and one thing must be done for a man to be saved. What he needs to know is, first, that he is a lost sinner and, second, that Christ is an all-sufficient Savior. What he needs to do is simply to accept this all-sufficient Savior whom God has provided. John 1:12 brings out this thought very clearly, *"As many as received him, to them gave he power to become the sons of God, even to them that believe on his name."* After the verse has been read, you can ask the one with whom you are dealing, "To whom does God give the power to become the sons of God?"

"As many as receive Him."

"What must you then do to become a son of God?"

"Receive Him."

"Well, will you receive Him as your Savior and Master now?"

Dealing with the Openhearted

Isaiah 55:7, Acts 16:31, and John 3:16, 36 are all useful in making the way of salvation plain. John 3:16 compared with Numbers 21:8–9 can often be used with good effect. When they are used, you should lead the inquirer to see what the serpent-bitten Israelite had to do to be saved—he had simply to look at the brazen serpent lifted up on the pole. Show him that the sin-bitten man has simply to do the same thing—look at Christ lifted up on the cross for his sins.

Romans 1:16 is another excellent verse to use. It makes the way of salvation very clear. You can ask the inquirer who it is, according to this verse, that the Gospel saves. He will see that it is *every one that believeth.* Then ask him, "What, then, is all that is necessary for one to do in order to be saved?" He will see that it is simply to believe. Ask him, "Believe what?" The answer is the Gospel.

What Is the Gospel?

This question is answered by 1 Corinthians 15:3–4. These verses show *"that Christ died for our sins according to the scriptures; and that he was buried, and that he rose again the third day according to the scriptures."* This is what he must believe in order to be saved. He must believe from his heart that Christ died for his sins and that He rose again. Ask the inquirer, "Do you believe that Christ died for your sins? Do you believe that He rose again?" If he says that he does, ask him if he will ask God by faith to forgive his sins for Christ's sake. He must believe it is done because God says so, and He must trust in the living Savior to save him day by day from the power of sin. Romans 10:9–10 also makes the way of salvation clear to many minds where other verses fail.

Romans 10:13 makes it, if possible, simpler still. This shows that all a man has to do to be saved is to *"call upon the name of the Lord."* You can ask the inquirer, "Are you ready now to call upon the name of the Lord for salvation and believe that God saves you because He says He will?"

The way of salvation can also be made plain by the use of Exodus 12:7, 13, 23. These verses show that it was the blood that made the Israelites safe. It is just the same today—the blood makes us safe. When God sees the blood, He passes over us. The only thing for us to do is to get under the blood. Show the inquirer that the way to be under the blood is by simple faith in Jesus Christ.

A Cry for Mercy

Luke 18:10–14 is useful in showing what a man may have and yet be lost (the Pharisee) and what a man may lack and yet be saved (the publican). Man simply must do as the publican did, that is, take the sinner's place and cry to God for mercy. Then he will return to his house justified.

This passage can be used in the following manner to make the meaning clearer. Ask the inquirer, "Which one of these two (the Pharisee or the publican) went home justified?" Ask him, "What did the publican do that the Pharisee did not do that brought him the forgiveness of his sins while the Pharisee went out of the temple unforgiven?"

When he studies the passage, he will soon see that the publican simply took the sinner's place before God and cried for mercy. As soon as he did this, he was "justified" or forgiven. Then you can ask him, "What must you do to find forgiveness? Will you do it here and now?" When he has done so, ask him if he believes God's Word and is now justified.

Saving faith is beautifully illustrated by Luke 7:48–50. The fiftieth verse tells us that this woman had saving faith. Now ask the inquirer, "What was the faith she had?" Show him that her faith was simply faith that Jesus could and would forgive her sins if she came to Him to do it. This is saving faith.

Galatians 3:10–13 also makes the way of salvation very simple. The tenth verse shows the sinner's position before accepting Christ: "under the curse." The thirteenth verse shows what Christ has done: He has been made a curse for us. What the sinner has to do is simply accept Christ.

5
Dealing with Difficulties

M any are anxious to be saved and know how, but they are confronted with difficulties that they think are insurmountable. One of the difficulties is, "I am too great a sinner." First Timothy 1:15 answers this objection fully.

One Sunday morning, a man who had led a reckless life and had lost $35,000 came to talk with me after church. He had been separated from his wife. I asked him why he was not a Christian.

"I am too great a sinner to be saved," he replied.

I turned at once to 1 Timothy 1:15: *This is a faithful saying, and worthy of all acceptation, that Christ Jesus came into the world to save sinners; of whom I am chief.*

He quickly replied, "Well, I am the chief of sinners."

"Well," I said, "that verse means you, then."

He replied, "It is a precious promise."

I said, "Will you accept it now?"

"I will."

We knelt down, and he confessed his sins to God and asked God for Christ's sake to forgive him. I asked him if he had really accepted Christ, and he said he had. I asked him if he really believed that he was saved, and he said he did. He took an early opportunity to confess Christ. He left the city in a short time, but I kept in touch with him. A most active Christian, he worked at his business during the day but engaged in some form of Christian work every night of the week. He was reunited with his wife, adopted a child, and had a happy Christian home.

Luke 19:10 is also a useful passage when a man says, "I am lost." You can say, "I have a passage intended especially for you.

If you really mean what you say, you are just the man Jesus is seeking. *'For the Son of man is come to seek and to save that which was lost.'*

Romans 5:6–8 is an effective passage. I stopped a man one night as he was hurrying out of a meeting. Laying my hand on his shoulder, I said, "Did you not hold your hand up tonight for prayer?"

He said, "Yes."

I said, "Why, then, are you hurrying away? Do you know God loves you?"

He replied, "You do not know who you are talking to."

"I do not care who I am talking to, but I know God loves you."

He said, "I am the meanest thief in Minneapolis."

I said, "If you are the meanest thief in Minneapolis, then I know God loves you." I opened my Bible to Romans 5:8 and read, *"But God commendeth his love toward us, in that, while we were yet sinners, Christ died for us."*

"Now," I said, "if you are the meanest thief in Minneapolis, you are a sinner, and this verse says that God loves sinners."

The man began to weep. Going into another room with me, he told me his story. He was just out of prison and had started out that night to commit one of the most daring burglaries ever in the city of Minneapolis. With his two companions in crime, he was passing a corner where he happened to hear an open-air meeting going on and stopped for a few minutes to listen. In spite of the protests and curses of his companions, he stayed through the meeting and went with us to the church.

After he told me his story, we knelt in prayer. Through tears, he cried to God for mercy, having been led by God's precious promise to believe that God loved a sinner even as vile as he.

Other useful passages are Matthew 9:12–13, Romans 10:13 (emphasize *"whosoever"*), John 3:16 (emphasize *"whosoever"*), Isaiah 1:18, 1 John 4:14, Isaiah 44:22, and Isaiah 43:25. Isaiah 1:18 and Psalm 51:14 are especially useful in dealing with men who have committed murder. Never tell anyone that his sins are not great. It is better to say, "Yes, your sins are great, greater than you think, but they have all been settled." Then show them Isaiah 53:6 and 1 Peter 2:24.

A woman once came to me who was very upset. After many ineffective attempts, she was at last able to unburden her heart. Fourteen years earlier, she had killed a man and had borne the memory of the act upon her conscience until it had almost driven her crazy. When she told the story to another Christian and myself, we turned to Isaiah 53:6.

After reading the verse carefully to her, I asked her what the Lord had done with her sin. After a few moments of deep and anxious thought, she said, "He has laid it on Christ."

I took a book in my hand. "Now," I said, "let my right hand represent you, and my left hand Christ, and this book your sin." I laid the book upon my right hand, and I said: "Where is your sin now?"

She said, "On me."

"Now," I said, "what has God done with it?"

She said, "Laid it on Christ."

I laid the book over on the other hand. "Where is your sin now?" I asked.

It was a long time before she could summon courage to answer; and then with a desperate effort, she said, "On Christ."

I asked, "Then, is it on you any longer?"

Slowly the light came into her face, and she burst out with a cry, "No, it is on Him! It is on Christ." John 1:29, Acts 10:43, and Hebrews 7:25 are also helpful in similar cases.

Facing Failure and Weakness

Another difficulty we frequently meet with is "I am afraid of failure." First Peter 1:5 is useful in showing that we are not to keep ourselves in the faith, but we are *kept by the power of God.*" John 10:28–29 shows that the safety of the one who accepts Christ does not depend on his ability to keep himself but on the keeping power of the Father and the Son.

Second Timothy 1:12 shows that it is Christ's business and not ours to keep that which is entrusted to Him and that He is able to do it. Isaiah 41:10, 13 are also helpful. Jude 24 shows that Christ is able to keep us from falling. Second Chronicles 32:7–8 and Romans 14:4, 11 are also good texts to use. First Corinthians 10:13 is especially useful when one is afraid that some great temptation will overtake him, and he will fall.

"I am too weak" is a similar difficulty. With such a person, use 2 Corinthians 12:9–10. Ask him, "Where is it that Christ's strength is made perfect?" When he answers, "In weakness," tell him, "Then, the weaker you are in your own strength the better." Philippians 4:13 shows that however weak we may be, we can do all things through Christ who strengthens us. First Corinthians 10:13 will show that God knows all about our weakness and will not permit us to be tempted above our strength.

"I cannot give up my evil ways or bad habits." Galatians 6:7–8 will show them that they must give them up or perish because we reap what we sow. Philippians 4:13 will show that they can give up their sin in Christ's strength. Point the one who fears that he cannot give up his bad habits to Christ as a risen Savior in 1 Corinthians 15:3–4.

A man once came to me and said, "I come to you to know if there is any way I can get power to overcome my evil habits." He told me his story. He had been converted in childhood but had come to Chicago, fallen in with evil companions, and now could not break away from his sins.

I said to him, "You know only half of the Gospel—the Gospel of a crucified Savior. Through trusting in the crucified Savior, you found forgiveness. But Jesus Christ is also a risen Savior. First Corinthians 15:4 says, *'All power is given unto him.'* Read Matthew 28:18. He has power to give you victory over your evil habits. Do you believe that?"

He said, "Yes."

"You trusted," I continued, "in the crucified Christ and found forgiveness, did you not?"

"Yes," he replied.

"Now," I said, "will you trust the risen Christ to save you from the power of your sins?"

"Yes, I will."

Dealing with Difficulties

"Let us kneel down then and tell Him so." We knelt and talked it all over with the Savior. When he stood up, his countenance was changed.

"I am so glad I came," he said. Sometime later I received a letter from him telling me how he found constant victory through trusting in the risen Christ.

What Will Others Say?

"I will be persecuted if I become a Christian." Never tell anyone that he will not be persecuted, but show him from such passages as 2 Timothy 2:12 and 3:12, Matthew 5:10–12, Mark 8:35, and Acts 14:22 that persecution is the only path to glory. Show him from Romans 8:18 that the sufferings of this present time are not worthy to be compared with the glory that will be revealed in us. Show him from Acts 5:41 and 1 Peter 2:20–21 that it is a privilege to be persecuted for Christ's sake. Hebrews 12:2–3 is useful in showing him where to look for victory in persecution.

"It will hurt my business" or "I cannot be a Christian in my present job." Point such a person to Mark 8:36. This will show him that it is better to lose his business than to lose his soul. After this thought has been sufficiently impressed upon his mind, show him Matthew 6:32–33. It contains God's promise that if we put God and His kingdom first, He will provide for all our real and temporal needs. Matthew 16:24–27, Luke 12:16–21 and 16:24–26 are also very effective passages to use here.

"I am afraid of my ungodly companions" or "I will lose my friends if I accept Christ." Proverbs 29:25 will show them the consequences of yielding to the fear of man and the security of the one who trusts in the Lord. Proverbs 13:20 will show them the results of holding on to their companions, and Psalm 1:1 will show the blessedness of giving up evil companions. First John 1:3 shows how one gets much better companionship than he loses by coming to Christ.

"I have too much to give up." Mark 8:36 will show them that they had better give up everything rather than lose their soul.

Philippians 3:7–8 and Psalm 16:11 will show them that what they give up is nothing compared with what they get. Psalm 84:11 and Romans 8:32 will show them that God will not ask them to give up any good thing. In other words, the only things God asks them to give up are the things that are hurting them.

A young woman once refused to come to the Savior, saying, "There is too much to give up."

"Do you think God loves you?" I asked.

"Certainly," she replied.

"How much do you think He loves you?"

She thought for a moment and answered, "Enough to give His Son to die for me."

"Do you think if God loved you enough to give His Son to die for you, He will ask you to give up anything that is good for you?"

"No."

"Do you wish to keep anything that is not good for you?"

"No."

"Then, you had better come to Christ at once."

She did.

First John 2:17 and Luke 12:16–21 will show people how worthless the things that they are trying to keep really are.

"The Christian life is too hard." Say to the inquirer, "Let me show you from God's Word that you are mistaken about the Christian life being hard." Turn to Matthew 11:30, Proverbs 3:17, Psalm 16:11, and 1 John 5:3 to show him that a Christian life is not hard but exceedingly pleasant. Then turn to Proverbs 13:15 and show him that it is the sinner's life that is hard.

Relying upon Feelings

"I have no feeling." Ask the inquirer what kind of feeling he thinks he must have before he comes to Christ. If it is the peace of which Christians speak, show him from Galatians 5:22, Ephesians 1:13, 1 Peter 1:8, and Matthew 10:32 that this feeling is the result of accepting Christ and confessing Him. He cannot expect the feeling until he accepts and confesses Christ.

Dealing with Difficulties

If the feeling he thinks he must have is the feeling that he is a sinner, show him by Isaiah 55:7 that it is not the feeling that we are sinners that God demands but a turning away from sin. Or from Acts 16:31 and John 1:12, show him that God does not ask us to feel that we are sinners but to confess that we are sinners and trust in Christ as Savior. Isaiah 55:1 and Revelation 22:17 will show the inquirer that all the feeling he needs is a desire for salvation. Passages recommended for use with indifferent inquirers could be used here if they do not believe they are sinners.

"I am seeking Christ but cannot find Him." Jeremiah 29:13 shows that when we seek Him with our whole heart, we will find Him. One evening after a meeting, a woman said to me, "I have been seeking Christ for two years and cannot find Him."

I replied, "I can tell you when you will find Him." She looked at me in surprise, and I turned to Jeremiah 29:13 and read, *"And ye shall seek me, and find me, when ye shall search for me with all your heart."* I said, "That shows you when you will find Christ. You will find Him when you search for Him with all your heart. Have you done that?"

After a little thought, she answered, "No."

"Well, then," I said, "let us kneel down right now."

She did this, and in a few moments she was rejoicing in Christ.

You can point one who has this difficulty to Luke 15:1–10 and 19:10. These passages show that Jesus is seeking the sinner, and you can say, "If you are really seeking Christ, it will not take a seeking Savior and a seeking sinner very long to find each other."

Excuses, Excuses

"I cannot believe." In most cases where one says this, the real difficulty lies in his unwillingness to forsake sin. John 5:44 and Isaiah 55:7 are good passages to use. When using the latter passage, hold the man's attention to the fact that all God asks of him is that he turn away from sin and turn to Him.

"My heart is too hard." Ezekiel 36:26–27 says that although their hearts are as hard as stone, it will make no difference because God will give them a new heart.

"God will not receive me" or "I am afraid I have committed the unpardonable sin." The people who honestly say this are, as a rule, about the most difficult to deal with of any that you will meet. John 6:37 is the great text to use with them, for it shows that Jesus will receive anyone who will come to Him. Hold them continually to that point, *"Him that cometh to me I will in no wise cast out."* If they keep saying, "He will not receive me," repeat the text, looking to the Spirit of God to make the truth real to them. Many utterly despondent souls have found light and peace through this verse in God's Word.

Revelation 22:17 is also useful because it shows that anyone who desires it can have the water of life freely. Isaiah 55:1 shows that anyone who desires salvation can have it. Isaiah 1:18 shows that no matter how great a man's sins are, they can still be forgiven. Acts 10:43 and John 3:16 say that "whosoever" will believe upon Christ will find pardon and eternal life. Romans 10:13 shows that anyone, no matter who or what he is, who will *"call upon the name of the Lord shall be saved."*

It is sometimes helpful to turn to Hebrews 6:4–6 and Matthew 12:31–32 to show the inquirer just what the unpardonable sin is and what its results are. Matthew 12:31–32 says the unpardonable sin is blasphemy against the Holy Spirit. Ask him squarely, "Have you ever blasphemed against the Holy Spirit?" Hebrews 6:4–6 shows that the difficulty is not in God's unwillingness to forgive, but in man's unwillingness to repent. Anyone who is concerned about his salvation evidently has not committed the unpardonable sin or sinned away his day of grace. A little instruction along this line is often all that is needed.

"It is too late." When an inquirer says this, use 2 Corinthians 6:2 and tell him that God says the time is right. Luke 23:39–43 is useful in showing that even at the last hour, Jesus will listen to the sinner's cry. Second Peter 3:9 will show that His will is that none should perish and that He is delaying the judgment to save as many as will come. Deuteronomy 4:30–31 is an especially helpful passage, as it promises, *"Even in the latter days,"* if you turn to the Lord, He will be merciful.

Isaiah 1:18 and Revelation 22:17 can also be used here.

6

Dealing with the Self-Righteous

Among those who entertain false hopes, perhaps the largest class are those who expect to be saved by their righteous lives. These persons are easily recognized by such sayings as these: "I am doing the best I can" or "I do more good than evil" or "I am not a great sinner" or "I have never done anything very bad." Galatians 3:10 is an excellent passage to use here, for it shows that all those who are trusting in their works are under the curse of the law. No hope is available on the ground of the law for anyone who does not continue *"in all things which are written in the book of the law to do them."* James 2:10 is also useful. Galatians 2:16 and Romans 3:19–20 are very effective by showing that *"by the deeds of the law there shall no flesh be justified"* in God's sight.

All these passages show the kind of righteousness God demands. No man's righteousness comes up to God's standard. If a man wishes to be saved, he must find some other means of salvation than by his own deeds. It is sometimes wise to use these passages to say to the inquirer, "You do not understand the kind of righteousness that God demands, or you would not talk as you do. Now let us turn to His Word and see what kind of righteousness God demands."

The Searching Eye of God

Another way of reaching this type of individual is by the use of such passages as Luke 26:15, Romans 2:16, and 1 Samuel 26:7. These passages show that God looks at the heart. Hold the inquirer right to that point. Every man, when brought face-to-face with that, must tremble because he knows that whatever his out-ward life may be, his heart will not stand the scrutiny of God's eye.

No matter how self-righteous a man is, somewhere in the depths of his heart is the consciousness of sin. All we have to do is to work until we touch that point. Every man's conscience is on our side.

Matthew 22:37–38 can be used when a man says, "I am doing the best I can, and I do more good than evil." Say to him, "You are greatly mistaken about that. Do you know that you have broken the first and greatest of God's laws?" Then show him Hebrews 6:6 or John 6:29. The one thing God demands is faith; without that, it is impossible to please Him.

John 16:9 shows that unbelief in Christ is the greatest sin. John 3:36 shows that the question of eternal life depends solely on a man's accepting or rejecting Jesus Christ. Hebrews 10:28–29 reveals that the sin that brings the heaviest punishment is that of treading *under foot the Son of God."*

Before using this last passage, you might say, "Do you know that you are committing the most awful sin in God's sight that a man can commit?" If he replies, "No," then say, "Well, let me show you from God's Word that you are." Turn to this passage and read it with great solemnity and earnestness.

Understanding God's Judgment

Those who think "God is too good to damn anyone" are also entertaining false hopes. When anyone says this, you can reply, "We know nothing of God's goodness except what we learn from the Bible, so we must go to that Book to find out the character of God's goodness. Let us turn to Romans 2:4–5." Having read the verses, you can say something like this, "The purpose of God's goodness is to lead you to repentance, not to encourage you to sin. When we trample His goodness, we are treasuring up *'wrath against the day of wrath and revelation of the righteous judgment of God.'"* John 8:21, 24 and John 3:36 will show the man that how-ever good God may be, He will reject all who reject His Son.

Still another way to approach this subject is to use John 5:40, 2 Peter 3:9–11, or Ezekiel 33:11, and show them that it is not so much God who damns men as men who damn themselves. This happens in spite of God's goodness because they will not come to Christ and accept the life freely offered. You can say, "God is not willing that any should perish. He offers life freely to you, but there is one difficulty in the way. Let us turn to John 5:40 to see what the difficulty is." Then read the passage: *Ye will not come to me, that ye might have life,"* and say, "My friend, your difficulty is that you won't come. Life is freely offered to you, but if you will not accept it, you must perish."

Second Peter 2:4–6, 9 and Luke 13:3 show how the "good" God deals with persons who persist in sin. Sometimes this last passage can be effectively used in this way: "You say God is too good to damn anyone. Now let us see what God Himself says in His Word." Then turn to the passage in Luke and read, *"Except ye repent, ye shall all likewise perish."* Repeat the passage over and over again until the person understands this.

Trusting versus Trying

A third type of those who entertain false hopes are those who say, "I am trying to be a Christian." John 1:12 will show them that it is not "trying" to be a Christian or "trying" to live a better life or "trying" to do anything that God asks of us, but simply to receive Jesus Christ who did it all.

You can ask the inquirer, "Will you now stop your trying and simply receive Jesus as Savior?" Acts 16:31 shows that God does not ask us to try what we can do, but to trust Jesus and what He has done and will do.

Romans 3:23–25 shows that we are not to be justified by trying but *"freely by his grace through the redemption that is in Christ Jesus"* on the simple condition of faith.

Still another group who entertain false hope are those who say, "I feel I am going to heaven" or "I feel I am saved." Show them from John 3:36 that it is not a question of what they feel but what God says. God says distinctly in His Word, *"He that believeth not the Son shall not see life; but the wrath of God abideth on him.*"

One afternoon I was talking with a lady who a few weeks before had lost her only child. At the time of the child's death, she had been deeply interested in salvation through Christ. But her serious desire to serve Him had since left her. I asked her the question, "Do you not wish to go where your little one has gone?"

She replied at once, "I expect to."

"What makes you think you will?" I said.

She replied, "I feel it. I feel that I will go to heaven when I die."

I asked her if she could point to anything in the Word of God that gave her reason to believe that she was going to heaven when she died.

"No," she said, "there is not." Then she turned and questioned me, saying, "Do you expect to go to heaven when you die?"

"Yes," I replied, "I know I will."

"How do you know it?" she said. "Have you any word from God for it?"

"Yes," I answered and turned to John 3:36. She was thus led to see the difference between a faith that rested on her feelings and a faith that rested on the Word of God.

Luke 18:9–14 can be used in the following way. You can say, "There was a man in the Bible who felt he was all right but was all wrong. Let me read to you about him." Then read about the Pharisee who was sure that he was all right, but he was all the time an unforgiven sinner. Make the inquirer see how untrustworthy our feelings are and what the ground of assurance is— God's Word. Proverbs 14:12 can also be used to show that "*there is a way which seemeth right unto a man, but the end thereof are the ways of death.*"

The last group of people who entertain false hopes are those who say they are saved although they are leading sinful lives. In the case of many forms of sin, a good passage to use is 1 Corinthians 6:9–10. First John 2:29 will also in many cases sweep away this false hope. First John 5:4–5 is useful to show that one who is born of God overcomes the world. The fact that they are living in sin and are not overcoming the world is evidence that they have not been born of God.

7

Dealing with the Uncertain

Sometimes lack of assurance is caused by ignorance. Scripture tells us that we may know we have eternal life. Often when you ask people if they know they are saved or if they know their sins are forgiven or if they know they have eternal life, they will reply, "Why, no one knows that." You can say to them, "Yes, the Bible says that all who believe may know it." Then show them 1 John 5:13:

> *These things have I written unto you that believe on the name of the Son of God; that ye may know that ye have eternal life, and that ye may believe on the name of the Son of God.*

John 1:12 shows that Christ gives to as many as receive Him power to become the sons of God. A good way to use this verse is to ask the inquirer questions regarding it: "What does everyone who receives Him receive power to become?" If the inquirer is attentively looking at the verse, he will answer, "A son of God." Then, ask the next question, "Have you received Him?" If he replies, "Yes," then ask him, "What are you, then?" It will probably be necessary to go over it several times, but at last the inquirer will see it and say, "I am a son of God."

John 3:36 can be used in a similar way. Ask the inquirer, "Who do these verses say has everlasting life?"

"He that believeth on the Son."

"Do you believe on the Son? What do you have, then?" In a little while he will see it and say, "Everlasting life." Then have him say over and over again, "I have everlasting life," and have him kneel down and thank God for giving him everlasting life.

One night I found a young man on his knees at the close of the service in great distress. I showed him from the Bible how Jesus Christ had borne his sins and asked him if he would accept Christ as his Savior. He said he would, but he seemed to have no joy and went out of the meeting in deep distress. The next night he was there again, professing to have accepted Christ but with no assurance that his sins were forgiven. I tried to show him from God's Word what God said of those who accepted the Savior, but the understanding did not come. Finally, he rose to leave the meeting. I had just shown him from John 3:36 that God said, *"He that believeth on the Son hath everlasting life."*

As he turned to leave, he said, "Will you pray for me?"

I said, "Yes."

He walked a little way down the aisle, and I called to him and said, "Do you believe I will pray for you?"

He turned with a look of astonishment and replied, "Yes, of course."

"Why do you think I will pray for you?" I asked.

"Because you said so," he replied.

I said, "Isn't God's Word as good as mine?" He saw immediately that while he had been willing to believe my word, he had not been willing to believe God's Word. He received assurance immediately and knew that he had everlasting life. John 5:24 and 1 John 5:12 can be used in a similar way. Acts 13:39 can be very useful. Ask the inquirer, "What does this verse say that all who believe are?" Then ask him, "Do you believe? What are you, then?" It will probably take two or three times going over it before he answers, "I am justified." Tell him to thank God for justifying him and confess Christ.

The Witness of the Spirit

Many inquirers stumble over not having the witness of the Holy Spirit. Show them from 1 John 5:10 that the witness of the Word concerning their acceptance is sufficient. If they do not believe this witness of God in His Word, tell them this makes Him a liar. Show them further from Ephesians 1:13 that after we believe the testimony of the Word, we are *"sealed with that holy Spirit of promise."*

The natural order in the assurance of salvation is this: first, assurance of our justification resting on the Word of God; second, public confession of Christ with the mouth; third, the witness of the Holy Spirit.

The trouble with many is that they wish to invert this order and have the witness of the Holy Spirit before they confess Christ with their mouth. From Matthew 10:32–33 we learn that when we confess Christ before men, He confesses us before the Father. We cannot expect the witness of the Spirit from the Father until we are confessed before the Father. So confession of Christ logically precedes the witness of the Spirit.

It is very important in using these texts to make clear what saving faith is. Many may say that they believe when they do not, in the sense of these texts. They get a false assurance and entertain false hopes, never finding deliverance. Often those who lack assurance are dealt with carelessly by workers who urge them on to assurance before they have really accepted Christ.

John 1:12 and 2 Timothy 1:12 clarify that believing means receiving Jesus or committing oneself to Him. Romans 10:10 serves a similar purpose by showing that *"with the heart man believeth unto righteousness."*

Often those who lack assurance are involved in some sin or questionable practice that they should confess and give up. John 8:12, Isaiah 55:7, Proverbs 28:13, and Psalm 32:1–5 are useful passages in dealing with this situation. When sin is confessed and forsaken and we follow Christ, we receive pardon, light, and assurance. Sometimes it works best to bluntly ask, "Do you know of any sin or anything in your life your conscience troubles you about?"

How to Deal with Backsliders

Many backsliders have no desire to come back to the Savior. With such people use Jeremiah 2:5 and drive the question home, "What iniquity have you found in the Lord?" Show them their ingratitude and folly in forsaking such a Savior and Friend. They may have wandered away because of unkind treatment by professing Christians. But hold them right to the point of how the Lord treated them and how they are now treating Him.

Use Jeremiah 2:13 to show them what they have forsaken. Have them read the verse and ask, "Is that verse true? When you forsook the Lord, did you not forsake the *'fountain of living waters'* and turn to *'broken cisterns, that can hold no water'*?" Illustrate the text by showing how foolish it would be to turn from a fountain of pure, living water to a broken cistern or muddy pool. God has used this verse many times to bring backsliders back to Himself.

Turn to Jeremiah 2:19 and ask them whether they have found it *"an evil thing and bitter"* to have forsaken the Lord their God. Proverbs 14:14, 1 Kings 11:9, Amos 4:11–12, and Luke 15:13–17 can often be used effectively with an impenitent backslider to show him the result of his wandering.

Other backsliders are sick of their wanderings and sin, and desire to come back to the Lord. These are perhaps as easy a group to deal with as we ever find. Jeremiah 3:12–13, 22 will show them how ready the Lord is to receive them back. All He asks of them is that they acknowledge their sin and return to Him. Hosea 14:1–4 is full of tender invitation to penitent backsliders and also shows the way back to God. Isaiah 43:22, 24–25 and 44:20–22, Jeremiah 29:11–13, Deuteronomy 4:28–31, 2 Chronicles 7:14, 1 John 1:9 and 2:1–2 set forth God's unfailing love for the backslider and His willingness to receive him back.

Mark 16:7, 2 Chronicles 15:4 and 33:1–9, 12–13 give illustrations of backsliders who returned to the Lord and how lovingly they were received. First John 1:9, Jeremiah 3:12–13, 2 Chronicles 15:12, 15 and 7:14 show the actual steps the backslider must take to come back to the Lord and be restored to His favor: humble himself, confess his sin, and turn from his sin.

Luke 15:11–24 is perhaps the most useful passage of all in dealing with a backslider who wishes to return. It illustrates both the steps that the backslider must take and the kind of reception he will receive. When a backslider has returned, he should always be given instructions on how to live so that he will not backslide again.

8
Dealing with Skeptics

Some skeptics simply take the Word of God lightly. If a man says the Bible is foolishness to him, you can say, "Yes, that is what the Bible says about itself." He will probably be surprised at this reply. Then you can show him the verse, *"The preaching of the cross is to them that perish foolishness"* (1 Cor. 1:18). You can say to him, "You see that the Bible says that it is foolishness to some—those who perish—and the reason it is foolishness to you is that you are perishing."

One night a man said to a Christian worker who was trying to persuade him to come to Christ, "All that you are saying is foolishness to me." The worker quickly replied, "Yes, that is what the Bible says." The man looked at him in astonishment and said, "What?" The worker turned to 1 Corinthians 2:14 and read, *"But the natural man receiveth not the things of the Spirit of God: for they are foolishness unto him; neither can he know them, because they are spiritually discerned."* The man said, "I never saw that before."

Second Corinthians 4:3–4 shows the doubter that he is lost and that his skepticism arises from the fact that the *"god of this world hath blinded"* his mind. Second Thessalonians 2:10–12 reveals the origin of skepticism—*"because they received not the love of the truth"*—and the consequences of skepticism—delusion and damnation. John 8:21–24 shows the terrible consequences of unbelief. John 5:44 and 3:18–20 expose the origin of skepticism. Psalm 14:1 is useful in some cases, although one needs to be cautious to use it only when it can be done with earnestness and tenderness. Second Thessalonians 1:7–8 can also be used with good results.

Dealing with Skeptics

Skepticism or Sin?

A large number of men and women in our day sincerely long to know the truth but are in an utter fog of skepticism. John 7:17 is a helpful passage to show the way through skepticism to faith. Get the skeptic to read that verse. Ask him, "Will you surrender your will to God and promise to search honestly and earnestly to find out what God's will is so that you can do it? Will you ask God to show you whether you need a Savior and whether Jesus is a divine Savior, the Son of God? And will you promise that, if God shows you that Jesus is the Son of God, you will accept Him as your Savior and confess Him before the world?" Have him make his promise definite by writing it down. If you get him to do this, his skepticism will soon take wings.

One evening at the close of a service I asked a gentleman why he was not a Christian. He replied, "I will tell you. I do not talk much about it, for I am not proud of it as some are, but I am a skeptic. I have lain awake nights thinking about this matter."

I asked him, "Do you believe there is a God?"

"Yes," he answered, "I never gave up my faith that there is a God."

"Well, if there is a God, you ought to obey Him. Tonight, will you take your stand to follow His will wherever it carries you, even if it carries you to the ends of the earth?"

"I will try to do as well as I know how," he said slowly.

"That is not what I asked. Will you follow God's will wherever it carries you?"

"I have never thought about it that way."

"Will you consider it tonight?"

"I will."

"Do you believe God answers prayer?"

"I don't know. I am afraid not."

"Well, since this is a possible clue to the truth, will you ask God to show you whether Jesus is His Son, and what your duty concerning Him is?"

"I will."

Not long after that, the man came into a meeting with a new look on his face. He stood up and said, "I was in a fog of doubt. I believed nothing." Then he told us he had done as he promised. "And now," he continued, "my doubts are all gone. I don't know where they have gone, but they are gone."

Knowing Right from Wrong

If the skeptic will not act in this way, you can silence him by showing him that he is not an honest skeptic. His trouble is not his skepticism but his sin. If the man does not believe there is a God, ask him if he believes there is an absolute difference between right and wrong. If he does not, he is merely foolish. If he says he does, ask him if he will take his stand for right and follow it wherever it carries him. He may try to put you off by saying, "What is right?" or "I am doing right as nearly as I know how." Get him to promise that he will take his stand for right, whatever he may find it to be. Then show him that if he is honest in this promise, he will find out what the truth is.

Say to him, "You do not know whether God answers prayer or not. I know He does, and you must admit that here is a possible clue to knowledge. If you are honest in your desire to know the truth, you will follow this clue. You can at least pray, 'O my God, if You are real, teach me Your will, and I will do it. Show me whether Jesus is Your Son or not. If You show that He is, I will accept Him as my Savior and confess Him before the world.'"

Tell the man to begin reading the gospel of John, slowly and thoughtfully, only a few verses at a time. He should ask God for the light of understanding each time he begins reading and promise God that he will follow the light the moment He makes it clear. If the skeptic will follow this rational course, he will come into the clear light of faith in the Bible as the Word of God and Jesus Christ as the Son of God. If the man is not an honest skeptic, it will become obvious. You can then show him that the difficulty is not with his skepticism but with his rebellious heart.

One afternoon I asked anyone who wished to talk with me to remain after the meeting. A young man with whom I had dealt some months before stayed behind. I asked him what his trouble was. He replied, "The same trouble that I told you in the spring. I cannot believe there is a God." I asked him if he had taken his stand to follow what was right regardless of the consequences. He replied that he did not know whether there was any difference between right and wrong.

I looked him in the eye and said, "Is there some sin in your life?"

He said, "Yes."

I asked, "What is it?"

He replied, "The same that I told you last spring."

I said, "You promised to give it up. Have you?"

"No, I have not."

"Well," I said, "the problem is not with your skepticism. Give up that sin, and your skepticism will take care of itself."

In some confusion he replied, "I guess that is the trouble."

Questioning God and His Word

The previously mentioned passages can also be used with those who do not believe in God. Three other passages are often effective with this type of skeptic. Before using Psalm 14:1, you can say, "Let me read to you from God's own Word what He says about those who deny His existence." Often it is sufficient to let the passage do its own work. Sometimes, however, it is wise to dwell a little on it. Call attention to the fact that it is *"in his heart"* that the fool says, *"There is no God."* He does not believe there is a God because he does not want to believe it.

You can add that the folly of saying in one's heart that there is no God is seen in two points: first, there is a God, and it is folly to say there is not one; second, the doctrine that there is not a God always brings misery and wretchedness. Ask the man if he ever knew a happy atheist. Psalm 19:1–2 and Romans 1:19–22 are also effective passages.

Romans 3:3–4 makes it plain that questioning the fact does not alter the fact. Matthew 24:35 is often used by the Spirit to convince the heart of the skeptic of the certainty and immutability of God's Word. Mark 7:13, Matthew 5:18, John 10:35, and Luke 24:27, 44 give Christ's testimony that the Old Testament is the Word of God. They are especially helpful in dealing with those who say that they accept the authority of Christ but not that of the Old Testament. Christ sets His seal on the Old Testament Scriptures. If we accept His authority, we must accept that of the Old Testament as well. Along the same line, John 14:26 and 16:12–13 also contain Christ's endorsement of the New Testament.

First Thessalonians 2:13 answers the skeptic's objection that Paul did not claim that his teaching is the Word of God. Second Peter 1:21, John 8:47, and Luke 16:30–31 can also be used. Second John 5:10 is very effective in showing the guilt of those who do not believe the record that God has given. Before using this passage, you can say, "You doubt that the Bible is the Word of God? Now let us see what God says about those who do not believe His testimony." Turn to the passage and have them read it.

Is There Life after Death?

Read 1 Corinthians 15:35–36, John 5:28–29, and Daniel 12:2. Some doubt the doctrine of future punishment or the conscious, endless suffering of the lost. Revelation 21:8 defines what death means when it is used in Scripture. Revelation 17:8, compared with Revelation 19:20, shows what perdition or destruction means in Scripture. Revelation 20:10 shows that those cast into the lake of fire do not cease to exist. The beast and false prophet are still there at the end of a thousand years. Far from being annihilated or losing conscious existence, they are tormented night and day forever. Revelation 13:7–8 shows that those subjected to terrible punishment are those whose names are not written in the Book of Life.

Matthew 10:28 refers to a destruction of the soul apart from the destruction of the body. Luke 12:5 shows that after one is dead, there is a punishment in hell. Mark 3:28–29 describes eternal sin. Luke 16:23–26 shows that the condition of the unsaved is one of conscious torment for eternity. Mark 14:21 shows that the retribution visited on the wicked is so severe that it would be better for them to have never been born.

Second Peter 2:4 and Jude 6 show that hell is not a place where the inhabitants cease to exist, but where they are kept alive for the purpose of God. Hebrews 10:28–29 shows that while the punishment of transgression under the Mosaic law was death, greater punishment awaits those who have *"trodden under foot the Son of God."* Matthew 25:41 sheds more light on the subject. The wicked go to the same place with the beast, false prophet, and the devil mentioned in Revelation 19:20 and 20:10. They share the same endless, conscious torment.

Is Jesus the Son of God?

In Acts 10:36, 1 Corinthians 2:8, Psalm 24:8–10, Hebrews 1:8, John 20:28, Romans 9:5, Revelation 1:17, and Isaiah 44:6, several divine titles are applied to Christ. These same titles applied to Christ in the New Testament were applied to Jehovah in the Old.

In Hebrews 1:10, 13, we find divine offices attributed to Christ. In Revelation 5:13, John 5:22–23, Hebrews 1:6, Philippians 2:10 and 5:22–23, it is taught that Jesus Christ should be worshipped as God.

In John 5:22–23 Jesus claims the same honor as His Father. Either He was divine, or He was the most blasphemous impostor that ever lived. One who denies Christ's divinity puts Him in the place of a blasphemous impostor. Mark 14:61–62 can be used in a similar way.

First John 2:22–23 and 5:1, 5 show that the one who denies the divinity of Christ, no matter who he may be, is a liar and an antichrist. First John 5:10–12 shows that he who does not believe that Jesus is divine makes God a liar, *"because he believeth not the record that God gave of his Son."*

Hebrews 10:28–29 shows the folly, guilt, and punishment of rejecting Christ as the Son of God. John 8:24 shows beyond a question that he who wants to be saved must believe in the divinity of

Jesus Christ. John 20:31 shows that we have life through believing that Jesus is the Christ, the Son of God.

There may be no need to take up specific questions, as for example, future punishment, until the inquirer has first decided whether he will accept Christ as his Savior.

9
Dealing with Objections

Many whom you wish to lead to Christ will try to suggest that God is unjust and cruel. Job 40:2 and Romans 9:20 are very pointed passages to use in this situation and need no comment. It may be wise to preface the reading of the passages with some remarks like this: "Do you know the enormous sin you are guilty of in accusing God of being unjust and cruel? Let me read what God says about it in His Word." Then read the passages.

Romans 11:33 will show the complaining person that the reason God's ways seem unjust and cruel is that His ways are so deep and unsearchable. The trouble is not with God's ways but with the limitations of human understanding. Hebrews 12:5, 7, and 10–11 are especially useful in cases where the inquirer complains because of his own misfortunes or sorrow. Isaiah 55:8–9 can often prove helpful.

You will often meet someone who will say, "God is unjust to create men and then damn them." Refer them to Ezekiel 33:11. This passage meets this complaint by showing that God has no pleasure in the death of the wicked but desires their welfare. The wicked bring damnation on themselves by their stubborn refusal to repent. First Timothy 2:3–4 shows that God—far from creating man to damn him—desires that all men be saved. Second Peter 3:9 teaches that God is not willing that any should perish and is delaying His purposes in order that all may come to repentance. John 5:40 and Matthew 23:37 show that the whole cause of man's damnation is his own willful and persistent refusal to come to Christ. John 3:36 and 3:16 are also helpful in many cases.

Is the Bible Reliable?

The Bible is often criticized as being contradictory and absurd. Scriptures that answer such criticisms are 1 Corinthians 1:18 and 2:14, 2 Corinthians 4:3–4, Daniel 12:10, and Romans 11:33–34. In extreme cases 2 Thessalonians 2:10–12, John 7:17, Psalm 25:14, and Matthew 11:25 will also help.

Sometimes the best thing to do with a man who says the Bible is full of contradiction is to hand him your Bible and ask him to show you one. In most cases, he will not attempt to do it. People who complain about the Bible usually know nothing about its contents.

One day I asked a certain man why he was not a Christian, and he replied, "The Bible is full of contradictions." I asked him to show me one. "Oh," he said, "it's full of them."

I said, "If it is full of them you ought to be able to show me one."

He said, "Well, there is one in Psalms."

I said, "Show it to me." He began looking in the back of the New Testament for the book of Psalms. I said, "You are not looking in the right part of the Bible for Psalms. Let me find it for you." I found the book of Psalms and handed it to him. After fumbling around he said, "I could find it if I had my own Bible here."

"Well," I said, "will you bring your Bible tonight?" He promised he would and agreed to meet me at a certain place in the church. The appointed hour came, but he did not.

Some months afterward in another series of meetings in the same church, one of the workers stopped me and said, "Here's a man I wish you would deal with. He is a skeptic." I looked at him and recognized him as the same man. "Oh," I said, "you are the man who lied to me." He admitted that he was, but he was still playing his old game of saying that the Bible was full of contradictions. In nine cases out of ten, men who say this know nothing about the Bible. When you ask them to show you a contradiction in the Bible, they are filled with confusion.

Dealing with Objections

Why Did Jesus Have to Die?

A great many men will say, "I do not see why God could not save men in some other way than by the death of His Son." Isaiah 55:8–9 and Romans 11:33 are useful in answering them. Romans 9:20 is also effective.

One night I asked a young student why he was not a Christian. He answered that he did not see why it was necessary for Christ to die for him, and why God did not save him in some other way. I opened my Bible and read Romans 9:20 asking him directly, *"Who art thou that repliest against God?"* Then I said to him, "Do you realize what you are doing? You are condemning God!"

The confused young man said, "I did not mean to do that."

"Well," I said, "that is what you are doing."

"If that is so," he replied, "I will take it back."

Using the passages given in the chapter "Dealing with the Indifferent" may also help. When anyone is led to see that he is a lost sinner, God's way of salvation will prove itself to be just the thing needed.

Too Many Hypocrites

Frequently when we try to persuade men to accept Christ as their Savior, they reply, "There are too many hypocrites in church." Romans 14:4 and 12 effectively deal with this remark. Romans 2:1 and Matthew 7:1–5 are also excellent. John 21:21–22 is useful in showing the objector that he is solely responsible for his own relationship to Christ, and what others do is none of his concern.

Sometimes the inquirer will complain of the way Christian people have treated him. In such a case, turn the attention of the inquirer from the people to the way God has treated him. For this purpose use Jeremiah 2:5, Isaiah 53:5, and Romans 5:6–8. Then ask him if the fact that Christians have treated him badly is any excuse for his treatment of a heavenly Father who has treated him so well.

One night I asked an elderly man if he was a Christian. He replied that he was a backslider. I asked him why he turned away from the Lord. He replied that Christian people had treated him badly. I opened my Bible and read Jeremiah 2:5 to him: *"Thus saith the LORD, What iniquity have your fathers found in me, that they are gone far from me, and have walked after vanity, and are become vain?"* I said, "Did you find any iniquity in God? Did God not treat you well?" In a voice that shook with emotion, the man admitted that God had not treated him badly. I held him right to this point of God's treatment of him and his treatment of God. Matthew 18:23–35, Ephesians 4:30–32, and Matthew 6:14–15 are also useful in showing the absolute necessity of forgiving others.

Now Is the Time

Many people want to put off making a decision. They say, "I want to wait" or "Not tonight" or "I will think about it." Read Isaiah 55:6 to the inquirer. Then ask him when he is to seek the Lord. When he answers, "While He may be found," ask him if he is sure that he will be able to find God tomorrow if he does not seek Him today.

You could also use Proverbs 29:1. After reading the verse, ask what becomes of the one who *"being often reproved hardeneth his neck."* When your inquirer answers, "He shall be destroyed," ask him how he will be destroyed. When he answers, "Suddenly," ask him if he is willing to run the risk.

Another good Scripture to use is Matthew 25:10, 12. Ask the inquirer who could attend the marriage feast. When he answers, "Those who were ready," ask him if he is ready. Have him tell you what happened after those who were ready went in. Then ask him, "Are you willing to be on the outside?"

Luke 12:19–20 might be used. Ask the inquirer for how long a time this man thought he had made provision. Then ask him, "If God called you tonight, would you be ready?" Matthew 24:44 is especially effective in dealing with those who say, "I am not ready." An excellent way to use 1 Kings 18:21 is by asking the person whether he would be willing to wait a year with no opportunity to accept Christ. When he answers, "No, I might die within a year," ask him if he would be willing to wait a month. Bring it down to a week and finally to a day. Ask him if he wants God, the Holy Spirit, and all Christians to leave him alone for a day without any opportunity to accept Christ.

Almost any thoughtful person will say, "No." Tell him that if that is the case, he had better accept Christ at once. This method has been used by many with great success. Proverbs 27:1, James 4:13–14, Job 36:18, Luke 13:24–28; 12:19–20, John 8:21; 12:35 and 7:33–34 can also be used for further reference. "I must get set up in business first; then I will become a Christian" or "I must do something else first." Matthew 6:33 is the great passage to use in such cases, because it shows that we must seek the kingdom of God first.

Others say, "I am waiting for God's time." If one says this, ask him if he will accept Christ in God's time if you will show him when God's time is. Then turn to 2 Corinthians 6:2 or Hebrews 3:15.

To the objection, "I am too young" or "I want to wait until I am older," Ecclesiastes 12:1 is a sufficient answer. Matthew 19:14 and 18:3 are also good passages to use, because they show that youth is the best time to come to Christ. All people must become like little children before they can enter into the kingdom of heaven. It is sometimes wise in dealing with persons who wish to put off a decision to use the passages given for the indifferent, until a deep impression is made of their need for Christ. Then they will not be willing to postpone accepting Him.

In some cases, using only one passage and driving it home by constant repetition works best. One night I was dealing with a man who was quite interested, but he kept saying, "I cannot decide tonight." I quoted Psalm 29:1, *"Give unto the LORD, O ye mighty, give unto the LORD glory and strength."* To every answer he made, I would come back to this passage. I must have repeated it a great many times in the course of the talk. Finally, the man realized not only his need of Christ, but also the danger of delaying and the necessity of a prompt decision. He tried to get away from the passage, but I held him to this one point. Later that night he was assaulted and seriously injured. The next night, he came to accept Christ. The pounding he received from his assailant would probably have done him little good if the Scripture had not been pounded into his mind beforehand.

10
Dealing with Excuses

Many people are willful or headstrong. They will say, "I do not want you to talk to me." In such a case, it is usually best to recommend a passage of Scripture. Then leave the person alone to reflect on it, allowing the Word to speak for itself. Romans 6:23, Hebrews 10:28–29; 12:25, Mark 16:16, Proverbs 29:1 and 1:24–33 are good passages for this purpose.

Others may protest, "I cannot forgive someone." Matthew 6:15 and 18:23–35 show that they must forgive or be lost. Philippians 4:13 and Ezekiel 36:26 will teach them how to forgive. Many people are kept from Christ by an unforgiving spirit. Sometimes this difficulty can be removed by getting the person to kneel in prayer and ask God to take away his unforgiving spirit.

I once reasoned a long time with an inquirer who was under deep conviction but was held back from accepting Christ by a hatred toward someone who had wronged her. She kept insisting that she could not forgive. Finally I said, "Let us tell God about this matter." She agreed, and the moment we knelt down, she burst into a flood of tears. The difficulty was removed, and she accepted Christ immediately.

Some will admit, "I love the world too much." Mark 8:36 is a great text to use with these people. Luke 14:33 shows the absolute necessity that the world be given up. Also see Luke 12:16–20. First John 2:15–17 shows the folly of holding on to the world. Psalm 84:11 and Romans 8:32 promise that the Lord will hold back no good thing from His children.

Another excuse is, "I cannot acknowledge a wrong that I have done." Proverbs 28:13 will show the misery that is sure to follow unless the wrong is confessed. Others will say, "I do not want to make a public confession." Romans 10:10 and Matthew 10:32–33 show that God will accept nothing else. Mark 8:38, John 12:42–43, and Proverbs 24:25 show the peril of not making it.

Still others say, "I want to have my own way." Isaiah 55:8–9 shows how much better God's way is, and Proverbs 14:12 shows the consequences of having our own way. Finally, some refuse to take a stand and say, "I neither accept Christ nor reject Him." Matthew 12:30 shows that they must do one or the other. This verse has been used to convict many people.

More than Religion

Under this category comes the churchgoer who believes he is saved through mere church membership. A good way to deal with this person is to show him the necessity of the new birth. The new birth is described in Ezekiel 36:25–27, 2 Corinthians 5:17, and 2 Peter 1:4. John 3:3, 5, 7 show the necessity of the new birth.

Many people who have always attended church understand the new birth to mean baptism, but it obviously means more than that. In 1 Corinthians 4:15, Paul told the Corinthian Christians that he had begotten them through the Gospel. If the new birth meant baptism, he must have baptized them. But in 1 Corinthians 1:14, he declared he had not baptized them. Acts 9:13, 21, 23 show that a man may be baptized while his heart is still not right in the sight of God, so he has *"neither part nor lot in this matter"* (v. 21).

It is good to go a step further and show the inquirer the evidence of the new birth. First John 2:29; 3:9–17, and 5:1–4 give the biblical evidence of the new birth. The next question that will arise is, "How can I be born again?" This question is answered in John 1:12, 1 Peter 1:23, and James 1:18.

Acts 3:19 is a good text to use with churchgoers because it shows the necessity of repentance and conversion. Examples of repentance are in Isaiah 55:7 and Jonah 3:10. Another approach is to show them that it is the believer's privilege to know that he has eternal life.

Nominal churchgoers almost always lack assurance of salvation. They do not know that they are forgiven but hope to be forgiven some day. If you can show them that we can know we are forgiven and that we have eternal life, a great many of them will want this assurance. First John 5:13 states that it is the believer's privilege to know. Acts 13:38–39, 10:43 and John 3:36 are useful in leading them to this assurance.

Still another approach to be used after you have already made some progress is to show them the advantage of Bible study. Good texts for this purpose are John 5:39, 1 Peter 2:1–2, 2 Timothy 3:13–17, James 1:21–22, Psalm 1:1–2, Joshua 1:8, Mark 7:7–8, 13, and Matthew 22:29.

You may want to deal with a churchgoer in the same way you would deal with any sinner—awaken the realization in him that he is a sinner who needs Christ. For this purpose, use Matthew 22:37–38, Galatians 3:10–13, and Isaiah 53:6.

Some people think there is no use talking with those who believe they are saved through church membership. This is a great mistake. Many churchgoers are longing for something they do not find in their dry churches. If you can show them from the Word of God how to find it, they will come to Christ very easily and become strong Christians. Do not attack their particular church. Give them the truth, and the errors will take care of themselves in time. Often our attacks only expose our ignorance.

We always have a particular advantage in dealing with churchgoers. We have peace and power in Christianity that they do not have, and they can see and appreciate the difference.

The best way to deal with a Jew is to show him that his own Bible points to Christ. The most helpful passages are Isaiah 53, Daniel 9:26, and Zechariah 12:10. The whole book of Hebrews relates to the Jews, especially chapters 7, 9, and 10, along with the whole gospel of Matthew. Many Jews today are inquiring into the claims of Jesus of Nazareth and are open to talking about

Him. The great difficulty in accepting Christ as the Messiah is the severe persecution a Jew must endure if he does. This difficulty can be met by the passages already given under the subject of persecution.

We also should be prepared to deal with spiritualists. Leviticus 19:31 and 22:6, Deuteronomy 18:10–12, 2 Kings 21:1, 2, 6, 1 Chronicles 10:13, Isaiah 8:19–20, 1 John 4:1–3, and 2 Thessalonians 2:9–12 are passages to be used here.

In dealing with people who are deceived, it is wise to begin with John 7:17 and bring them to the place where they heartily desire to know the truth. A man cannot be brought out of his deception unless he wants to know the truth.

11
Helpful Soulwinning Hints

1. Deal with people of your own gender and about your own age. There are exceptions to this rule. One should always look to the Holy Spirit for His guidance concerning whom to approach. He may lead us to someone of the opposite sex. But unless there is clear guidance in the matter, experienced Christian workers agree that men do the most satisfactory work with men, and likewise women with women. This is especially true of the young. Many unfortunate complications can arise when young men try to lead young women to Christ or vice versa. Of course, an elderly, motherly woman may do excellent work with a young man or boy, and an elderly, fatherly man may do good work with a young woman or girl. It is not ordinarily wise for a young and inexperienced person to approach one much older and wiser than themselves.

2. Whenever it is possible, talk to the person alone. No one likes to open his heart freely to another on this personal and sacred subject when others are present. Many who would defend themselves out of pride when their friends are with them would admit their sin and need if they were alone with you. One worker can deal better with one unconverted person than several workers can deal with a single inquirer. A single worker cannot deal effectively with several people at once. But you may succeed in leading them one by one to Christ when you take the individuals off by themselves.

3. Rely wholly on the Spirit and the Word of God.

4. Do not merely quote or read passages from the Bible, but have the one with whom you are speaking read them himself. The truth may enter his heart through the eye as well as the ear.

143

5. It is best to emphasize a single passage of Scripture, repeating and discussing it until the inquirer cannot forget it. He will hear it ringing in his memory long after you have ceased talking. A friend of mine who was dealing with a young man who had many doubts and fears kept quoting the passage, *"Now is the accepted time; behold, now is the day of salvation"* (2 Cor. 6:2). The young man tried to get my friend to talk about something else, but he just kept repeating the words. The next day the young man returned, rejoicing in Christ. He thanked my friend for hammering him with that text. The words kept ringing in his ears during the night, and he could not rest until he had settled the matter by accepting Christ.

It is a good thing when a person can point to some definite verse in the Word of God and say, "I know on the authority of that verse that my sins are forgiven, and I am a child of God." Sometimes, however, a powerful effect is produced by grouping together passages along a particular subject until the mind is convinced and the heart conquered.

6. Always hold the person with whom you are dealing to the main point of accepting Christ. If he wishes to discuss the claims of various denominations, the question of baptism, theories of future punishment, or any question other than the central one of his need of a Savior, tell him that the time to settle those questions is after he has decided to accept or reject Christ. Many opportunities for repentance have been lost by an inexperienced worker allowing himself to become involved in an argument over some side issue.

7. Be courteous. Many well-meaning but indiscreet Christians, by their rudeness and impertinence, repel those whom they desire to win to Christ. We can be perfectly frank and perfectly courteous at the same time. You can point out to men their sin without insulting them. The gentler our manner is, the deeper our words will go, for they will not stir up opposition in the hearts of others. Some overzealous workers cause the people they approach to become defensive and clothe themselves with an armor that is impossible to penetrate.

8. Be earnest. Only the earnest Christian can make the unsaved person realize the truth of God's Word. We should let the passages we want to use with others first sink into our own souls. I know of a very successful worker who for a long time used the one passage, *"Prepare to meet thy God"* (Amos 4:12), whenever she witnessed for Christ. That passage had taken such complete possession of her heart and mind that she used it with tremendous effect. A few passages that have become real to us are better than many passages memorized from some textbook.

Take time to kneel and ponder some of the passages suggested in this book until you feel their power. Paul *"ceased not to warn every one night and day with tears"* (Acts 20:31). Genuine earnestness means more than any skill learned in a training class or even from the study of such a book as this.

9. Never lose your temper when trying to lead a soul to Christ. Some people are exasperating, but even they can be won by patience and gentleness. They certainly cannot be won if you lose your temper. Nothing will delight them more or give them more comfort in their sins. The more irritating they are in their words and actions, the more impressed they will be if you answer their insults with kindness. Often the one who has been most insufferable will come back in penitence.

One of the rudest men I ever met later became one of the most patient, persistent, and effective workers for Christ.

10. Never have a heated argument with anyone you desire to lead to Christ. This always comes from the flesh and not from the Spirit. (See Galatians 5:20, 22–23.) It arises from pride and unwillingness to let the other person get the best of you in an argument. Refuse to argue. If the one with whom you are talking has mistaken notions that must be removed before he can be led to Christ, quietly and pleasantly show him his error. If the error is not essential to the doctrine of salvation, refuse to discuss it, and hold the person to the main question.

11. Never interrupt anyone else who is leading someone to Christ. You may think he is not doing it in the best way. But if you can do any better, wait quietly, and you will have the opportunity. Many unskilled workers have someone at the point of

decision when a meddler breaks in and upsets the whole work. On the other hand, do not let others interrupt you. Just a little word plainly but courteously spoken will usually prevent it.

12. Don't be in a hurry. One of the great faults of Christian work today is haste. We are too anxious for immediate results and therefore do superficial work. Many of those who followed Christ came to Him slowly. Nicodemus, Joseph of Arimathea, Peter, and even Paul—although the final step in Paul's case seems very sudden—are cases in point. Three days after Jesus appeared to Paul on the way to Damascus, Paul came out into the light and openly confessed Christ. (See Acts 22:16.) One man with whom slow but thorough work has been done, and who at last has committed his life to Christ, is better than a dozen who are rushed through the sinner's prayer and think they have accepted Christ when in reality they have not. It is often wise to plant a truth in a man's heart and leave it to work. The seed on rocky ground springs up quickly, but it withers just as quickly.

13. Whenever possible, ask the person to pray with you. Difficulties can disappear in prayer, and many stubborn people yield when they are brought into the presence of God. I remember talking with a young woman for two hours and making no apparent headway. At last we knelt in prayer, and she was rejoicing in her Savior in less than five minutes.

14. Whenever you seem to fail, go home, pray about it, and find out why you failed. If you did not know what Scripture verse to use, study the portion of this book that describes the different types of people we meet and how to deal with them. See where your particular case belongs and how you should have responded. Then go back, if you can, and try again. In any case, you will be better prepared next time. The greatest successes in Christian work come through many apparent defeats. Study these hints and suggestions often to see if your failures come from a lack of preparation.

15. Before parting from the one who has accepted Christ, be sure to give him definite instructions as to how to succeed in the Christian life. The following points should always be insisted upon:

(a) Confess Christ openly before men every opportunity you get (Romans 10:9–10; Matthew 10:32–33).

(b) Be baptized and partake regularly of the Lord's Supper (Acts 2:38–42; Luke 22:19; 1 Corinthians 11:24–26).

(c) Study the Word of God daily (1 Peter 2:2; Acts 20:32; 2 Timothy 3:13–17; Acts 17:2).

(d) Pray daily, often, and in times of temptation (Luke 11:9–13, 22:40; 1 Thessalonians 5:17).

(e) Put every sin, even the smallest, and every doubt out of your life, and obey every word of Christ (1 John 1:6–7; Romans 14:23; John 14:23).

(f) Seek the fellowship of other Christians (Ephesians 4:12–16; Acts 2:42, 47; Hebrews 10:24–25).

(g) Go to work for Christ (Matthew 25:14–29).

(h) When you fall into sin, don't be discouraged, but confess it at once and believe it is forgiven because God says so. Then get up and go on with God (1 John 1:9; Philippians 3:13–14).

You should give these instructions to the one you have led to Christ. You can write them out or give a little tract or book that lists these and other helpful points for living the Christian life.

16. When you have led anyone to Christ, help him grow in his Christian life. Many who are led to Christ are then neglected, and their Christian growth is poor. The work of following up on those who are converted is as important as the work of leading them to Christ. As a rule, no one can do it as well as the person God used in their conversion.

12
Power for Soulwinning

One important condition for successful soulwinning demands a separate chapter. In Acts 1:5, Luke 24:49, and Acts 2:4, we have three expressions: *"baptized with the Holy Ghost," "endued with power from on high,"* and *"filled with the Holy Ghost."* By a careful comparison of these and related passages, we will find that these various expressions refer to one and the same experience. This experience is an absolutely necessary condition of acceptable and effective service for Christ.

Filled with the Spirit

The infilling of the Holy Spirit is a definite and distinct experience. A Christian will know whether he has received the Spirit or not. Jesus commanded His disciples to wait in Jerusalem until they received power from on high. (See Luke 24:49 and Acts 1:8.) If this were not a definite and distinct experience, the disciples would not know whether they had complied with Christ's command.

The baptism in the Holy Spirit is separate from His regenerating work. The disciples were told in Acts 1:5, *"Ye shall be baptized with the Holy Ghost not many days hence."* In Acts 8:15–16, we are told that some of them had already believed and were baptized with water, but the Holy Spirit had not yet fallen upon them. Again in Acts 19:1–6 some of the disciples had not received the Holy Spirit since they believed.

A believer may be regenerated by the Holy Spirit without being baptized with the Holy Spirit. Such a soul is saved but is not yet ready for service. Although every believer has the Holy Spirit according to Romans 8:9, not every believer has the baptism of the Holy Spirit. (See Acts 8:12–16 and 19:1–2.) Nevertheless, the baptism is available to everyone who has been born again.

The baptism of the Holy Spirit is always connected with testimony or service. (See 1 Corinthians 12:4–13; 2:4; 4:8, 31; 7:55; 9:17, 20; 10:45–46; and 19:6.) The baptism of the Holy Spirit has no direct reference to cleansing from sin. Some teaching on this subject leads men to expect that if they receive the baptism of the Holy Spirit, the old carnal nature will be eradicated. No Scripture supports this position. If you examine all the passages in which the baptism of the Holy Spirit is mentioned, you will see that it is always connected with testimony and service. A great moral and spiritual uplifting accompanies the baptism and often brings about an entire surrender of the will to Christ. But its primary purpose is for service.

We will get a better understanding of the baptism of the Holy Spirit if we consider its manifestations and results recorded in the Bible. Let us look first at the passage that goes into the most detail on this subject—1 Corinthians 12:4–13. The manifestations or results of the baptism of the Holy Spirit are not precisely the same in every person. For example, the baptism of the Holy Spirit will not make everyone who receives it a successful evangelist or teacher. A different gift may be imparted instead. This fact is often overlooked, resulting in disappointment and doubt. The manifestations or results vary with the lines of service to which God has called different individuals. One may receive the gift of being an evangelist, another a teacher, and another a helper. (See 1 Corinthians 12:28–31 and Ephesians 4:8, 11.) Some gift will be given in every case. (See 1 Corinthians 12:7, 11.) It may not be the same gift, but there will be a gift.

The Holy Spirit is the One who decides what gift or gifts will be imparted to each individual. (See 1 Corinthians 12:2.) It is not for us to select some place of service and then ask the Holy Spirit to qualify us for that service. We should not select some gift and then ask the Spirit to impart to us that gift. We are called to put ourselves entirely at the disposal of the Holy Spirit to send us where He will, into what line of service He will, and to impart what gift He will. He is absolutely sovereign, and our rightful position is one of absolute and unconditional surrender to Him.

Many fail to allow God to choose how He will use them, and they meet with disappointment. I know a sincere and self-sacrificing man who gave up a prosperous business and began the work of an evangelist. He had heard of the baptism of the Holy Spirit and supposed that if he received it, he would be qualified to be an evangelist. The man traveled more than four thousand miles to another country, but the work did not open up for him. He was confused and in doubt until he was led to see that it was not for him to select the work of an evangelist, as good as that work was, and then expect the Holy Spirit to qualify him for it. He gave himself up to be used in whatever work the Spirit would choose. The power of the Spirit came upon him, and he received the gift of an evangelist that he had coveted.

Power for Bold Service

The baptism of the Holy Spirit always imparts power for the service God calls us to fulfill. In a large American city, an uneducated boy was led to Christ. In his humble occupation, he began witnessing for Jesus. He grew one step at a time in Christ's work. A gentleman told me about him and said he would like me to meet him. The gentleman brought him to Chicago, and I invited him to speak one night in one of our tent meetings. The meeting was in a rough neighborhood, and it was usually difficult to hold the audience's attention for very long.

The young man began his message in a simple way. I was afraid I had made a mistake in asking him to speak, but I prayed and watched the audience. There was nothing remarkable in his address as he continued. But I noticed that all the people were listening. They continued to listen to the end. When I asked if there was anyone who wished to accept Christ, people stood in different parts of the tent to signify that they did. A man who had known the speaker before whispered to me, "It is the same wherever he goes." What was the explanation? This uneducated boy had received the baptism of the Holy Spirit and had received power.

One night at the close of a message on the baptism of the Holy Spirit, a minister came to me on the platform and said, "I need this power. Please pray for me."

"Let us kneel right now," I replied, and we did. A few weeks later, I met a gentleman who had been standing near us. "Do you remember," he said, "the minister with whom you prayed at New Britain? He went back to his church, and it is now packed every Sunday. People are being converted right and left." He had received the baptism of the Holy Spirit and power.

The baptism of the Holy Spirit always imparts boldness in testimony and service. (See Acts 4:29–31.) Contrast Peter in Acts 4:8–12 with Peter in Mark 14:66–72. Perhaps you have a great desire to speak to others and win them to Christ, but an insurmountable timidity stands in the way. If you receive the baptism of the Holy Spirit, all your shyness and fear will be overcome.

We are now ready to define the baptism of the Holy Spirit. The baptism of the Holy Spirit is the Spirit of God falling on the believer, taking possession of his faculties, imparting to him gifts not naturally his own but that qualify him for the service to which God has called him.

Who Needs the Baptism?

In Luke 24:49, Jesus told the apostles to remain in Jerusalem until they were filled with power from on high. These men had been appointed to be witnesses of the life, death, and resurrection of Christ. (See Luke 24:45–48 and Acts 1:22; 10:39–41.) They had received what would seem to be splendid and sufficient training for this work. For more than three years, they were instructed by Jesus Himself. They saw His miracles, death, burial, resurrection, and ascension.

But one thing was still needed. Jesus would not permit them to begin their appointed work until they were baptized in the Holy Spirit. The apostles with their unparalleled qualifications for service were not permitted to begin their work until they received the baptism of the Holy Spirit. What presumption it is for any of us with our inferior training to attempt service without it. Even Jesus did not begin His ministry until He was anointed with the Holy Spirit and power. (See Acts 10:38; Luke 3:22; 4:1, 14.)

This baptism is an absolutely essential preparation for Christian work. Only ignorance of the requirements of God's Word or daring presumption on our part would cause us to try to work for Christ before being baptized with the Holy Spirit.

It is the privilege of every believer to be baptized with the Holy Spirit. *"For the promise is unto you, and to your children, and to all that are afar off, even as many as the Lord our God shall call"* (Acts 2:39). The *"promise"* of this verse means the promise of the baptism of the Holy Spirit. The verse tells us that this promise is for everyone in all ages of the church's history whom God calls to Himself. If we do not have this baptism, it is our own fault. The baptism of the Holy Spirit is for us. We are responsible before God for all the work we could have done and all the souls we could have won if we would have received the baptism.

13

Obtaining the Baptism in the Holy Spirit

We now come to the practical question: How can we obtain this baptism of the Holy Spirit that is absolutely necessary in our service for Christ? Fortunately, the answer is plainly stated in the Bible.

"Repent, and be baptized every one of you in the name of Jesus Christ for the remission of sin, and ye shall receive the gift of the Holy Ghost" (Acts 2:38). The first step toward obtaining this baptism is repentance. Repentance means a change of mind—a change of mind about sin, about God, and in this case especially (as the context shows) a change of mind about Christ. A real change of mind leads to action. We turn away from all sin and turn to God. We turn away from rejecting Jesus Christ to accepting Him.

The second step is the rejection of our sin and acceptance of Jesus Christ by baptism in His name. The baptism with the Holy Spirit in at least one instance preceded the baptism with water, but this was apparently an exceptional case. (See Acts 10:44–48.)

How to Surrender All

"The Holy Ghost, whom God hath given to them that obey him" (Acts 5:32). The condition of the gift of the Holy Spirit stated here is that we obey Him. Obedience means more than the mere performance of some of the things God commands us to do. It means the entire surrender of our wills, ourselves, and everything we have to Him. We come to Him and say from the heart, "Here I am, Lord. I am Yours. You bought me with a price, and I acknowledge Your ownership. Take me and do with me whatever

You desire. Send me wherever You want. Use me as You wish." This entire yielding of ourselves to God is the condition of our receiving the baptism of the Holy Spirit.

At the close of a revival service, a gentleman hurried to the platform and said there was a lady in great distress who wished to speak with me. It was an hour before I could get to her, and she was anxious to receive the baptism of the Holy Spirit. Others had talked to her, but it seemed to do no good. I sat down beside her and said, "Is your will completely surrendered?" She did not know.

"Do you want to work for Jesus?" I asked.

"Yes."

"Are you willing to go back home and be a servant girl if it is God's will?"

"No!"

"You will never receive this blessing until your own will is completely laid down."

"I cannot lay it down."

"Would you like to have God lay it down for you?"

"Yes."

"Well, let us ask Him to do it." We did, and God heard her prayer. She received the baptism of the Holy Spirit and went from the church rejoicing.

Obedience means following the will of God as revealed in His Word or by His Spirit in every circumstance. Any refusal to do what God tells us to do, any conscious doing of what He tells us not do do—even in very little matters—will shut us out of this blessing. If even the smallest thing troubles us as we pray over this matter, we should set it right with God at once.

Asking and Receiving

We must make a definite request for the Father to fill us with the Holy Spirit. *"How much more shall your heavenly Father give the Holy Spirit to them that ask him"* (Luke 11:13). Ministers often say that because the Holy Spirit is already here and every believer has the Spirit, we do not need to pray for Him to come. This argument overlooks the distinction between having the Holy Spirit and being baptized in the Holy Spirit. It also contradicts the plain teaching of God's Word that He gives the Holy Spirit to those who ask Him. Furthermore, the baptism of the Holy Spirit in the book of Acts was constantly given in connection with and in answer to prayer. (See Acts 1:14; 2:1–4; 4:31; and 8:15, 17.)

Prayer implies desire. There is no real prayer for the baptism of the Spirit unless there is a deep desire for it. As long as a man thinks he can get along somehow without this blessing, he is not likely to obtain it. But when he reaches the place where he feels he must have this no matter what it costs, he is on his way toward receiving it. Many ministers of the Gospel have realized that they could not go on with their ministry without this gift. The gift soon came in answer to prayer, and the character of their work was entirely transformed.

Effective prayer must be in faith. (See Mark 1:24.) James said this in regard to the prayer for wisdom: *"Let him ask in faith, nothing wavering. For he that wavereth is like a wave of the sea driven with the wind and tossed. For let not that man think that he shall receive any thing of the Lord"* (James 1:6–7). The same principle holds true regarding the prayer for the Holy Spirit.

Many miss the blessing at this point. The way to approach God in faith is clearly taught in 1 John 5:14–15. *"This is the confidence that we have in him, that, if we ask any thing according to his will, he heareth us: and if we know that he hear us, whatsoever we ask, we know that we have the petitions that we desired of him."* When we ask the Father for the baptism of the Holy Spirit, we know that we have asked something according to His will because it is definitely promised in His Word. Therefore, when I ask God in faith, I have a right to count this blessing as mine. The prayer is heard, and I have the petition I asked of Him. I can get up and begin my work, assured that the Spirit's power will be with me.

You may ask, "Should I expect any evidence of the Spirit's presence?" The answer is yes, but only in your service to Him. When I know on the authority of God's Word that my prayer is heard, I have the right to begin any service to which He calls me. I confidently expect the manifestation of the Spirit's power in that service. It is a mistake to wait—as so many do—for the manifestation in special emotional experiences. These may and often do accompany the baptism of the Holy Spirit. But the Bible clearly teaches in 1 Corinthians 12:4–11 that the place to look for manifestation is in service. The most important, reliable, and scriptural manifestations are found in our work.

The Word on Waiting

"Must we not wait," it may be asked, "until we know that we have received the baptism of the Holy Spirit?" The answer is yes, but how are we to know? We know in the same way we know we are saved—by the testimony of God's Word. When I have met His conditions and have asked for this gift that is according to His will, I know by God's Word in 1 John 5:14–15 that my prayer is heard and that I have received the answer. I have a right to proceed with no other evidence than the all-sufficient evidence of God's Word. I can enter into the service to which God calls me.

The disciples waited ten days, and the reason is clearly given in Acts 2:1: *"When the day of Pentecost was fully come."* In the Old Testament types, the Day of Pentecost had been appointed as the day for the first giving of the Holy Spirit and the offering of the first fruits (the church). Therefore, the Holy Spirit could not be given until that day. (See Leviticus 23:9–17.) But after the Spirit was given, we find no lengthy period of waiting on the part of those who sought this blessing. (See Acts 4:31; 8:15, 17; 9:17, 20; and 19:6.) Men are obliged to wait today, but it is only because they have not met the conditions or do not believe and claim the blessing simply on the Word of God. The moment we meet the conditions and claim the blessing, it is ours. (See Mark 11:24.) Any child of God may lay down this book, meet the conditions, ask for the blessing, claim it, and have it.

A student came to talk with me about the baptism of the Holy Spirit. He said he had heard of this before and had been seeking it for months but could not get it. I found that his will was not surrendered, but we soon settled the matter. I said, "Let us kneel down and ask God for the baptism of the Holy Spirit."

After we prayed, I asked the student, "Was that petition according to God's will?"

"Yes."

"Was the prayer heard?"

After some hesitation he replied, "It must have been."

"Have you received what you asked of Him?"

"I do not feel it." I read 1 John 5:15 from the Bible that lay open before us: *"If we know that he hear us, whatsoever we ask, we know that we have the petitions that we desired of him."*

"Now, have you received what you asked?"

A smile spread over his face, and he said, "I must have, for God says so." He left a few minutes later. When I went back to the school in a few days, I met the young man again. His face was all aglow. He knew he had received what at first he took on the Word of God alone.

We must be filled continually with the Spirit to work for God. Many Christians who once experienced the baptism of the Holy Spirit are today trying to work in the power of that old experience and are working without God. A constant fellowship must be maintained so that the Spirit is allowed to work in and through the believer. By the power that works within us, we will be able to do mighty exploits for the kingdom of God.

The Power of Prayer

Contents

Introduction

The great need of the church today, and of human society as a whole, is a genuine, God-sent revival. It is either revival or revolution—a revolution that will plunge human society and civilization into chaos and utter confusion. It is a time of widespread apostasy. This may be the last apostasy from which we will be saved by the return of our Lord Jesus to this earth to take the reins of government into His own thoroughly competent hands. That would, of course, be the greatest and most glorious of all revivals, and a revival that would never end.

But we do not know that this is the final apostasy. There have been more thoroughgoing and appalling apostasies in the past than this one is at the present hour. The apostasy in England at the time of the Wesleys, and in America at the time of Jonathan Edwards, was far more complete than the present apostasy is. The apostasy in this country at the opening of the nineteenth century was far more appalling, at least as regards university life, than the apostasy of today. It was the revival under the Wesleys and their associates that saved the church and saved civilization in their day. Even a rationalist as absolute as William Lecky, the Irish historian (1838–1903), admits that it was the revival under the Wesleys that saved civilization in England. And it was the Great Awakening under the leadership of Jonathan Edwards and others that saved the church in America.

Our sorest need today is a deep, thorough, Spirit-worked, God-sent revival. Such revivals, as far as man's agency is concerned, always come in one way—by prayer. It was Jonathan Edwards' *Call to Prayer* that brought the Great Awakening. The wondrous revival of 1857 was brought by city missionary Landfear's stirring the Christians of New York City to prayer. It was the prayer of the four humble Christians of Kells, and the prayers of others, that brought the marvelous Ulster Revival of 1859–60.

Late in the nineteenth century, at the request of D. L. Moody, I wrote a book entitled *How to Pray*. God used that book to stir many thousands to pray; and the great work in Australia and New Zealand in 1902, extending over to England, Scotland, Ireland, and Wales (the great Welsh revival of 1904), and to India and many lands, resulting in the conversion of hundreds of thousands of souls, was the direct outcome of the publication of that book.

The present book is much fuller and more complete than *How to Pray*, and it covers the whole subject of prayer, not only in its relationship to revivals, but in its relationship to the various departments of Christian life and activity. The chapters are composed largely of addresses on prayer that I have given as I have gone around the world preaching the Gospel. They have expanded through the twenty-two years and more that I have been engaged in this work. In their present, completed form, they were delivered to my own congregation in the Church of the Open Door, Los Angeles, and they were broadcast over the radio to perhaps 100,000 people (some say far more) each week in places from one mile to 3,000 miles away. These were "listening in" Sunday after Sunday, in the autumn, winter, and spring of 1923 and 1924.

As I write this preface, I am in the midst of a revival in Winnipeg, Canada, where last night 5,000 people crowded into a rink that seats only 4,100, and many were unable to get in. Many men, women, and children made a public confession of having accepted Christ in that hour. Will we have a revival of great power extending over many lands? I believe we will. God grant that this book may hasten it!

—R. A. Torrey

1

The Power of Prayer

Ye have not, because ye ask not.
—James 4:2

A message from God is contained in these seven short words. Six of the seven are monosyllables, and the remaining word has only two syllables and is one of the most familiar and most easily understood words in the English language. Yet there is so much in these seven short, simple words that they have transformed many lives and brought many inefficient Christian workers into a place of great power.

These seven words in James 4:2 contain the answer to the poverty and powerlessness of the average Christian, of the average minister, and of the average church. "Why is it," many Christians are asking, "that I make such poor progress in my Christian life? Why do I have so little victory over sin? Why do I win so few souls to Christ? Why do I grow so slowly into the likeness of my Lord and Savior Jesus Christ?" And God answers in the words of our text: "Neglect of prayer. You do not have because you do not ask."

"Why is it," many ministers are asking, "that I see so little fruit from my ministry? Why are there so few conversions? Why does my church grow so slowly? Why are the members of my church so little helped by my ministry and built up so little in Christian knowledge and life?" And again God replies: "Neglect of prayer. You do not have because you do not ask."

"Why is it," both ministers and churches are asking, "that the church of Jesus Christ is making such slow progress in the world today? Why does it make so little headway against sin, against unbelief, against error in all its forms? Why does it have so little victory over the world, the flesh, and the devil? Why is the average church member living on such a low plane of Christian living? Why does the Lord Jesus Christ get so little honor from the state of the church today?" And, again, God replies: "Neglect of prayer. You do not have because you do not ask."

When we read the only inspired church history that was ever written, the history of the early church as it was recorded by Luke (under the inspiration of the Holy Spirit) in the Acts of the Apostles, what do we find? We find a story of constant victory, a story of perpetual progress. We read, for example, such statements as these: *"The Lord added to the church daily such as should be saved"* (Acts 2:47); *"Many of them which heard the word believed; and the number of the men was about five thousand"* (Acts 4:4); and *"Believers were the more added to the Lord, multitudes both of men and women"* (Acts 5:14). We also read in Acts 6:7, *"And the word of God increased; and the number of the disciples multiplied in Jerusalem greatly; and a great company of the priests were obedient to the faith."*

We can go on, chapter after chapter, through the book of Acts, and in every one of the twenty-seven chapters after the first, we find the same note of victory. I once went through the Acts of the Apostles, marking the notes of victory, and without a single exception, the triumphant shout of victory rang out in every chapter. How different the history of the church as recorded here is from the history of the church of Jesus Christ today. Take, for example, that first statement, *"The Lord added to the church daily* [that is, every day, or as the Revised Version puts it, *"day by day"*] *such as should be saved"* (Acts 2:47). How different it is today! If we have a revival once a year and acquire fifty or sixty members, though we spend the rest of the year slipping back to where we were before, we think we are doing pretty well. But in those days there was a revival all the time, and every day those who not only "hit the trail" but were really being saved were added to the church.

Why this difference between the early church and the church of Jesus Christ today? Someone will answer, "Because there is so much opposition today." Ah, but there was opposition in those days: bitter, determined, relentless opposition—opposition that turns what you and I meet today into child's play. But the early church went right on beating down all opposition, surmounting every obstacle, conquering every foe, always victorious, right on without a setback from Jerusalem to Rome, in the face of the most firmly entrenched and mightiest heathenism and unbelief. I repeat the question, "Why was it?" If you will turn to the chapters to which I have already referred, you will get your answer.

Turn, for example, to Acts 2:42: *"And they continued stedfastly in the apostles' doctrine and fellowship, and in breaking of bread, and in prayers."* This is a brief but very suggestive picture of the early church. It was a praying church. It was a church in which they prayed not merely occasionally, but where they all *"continued stedfastly...in prayers."* They all prayed—not a select few, but the whole membership of the church—and all prayed continuously with steadfast determination. Now turn to Acts 6:4, and you will get the rest of your answer: *"But we will give ourselves continually to prayer."* That is a picture of the apostolic ministry—it was a praying ministry, and a ministry in which they gave themselves *"continually to prayer"* and *"continued stedfastly...in prayers"* (Acts 2:42). A praying church and a praying ministry! Ah, such a church and such a ministry can achieve anything that ought to be achieved. It will go steadily on, beating down all opposition, surmounting every obstacle, conquering every foe, just as much today as it did in the days of the apostles.

There is nothing else in the church of today, nothing in the ministry of today, nothing in which you and I have departed more notably and more lamentably from apostolic precedent than in this matter of prayer. We do not live in a praying age. A considerable proportion of the membership of our evangelical churches today do not believe even theoretically in prayer; that is, they do not believe in prayer as bringing anything to pass that would not have come to pass even if they had not prayed. They believe in prayer as having a beneficial "reflex influence," that it benefits the person who prays by a sort of lifting yourself up by your spiritual bootstraps. But as for prayer bringing anything to pass that would not have come to pass if no one had prayed, they do not believe in it, and many of them, even some of our modern ministers, frankly say so.

And with the part of our church membership that does believe in prayer theoretically—and thank God, I believe it is still the vast majority in our evangelical churches—even they do not make use of this mighty instrument that God has put into our hands as one would naturally expect. As I said, we do not live in a praying age. We live in an age of hustle and bustle, of man's efforts and man's determination, of man's confidence in himself and in his own power to achieve things, an age of human organization, human machinery, human scheming, and human achievement. In the things of God, this means no real achievement at all. I think it would be perfectly safe to say that the church of Christ was never in all its history so fully and so skillfully, so thoroughly and so perfectly organized as it is today. Our machinery is wonderful; it is just perfect. Unfortunately, it is machinery without power; and when things do not go right, instead of going to the real source of our failure, which is our neglect to depend upon God and to look to God for power, we look around to see if there is not some new organization we can set up, some new wheel that we can add to our machinery. We have altogether too many wheels already. What we need is not so much some new organization, some new wheel, but *the spirit of the living creature...in the wheels*" (Ezek. 1:20), whom we already possess.

Prayer has as much power today, when men and women are themselves on praying ground and meeting the conditions of prevailing prayer, as it has ever had. God has not changed; His ear is just as quick to hear the voice of real prayer, and His hand is just as long and strong to save, as it ever was. *"Behold, the LORD's hand is not shortened, that it cannot save; neither his ear heavy, that it cannot hear: but* [our] *iniquities* [may] *have separated between* [us] *and* [our] *God, and* [our] *sins* [may] *have hid his face from* [us], *that he will not hear"* (Isa. 59:1–2). Prayer is the key that unlocks all the storehouses of God's infinite grace and power. All that God is, and all that God has, is at the disposal of prayer. But we must use the key. Prayer can do anything that God can do, and, since God can do anything, prayer is omnipotent. No one can stand against the man who knows how to pray and who meets all the conditions of prevailing prayer and who really prays. *"The Lord God omnipotent"* (Rev. 19:6) works for him and works through him.

Prayer Promotes Our Personal Holiness

But what, specifically, will prayer do? We have been dealing in generalities, so let us come down to the definite and specific. The Word of God plainly answers the question.

In the first place, prayer will promote our personal piety, our individual holiness, and our individual growth into the likeness of our Lord and Savior Jesus Christ as nothing else but the study of the Word of God will do. These two things, prayer and study of the Word of God, always go hand in hand, for there is no true prayer without study of the Word of God, and there is no true study of the Word of God without prayer.

Other things being equal, your growth and mine into the likeness of our Lord and Savior Jesus Christ will be in exact proportion to the time and to the heart we put into prayer. Please note exactly what I say: your growth and mine into the likeness of our Lord and Savior Jesus Christ will be in exact proportion to the time and to the heart we put into prayer. I put it this way because there are many who put a great deal of time into praying, but they put so little heart into their praying that they do little actual praying in the long time they spend at it. There are others who may not put so much time into praying but who put so much heart into their praying that they accomplish vastly more by their praying in a short time than the others accomplish by their praying a long time. God Himself has told us in Jeremiah 29:13, *"And ye shall seek me, and find me, when ye shall search for me with all your heart."*

We are told in the Word of God in Ephesians 1:3 that God *"hath blessed us with all spiritual blessings in heavenly places in Christ."* In other words, Jesus Christ, by His atoning death and by

His resurrection and ascension to the right hand of the Father, has obtained for every believer in Him every possible spiritual blessing. There is no spiritual blessing that any believer enjoys that may not be yours. It belongs to you now; Christ purchased it by His atoning death, and God has provided it in Him. It is there for you; but it is your part to claim it, to put out your hand and take it. God's appointed way of claiming blessings, or putting out your hand and taking hold of the blessings that are procured for you by the atoning death of Jesus Christ, is by prayer. Prayer is the hand that takes to ourselves the blessings that God has already provided in His Son.

Go through your Bible, and you will find it definitely stated that every conceivable spiritual blessing is obtained by prayer. For example, it is in answer to prayer, as we learn from Psalm 139:23–24, that God searches us and knows our hearts, tries us and knows our thoughts, brings to light the sin that there is in us, and delivers us from it. As we learn from Psalm 19:12–13, it is in answer to prayer that we are cleansed from secret faults and God keeps us back from *"presumptuous sins"* (v. 13). It is in answer to prayer, as we learn from verse fourteen, that the words of our mouths and the meditations of our hearts are made acceptable in God's sight. And it is in answer to prayer, as wc learn from Psalm 25:4–5, that God shows us His ways, teaches us His path, and guides us in His truth. We also learn from the prayer our Lord Himself taught us, that we are kept from temptation and delivered from the power of the *"evil one"* in answer to prayer (Matt. 6:13 RV). As we learn from Luke 11:13, it is in answer to prayer that God gives us His Holy Spirit. In this way, we might go on through the whole catalog of spiritual blessings, and we would find that every one is obtained by asking for it. Indeed, our Lord Himself has said in Matthew 7:11, *"If ye then, being evil, know how to give good gifts unto your children, how much more shall your Father which is in heaven give good things to them that ask him?"*

One of the most instructive and suggestive passages in the entire Bible, showing the mighty power of prayer to transform us into the likeness of our Lord Jesus Himself, is found in 2 Corinthians 3:18: *"But we all, with open face beholding as in a glass* [the

Revised Version reads better, *"reflecting as a mirror"*] *the glory of the Lord, are changed into the same image from glory to glory, even as by the Spirit of the Lord."* The thought is that the Lord is the Sun, and you and I are mirrors. Just as a mischievous boy on a bright sunshiny day will catch the rays of the sun in a piece of a broken mirror and reflect them into your eyes and mine with almost blinding power, so we as mirrors, when we commune with God, catch the rays of His moral glory and reflect them out upon the world *"from glory to glory."* That is, each new time we commune with Him, we catch something new of His glory and reflect it out upon the world.

Consider Moses, who went up into the Mount and tarried alone for forty days with God, gazing upon that ineffable glory. He caught so much of the glory in his own face that when he came down from the Mount, though he himself did not know it, his face shone so much that he had to put a veil over it to hide the blinding glory of it from his fellow Israelites. Likewise we, going up into the mount of prayer, away from the world, alone with God, and remaining long alone with God, catch the rays of His glory. When we come down to our fellowmen, it is not so much that our faces shine (though I do believe that sometimes even our faces shine), but our characters shine with the glory that we have been beholding.

We reflect out upon the world the moral glory of God *"from glory to glory,"* each new time of communion with Him catching something new of His glory to reflect out upon the world. Oh, here is the secret of becoming much like God: remaining long alone with God. If you won't stay long with Him, you won't be much like Him.

One of the most remarkable men in Scotland's history was John Welch, son-in-law of John Knox, the great Scotch reformer. He was not so well-known as his famous father-in-law, but in some respects he was a far more remarkable man than John Knox himself. Most people have the idea that it was John Knox who prayed, "Give me Scotland or I die." It was not; it was John Welch, his son-in-law. John Welch put it on record, before he died, that he counted a day ill-spent if he did not spend seven or eight hours in secret prayer; and when John Welch came to die, an old Scotchman who had known him from his boyhood said of him, "John Welch was a type of Christ." Of course that was an inaccurate use of language, but what the old Scotchman meant was that Jesus Christ had stamped the impression of His character upon John Welch. When had Jesus Christ done it? In those seven or eight hours of daily communion with Himself.

I do not suppose that God has called many of us, if any of us, to spend seven or eight hours a day in prayer, but I am confident God has called most of us, if not every one of us, to put more time into prayer than we now do. This is one of the great secrets of holiness; indeed, it is the only way in which we can become really holy and continue to be holy.

We often used to sing the hymn, "Take Time to Be Holy." I wish we sang it more in these days. It takes time to be holy; one cannot be holy in a hurry, and much of the time that it takes to be holy must go into secret prayer. Some people express surprise that professing Christians today are so little like their Lord, but when I stop to think how little time the average Christian today puts into secret prayer, the thing that astonishes me is not that we are so little like the Lord, but that we are as much like the Lord as we are.

Prayer Brings God's Power into Our Work

Prayer will not only promote our personal holiness as almost nothing else will, but prayer will also bring the power of God into our work. We read in Isaiah 40:31, *"But they that wait on the LORD shall renew their strength; they shall mount up with wings as eagles; they shall run, and not be weary; and they shall walk* [plod right along day after day, which is far harder than running or flying], *and not faint."*

It is the privilege of every child of God to have the power of God in his service. And the verse just quoted tells us how to obtain it, and that is by waiting on the Lord. Sometimes you will hear people stand up in a meeting, not so frequently perhaps in these days as in former days, and say, "I am trying to serve

God in my poor, weak way." Well, if you are trying to serve God in your poor, weak way, quit it; your duty is to serve God in His strong, triumphant way. But you say, "I have no natural ability." Then get a supernatural ability. The religion of Jesus Christ is a supernatural religion from start to finish, and we should live our lives in supernatural power, the power of God through Jesus Christ. We should perform our service with supernatural power, the power of God ministered by the Holy Spirit through Jesus Christ. You say, "I have no natural gifts." Then get supernatural gifts. The Holy Spirit is promised to every believer so that he may obtain the supernatural gifts that equip him for the particular service to which God calls him. The Holy Spirit distributes *"to every man* [that is, to each and every believer] *severally as he will"* (1 Cor. 12:11). It is our privilege to have the power of God, if only we will seek it by prayer, in any and every line of service to which God calls us.

Are you a mother or a father? Do you wish power from God to bring your own children up in the *"nurture and admonition of the Lord"* (Eph. 6:4)? God commands you to do it, and He especially commands the father to do it. The whole of verse four reads, *"Ye fathers, provoke not your children to wrath: but bring them up in the nurture and admonition of the Lord."*

Now God never commands the impossible, and as He commands us fathers and mothers to bring our children up in the nurture and admonition of the Lord, it is possible for us to do it. If any one of your children is not saved, the first blame lies at your own door. Paul said to the jailer in Philippi, *"Believe on the Lord Jesus Christ, and thou shalt be saved, and thy house"* (Acts 16:31). Yes, it is the solemn duty of every father and mother to lead every one of their children to Jesus. But we can never accomplish it unless we are much in prayer to God for power to do it.

In my first pastorate, I had as a member of my church a most excellent Christian woman. She had a little boy of six who was one of the most incorrigible youngsters I have ever known. He was the terror of the community. One Sunday at the close of the morning service, his mother came to me and said, "You know ———" (calling her boy by his first name).

"Yes," I replied, "I know him." Everybody in town knew him.

Then she said, "You know he is not a very good boy."

"Yes," I replied, "I know he is not a very good boy." Indeed, that was a decidedly euphemistic way of putting it; in fact, he was the terror of the neighborhood.

Then his heavyhearted mother said, "What shall I do?"

I replied, "Have you ever tried prayer?"

"Why," she said, "of course I pray."

"Oh," I said, "that is not what I mean. Have you ever asked God definitely to regenerate your boy and then expected Him to do it?"

"I do not think I have ever been as definite as that."

"Well," I said, "you go right home and be just as definite as that."

She went home, and she was just as definite as that. I think it was from that very day, certainly from that week, that her boy was a transformed boy and grew up into a fine young man.

Oh, mothers and fathers, it is your privilege to lead every one of your children to the Savior. But it costs something to have them saved. It takes much time alone with God, to be much in prayer. It costs also your making those sacrifices, and straightening out those things in your life that are wrong; it costs fulfilling the conditions of prevailing prayer. And if any of you have unsaved children, get alone with God and ask Him to show you what in your own life is responsible for the present condition of your children, and straighten it out at once. Then get down alone before God and hold on to Him in earnest prayer for the definite conversion of each one of your children. Do not rest until, by prayer and by your putting forth every effort, you know beyond question that every one of your children is definitely and positively converted and born again.

Are you a Sunday school teacher? Do you wish to see every one of your Sunday school students converted? That is primarily your duty as a Sunday school teacher. You are not merely to teach Bible geography and Bible history, or even Bible doctrine, but to get the students in your class saved, one and all. Do you want power from on high to enable you to save them? Ask God for it.

When my associate, Mr. Alexander, and I were in Sydney, Australia, the meetings were held in the town hall, which seated about 5,000 people. But the crowds were so great that some days we had to divide the group and have women only in the afternoon, and men only at night. One Sunday afternoon the Sydney town hall was packed with women. I gave the invitation for all who wished to accept Jesus Christ as their personal Savior to surrender to Him as their Lord and Master, begin to confess Him as such before the world, and strive to live from this time on to please Him in every way from day to day. On my left a whole row of young women, all about twenty years of age, rose to their feet, eighteen of them in all. As I saw them stand side by side I said to myself, "That is someone's Bible class." Afterward they came forward with the other women who came to make a public confession of their acceptance of Jesus Christ. When the meeting was over, a young lady came to me, her face wreathed in smiles, and she said, "That is my Bible class. I have been praying for their conversion, and every one of them has accepted Jesus Christ today."

We were holding meetings in Bristol, England. A prominent manufacturer in Exeter had a Bible class in that city, a class of twenty-two men. He invited all of them to go to Bristol with him and hear me preach. Twenty-one of them consented to go. At that meeting twenty of them accepted Christ. The twenty-first accepted Christ in the train on the way home, and then they all, on their return, gathered around the remaining one who would not go, and he also accepted Christ. That teacher was praying for the conversion of the members of his class and was willing to make the sacrifices necessary to get his prayers answered. What a revival we would have if every Sunday school teacher would begin praying the way he or she ought for the conversion of every student in his or her class!

Are you in more public work, a preacher perhaps, or speaking from the public platform? Do you long for power in that work? Ask for it.

The Power of Prayer

I will never forget a scene I witnessed many years ago in the city of Boston. It was at the International Christian Workers' Convention, which was held in the old Tremont Temple, seating 3,500 people. It was my privilege to preside at the Convention. On a Saturday morning at eleven o'clock, the Tremont Temple was packed to its utmost capacity. Every seat was taken, every inch of standing room where men and women were allowed to stand was taken, and multitudes outside still clamored for admission. The audience was as fine in quality as it was large in numbers. As I looked behind me on the platform, it seemed as if every leading minister and clergyman, not only of Boston, but also of New England, was on that platform. In front of me were seated the leaders not only in the church life, but also in the social, commercial, and political life of Boston and the surrounding area.

I arose to announce the next speaker on the program; and my heart sank, for the next speaker was a woman. In those days I had a prejudice against any woman speaking in public under any circumstances. But this particular woman was a professing Christian, and a Presbyterian at that (and I suppose that is orthodox enough for most of us), but she had been what we call a "worldly Christian," a dancing, card-playing, theater-going Christian. She had, however, had an experience of which I had not heard. One night, sitting in her beautiful home in New York City (she was a woman of wealth), she turned to her husband as he sat reading the evening paper, and said, "Husband, I hear they are doing a good work down at Jerry McAuley's Mission at 316 Water Street. Let's go down and help them." He was very much like her: kindhearted, generous, but very much of a worldling. He laid aside his paper and said, "Well, let's go." They put on their coats and started for 316 Water Street.

When they arrived they found the mission hall full and took seats back by the door. As they sat and listened to one after another of those rescued men, they were filled with new interest. A new world seemed to open to them; at last the woman turned to her husband and whispered, "I guess they will have to help us instead of our helping them. They've got something we haven't."

The Power of Prayer

And when the invitation was given out, this finely dressed, cultured gentleman and his wife went forward and knelt at the altar in the sawdust along with the drunken "bums" and other outcasts of Water Street.

But of this I knew nothing. I only knew the type of woman she had been. When I saw her name on the program, as I said, my heart sank and I thought, "What a waste of a magnificent opportunity; here is this wonderful audience and only this woman to speak to them." But I had no authority to change the program; my business was simply to announce it. Summoning all the courtesy I could command under the circumstances, I introduced this lady, and then sank into the chairman's seat and buried my face in my hands and began to pray to God to save us from disaster.

Some years afterward I was in the city of Atlanta, and one of the leading Christian workers of that city, who had been at the Boston Convention, came to me laughing and said, "I shall never forget how you introduced Mrs. ——— at the Boston Convention, and then dropped into your chair and covered your face with your hands as if you had done something you were ashamed of."

Well, I had. But as I said, I began to pray. In a short while, I took my face out of my hands and began to watch as well as pray. Every one of those 3,500 pairs of eyes were riveted on that woman as she stood there and spoke. Soon I saw tears come into eyes that were unaccustomed to weeping, and I saw men and women taking out their handkerchiefs and at first trying to pretend they were not weeping. Then, throwing all disguise to the wind, they bowed their heads on the backs of the seats in front of them and sobbed as if their hearts would break. Before that wonderful address was over, that whole audience was swept by the power of that woman's words as the trees of our forests are sometimes swept by a cyclone.

This was a Saturday morning. The following Monday morning, Dr. Broadbeck, at that time pastor of the leading Methodist church in Boston, came to me and said with a choking voice, "Brother Torrey, I could not open my mouth to speak to my own people in my own church yesterday morning without bursting into tears as I thought of that wonderful scene we witnessed here on Saturday morning."

When that wonderful address was over, some of us went to this woman and said to her, "God has wonderfully used you this morning."

"Oh," she replied, "would you like to know the secret of it? Last night as I thought of the great throng that would fill the Tremont Temple this morning, and of my own inexperience in public address, I spent the whole night on my face before God in prayer."

Oh, men and women, if we would spend more nights before God on our faces in prayer, there would be more days of power when we faced our congregations!

2
The Results of Definite and Determined Prayer

The effectual fervent prayer of a righteous
man availeth much.
—James 5:16

These words of God set forth prayer as a working force, as a force that brings things to pass that would not come to pass if it were not for prayer. This truth comes out even more clearly in the Revised Version: *"The supplication of a righteous man availeth much in its working."* While this translation means practically the same thing as the King James Version, it is not only a more accurate translation, but it is also a more suggestive one. It tells us that prayer is something that works, and that it avails much because of its *"working."* Yes, prayer certainly does work.

A contrast is often drawn by many between praying and working. I knew a man once, an officer in a Sunday school in Brooklyn. One day the superintendent called on him to pray. He arose and said, "I am not a praying Christian; I am a working Christian." But praying is working. It is the most effective work that anyone can do; that is, we can often bring more to pass by praying than we can by any other form of effort we might put forth.

Furthermore, prayer, if it is real prayer, the kind of prayer that avails much with God, oftentimes is harder work than any other kind of effort; it takes more out of a person than any other kind of effort. When Mr. Alexander and I went to Liverpool for our second series of meetings there, Rev. Musgrave Brown, vicar

177

of one of the leading Church of England parishes in the city, was chairman of our committee. His health gave out the very first week of the meetings, and he was ordered to Switzerland by his doctor. Soon after reaching Switzerland he wrote me saying, "I hoped to be of so much help in these meetings and anticipated so much from them, but here I am, way off here in Switzerland, ordered here by my doctor, and now all I can do is to pray." Then he added, "But after all, that is the greatest thing anyone can do, is it not? And real prayer takes more out of a person than anything else, does it not?" Yes, it often does. Real praying is a costly exercise, but it pays far more than it costs. It is not easy work, but it is the most profitable of all work. We can accomplish more by time and strength put into prayer than we can by putting the same amount of time and strength into anything else.

You will notice that in the Revised Version the word *"supplication"* is substituted for the word *"prayer."* The reason for this is that there are a number of Greek words that are translated *"prayer"* in the King James Version, and they have different shades of meaning, sometimes very significant shades of meaning. The Greek word that the King James Version translates *"prayer"* in this passage is a very significant word: it sets forth prayer as the definite expression of a deeply felt need. Indeed, the primary meaning of the word is "need." Therefore, our text teaches that definite and determined prayer to God *"availeth much."*

The Greek word translated *"availeth"* is also an expressive and significant word. Its primary meaning is "to be strong," "to have power or force," and then "to exercise power." So the thought of our text is that definite and determined prayer exerts much power in its working, that it achieves great things. Then in the verses that immediately follow our text, we are told of the astounding things Elijah brought to pass by his prayers, how he shut up heaven for three years and six months so that there was not a drop of rain for that long period. The Old Testament account tells us that not only was there not a drop of rain, but furthermore, not a drop of dew (1 Kings 17:1). When the proper time had come, Elijah *"prayed again, and the heaven gave rain, and*

The Results of Definite and Determined Prayer

the earth brought forth her fruit" (James 5:18). Or, as Mr. Moody used to put it in his graphic way, "Elijah locked up heaven for three years and six months and put the key in his pocket."

Now there is no particular reason that you or I know of why we should shut up heaven for three years and six months, or, for that matter, for three days; but there is a most imperative need that we bring some other things to pass. There is no other way in which we can bring them to pass than by praying for them, by definite and determined prayer. So we are brought face-to-face with the tremendously important question: What are some of the definite things that are greatly to be desired at the present time that prayer will bring to pass?

We have already seen two immeasurably important things that prayer will accomplish: first, it will promote our own personal piety, our individual holiness, our individual growth into the likeness of our Lord and Savior Jesus Christ; second, it will bring the power of God into our work. Now we will discover from a study of the Bible some other exceedingly important things that the right sort of praying will bring to pass.

Prayer Will Save Others

Turn to 1 John 5:16, where we read, *"If any man see his brother sin a sin which is not unto death, he shall ask, and he shall give him life for them that sin not unto death."*

This is one of the most remarkable statements in the whole Bible on the subject of prayer and its amazing power. The statement of this verse is not only most remarkable, but it is also most cheering and most gladdening. Here God tells us that prayer will not only bring blessing to the one who prays, but that it will also bring the greatest of all blessings to others, even the blessing of eternal life to those for whom we pray. It tells us that if we see another sinning a sin not unto death—that is, committing sin, any sin except the one unpardonable sin—we can go to God in prayer for that person, and in answer to our prayers, God will give eternal life to this one for whom we have prayed.

The Power of Prayer

This passage, of course, is often taken to teach divine healing and is interpreted as if the thought were that the *"life"* here spoken of was mere natural or physical life. People take this verse to mean that by our prayer, we can get physical life for one who is sick because of his sinning, but who has not committed the sin that would bring about his being removed from this world. But this interpretation is not only incorrect but also impossible. The apostle John in his writings used two different Greek words for "life." One signifies physical life, and the other signifies spiritual or eternal life. I have looked up every passage where John used this latter word in his gospel, in his epistles, and in the book of Revelation, and in not one single instance did he use the word used in this verse of anything but spiritual or eternal life. This is the word John used in this passage, and the thought of this passage then is, not that one may obtain physical life, deliverance from natural death, by praying for one who has sinned, but that he can obtain eternal life, salvation in its fullest sense, for the one who has sinned but has not sinned unto death. This is a wonderful thought and a thought full of comfort and encouragement.

We can accomplish more for the salvation of others by praying for them than we can in any other way. I do not mean by this that when we feel our responsibility for the salvation of someone else we should merely pray for them and do nothing else. That is what many do; they are not willing to do their duty and go to them and speak to them about Christ, and so they go to God in prayer. Then, when they have prayed for their salvation, they flatter themselves that they have done their whole duty, and thus make their prayer an excuse for their cowardice and laziness and neglect of duty. That kind of praying is a mockery. It is simply an attempt to cover up and excuse our neglect of duty, and God will pay no attention whatsoever to prayers of that sort. God never gave us the wonderful privilege of prayer to cover up our laziness and neglect of duty. But if we are willing that God should use us in answering our own prayers, willing to do anything that God may guide us to do in order to secure the salvation of those for whom we are praying, willing to do anything in our power to bring about the salvation of those for whom we pray, then we can

The Results of Definite and Determined Prayer

accomplish far more for their salvation by praying for them than in any other way.

Did you ever think how our Lord Jesus Himself accomplished things by praying that even He could not accomplish in any other way? Take for example the case of Simon Peter. He was full of self-confidence and therefore was in imminent danger. Our Lord endeavored by His teachings and by His warnings to deliver Peter from his self-confidence. He told Peter definitely of his coming temptation and of his fall, but Peter, filled with self-confidence, replied, *"Though all men shall be offended because of thee, yet will I never be offended"* (Matt. 26:33), and again, *"I will lay down my life for thy sake"* (John 13:37). Teaching failed, warning failed, and then our Lord took to prayer. He said,

> *Simon, Simon, behold, Satan hath desired to have you, that he may sift you as wheat: but I have prayed for thee, that thy faith fail not: and when thou art converted, strengthen thy brethren.*
> (Luke 22:31–32)

Satan got what he asked—he had Simon in his sieve and sifted him; and, oh, how poor Simon was battered and bruised against the edges of Satan's sieve! But all the time Satan sifted, our Lord Jesus prayed, and Simon was perfectly safe even though he was in Satan's sieve. All that Satan succeeded in doing with him was to sift some of the chaff out of him, and Simon came out of Satan's sieve purer than he ever was before.

It was our Lord's prayer for him that transformed the Simon who denied his Lord three times, and denied Him with oaths and curses, in the courtyard of Annas and Caiaphas, into Peter, the man of rock. This transformed Peter faced the very court that sentenced Jesus to death and hurled defiance in their teeth and said,

> *Rulers of the people, and elders of Israel, if we this day be examined of the good deed done to the impotent man, by what means he is made whole; be it known unto you all, and to all the people of Israel, that by the name of Jesus Christ of Nazareth, whom ye crucified,*

The Power of Prayer

*whom God raised from the dead, even by him doth this man stand
here before you whole.* (Acts 4:8–10)

Prayer will reach down, down, down into the deepest depths of sin and ruin and take hold of men and women who seem lost beyond all possibility or hope of redemption, and lift them up, up, up until they are fit for a place beside the Son of God upon the throne.

Many years ago in Chicago, in the early days of D. L. Moody's work in that city, there was a desperate man who used to attend the meetings and try to disturb them. He was a Scotchman and had been reared in a Christian home by a godly mother, but he had wandered far from the teachings of his childhood. This man was dreaded even by other dissolute men in Chicago. One night he stood outside the old Tabernacle with a pitcher of beer in his hand, offering a free drink to everyone who came out of the Tabernacle. At other times he would come into the meetings and into the after-meetings and try to disturb the workers.

One night Major Whittle was dealing with two young men, and this desperate Scotchman stood nearby mocking, until Major Whittle turned to the young men and said, "If you set any value upon your souls, I advise you not to have anything to do with that desperate man." The Scotchman only laughed, but his old mother over in Scotland was praying. One night he went to bed just as wicked and godless as ever, and in answer to his mother's prayer God awakened him in the middle of the night and brought to his mind a text of Scripture that he had forgotten was in the Bible, Romans 4:5: *"But to him that worketh not, but believeth on him that justifieth the ungodly, his faith is counted for righteousness."* That verse of Scripture went home to his heart, and he accepted Christ without getting out of bed. He became one of the most active and most useful members of the Moody Church. When I was pastor of the church, he was one of the elders, and he afterward became visitor for the church and was used by God to lead many to Christ.

Sometime after his own conversion, he went to Scotland to visit his old mother. He had a brother in Glasgow in business, and this brother was trying to be an agnostic. But the godly mother and converted son prayed for this brother, and he was converted and gave himself up to God's work. This brother went to the Free Church College to prepare for foreign missionary work, and for thirty years he was a medical missionary in India under the Free Church of Scotland Missionary Board. But there was still another brother, a wanderer on the face of the earth. They did not know where he was, though they supposed he was somewhere on the high seas, but the godly mother and converted brother knelt and prayed for this wandering son and brother. As they prayed, that son, unknown to them, was on the deck of a vessel on the other side of the globe, in the Bay of Bengal, not far from Calcutta. The Spirit of God fell upon that son on the deck of that vessel, and he was converted. He was for many years a member of the Moody Church when I was pastor there. When I went out to Los Angeles he followed me and became a member of our church in Los Angeles, and then died a triumphant death. Prayer had reached halfway around the world and instantly saved a man who seemed utterly beyond hope.

When I was in England holding meetings in the city of Manchester, one of the leading businessmen came to me and asked me to pray for the conversion of his son. He said, "My son is a graduate of Cambridge University and a brilliant lawyer. He has a wife and two children, but he has left them, and we do not know where he is. Will you pray for his conversion?" I promised him that I would. Some months afterward this man came to me at the Keswick Convention and said, "I have found my boy. He is in Vancouver, British Columbia. Do you know any minister in Vancouver to whom I could cable?" I told him the name of a friend who was a minister of the Gospel in Vancouver, and he cabled him. The next day he came to me and said, "We were too late; the bird has flown; he has left Vancouver. Will you continue to pray for him?" I said I would. At the close of the same year, when we began our second series of meetings in Liverpool, unknown to his father, this son had returned to England and was in Liverpool. He came to our first Sunday afternoon meeting and was one of the first ones to accept

Christ. Immediately he began to study for holy orders under the Bishop of Liverpool.

Do you have loved ones who are unsaved? There is a way to reach them: that way is by the throne of God. By the way of the throne of God, you can reach out to the uttermost parts of the earth and get hold of your loved ones of whom you have lost track. God knows where they are, and God hears and answers prayer. At the close of the meeting in a certain city, a lady came to me and said, "I have a brother above sixty years of age. I have been praying for his salvation for years, but I have given up. I will begin again." Within two weeks she came to me and said, "I have heard from my brother, and he has accepted Christ."

Yes, yes, yes, *the supplication of a righteous man availeth much in its working*" (James 5:16 RV), and if we would only pray more and be more sure that we had met the conditions of prevailing prayer, we would see multitudes more of men and women flocking to Jesus Christ. Oh, that we might pray as we ought, as intelligently as we ought, as definitely as we ought, as earnestly and determinedly as we ought, for the salvation of the men, women, and children whom we know are unsaved!

Prayer Brings Blessing and Power

And take the helmet of salvation, and the sword of the Spirit, which is the word of God: praying always with all prayer and supplication in the Spirit, and watching thereunto with all perseverance and supplication for all saints; and for me, that utterance may be given unto me, that I may open my mouth boldly, to make known the mystery of the gospel, for which I am an ambassador in bonds: that therein I may speak boldly, as I ought to speak. (Eph. 6:17–20)

Here Paul urgently requested the earnest prayers of the believers in Ephesus for himself, that in answer to their prayers he might preach the Gospel with boldness and with power. Paul made a similar request of every church to which he wrote with one striking exception; that one exception was the church in Galatia. That church was a backsliding church, and he did not care to have a backsliding church praying for him. In every other case he urged the church to pray for him. Here we see the power of prayer to bring blessing and boldness and effectiveness to ministers of the Gospel. A minister may be made a man of power by prayer, and he may be bereft of power by people failing to pray for him. Any church may have a mighty man of God for its pastor, if it is willing to pay the price, and that price is not a big salary but great praying.

Do you have a pastor you do not like, a pastor who is perhaps inefficient or does not clearly know or preach the truth? Do you want a new minister? I can tell you how to get him. Pray for the one you have until God makes him over.

Many years ago in one of the Cornish parishes of the Church of England, the vicar was not even a converted man. He had little interest in the real things of God; his interest was largely in restoring old churches and in matters of ritual. There were many godly people in that parish, and they began to pray to God to convert their minister, and then they would go to church every Sunday and watch for the answer to their prayers. One Sunday when he rose to speak, he had not uttered many sentences before the people of spiritual discernment realized that their prayers had been answered and a cry arose all over the church, "The parson's converted, the parson's converted!" And it was true. He was not only converted, but he was filled with *"power from on high"* (Luke 24:49). For many years afterward, God used that man all over England for the conversion of sinners, for the blessing of all saints, and for the quickening of churches, as almost no other man in the Church of England.

There was a church in the city of Hartford, Connecticut, that had a very brilliant man for its pastor. But the pastor was not sound in doctrine. There were three godly men in that church who realized that their pastor was not preaching the truth. However, they did not go around the congregation stirring up dissatisfaction with the pastor. They covenanted together to meet every Saturday night to pray long into the night for their minister. So Saturday night after Saturday night they met in earnest and extended prayer; then Sunday morning they would go to church and sit in their places and watch for an answer to their prayers.

The Power of Prayer

One Sunday morning when the minister rose to speak, he was just as brilliant and just as gifted as ever, but it soon became evident that God had transformed his ideas and transformed the man. Through that minister who was transformed by the prayers of his members, God sent to the city of Hartford the greatest revival that city ever had. Oh, if we would talk less to one another against our ministers, and more to God on their behalf, we would have far better ministers than we have now.

Do you have a minister whom you do like? Do you wish him to be even better; do you wish him to be far more effective than he is today? Pray for him until God gives him new wisdom and clothes him with new power.

Have you ever heard how D. L. Moody became a worldwide evangelist? After the great fire in Chicago, Mr. Moody stayed in Chicago long enough to get money together to feed the poor and to provide a new building for his own work, and then he went to England for a rest. He did not intend to preach at all, but to hear some of the great preachers on the other side of the water—Charles Spurgeon, George Müller, and others. He was invited to preach one Sunday in a Congregational church in the north part of London, of which a Mr. Lessey was the pastor. He accepted the invitation. Sunday morning as he preached, he had great difficulty. As he told the story to me many years afterward, he said,

> I had no power, no liberty; it seemed like pulling a heavy train up a steep grade, and as I preached I said to myself, "What a fool I was to consent to preach. I came here to hear others, and here I am preaching." As I drew to the close of my sermon, I had a sense of relief that I was so near through, and then the thought came to me, "Well, I've got to do it again tonight." I tried to get Mr. Lessey to release me from preaching that night, but he would not consent. I went to the evening service with a heavy heart. But I had not been preaching long when it seemed as if the powers of an unseen world had fallen upon that audience. As I drew to the close of my sermon, I got courage to draw the net. I asked all who would then and there accept Christ to rise, and about five hundred people

rose to their feet. I thought there must be some mistake; so I asked them to sit down, and then I said, "There will be an after-meeting in the vestry, and if any of you will really accept Christ, meet the pastor and me in the vestry."

There was a door at each side of the pulpit into the vestry, and people began to stream through these doors into the vestry. I turned to Mr. Lessey and said, "Mr. Lessey, who are these people?" He replied, "I do not know." "Are they your people?" "Some of them are." "Are they Christians?" "Not as far as I know." We went into the vestry, and I repeated the invitation in a stronger form, and they all rose again. I still thought that there must be some mistake and asked them to be seated, and repeated the invitation in a still stronger form, and again they all rose. I still thought there must be some mistake and I said to the people, "I am going to Ireland tomorrow, but your pastor will be here tomorrow night if you really mean what you have said here tonight meet him here." After I reached Ireland I received a telegram from Mr. Lessey saying, "Mr. Moody, there were more people out on Monday night than on Sunday night. A revival has broken out in our church, and you must come back and help me."

Mr. Moody hurried back from Dublin to London and held a series of meetings in Mr. Lessey's church that added hundreds of people to the churches of North London. That was what led to the invitation that took him over to England later for the great work that stirred the whole world.

After Mr. Moody had told me that story, I said, "Mr. Moody, someone must have been praying." He said,

Oh, did I not tell you that? That is the point of the whole story. There were two sisters in that church, one of whom was bedridden; the other one heard me that Sunday morning. She went home and said to her sister, "Who do you suppose preached for us this morning?" The sister replied, "I do not know." Then she said, "Guess," and the sister guessed all the men that Mr. Lessey was in the habit of exchanging with, but her sister said it was none of them. Then her sister asked, "Who did preach for us this morning?" And she replied, "Mr. Moody of Chicago." No sooner had she said it than her sister turned pale as death and said, "What! Mr. Moody of Chicago! I have read of him in an American paper, and I have been praying God to send him to London, to our church. If I had known he was to preach this morning, I would have eaten no breakfast; I would have spent the whole morning in fasting and prayer. Now, sister, go out, lock the door, do not let any one come to see me, do not let them send me any dinner; I am going to spend the whole afternoon and evening in fasting and prayer!" And pray she did, and God heard and answered.

God is just as ready to hear and answer you as He was to answer that bedridden saint. To whatever church you belong, and whoever your pastor is, you can make him a man of power. If he is a man of power already, you can make him a man of even greater power.

Will you bear with me while I give you a page out of my own experience? When I went to Chicago, it was not to take the pastorate of a church but to be superintendent of the Bible Institute and of the Chicago Evangelization Society. After I had been there four years, the pulpit of the Moody Church became vacant, and Mr. Moody and I asked them to call a very gifted preacher from Aberdeen, Scotland, which they did. While we waited to hear from him as to whether he would accept the call, I filled the pulpit; and God so blessed the preaching of His Word that quite a number of the people were praying that the minister from Scotland would not accept the call, and he did not. Then they called me to the pastorate. I could not see how I could take it; my hands were full with the Institute, the lectures, the correspondence, and other duties. But Mr. Moody urged me to accept the call; he said, "That is what I have been wanting all the time. If you will only accept the call, I will give you all the help that you ask for, and provide men to help you in the Institute." And so I accepted the call.

The first sermon I preached after taking the pastorate of the church was upon prayer, and in it I said some of the things that I have said here. As I drew toward the close of my sermon I said, "How glad your new pastor would be if he knew that some of you men and women of God sat up late Saturday night, or rose early Sunday morning, to pray for your new pastor." Many of those dear saints of God took me at my word. Many of them sat up late Saturday night praying for their minister, and many of them rose early Sunday morning to pray for their minister, and God answered their prayers.

When I took the pastorate, the church building would seat 2,200 people—1,200 on the first floor and 1,000 in the gallery. But in the preceding years, only the first floor of the church had been filled, and the gallery opened only on special occasions, when Mr. Moody was there or something of that kind. Almost immediately upon my being instated, it became necessary to open the gallery. Then in the evening service, every inch of standing room would be taken, until we packed 2,700 people into that building by actual count, and the police authorities allowed us no longer to let people sit on the stairs or stand in the aisles. Then we had an overflow meeting in the rooms below, which would seat 1,100, and oftentimes into the Institute Lecture Hall also.

But that was not the best of it. There were conversions every Sunday; indeed, there were conversions in and around the church practically every day in the week. The great majority of those who were converted did not unite with the Moody Church; they were strangers passing through the city, or people who came from other churches. It came to be quite a custom for some ministers to send their people over to our church to have them converted, then they would go back and join the churches to which they properly belonged. So only a comparatively small proportion of those converted united with our church, and yet the smallest number that we ever received into the church in any one of the eight years I remained there as active pastor was 250. And in those eight years I had the joy of giving the right hand of fellowship to over 2,000 new members.

And it went on just the same way the four years that I was only nominally pastor and not at the church at all, under the different men who came and whom the people prayed into power. It went on the same way under Dr. Dixon's pastorate. It was not so much the men who were preaching as the people behind them who were praying that accomplished such great things for God. Then, when I started around the world, those people still followed me with their prayers; and it was reported when I came back, by one who claimed to know, that there were more than 102,000 people who made a definite profession of accepting Christ in the different places I visited in those months that I was away. When I came back after my first eighteen months' absence, Dr. Dixon met me one day, and he said to me (this was before he became pastor of the church), "Brother Torrey, when we heard the things that were done in Australia and elsewhere, we were all surprised. We didn't think it was in you." He was perfectly right about that; it wasn't in me. Then he added, "But when I went out and supplied your church for a month and heard your people pray for you, I understood." Oh, any church can have a minister who is a man of power, a minister who is baptized and filled with the Holy Spirit, if they are willing to pay the price, and the price is prayer, much prayer, and much real prayer, prayer in the Holy Spirit.

3

What Prayer Can Do for
Churches and All Nations

*Praying always with all prayer and supplication in the
Spirit, and watching thereunto with all perseverance
and supplication for all saints.*
—Ephesians 6:18

What a tremendous emphasis Paul here put on the importance and power of prayer, and on the imperative need of intense earnestness and never-wearying persistence in prayer. Read the text again: *"Praying always with all prayer and supplication in the Spirit, and watching thereunto with all perseverance and supplication for all saints."*

We have already seen some of the things of great importance that are brought about by prayer, things that cannot be brought to pass in any other way. We have seen that true prayer will promote our own personal piety, our individual holiness, and our individual growth into the likeness of our Lord and Savior Jesus Christ, as nothing else will but the study of the Word of God. We have seen that prayer will bring power into our work, that it is the privilege of every child of God to have the power of God manifested in his work in whatever line of service he is called, and that this power is obtained by prayer and in no other way. We have seen that prayer avails mightily for others as well as for ourselves, that we can accomplish more for the salvation of others by praying for them than we can in any other way, and that prayer avails for the salvation of men and women who are so sunken in sin and so far from God that there seems no possible hope of their redemption. Furthermore, we have seen that prayer brings power to the minister of the Gospel, that any church can have a man of power for its pastor if they are willing to pay the price, and that the price is not a big salary but big praying.

We will make other discoveries in this chapter—things that are greatly to be desired, that can be brought to pass by prayer, and that can be brought to pass in no other way.

Andrew Murray has said, "God's child can conquer everything by prayer. Is it any wonder that Satan does his utmost to snatch that weapon from the Christian or to hinder him in the use of it?" Well, if the devil is doing "his utmost to snatch that weapon from the Christian or to hinder him in the use of it," I wish to do my utmost to restore that mighty weapon to the hands of the church, and to stir you up to use this weapon in mighty and victorious onslaught on Satan and his forces.

It is true that we have a terrific fight on our hands, that *"we wrestle not against flesh and blood, but against principalities, against powers, against the rulers of the darkness of this world, against spiritual wickedness in high places"* (Eph. 6:12), but we can win this fight by prayer; for prayer brings God on the field, and the devil is no match for Him. I say we can win this fight, as terrible as it is and as mighty and cunning as our enemies are, by praying, and we cannot win it in any other way. Men are constantly appearing who have discovered some new way of defeating the devil by some cunning scheme that they have devised—by the social gospel, for example, or by some other humanly devised method. But there is no new way that will win; the old way, the Bible way, the way of definite, determined, and persistent prayer in the Holy Spirit, will win every time.

Blessing to Churches

Let us now look at something else in addition to the important things already mentioned that prayer will do. Turn to 1 Thessalonians 3:11–13:

What Prayer Can Do for Churches and All Nations

Now God himself and our Father, and our Lord Jesus Christ, direct our way unto you. And the Lord make you to increase and abound in love one toward another, and toward all men, even as we do toward you: to the end he may stablish your hearts unblameable in holiness before God, even our Father, at the coming of our Lord Jesus Christ with all his saints.

In the last chapter we saw the church praying for Paul; in this passage we see Paul praying for the church. Prayer will bring blessing, definite and rich and immeasurable blessing, to the church; praying will do more to make the church what it ought to be than anything else we can do. Prayer will do more to root out heresy than all the heresy trials ever held. Prayer will do more to straighten out tangles and misunderstandings and unhappy complications in the life of a church than all the councils and conferences ever held. Prayer will do more to bring a deep and lasting and sweeping revival, a revival that is real and lasting and altogether of the right sort, than all the organizations ever devised by man.

The history of the church of Jesus Christ on earth has been largely a history of revivals. When you read many of the church histories that have been written, the impression that you naturally get is that the history of the church of Jesus Christ here on earth has been largely a history of misunderstandings, disputes, doctrinal differences, and bitter conflicts. But if you will study the history of the living church, you will find it has been largely a history of revivals. Humanly speaking, the church of Jesus Christ owes its very existence today to revivals. Time and time again the church has seemed to be on the verge of utter shipwreck; but just then God has sent a great revival and saved it. And if you will study the history of revivals, you will find that every real revival in the church has been the result of prayer. There have been revivals without much preaching; there have been revivals with absolutely no organization, but there has never been a mighty revival without mighty praying.

Take the great revival that so marvelously blessed our nation in 1857. How did that revival come about? A humble city missionary in the city of New York, a man named Landfear, became greatly burdened because of the state of the church. He and two other men who were like-minded began to pray for a revival. Then they opened a daily noontime meeting for prayer and invited others. These meetings were poorly attended at first. On one occasion, if I remember correctly, there were only two individuals present, and I think that on one occasion there was only one person present, this humble city missionary himself, this very obscure man Landfear. But soon the interest began to deepen and large crowds began to flock to the meetings for prayer. Such throngs came that it became necessary to set up other prayer meetings.

I have been told (and I think correctly told) that, after a while, prayer meetings were held every hour of the day and night in New York City, and not only the churches were used for prayer meetings, but also theaters and other public places. And these places were crowded with praying men and praying women. The fire spread from New York to Philadelphia and to other cities, and then swept over the entire country. A young man came into one of the meetings in Chicago on one occasion and said that he had just come back from a trip to the far West, and that at every place where he had stopped on the way back to Chicago, prayer meetings were being held.

In New York City, at one of the Presbyterian ministers' meetings, Dr. Gardiner Spring, who was perhaps at that time the most prominent minister in New York, said to the assembled believers, "It is evident that a revival has come to us, and we ministers must preach." Someone replied, "Well, if anyone must preach, you must preach the first sermon, for you are the best qualified to do it of any man in the city." So it was announced that on a certain day Dr. Gardiner Spring would preach, but no more people came out to hear the preaching than came out to the prayer meetings, so they stopped the preaching and went on praying. The whole emphasis was on prayer, and our whole nation was shaken by the power of God as it had never been shaken before, and perhaps has never been shaken since.

That is the kind of a revival I am longing to see here in our city; yes, throughout our whole land and even throughout the world. I do not mean a revival where there is great preaching and marvelous singing and all kinds of bewildering antics by preachers or singers, or skillful managers or manipulators; but a revival where there is mighty praying and wonderful displays of the convicting and converting and regenerating power of the Holy Spirit in answer to prayer.

Don't come to me and tell me what this man or that man, or this woman or that woman, is doing that you think is wrong or right. Go to God and tell Him if you like, but it is far more important that you pray to Him. Pray, pray, pray for Him to bless your church and to bless other churches of your city, and to bless the whole land; yes, and to bless every land.

The news of what God was doing in 1857 in America spread to Northern Ireland, and the General Assembly of the Presbyterian Church of Ireland sent a commission to America to study the work and to come back with a report. When they came back they gave the next General Assembly a glowing report of what was being done in America. People began to pray that Ireland might also have a similar visitation from God.

Four men in the little town of Kells, in Northern Ireland, banded themselves together and met every Saturday night for prayer for a revival. They spent the whole night in prayer. They were humble men: one of them was a farmer, one was a blacksmith, one was a school teacher, and I do not recall what the fourth was, but I know he was in some humble sphere of life. When Mr. Alexander and I were holding meetings in London, and God was working there in great power, one of these four men, at that time living in Glasgow, sent his grandson down to London to consult with Mr. Alexander and me and to observe the work and bring back a report to him as to whether it was a real work of God or not.

After these men had been praying for some time, they went out to try and preach, but their attempt was a failure, so they went back and kept on praying. God heard their prayer, and the fire of God fell. The work went on in such marvelous power in some parts of Ireland that courts adjourned because there were no cases to try, jails were closed because there were no prisoners to incarcerate, and in some places even the grain stood unharvested in the fields because men were so taken up with things of God and of eternity that they had no time to attend even to the things that ordinarily are so necessary. Many of the most notorious and hardened and hopeless sinners in the land were converted and thoroughly transformed.

Let me tell you how the revival came to Coleraine, in Northern Ireland. I know something about this because when Mr. Alexander and I were in Belfast, Ireland, in 1903, the residents of Coleraine were about to celebrate the forty-third anniversary of how the revival came to Coleraine, and they sent a committee down to Belfast to invite Mr. Alexander and me to go up and celebrate the anniversary. We were unable to go; but I read very carefully the account of the revival as it was given by Rev. William Gibson, Moderator of the General Assembly of the Presbyterian Church in Ireland for 1860, in his book, *The Year of Grace.* It was reported on a certain day in Coleraine that three young men were coming to Coleraine that evening to hold an open-air meeting in the marketplace. At the appointed hour the ministers of the city went down to the marketplace out of curiosity, to see what was done. To their amazement they saw the people pouring into the marketplace from every quarter until there were no less than 15,000 people gathered together in the marketplace. The ministers looked at one another in bewilderment and dismay and said, "We must preach; these young men can never deal with a vast throng like this."

So they put up four pulpits at the four corners of the marketplace, and a preacher ascended each pulpit. They had not been preaching long when a very solemn awe fell upon the entire throng, and soon in one section of the marketplace there was a loud cry, and a man fell to the ground under such overwhelming conviction of sin that he could not stand on his feet. He was carried out to the town hall that was not yet completed. Soon a cry arose in another part of the marketplace, and another man fell under the power of conviction of sin, and he too was taken to the town hall. Then another, and then another, and then another fell in different parts of the marketplace until conviction became so general that the meeting broke up and the ministers adjourned to the town hall to deal individually with stricken souls.

The Presbyterian minister who described the incident said that he was in the town hall all night dealing with souls overwhelmed with deep conviction of sin. When the morning dawned, he started for his home, but as he went up the street he found people standing on their doorsteps waiting for him to pass, because there were people under conviction of sin in their homes and they wanted to invite him in to deal with them. He went into one home after another, and there were so many to deal with that the sun had set before he reached his own home. The whole town of Coleraine was so transformed and so impressed that in completing the town hall, they put in an inscribed tablet dedicating the hall to the memory of the revival, and for every year of the forty-three years up to that time, they were commemorating the coming of the revival to Coleraine. I think they have kept up the commemoration annually to this present day.

I think it was at the close of the week of prayer in January 1901, that Miss Strong, Superintendent of Women of the Bible Institute of Chicago, came to me and said, "Why not keep up these prayer meetings at least once a week after the week of prayer is over, and pray for a worldwide revival?" This suggestion seemed appropriate to the faculty, and we scheduled a prayer meeting every Saturday night from nine to ten o'clock (after the popular Bible class was over) at which people could gather to pray for just one thing—a worldwide revival. Three or four hundred gathered every Saturday night for that purpose, and God gave us great liberty and great expectation in prayer. Soon we began to hear of the working of God in Japan and other lands, and yet the work was not as general as we wanted to see. People would come to me and to my colleague who was most closely associated with me in the conduct of the meetings, and ask, "Has the revival come?"

We replied, "No, not as far as we know."

"When is it coming?"

"We do not know."

"How long are you going to keep praying?"

"Until it comes."

197

The Power of Prayer

After we had been praying for some months, two men from Australia appeared in our lecture room. After they had been attending the lectures for some time, they asked for a private conversation with me. They told me that in leaving Australia they had been commissioned to go to England, to Keswick and other places, and to other gatherings in America, and select someone to invite to Australia to conduct an evangelistic campaign. They said further that they had both agreed upon me: would I go? I replied, "I do not see how I can leave Chicago. I have the Bible Institute to look after, and also the Chicago Avenue Church (the Moody Church), and I do not see how I can possibly get away from Chicago."

"Well," they said, "you are coming to Australia." Some months passed and I was in a Bible Conference in St. Louis. I received a letter from Australia asking me to cable my acceptance of their invitation. They said they would at once cable me the money to come. I laid the matter before the Conference, asked them to pray over it, and withdrew from the Conference to be alone in prayer. God made it clear that I should go, and so I cabled them. When Mr. Alexander and I reached Australia, we found that there was a group of about ten or twelve men who had been praying for years for a great revival in Australia. They had banded together to pray for "the big revival," as they called it in their prayers—to pray for the revival no matter how long it took. The group was led by the Rev. John McNeil, the author of *The Spirit-Filled Life*, but he had died before we reached Australia. A second member of the group, Rev. Allan Webb, died the first week of our meetings in Melbourne. He had come to Melbourne to assist in the meetings, and died on his knees in prayer. A third member of the group, even before we had been invited to Australia, had been given a vision of great crowds flocking to the Exposition Hall, people hanging on to the loaded street cars wherever they could. When that vision was fulfilled, he came a long distance to Melbourne just to see with his own eyes what God had revealed to him before.

We also found that a lady in Melbourne had read a book on prayer and had been very deeply moved by one short sentence in the book: "Pray through." She had organized prayer meetings all over the city before we reached it; indeed, we found when we reached Melbourne that there were 1,700 neighborhood prayer meetings being held there every week. We remained in that city for four weeks. The first two weeks the meetings were held by many different pastors and evangelists in some forty or fifty different centers throughout the city, though meetings for the whole city were held at one o'clock, two o'clock, and three o'clock each day in the town hall. The last two weeks, the meetings were all concentrated in the Exposition Hall, which seated about 8,000 people.

At the very first meeting in the Exposition Hall, the crowd was so great that they swept the police before them, packed the building far beyond its proper capacity, and great crowds still could not get in. In the four weeks, 8,642 people made a definite profession of having accepted the Lord Jesus Christ as their Savior. And when we went back to Melbourne some months later and held a meeting of the converts, 6,000 of them were present at that meeting, most of whom had already joined the church. Almost all those who had not united with the church as yet promised to do so at once. The report of what God had done in Melbourne spread not only all over Australia, but also to India, England, Scotland, and Ireland. This resulted in a wonderful work of God in the leading cities of England, Scotland, and Ireland; and the whole worldwide work was the outcome of the prayer meetings held in Chicago, and of the prayers of the little group of men in Australia.

The great Welsh revival in 1904, the beginning of which I was an eyewitness, came in a similar way. Mr. Alexander and I had been invited to Cardiff, Wales, for a month's mission. The announcement that we were going there was made about a year before we went, and prayer began to go up all over England and Scotland and Wales that God would send a revival not only to Cardiff but to all of Wales. When we reached Cardiff, we found that for almost a year some people there had been holding a prayer meeting from six to seven o'clock every morning in Penarth, a suburb of Cardiff, praying for a great revival. For the first two weeks or so, things dragged. Great crowds came, and there was great enthusiasm in the singing, but we could not get the people to do personal work. Then we appointed a day of fasting and prayer, and the day was observed in other parts of Wales as well as in Cardiff.

In one place, Seth Joshua, who was afterward so greatly used in the revival, was the leading figure and had charge of the meeting. He wrote me a most glowing and cheerful account of what God had done in that place on that day. I think it was on that very day that he was kneeling beside Evan Roberts, and as he prayed, the power of God fell upon Evan Roberts. The power of God came down in Cardiff in such a wonderful way that when Mr. Alexander and I were compelled to leave at the end of the month to keep an engagement in Liverpool, the meetings went right on without us, and they went on for one whole year—meetings every night for a whole year—and multitudes were converted.

From Cardiff, the fire spread up and down the valleys of Wales. Soon after we had reached Liverpool, the next city that we visited, I received a letter from the minister who was secretary of our mission in Cardiff. The letter said that the preceding Sunday night his assistant had gone up one of the valleys of Wales and that as he preached, the power of God fell on him, and 100 people were converted while he was preaching. The fire spread over the entire country under Evan Roberts and others, and it is said that more than 100,000 souls were converted in twelve months.

This is what we need more than anything else today, in our own land and in all lands—a mighty outpouring of the Spirit of God. The most fundamental trouble with most of our present-day so-called revivals is that they are man-made and not God-sent. They are worked up (I almost said faked up) by man's cunningly devised machinery—not prayed down. Oh, for an old-time revival, a revival that is really and not spuriously of the Pentecostal pattern—for that revival was born of a fourteen days' prayer meeting. But let us not merely sigh for it; let us cry for it, cry to God, cry long and cry loud if need be, and then it will surely come.

Blessing and Victory to Foreign Missions

But when he saw the multitudes, he was moved with compassion on them, because they fainted, and were scattered abroad, as sheep having no shepherd. Then saith he unto his disciples, The harvest truly is plenteous, but the labourers are few; pray ye therefore the Lord of the harvest, that he will send forth labourers into his harvest.

(Matt. 9:36–38)

Here we see from our Lord's own teaching that prayer will bring blessing to foreign missions. It will get the needed men and women, and the right kind of men and women, for the work in all the fields that are now ripe for the harvest in many lands. It will also bring blessing and power to the men and women who go to the field. The greatest need of foreign missions today is prayer. It is true that men are greatly needed, and it is true that money is needed; but prayer is needed far more. When we pray as we ought, the men and the women will come, and the money will come. Even if men came in crowds, without prayer they would be of no use; they will be of no use whatsoever unless they are backed by prayer.

In this country, men of great force of character and mind have greatly stirred students their to have an interest in foreign missions. They have gathered large numbers of men and women for the foreign field, without much prayer. These men and women, though gifted, some of them greatly talented, have oftentimes been an actual curse to the work. It is my conviction, founded upon much observation, that the work of foreign missions would be far better off today if these men had gone into secular work and left missions alone. The results of their work have been most sinister. I have seen much of it with my own eyes in China and elsewhere, and I am convinced that one of the most discouraging problems that faces foreign mission work has arisen from the large number of men and women who have gone into the foreign work not because they were sent by God in answer to prayer, but because they were stirred up by a man of attractive personality and rare power.

The Power of Prayer

What I have said of men is just as true of money. No matter how much money may be put into foreign missions, the money will be of no real use unless the misionary men and women who are supported by the money are backed by prayer. Indeed, without prayer, the money will be a curse rather than a blessing. Probably no other missionary society in all this world's history ever accomplished as much good, all things considered (that is of real and lasting value), as the China Inland Mission; and that is so because this Mission was born of so much prayer and backed by so much prayer.

Prayer for Foreign Missions

But what should we pray for in connection with foreign missions?

PRAY FOR WORKERS

First of all we should pray, just as the words of our Lord Jesus we are studying command us to pray, for men and women. Read our Lord's words again: *"The harvest truly is plenteous, but the labourers are few; pray ye therefore the Lord of the harvest, that he will send forth labourers into his harvest."* It is not so much a large number of men and women who are needed; it is the right kind of men and women. A large number of men and women are needed, no question about that. The fields were never so ripe for the harvest before as they are today, and the laborers are indeed few; but the greatest need is the right kind of men and women. Missions in China and elsewhere would be far better off today if many of the men and women who have gone out had remained at home. Earnest-minded men and women from this country who visited China and were brought in close contact with some of the young men and women who were being poured into China by certain missionary societies were appalled at the thought that men and women of this type should be sent out for foreign mission work. Many of the older missionaries who have made great sacrifices for the work, and by much effort and prayer have gathered together bodies of believers who really know the Lord, trembled as they thought what the influence of this type of missionary would be upon the doctrine and the life of the Chinese converts. Many of the Christian Chinese themselves felt they must protest against the teaching and the manner of life of these would-be missionaries.

PRAY FOR WORKERS ALREADY IN THE FIELD

In the second place, we should pray for the missionaries who have already gone out. I have already stated how much is done by prayer to make a minister of the Gospel what he ought to be. If possible, prayer is even more effective in making missionaries what they ought to be, and the neglect of prayer on the part of the people at home has much to do with the comparative failure of many of the missionaries in the field. Every Christian at home should have some missionaries in the field for whom he is praying definitely, constantly, persistently, and intensely. The man or woman at home who prays often has as much to do with the effectiveness of the missionary on the field, and consequently with the results of his labors, as the missionary himself.

PRAY FOR THE SPIRIT'S OUTPOURING

In the third place, we should pray for the outpouring of the Spirit on different fields. Oh, how much the various missionary fields of the world need genuine revivals of religion in the power of the Holy Spirit! And revivals on the foreign field come in exactly the same way we have just seen revivals come at home—in answer to prayer. This could be proved by many illustrations. Charles Finney tells of a mighty man of prayer who was interested in the work not only at home, but also abroad. After this man's death, his diary was found; in examining it, it was found that on certain days he had recorded that he had a great burden of prayer for some specific foreign missionary field. Upon inquiry it was found that in each instance, revivals on the foreign field had followed this man's insistent intercession, and followed in the exact order of his petitions as recorded in his diary.

Many of us are tempted to criticize the foreign work because of the meagerness of the results, but ought not our criticism to begin with ourselves? May it not be that the meagerness of the results is the consequence of the meagerness of our own prayers? We can increase the blessed and glorious results of the work in foreign fields by giving more time to real prayer here at home.

PRAY FOR CONVERTS IN THE FIELD

Fourth, we should pray for the converts in the mission field. It is difficult for us to realize how many and how great are the obstacles put in the way of a convert's standing steadfast in the new life, and the difficulties that lie in the way of his living such a life as a Christian ought to live, in the atmosphere that he daily breathes. Many of the converts in many fields are men and women of an unusually high character. My son has told me that some of the Christian Chinese he knows intimately put him to shame by their clearness of understanding of the deep things of God and by the Christlikeness and devotion of their lives. But while this is true, we should never forget that it is far more difficult for one converted in a heathen land to lead the life a Christian ought to live than it is for one converted in this land, and, therefore, the converts greatly need our prayers. And prayer *"availeth much in its working"* (James 5:16 RV) in the lives of those who are won to Christ in the foreign field.

PRAY FOR CHURCHES IN THE FIELD

In the fifth place, we should pray for the churches in these mission fields. We should pray not only for the converts as individuals, but also for the churches as organizations. Every church has its particular problems. Take, for example, the church of Christ in Korea. It is difficult for anyone who has not visited that land, so wonderfully favored by God in missionary work and at the same time so amazingly resisted by the devil in various ways, to realize how much the church of Christ in Korea needs the prayers of those in the homeland who believe in Christ and in prayer. And so do the churches in Africa and India, and elsewhere, greatly need our prayers here at home.

PRAY FOR OFFICIALS AT HOME

In the sixth place, we should pray for the secretaries and official members of the various boards here at home.

PRAY FOR FUNDS

Finally, we should pray for money. Many of the boards and missionary societies are in extreme distress for funds today. This is true even of boards and councils of whose loyalty to the faith there is no question: they are in great need of increased gifts. The way to get the money is to pray for it—not only for those who are immediately responsible for the money to pray for it, but for us all to pray for it. Very likely, if we pray as we ought, God will bring us to see that we ourselves ought to go down into our own pockets as we never have done to aid in answering our own prayers.

There are many other specific things, and things greatly to be desired, that definite and determined prayer will bring to pass; but I wish to concentrate your attention on just these two things in this chapter: first, that prayer will bring blessing to the churches; second, that prayer will bring blessing and victory to foreign missions.

Oh, how much we need the blessing that includes all other blessings for the church—a great, deep, thorough, widespread revival! And how we need larger blessing and more complete victory in the work of foreign missions. We can have both if we will pay the price; and the price is prayer—real prayer, determined prayer, extensive prayer, heart-wringing, crying to God in the power of the Holy Spirit.

4

How to Get What You Pray For

But prayer was made without ceasing of the church
unto God for him.
—Acts 12:5

Our subject is how to pray so as to get what you ask for. I can think of nothing more important than this to discuss with you. Suppose it had been announced that I was to tell the businessmen of Los Angeles how they could go to any bank in the city and get all the financial accommodation they desired any day of the year. Suppose, also, that I really knew that secret and could really tell it. Do you think that the businessmen of that city would consider it important? It would be difficult to think of anything they would consider more important! In the same way, praying is going to the bank that has the largest capital of any bank in the universe, the Bank of Heaven, a bank that has absolutely unlimited capital. And if I can show you how you can go to the Bank of Heaven any day in the year, and any hour of the day or night, and get from that Bank all that you desire, that will certainly be of incalculable importance.

Now the Bible tells us this very thing. It tells us how we can go to the Bank of Heaven, how we can go to God in prayer any day of the year and any hour of the day or night, and get from God the very things that we ask. What the Bible teaches along this line has been put to the test by tens of thousands of people, and has been found in their own experience to be absolutely true. And this is what we are about to discover in God's own Word.

In Acts 12 we have the record of a most remarkable prayer, remarkable because of what was asked for and remarkable

206

because of the results of the asking. King Herod had killed James, the brother of John. This greatly *"pleased the Jews"* (v. 3), so he proceeded further to arrest the leader of the whole apostolic company—the apostle Peter—with the intention of killing him also. But the arrest was made during Passover Week, the Holy Week of the Jews; and, while the Jews were perfectly willing, even eager, to have Peter assassinated, they were not willing to have their Holy Week desecrated by his violent death. So Peter was cast into prison to be kept until the Passover Week was over, and, then, to be executed. The Passover Week was nearly over; it was the last night of the Passover Week. Early the next morning Peter was to be taken out and beheaded.

There seemed to be little hope for Peter, indeed no hope at all. He was in a secure dungeon, in an impregnable fortress, guarded by sixteen soldiers, and chained by each wrist to a soldier who slept on either side of him. There appeared to be no hope whatsoever for Peter. But the Christians in Jerusalem undertook to get Peter out of his perilous position, to completely deliver him. How did they go about it? Did they organize a mob and storm the castle? No, there was no hope of success along that line; the castle was impregnable against any mob, and furthermore, it was garrisoned by trained Roman soldiers who would be more than a match for any mob. Did they circulate a petition and get the names of the leading Christians in Jerusalem signed to it to present to Herod, asking that he would release Peter? No. That might have had weight, for the Christians in Jerusalem at that time were numbered by the thousands and among them were not a few influential persons. A petition signed by so many people and by people of such weight would have had influence with a wily politician such as Herod. But they did not attempt that method of deliverance. Did they take up a collection and gather a large amount of money from the believers in Jerusalem to bribe Herod to release Peter? Quite likely that might have proved successful, for Herod was open to that method of approach. But they did not do that.

What did they do? They held a prayer meeting to pray Peter out of prison. Was anything apparently more futile and ridiculous ever undertaken by a company of fanatics? Praying a man so securely incarcerated, and so near his execution, out of prison? If the enemies of Peter and the church had known of that attempt, they undoubtedly would have been greatly amused, and laughed at the thought of these fanatical Christians praying Peter out of prison. Undoubtedly they would have said to one another, "We'll see what will become of the prayers of these foolish Christians!"

But the attempt to pray Peter out of prison was entirely successful. Apparently Peter himself had no fears, but he was calmly resting in God; for he was fast asleep on the very eve of his proposed execution. While Peter was sound asleep, guarded by the sixteen soldiers, chained to a soldier sleeping on either side of him, suddenly there shone in the prison a light, a light from heaven; and there could have been seen standing by Peter *"the angel of the Lord"* (Acts 12:7). The angel *"smote Peter on the side"* (v. 7) as he slept and awakened him and said, *"Arise up quickly"* (v. 7). Instantly Peter's chains fell from his hands, and he rose to his feet. The angel said to him, *"Gird thyself, and bind on thy sandals"* (v. 8). Peter did so, and then the angel said, *"Cast thy garment about thee, and follow me"* (v. 8). Peter, dazed and wondering, thought he was dreaming; but he was wise enough to obey God even in his sleep, and he went out and followed the angel, though he *"thought he saw a vision"* (v. 9). The soldiers were all asleep, but Peter, not being prevented, passed the first guard and the second guard and came to the strong iron gate that led into the city. Moved by the finger of God, the gate *"opened to them of his own accord"* (v. 10). They went out and silently passed through one street.

Now Peter was safe and the angel left him. Standing there in the cold night air, Peter came to himself. He realized that he was not dreaming, and said, *"Now I know of a surety, that the Lord hath sent his angel, and hath delivered me out of the hand of Herod, and from all the expectation of the people of the Jews"* (v. 11). Stopping a few moments to reflect, he said to himself, "There is a prayer meeting going on. It must be at Mark's mother's house; I will go there."

Soon those in prayer were startled by a heavy pounding at the outside gate of Mark's mother's home. There was a little servant girl named Rhoda kneeling among the them. Instantly she sprang to her feet and rushed to the gate, saying to herself, "That's Peter! That's Peter! I knew God would hear our prayers. God has delivered him, and he is at the gate." Reaching the gate she excitedly cried, "Is that you, Peter?" "Yes." Too excited even to open the gate, she left Peter standing outside. She dashed back and said to the startled others, "Our prayers are answered—Peter is at the gate."

"Oh, Rhoda, you are crazy," cried the unbelieving company.

"No," Rhoda said, "I am not crazy. It is Peter. God has answered our prayers. I know his voice. I knew he would come, and he is here."

Then they all cried, "It is not Peter; it is his ghost. He has been killed in the night, and his ghost has come around and is rapping at the gate." But Peter kept on knocking, and they opened the gate, and there stood Peter, the living evidence that God had answered their prayers. (See Acts 12:12–16.)

By the way, have you ever noticed that among all the people who were present at that prayer meeting, only one person is mentioned by name, and that one person only a servant girl, Rhoda? Undoubtedly the bishops and elders of the church in Jerusalem were there, but not a single name of theirs has gone down in writing. Probably some of the leading people of Jerusalem, who had now become Christians, were there, but not a single name is mentioned. Rhoda, and Rhoda only. Why? Because Rhoda was the only one who really had faith and was therefore the only one worth mentioning, even though she was just a servant girl. The name Rhoda means "rose," and this Rhoda was a rose who was very fragrant to God, although she was only a servant girl; for there is no sweeter fragrance to God than the fragrance of faith.

Now if we can find out how these people prayed, then we will know just how we too can pray so as to get what we ask. In the fifth verse of Acts 12, we are told exactly how they prayed. Read it again: *"Prayer was made without ceasing of the church unto God for him."* The whole secret of prevailing prayer, the prayer that gets what it asks, is found in four phrases in this brief description of their prayer. The first phrase is *"unto God"*; the second, *"of the church"*; the third, *"without ceasing"*; the fourth, *"for him."* Let us take up these four phrases and study them.

"Unto God"

The first phrase is really the most important one: *"unto God."* The prayer that gets what it asks is the prayer that is prayed to God. But someone will say, "Is not all prayer made to God?" No. Comparatively few of the prayers that go up from this earth today are really made to God. I sometimes think that not one prayer in a hundred is really made *"unto God."* You ask, "What do you mean?" I mean exactly what I say, that not one prayer in a hundred is really prayed to God. "Oh," you say, "I know what you mean. You are talking about the prayers of the heathen to their idols and their false gods." No, I mean the prayers of people who call themselves Christians. I do not think that one in a hundred of them are really prayed to God. "Oh," you say, "I know what you mean. You are talking of the prayers of the Roman Catholics to the Virgin Mary and to the saints." No, I mean the prayers of people who call themselves Protestants. I do not believe that one in a hundred of the prayers of Protestant believers are really prayed to God. "What do you mean?" you ask. I mean exactly what I say.

Stop a moment and think. Is it not often the case when men stand up to pray in public, or kneel down to pray in private, that they are thinking far more of what they are asking for than they are of the great God who made heaven and earth, and who has all power, of whom they are asking it? Is it not often the case that in our prayers we are not thinking much either of what we are asking for or of Him from whom we are asking it, but our thoughts are wandering off woolgathering everywhere? We take the name of God upon our lips, but there is no real conscious approach to God in our hearts. We are really taking the name of God in vain while we imagine we are praying to Him. If there is to be any power in our prayers, if our prayers are to get anything, the first thing to be sure of when we pray is that we have really come into the presence of God and are really speaking to Him.

How to Get What You Pray For

We should never utter one syllable of prayer, either in public or in private, until we are definitely conscious that we have come into the presence of God and are actually praying to Him. Oh, let those two words, *"unto God,"* sink deep into your heart. From this time on, never pray, never utter one syllable of prayer, until you are sure that you have come into the presence of God and are really talking to Him.

There was a time when I had wandered far from God and had definitely decided that I would not accept Jesus Christ. Nevertheless, I prayed every night. I had come to a place where I doubted whether the Bible was the Word of God and whether Jesus Christ was the Son of God, and even doubted whether there was a personal God. Nevertheless, I prayed every night. I am glad that I was brought up that way, and that the practice of prayer was so instilled in me that it became habitual; for it was along that line that I came back out of the darkness of agnosticism into the clear light of an intelligent faith in God and His Word. Nevertheless, prayer was largely a mere matter of ritual. There was little real thought of God, and no real approach to God. And even after I was converted, yes, even after I had entered the ministry, prayer was largely a matter of ritual.

But the day came when I realized what real prayer meant, realized that prayer was having an audience with God, actually coming into the presence of God and asking for and getting things from Him. And the realization of that fact transformed my prayer life. Before that, prayer had been a mere duty, and sometimes a very irksome duty. But from that time on, prayer has been not merely a duty but a privilege, one of the most highly esteemed privileges of life. Before that the thought I had was, "How much time must I spend in prayer?" The thought that now possesses me is, "How much time may I spend in prayer without neglecting the other privileges and duties of life?"

Suppose some Englishman were summoned to Buckingham Palace to meet the Queen. He answers the summons and is waiting in the anteroom to be ushered into her presence. What do you think that man would say to himself as he waited to be brought in? Do you think he would say, "I wonder how much time I must spend with the Queen?" No, indeed; he would rather think, "I wonder how much time the Queen will give me." But prayer is having an audience with the King of Kings, that eternal, omnipotent King in comparison with whom all earthly kings and queens are as nothing. Would any intelligent person who realizes this fact ever ask himself, "How much time must I spend in prayer?"

No, our thought will be, "How much time may I spend in prayer? How much time will the King give me?"

So let these two words, *"unto God,"* sink deep into your heart and govern your prayer life from this day on. Whenever you kneel in prayer, or stand in prayer, whether it be in public or in private, be absolutely sure before you utter a syllable that you have actually come into the presence of God and are really speaking to Him. Oh, it is a wondrous secret.

But at this point questions arise: How can we come into the presence of God, and how can we be sure that we have come into the presence of God, and that we are really talking to Him? Some years ago I was speaking on this verse of Scripture in Chicago, and at the close of the address an intelligent Christian woman, one of the most intelligent and deeply spiritual women I ever knew, came to me and said, "Mr. Torrey, I like that thought of *'unto God,'* but how can we come into the presence of God, and how can we be absolutely sure that we have come into the presence of God, and that we are really talking to Him?" It was a wise question and a question of great importance; and it is clearly answered in the Word of God. There are two parts to the answer.

By the Blood of Jesus Christ

You will find the first part of the answer in Hebrews 10:19: *"Having therefore, brethren, boldness to enter into the holiest by the blood of Jesus."* We come into the presence of God *"by the blood of Jesus,"* and we can come into the presence of God in no other way. Just what does this mean? It means that you and I are sinners, the best of us are great sinners, and God is infinitely holy—so holy that even the seraphim, those wonderful burning ones (for that is what *seraphim* means), burning in their own intense holiness, must veil their faces and their feet in His presence. (See Isaiah 6:2.) But our sins have been laid upon Another, upon the Lord Jesus when He died upon the cross of Calvary and made a perfect atonement for our sins. When He died there, He took our place, the place of rejection by God, the place of the "curse." (See Galatians 3:13.) The moment we accept Him and believe in God's testimony concerning His blood, that by His shed blood He made perfect atonement for our sins, and trust God to forgive and justify us because the Lord Jesus died in our place, that moment our sins are forgiven and we are considered righteous and enter into a place above the seraphim, the place of God's only and perfect Son, Jesus Christ.

We do not need to veil our faces or our feet when we come into His presence, for we are made perfectly *"accepted in the beloved"* (Eph. 1:6). Therefore, *"to enter into the holiest"* (Heb. 10:19), to come into the very presence of God *"by the blood of Jesus"* (v. 19), means that when we draw near to God, we should give up any and every thought that we have any acceptability before God in ourselves. We must realize that we are miserable sinners, but we must also believe that every sin of ours has been atoned for by the shed blood of Jesus Christ. Consequently, we come with *"boldness"* into the very presence of God, into *"the holiest by the blood of Jesus"* (v. 19). The best man or woman on earth cannot come into the presence of God on the ground of any merit of his own, not for one moment; nor can he get anything from God on the ground of his own goodness, not even the smallest blessing. But on the ground of the shed blood of Jesus Christ, the vilest sinner who ever walked this earth, who has turned from his sin and accepted Jesus Christ and trusts in the shed blood as the ground of his acceptance before God, can come into the presence of God any day of the year, any hour of the day or night, and with perfect boldness speak out every longing of his heart and get what he asks from God. Isn't that wonderful? Yes, and thank God, it is true.

The Christian Scientist cannot really pray. What he calls prayer is simply meditation or concentration of thought. It is not asking a personal God for a definite blessing. Indeed, Mrs. Eddy denied the existence of a personal God, and she denied the atoning power of the blood. She said that the blood of Jesus Christ, when it was shed on the cross of Calvary, did no more good than when it was running in His veins. So a Christian Scientist cannot really pray; he is not on praying ground.*

Neither can a Unitarian really pray. Oh, he can take the name of God upon his lips and call Him Father and say beautiful words, but there is no real approach to God.† Our Lord Jesus Christ Himself said, *"I am the way, the truth, and the life: no man cometh unto the Father, but by me"* (John 14:6).

Some years ago I was on a committee in Chicago of three persons, one of whom was a leading Unitarian minister of the city. He was a charming man in many ways. One day at the close of our committee meeting, this Unitarian minister turned to me and said, "Brother Torrey, I often come to your church to hear you."

I replied, "I am very glad to hear it."

Then he continued, "I especially love to go to your prayer meetings. On many Friday nights I drop into your prayer meeting and sit down by the door, and I greatly enjoy it."

I replied, "I am glad that you do. But tell me something. Why don't you have a prayer meeting in your own church?"

"Well," he said, "you have asked me an honest question, and I will give you an honest answer. Because I can't. I have tried it, and it has failed every time." Of course it failed; they had no ground of approach to God—they denied the atoning blood.

But there are many supposedly orthodox Christians, and often in these days even supposedly orthodox ministers, who deny the atoning blood. They do not believe that the forgiveness of our sins is solely and entirely on the ground of the shedding of

---

* Christian Science, founded by Mary Baker Eddy in 1866, denies the diety of Christ and teaches that sin, sickness, and death are illusions that can be done away with through mental efforts.
† Unitarianism came to prominence in the eighteenth and nineteenth centuries. It denies the Christian doctrines of the Trinity and the deity of Jesus Christ, and ascribes divinity to God the Father only.

Jesus' blood as an atonement for sin on our behalf on the cross of Calvary. Therefore, they cannot really pray. There are some who call the theology that insists upon the truth so very clearly taught in the Word of God (of the substitutionary character of Christ's death and that we are saved by the shedding of His blood) a "theology of the slaughterhouse."

Mr. Alexander and I were holding meetings in the Royal Albert Hall in London. One day, I received through the mail one of our hymnals that some man had taken from the meeting. He had gone through it and cut out every reference to the blood of Christ. With the hymnal was an accompanying letter, and in this letter the man said, "I have gone through your hymnal and cut out every reference to the blood in every place where it is found, and I am sending this hymnal back to you. Now sing your hymns this way with the blood left out, and there will be some sense in them." I took the hymnal to the meeting with me that afternoon and displayed it; it was a sadly mutilated book. I read the man's letter, and then I said, "No, I will not cut the blood out of my hymnology, and I will not cut the blood out of my theology; for when I cut the blood out of my hymnology and my theology, I will have to cut all access to God out of my experience." No, you cannot approach God on any other ground than the shed blood; and until you believe in the blood of Jesus Christ as a perfect atonement for your sins, and as the only ground upon which you can find forgiveness and justification, real prayer is an impossibility.

ENTERING GOD'S PRESENCE BY THE SPIRIT

You will find the second part of the answer to the questions, "How can we come into the presence of God, and how can we be sure that we have come into His presence?" in Ephesians 2:18: *"For through him we both have access by one Spirit unto the Father."* Here we have the same thought repeated, that it is *"through him."* Through Jesus Christ we have our access to the Father. But we have an additional thought, and that is the thought that while we come into the presence of God through Jesus Christ, we come by one Spirit, the Holy Spirit. Just what does this mean? It means that, when you and I pray, it is the work of the Holy Spirit to take us by the hand, as it were, and lead us into the very presence of God, to introduce us to Him, and to make God real to us. The Greek word translated *"access"* is the exact equivalent in its etymology of the word "introduction," which is really a Latin word transliterated into English.

It is the work of the Holy Spirit to introduce us to God, that is, to lead us into God's presence and to make God real to us as we pray, as we return thanks, or as we worship. When we pray, in order that we may really come into the presence of God and be sure that we have come into His presence, we must look to the Holy Spirit to make God real to us.

Have you ever had this experience—that when you knelt to pray it seemed as if there were no one there, as if you were just talking to the air or into empty space? What should we do at such a time as that? Should we stop praying and wait until a time when we feel like praying? No, when we least feel like praying, and when God is least real to us, that is the time we need to pray most. What should we do then? Simply be quiet, look up to God, and ask God to fulfill His promise and to send His Holy Spirit to lead us into His presence and to make Him real to us. Then wait and expect. And He will come. He will take us into God's presence, and He will make God real to us. I can testify today that some of the most wonderful seasons of prayer I have ever had have been times when, as I first knelt to pray, I had no real sense of God. There seemed to be no one there; it seemed as if I were talking into empty space. Then I have just looked up to God and asked Him and trusted Him to send His Holy Spirit to teach me to pray, to lead me into His presence, and to make Him real to me. Then the Spirit has come, and He has made God so real to me that it almost seemed if I opened my eyes I could see Him; in fact, I did see Him with the eyes of my soul.

One night at the close of a sermon in Chicago in one of the churches on the South Side, I went down the aisle to speak to different individuals. I stepped up to a middle-aged man and asked him, "Are you a Christian?"

"No," he replied, "I am an infidel. Did you ever see God?"

I quickly replied, "Yes, I have seen God."

The man was startled and silenced. Did I mean that I had seen God with these eyes of my body? No. But, thank God, I have two pairs of eyes; not only does my body have eyes, but my spirit also has eyes. I pity the person who has only one pair of eyes, no matter how good those eyes are. I thank God I have two pairs of eyes, these bodily eyes with which I see you, and the eyes of my spirit with which I see God. God has given me wonderful eyes for my body, that at sixty-seven years of age I have never had to wear glasses. I do not know what it means to have my eyes weary or painful under any circumstances. But I will gladly give up my physical eyes rather than those other eyes that God has given me, the eyes with which I see Him.

This, then, is the way to come into the presence of God and to be sure that we have come into His presence: first, to come by the blood; second, to come in the Holy Spirit, looking to the Holy Spirit to lead us into the presence of God, and to make God real to us.

Let me quickly call your attention to the great practical importance of the doctrine of the Trinity. There are many who think that the doctrine of the Trinity is a purely abstract, theoretical, and utterly impractical doctrine. Not at all. It involves our whole spiritual life, and it is of the highest importance in the practical matter of praying. We need God the Father to pray to; we need Jesus Christ the Son to pray through; and we need the Holy Spirit to pray by. It is the prayer that is to God the Father, through Jesus Christ the Son, and under the guidance and by the power of the Holy Spirit, that God the Father answers.

With Intense Earnestness

Now let us consider another of the phrases used in Acts 12:5 that contains the whole secret of prevailing prayer: *"without ceasing."* *"Prayer was made without ceasing of the church unto God for him."* If you have the Revised Version, you will notice that it reads differently: *"Prayer was made earnestly of the church unto God for him."* The word *"earnestly"* comes far closer to the force of the original than the words *"without ceasing,"* but even *"earnestly"* does not give the full force of the Greek word used. The Greek word is *ektenos,* and it means literally "stretched-out-edly." You can see how the King James Version's translators came to translate it *"without ceasing."* They thought of the prayer as stretched out a long time, unceasing prayer. But that is not the thought at all. The Greek word is never used in that sense anywhere in the New Testament. And I do not know of a place in Greek literature outside of the Bible where it is so used. The word is a pictorial word, as so many Bible words are. It represents the soul stretched out in the intensity of its earnestness toward God.

Did you ever see a foot race? The racers are all toeing the mark waiting for the starter to say "go," or to shoot the starting pistol as a signal to go. As the critical moment approaches, everything about the runners becomes more and more tense, until when the word "go" comes, or the revolver cracks, they go charging down the track with every nerve and muscle stretched toward the goal. Sometimes the veins stand out on their foreheads like whipcords—every runner wants to be the winner. That is the picture of this verse in Acts 12, the soul stretched out in intense earnestness toward God.

It is the same word that is used in the comparative mood in Luke 22:44, where we read, *"And being in an agony he prayed more earnestly* [literally, more stretched-out-edly]: *and his sweat was as it were great drops of blood falling down to the ground."* The thought is, as I have pointed out, of the soul being stretched out toward God in intense earnestness of desire.

Probably the most accurate translation that could be given in a single word would be "intensely." "Prayer was made intensely by the church unto God for him." In fact, the word *intensely* is from the same root, only it has a different prefix. In the 1911 Bible, the passage is translated, *"Instant and earnest prayer was made by the church unto God for him,"* which is not a bad paraphrase though it is not a translation. "Intensely earnest prayer was made of the church unto God for him" would be an even better rendering.

How to Get What You Pray For

It is the intensely earnest prayer to which God pays attention, and which He answers. This thought comes out again and again in the Bible. We find it even in the Old Testament, in Jeremiah 29:13: *"Ye shall seek me, and find me, when ye shall search for me with all your heart."* Here we discover the reason why so many of our prayers are unheard by God. There is so little heart in them, so little intensity of desire for the thing asked, that there is no reason why God should pay any attention to them. Did you pray this morning? Undoubtedly almost every one of you would reply, "Yes, I did." Then suppose I ask you again, "For what did you pray this morning?" I fear that some of you would hesitate and ponder and then have to say, "Really, I forget what I did pray for this morning." Well, then, God will forget to answer.

But if I were to ask some of you if you prayed this morning, you would say, "Yes." Then if I asked you for what you prayed, you could tell me at once, for you always pray for the same thing. You have just a little rote prayer that you go through each morning or each night. You fall on your knees, go through your little prayer automatically, scarcely thinking of what you are saying; in fact, oftentimes you do not think of what you are saying but are thinking of a dozen other things while you are repeating your prayer. Such prayer is profanity, taking the name of God in vain.

When Mrs. Torrey and I were in India, she went up to Darjeeling, in the Himalayas, on the border of Tibet. I was unable to go because I was so busy with meetings in Calcutta. When she came back she brought with her a Tibetan praying wheel. It is a little round brass cup on the top of a stick, and the cup revolves when the stick is whirled. The Tibetan writes out his prayers, drops them into the cup, and then he whirls the stick. The wheel goes round, and the prayers are said. That is just the way a great many Americans pray—except that the wheel is in their heads instead of being on the top of a stick. They kneel down and rattle through a rote prayer, day after day the same thing, with scarcely any thought of what they are praying about. This kind of prayer is profanity, taking the name of God in vain, and it has no power whatsoever with God. It is a pure waste of time, or worse than a waste of time.

But if I should ask some of you what you prayed for this morning, you could tell me, for as you were in prayer, the Spirit of God came upon you, and with a great heartache of intensity of desire you cried to God for that thing that you must have. Well, God will hear your prayer and give you what you asked.

If we are to pray with power, we must pray with intense earnestness, throwing our whole souls into the prayer. This thought comes out again and again in the Bible. For example, we find it in Romans 15:30: *"Now I beseech you, brethren, for the Lord Jesus Christ's sake, and for the love of the Spirit, that ye strive together with me in your prayers to God for me."* The word translated *"strive together"* in this verse is *sunagonizo.* The word *agonizo* means "to contend, strive, wrestle, or fight." This verse could therefore be properly translated, "Now I beseech you, brethren, for the Lord Jesus Christ's sake, and for the love of the Spirit, that ye wrestle together with me in your prayers to God for me."

We hear a great deal these days about the "rest of faith." By this, one usually means that we should take things very calmly in our Christian lives; and when we pray we should simply come into God's presence as little children, quietly and trustfully ask Him for the thing desired, consider it ours, and go away calmly and assume the thing is ours. Now there is truth in that, a great truth; but it is only one side of the truth, and a truth usually has two sides. The other side of the truth is that there is not only the "rest of faith," but also the "fight of faith," and my Bible has more to say about the fight of faith than it does about the rest of faith. The thought of wrestling or fighting in prayer is not the thought that we have to wrestle with God to make God willing to grant our prayers. No, our wrestling is *"against principalities, against powers, against the rulers of the darkness of this world, against spiritual wickedness in high places"* (Eph. 6:12), against the devil and all his mighty forces, and there is no place where the devil so resists us as when we pray. Sometimes when we pray, it seems as if all the forces of hell sweep in between us and God. What should we do? Give up? No! A thousand times, no! Fight the thing through on your knees, wrestle in your prayer to God, and win.

How to Get What You Pray For

Some years ago I was attending a Bible conference in Dr. James H. Brooks' old church in St. Louis. On the program was one of the most distinguished and most gifted Bible teachers America ever produced, and he was speaking this day on "The Rest of Faith." In his address he said, "I challenge anyone to show me a single passage in the Bible where we are told to wrestle in prayer." Now one speaker does not like to contradict another, but here was a challenge, and there I was sitting on the platform. I was obliged to take it up. So I said in a low voice, "Romans 15:30, brother." He was a good enough Greek scholar to know that I had him, and what is rarer still, he was honest enough to admit it on the spot. Yes, the Bible tells us to wrestle in prayer, and it is the prayer in which we actually wrestle in the power of the Holy Spirit that wins out with God. The word that is the root of the word translated *"strive together"* (Rom. 15:30) is *agōnē*, from which our word *agony* comes. In fact, in Luke 22:44, to which I have already referred, this is the very word that is translated *"agony"*: *"And being in an agony he prayed more earnestly: and his sweat was as it were great drops of blood falling down to the ground."* Oh, that we might have more agonizing prayer!

Turn now to Colossians 4:12–13, and you will find the same thought again, put in other words:

> *Epaphras, who is one of you, a servant of Christ, saluteth you, always labouring fervently for you ["striving for you," RV] in prayers, that ye may stand perfect and complete in all the will of God. For I bear him record, that he hath a great zeal for you.*

Notice that the Revised Version puts it, *"striving for you,"* the same word as in Romans 15:30. Also, the words translated *"great zeal"* in this version are translated in the Revised Version as *"much labour,"* which is an accurate translation. The word translated *"labour"* is a very strong word; it means intense toil, or painful labor. Do you know what it means to toil in prayer, to labor with painful toil in prayer? Oh, how easily most of us take our praying, how little heart we put into it, how little it takes out of us, and how little it counts with God!

The Power of Prayer

The mighty men of God, who throughout the centuries have brought about great things by prayer, are the men who have had much painful toil in prayer. Take, for example, David Brainerd, that physically feeble but spiritually mighty man of God. Trembling for years on the verge of tuberculosis, from which he ultimately died at an early age, Brainerd felt led by God to labor among the North American Indians in the early days, in the primeval forests of northern Pennsylvania. Sometimes on a winter night he would go out into the forest and kneel in the cold snow when it was a foot deep, and he would so labor with God in prayer that he would be wringing wet with perspiration even out in the cold winter night hours. God heard David Brainerd and sent such a mighty revival among the North American Indians as had never been heard of before, as indeed had never been dreamed about.

Not only did God send in answer to David Brainerd's prayers this mighty revival among the North American Indians, but also in answer to David Brainerd's prayers he transformed Jonathan Edwards, who would have been his father-in-law had Brainerd not died of tuberculosis. Edwards, that mighty prince of theology, probably the mightiest thinker that America has ever produced, was transformed into Jonathan Edwards, the evangelist on fire for God. Edwards so preached on the subject of "Sinners in the Hands of an Angry God," in the church at Enfield, in the power of the Holy Spirit, that the strong men in the audience felt as he preached as if the very floor of the church were falling out and they were sinking into hell. They sprang to their feet and threw their arms around the pillars of the church and cried to God for mercy. Indeed, if we had more men who could pray like David Brainerd, then we would have more men who could preach like Jonathan Edwards.

Speaking at a conference in New York State, I once used this illustration of David Brainerd. Dr. Park, the grandson and biographer of Jonathan Edwards, was in my audience, and he came to me at the close and said, "I have always felt that there was something abnormal about David Brainerd."

I replied, "Dr. Park, it would be a good thing for you and a good thing for me if we had a little more of that kind of abnormality."

How to Get What You Pray For

Indeed it would; and it would be a good thing if many of us had that kind of so-called abnormality that bows a man down with intensity of longing for the power of God, that would make us pray in the way that David Brainerd prayed.

But a practical question arises at this point. How can we get this intense earnestness in prayer? The Bible answers the question plainly and simply. There are two ways of having earnestness in prayer—a right way and a wrong way. The wrong way is to work it up in the energy of the flesh. Have you never seen this done? A man kneels down by a chair to pray; he begins calmly, and then he begins to work himself up and begins to shout and scream and pound the chair, and sometimes he sputters; and he screams until your head is almost splitting with the loud uproar. That is the wrong way; that is false fire; that is the energy of the flesh, which is an abomination to God. If possible, that is even worse than the careless, thoughtless prayers that I mentioned earlier.

There is a right way to obtain real, heart-stirring, heart-wringing, and God-moving earnestness in prayer. The Bible tells us the right way in Romans 8:26–27:

> *Likewise the Spirit also helpeth our infirmities: for we know not what we should pray for as we ought: but the Spirit itself maketh intercession for us with groanings which cannot be uttered. And he that searcheth the hearts knoweth what is the mind of the Spirit, because he maketh intercession for the saints according to the will of God.*

That is the right way—look to the Spirit to create the earnestness. The earnestness that counts with God is not the earnestness that you or I work up; it is the earnestness that the Holy Spirit creates in our hearts. Have you ever gone to God in prayer with no earnestness in your prayer at all? It was just words, words, words, a mere matter of form; there seemed to be no real prayer in your heart. What do you do at such a time as that? Stop praying and wait until you feel more like praying? No. If there is ever a time when one needs to pray, it is when he does not feel like praying. What should you do? Be silent and look up to God to send His Holy Spirit, according to His promise, to move your heart to prayer and to awaken and create real earnestness in your heart in prayer. Then God will send His Spirit, and you will pray with intense earnestness, very likely *"with groanings which cannot be uttered."*

Oh, that is how we must pray if we want to get what we ask in prayer. Pray with the intense earnestness that the Holy Spirit alone can inspire.

"Of the Church"

Now let us look briefly at another one of the four phrases, the phrase, *"of the church."* The prayer that God particularly delights to answer is united prayer. There is power in the prayer of a single individual, and the prayer of individuals has brought about great things, but there is far greater power in united prayer. Our Lord Jesus taught this same great truth in Matthew 18:19–20:

> *Again I say unto you, that if two of you shall agree on earth as touching any thing that they shall ask, it shall be done for them of my Father which is in heaven. For where two or three are gathered together in my name, there am I in the midst of them.*

God delights in the unity of His people, and He does everything in His power to promote that unity. Thus, He especially honors unity in prayer. There is power in the prayer of one true believer; there is far more power in the united prayer of two, and greater power in the united prayer of still more.

But it must be real unity. This comes out in the exact words our Lord used; He said, *"If two of you shall agree on earth as touching any thing that they shall ask, it shall be done for them of my Father which is in heaven."* This verse contains one of the most frequently misquoted and most constantly abused promises in the whole Bible. It is often quoted as if it reads, "Again I say unto you, if two of you shall agree on earth to ask anything, it shall be done for them by My Father who is in heaven." But it actually reads, *"Again I say unto you, if two of you shall agree on earth as touching any thing that they shall ask, it shall be done for them of my Father which is in heaven."*

Someone may say, "I do not see any essential difference." Let me explain it to you. Someone else has a burden on his heart. He comes to you and asks you to unite with him in praying for this thing, and you consent, and you both pray for it. Now you are "agreed" in praying, but you are not agreed at all *"as touching"* the thing that you ask. He asks for it because he intensely desires it; you ask for it simply because he asks you to ask for it. You are not at all agreed *"as touching"* the thing that you ask. But when God, by His Holy Spirit, puts the same burden on two hearts, and they, then, in the unity of the Spirit pray for the same thing, there is no power on earth or in hell to keep them from getting it. Our heavenly Father will do for them the thing that they ask.

"For Him"

Now let us look at the fourth phrase in Acts 12:5, *"for him."* The prayer was definite prayer for a definite person; and that is the kind of prayer God answers—definite prayer. Oh, how general and vague many of our prayers are! They are pretty; they are charmingly phrased, but they ask no definite, specific thing, and they get no definite, specific answer. When you pray to God, have a definite, clear-cut idea of exactly what it is you want from God. Ask Him for that definite and specific thing; and, if you meet the other conditions of prevailing prayer, you will get that definite, specific thing for which you asked. God's answer will be just as definite as your prayer.

In closing, let me call your attention to our dependence on the Holy Spirit in all our praying, if we are to accomplish anything by our prayers. It is the Holy Spirit, as we saw in our study of the first phrase, who enables us to really pray *"unto God,"* who leads us into the presence of God and makes God real to us. It is the Holy Spirit who gives us the intense earnestness in prayer that prevails with God. It is the Holy Spirit who brings us into unity so that we know the power of really united prayer. And it is the Spirit who shows us the definite things for which we should definitely pray.

To sum it all up, the prayer that God answers is the prayer that is to God the Father, that is on the ground of the atoning blood of God the Son, and that is under the direction and in the power of God the Holy Spirit.

5

Can You Get What You Pray For?

And whatsoever we ask, we receive of him, because we keep his
commandments, and do those things that are pleasing in his sight.
—1 John 3:22

In the last chapter we discussed what God tells us in His Word as to how to pray so as to get what we ask. Now we take up the concern, "Who can pray so as to get what they ask? Can I get what I pray for?"

The impression that many people have is that all the promises in the Word of God in regard to His answering prayer are made to everyone, and that anyone can claim these promises; but this is far from the truth. God's promises to answer prayer are made to certain specified persons, and God is very careful in His Word to tell us just who these persons are whose prayers He promises to answer. One of the most common sources of misinterpretation of the Word of God is the taking of promises that are made to one class of people and applying them to an entirely different class. Of course, when this is done, and people to whom the promises were never made claim them, disappointment is the inevitable result; they do not get what they ask, and they think that God's promise has failed. But God's promise has not failed! Someone has claimed the fulfillment of a promise that he had no right to take as belonging to himself. God tells us in the plainest possible words, words that any intelligent person can understand, just whose prayers He promises to answer.

One of the most definite and clearest descriptions to be found in the Bible of whose prayers God will answer is found in our text verse: *"And whatsoever we ask, we receive of him, because we keep his commandments, and do those things that are pleasing in his sight."*

Have you ever noticed what a remarkable statement the apostle John made in this verse? He said that whatever he asked of God, he got: *"Whatsoever we ask, we receive of him."* John here said that he never asked one single thing of God without getting that very thing for which he asked. How many of us could say that: "Whatever I ask of God, I get"? Many of us could undoubtedly say, "Many of the things I ask of God I get." Others could say, "Some of the things I ask of God I get"; and some of us would probably have to say, "I do not know that I have ever gotten one thing I asked of God." But John said, "Whatever I ask of God, I get." Then John went on to tell us why he could say it, and by telling us why he could say it he told us how we, too, can get into such a relationship with God that we can say, "Whatever I ask of God, I get."

Those Who Keep His Commandments

Whenever you find the words *because* or *therefore* in the Bible, you should take careful notice, for these words point out the reason of things. John said that the reason that God gave him whatever he asked was *"because"* he, and the others that he included with himself in the word *"we,"* kept His commandments and did the things that are pleasing in His sight.

There are two parts to John's description of those whose prayers God always answers. The first part of the description is, *"we keep his commandments."* God hears the prayers of those who *"keep his commandments,"* that is, those who study His Word each day to find out what His will is, and who, when they discover what His will is, do it every time they find it. God demands reciprocity: He demands that we listen to His Word before He listens to our prayers. If we have a sharp ear for God's commandments, then God will have a sharp ear for our petitions; but if we turn a deaf ear to one of God's commandments, God will turn a deaf ear to every one of our petitions. If we do the things that God bids us to do, then God will do the things that we ask Him to do;

but if we do not pay close attention to God's Word, God will pay no attention whatsoever to our prayers. To put it all in a single sentence, if we wish God to answer our prayers, we must study God's Word diligently each day to find out what the will of God is, and do that will every time we find it.

Here we touch upon one of the most common reasons why prayers are not answered: those who pray are neglecting the study of the Word of God, or they are not studying it for the particular purpose of finding out what God's will is for them, or else they are not doing that will every time they find it out. In my first pastorate there was a lady who always attended the church services but was not a member of the church. She was one of the most intelligent women in the community. One day someone told me that this lady had formerly been a member of the church of which I was pastor. So one Sunday morning, as I was walking home from church, I walked along with this lady, who lived on the same street as I. When we reached my front gate and I was about to turn in, I said to her, "They tell me you were formerly a member of this church of which I am pastor."

She replied, "Yes, I was."

"Well," I said, "why are you not a member now?"

She answered, "Because I do not believe the Bible."

I said, "Do not believe the Bible?"

"No," she said, "I do not believe the Bible."

I asked, "Why do you not believe the Bible?"

She replied, "Because I have tried its promises and found them untrue."

I said, "Will you tell me one single promise in the Word of God that you ever tried and found untrue?"

She said, "Does it not say somewhere in the Bible that whatever things you desire when you pray, believe that you receive them and you shall have them?"

I said, "It says something that sounds a good deal like that."

She said, "My husband was very ill. I prayed for his recovery, and I fully believed God would raise him up, but he died. Did not the promise fail?"

"No, not at all," I said.

"What?" she exclaimed. "The promise did not fail?"

"No," I replied, "the promise did not fail."

"But," she said, "does it not say that whatever you desire when you pray, believe that you receive it and you shall have it?"

I said, "It says something that sounds a good deal like that."

"Just what does it say?"

I replied, "It says, *'What things soever ye desire, when ye pray, believe that ye receive them, and ye shall have them'* (Mark 11:24). Are you one of the *'ye's'*?"

She asked, "What do you mean?"

I replied, "Are you one of the people to whom this promise is made?"

"Why," she exclaimed, "isn't it made to every professing Christian?"

I replied, "Certainly not. God defines very clearly in His Word just to whom He makes His promises to answer prayer."

"I would like to see God's definition," she said.

I said, "Let me show it to you," and I opened my Bible to 1 John 3:22, and read, *"Whatsoever we ask, we receive of him, because we keep his commandments, and do those things that are pleasing in his sight."* Then I said, "That is God's definition of the *'we's'* and the *'ye's'* whose prayers God promises to answer—those who *'keep his commandments, and do those things that are pleasing in his sight.'* Were you keeping His commandments? Were you doing the things that are pleasing in His sight? Were you living for the glory of God in everything?"

"No," she said, "I certainly was not."

"Then," I said, "the promise was not made to you, was it?"

"No," she said, "it was not."

"Then did it fail?"

"No, it did not." She saw her error and came back to God and became one of the most active and most useful members of that church.

There is a multitude of men and women just like that woman: they take a promise that is made to someone else and apply it to themselves, and of course it fails. Are you one of the "ye's"? That is, are you studying the Word of God every day of your life, earnestly and carefully, to find out what God's will is for you, and are you doing it every time you find it? If so, you are on praying ground and belong to the class whose prayers God will answer; God will give you what you ask. If not, you do not belong to the class whose prayers God promises to answer.

I had another illustration of this same thing in our church in Chicago. I had in my church two women, one the mistress, the other the maid. The mistress was an earnest and intelligent Christian. One night at the close of a meeting the maid came to me and said, "My mistress, Miss W———, thinks that I ought to have a talk with you."

"Why, Jennie, does Miss W——— think that you ought to have a talk with me?"

"Because I am in great perplexity."

I said, "What are you perplexed about?"

She replied, "I am perplexed because God does not answer my prayers."

"Oh," I said, "there is nothing to be surprised about in that. Does God anywhere promise to answer your prayers? God does tell us very plainly in His Word whose prayers He will answer." Then I quoted 1 John 3:22: *"Whatsoever we ask, we receive of him, because we keep His commandments, and do those things that are pleasing in his sight."*

"Now, Jennie," I said, "does that describe you? Are you studying the Word of God every day of your life to find out what God wishes you to do, and do you do it every time you find it?"

"No," she replied, "I do not."

"Then," I said, "there is nothing mysterious, is there, about God's not answering your prayers?"

"No," she said, "there is not."

I put the same question to each one of you. Are you studying the Word of God every day of your life to find out what the will of God is, and doing it every time you find it? If you are, as I have said, you are on praying ground, and God will heed your prayers and give you the things that you ask of Him. But if you are neglecting the study of the Word of God, to find out what His will is, or failing to do that will every time that you discover it, then you have no right whatsoever to expect God to answer your prayers. He does not promise to do so. Indeed, He distinctly says in His Word that He will not.

You may go right through your Bible, and you will find, in regard to every one of the great promises of God to answer our prayers, that this same thought comes out in the context in which the promise is found. Take, for example, that wonderful promise of Jesus Christ to answer prayer, which is so often quoted and is so familiar to us all, John 14:13–14: *"And whatsoever ye shall ask in my name, that will I do, that the Father may be glorified in the Son. If ye shall ask any thing in my name, I will do it."* Now most people, when they quote this promise, stop there, and therefore get the impression that if anyone asks anything in Christ's name, Jesus Christ offers to do it. But Jesus Christ did not stop there; He went on. Look at it again in its context:

> *And whatsoever ye shall ask in my name, that will I do, that the Father may be glorified in the Son. If ye shall ask any thing in my name, I will do it. If ye love me, keep my commandments* [or, as the Revised Version reads, *"If ye love me, ye will keep my commandments"*]. *And I will pray the Father, and he shall give you another Comforter, that he may abide with you for ever; even the Spirit of truth; whom the world cannot receive, because it seeth him not, neither knoweth him: but ye know him; for he dwelleth with you, and shall be in you.* (John 14:13–17)

In other words, Jesus Christ told His disciples that if they had the love for Him that led them to keep His commandments (that is, to study His Word and find out what His commandments were, and to do them every time they discovered them), He would pray to the Father; and the Father, in answer to His prayers, would give them the Holy Spirit; and the Holy Spirit would guide them in their prayers, so that they would pray according to the will of God. Then, whatever they—those who keep His commandments and were therefore led by the Holy Spirit—should ask in His name, that He would do.

Turn to another familiar promise, one of the most remarkable promises in the whole Bible regarding God's answering prayer, John 15:7: *"If ye abide in me, and my words abide in you, ye shall ask what ye will, and it shall be done unto you."* This verse is constantly quoted as if it read, "If you abide in me, you shall ask what you will, and it shall be done unto you," but it does not read that way. This reading leaves out one of the most important clauses in the verse. Read it again as it really reads: *"If ye abide in me, and my words abide in you, ye shall ask what ye will, and it shall be done unto you."* So the Lord Jesus tells us that it is necessary not only that we abide in Him, but also that His words abide in us, if we are to get what we ask.

Now in order that Christ's words may abide in us, we must study these words, must we not? Unless we get them in us, they certainly cannot stay in us, and we certainly cannot get Christ's words in us unless we study them diligently.

But it is not enough to get Christ's words in us; His words must *"abide"* in us, that is, stay in us. There is only one possible way in which Christ's words can stay in us, and that is by our diligently obeying them. Three verses later in this same chapter, Jesus says again, *"If ye keep my commandments, ye shall abide in my love; even as I have kept my Father's commandments, and abide in his love"* (John 15:10). So you can go straight through your Bible, and you will find that every promise of God to answer our prayers is made to those who diligently study His Word so that they may know His will, and who always obey His will every time they find it. Are you greatly perplexed as to why God does not give you the things you ask? There is no mystery at all about it; you are not studying God's Word to find out His will for you, or else you are not doing it every time you find it. You are doing it in many instances, but there is some particular thing you are not doing that you know God wishes you to do, and there is not the slightest reason why you should expect God to answer your prayers.

Those Who Do the Things That Are Pleasing to God

But it is not enough that we keep His commandments. There is something further than that in the verse we are studying. Read

The Power of Prayer

1 John 3:22 again: *"And whatsoever we ask, we receive of him, because we keep his commandments and* [notice this *and*—a little word but a very important word] *do those things that are pleasing in his sight."* It is not enough that we do the things that God specifically commands us to do; in addition to that, we must *"do those things that are pleasing in his sight,"* even though He has not commanded us to do them. There are many things that it would please God for us to do that He does not specifically command us to do.

The idea that many people have of God's government is this: God is a great moral Governor, and He lays down a lot of laws for us to obey. It's "Thou shalt do this" and "Thou shalt not do that." In this way, we end up thinking that the whole of Christian duty lies in our doing the things that God specifically tells us to do, and leaving undone the things that God specifically tells us not to do. What a strange idea of God's government! God is not a mere moral governor. He is that, but He is far more than that—something infinitely better than that. God is our Father. That is the thought that lies at the very foundation of the Bible doctrine of prayer—the thought of the fatherhood of God. All the apparently philosophical and learned arguments that men bring against the doctrine of God's answering prayer, from "the uniformity of law" to "the established course of things in nature and in providence," are all utterly foolish. In fact, they are also unphilosophical, for all their ostentatious parade of being profoundly scientific and philosophical, because they lose sight of the great fundamental truth about God that lies at the very foundation of answered prayer. This truth is that God is not merely a Creator and the Governor of the physical universe and the moral universe, but that God is also our Father.

Now how does a father govern his children? Does he lay down a lot of laws—"Thou shalt do this" and "Thou shalt not do this"? Does he rest content when his children do the things that he specifically tells them to do, and leave undone the things he specifically tells them not to do? No, not if he is a wise father. If he is a wise father, he will lay down some rules for the conduct of his children, which he, because of superior knowledge, knows to be wise. But those rules will not be very many, and certainly he will not be content if his children simply obey those rules. No, the wise father expects his children to become thoroughly acquainted with him, so that they know instinctively what pleases him and, when they know what pleases him, do it without waiting to be told.

Take, for example, my own government of my children. Did my wife and I lay down a lot of laws for our children to follow, as to what they should do and what they should not do? No, certainly not. We did lay down a few principles of action, which we, in our superior wisdom, knew to be best for our children. We did not always explain to our children why we laid down these laws, for we wished our children to learn obedience to authority. In much of the home life of Americans today, in much of the school life, and in much of our national life, we have entirely lost sight of the great and wholesome principle of authority. Some of our modern would-be educators tell us that we ought to explain everything that we command our children to do, in the home or in the school, and that we ought to let our children "follow out their own individuality," and "not enslave them by parental or school authority."

That is one of the most dangerous principles in modern teaching. By it we are training a lot of rebels—rebels in the home, rebels in the schools, and afterward rebels in society and in civil government. If there is anything the present generation needs to learn, and that we, who are in authority of one kind or another, need to teach our children, it is the principle of rightful authority: the authority of the parent in the home, the authority of teachers in schools, and the authority of civil rulers in our government.

My children were taught to obey when they were told to do anything, without asking why. And if either my wife or I had told our children to do anything, and they had not done it, we would not have known what to make of it; or if we had told them not to do anything and they had done it, we would not have known what to make of that. I cannot recall an instance in many years in which our children disobeyed us in a single matter.

But we were not satisfied with that. Over and above the few rules we laid down for the guidance of our children, we expected our children to become thoroughly acquainted with us, so that they would know instinctively what would please their father or their mother and, when they knew it, do it without waiting to be told. We should have been much grieved if our children had only done the things that pleased us when they were specifically told to do them.

Now when we are careful to consider, in all our actions and in all our decisions, what would please God and what would displease Him; and when we always do the things we think would please Him, and refuse to do the things we think would displease Him, even though He has not specifically told us to do the one, or leave the other undone; then God will listen to our prayers. If we always aim to *do those things that are pleasing in his sight,* He will always study to do the things that please us and, therefore, grant our requests. Are you always, in all your decisions, carefully considering what would please or displease God, doing every time the things that you think would please Him, and leaving undone every time the things you think would displease Him, whether or not He has told you to do the one or not to do the other?

Here we find a very simple way of deciding the questions that are perplexing so many Christians today: "Should Christians go to the theater?" or "Should Christians dance?" or "Should Christians play cards?" or "Should Christians go to the movies?" and so on. Many people attempt to decide these questions in the following way. They ask, "Does God anywhere say in His Word, 'You shall not go to the theater' or 'You shall not dance' or 'You shall not play cards'?" But that is not the question. If you were a loyal child of God, you would not ask such questions. The real question is, "Will it please my Father? Will it please God?"

Take, for example, the question of the theater. If I thought it would please God for me to go to the theater, more than for me to stay away, I would go, no matter what anyone else might think of it, or what anyone else might do. But if I thought it would please God more for me to stay away than for me to go, I would stay away no matter who else went.

Can You Get What You Pray For?

When I lived in Chicago, I frequently received complimentary tickets from different theaters, especially from one of the highest class theaters. With the tickets oftentimes would come a note saying that the play was of a very high moral character, and that Bishop So-and-so, in some city, or Dr. So-and-so, highly approved of it and had gone to the play, and that they would be highly complimented if I would occupy a box at the play. However, I could not be caught by any such chaff as that. It made no difference to me what Bishop or Dr. So-and-so had done. The only question with me was, "Will it please God more for me to go than for me to stay away?" Had I thought that it would please God more for me to go than for me to stay away, I would have gone, whether Bishop So-and-so had gone or not. But if, on the other hand, I had thought it would please God more for me to stay away, I would have stayed away, even though every bishop and every minister in Chicago had gone.

Each one of us must decide these questions for himself. No one of us can be a conscience for someone else. But these questions are not difficult to decide if we decide them based on the biblical principle of doing what would please our Father, and leaving undone the things that would not please Him.

Does it please God for a child of His to attend the theater? There are certain things that we all know about the theater, or that we may easily learn if we do not already know them. We all know there are great differences among the plays that are put on the stage. Some of them are of a high moral character, and the natural effect of them would be uplifting. Others are morally not so good, and others are as vile as the theatrical people dare to make them. We know, too, that there is a great difference among the actors and the actresses. We know that some actors and actresses try to maintain a high moral standard, and that others are among the most corrupt members of modern society. We know that some actresses go on the stage with lofty moral ideals, and that other actresses have no moral ideals at all. "Well, then," someone may say, "the way to decide it is this: go to those plays, and only to those plays, where the play itself is of a high, elevating moral character, and where all the actors and actresses are men and women who are trying to maintain high moral ideals."

Well, if you decided it in that way, you would not go to many plays. But the question is not quite that simple. The theater is an institution, and we must judge it as an institution, judge it as it really exists today. It is possible to imagine a stage of the purest and loftiest character, and to imagine plays that would be among the most elevating of all the influences in society; but the question is not of the stage, and the plays, as we can imagine them, but of the stage as it actually exists today.

Now there are certain things that all of us who have studied the problem at all know about the stage as it exists today. We know that the influence of the stage upon the men and women who perform upon it is of a most demoralizing character. We know that many women have gone on the stage with a determination to maintain the highest moral ideals, and that they have all found out, after they have been on the stage a while, that they must do one of two things—they must either lower their standards, or else quit the stage. Some have quit the stage. Others have lowered their standards.

Clement Scott (1841–1904), who was the leading dramatic critic of his day in England, and whose whole life was given to dramatic criticism, said some years ago in a leading London paper that it was practically impossible for any woman to remain on the stage and retain her womanly modesty. This statement naturally roused great excitement and great indignation among theatrical people. By threats of one kind and another, they compelled Clement Scott to say that he was sorry that he made the statement, but they could never make him say that it was not true.

When Mr. Alexander and I were holding meetings in London, Herbert Beerbohm Tree (1853–1917), who stood at the top of the dramatic profession of that day, and who was afterward knighted by the king because of his prominence and talent, came to see me at my lodgings. He came with one of the leading newspaper men of London in order to convince me that I was wrong in my attitude toward the stage. We had a long conversation. I invited

Can You Get What You Pray For?

Mr. Alexander in to listen to the conversation, and he took part in it. In that conversation, both Mr. Alexander and I put some very direct questions to Beerbohm Tree, and he answered them frankly. The admissions that he made (not, of course, regarding any matter in his own moral conduct, but regarding what was necessary to be done in the conduct of the stage), made me think worse of the theater than I ever had before.

When I was holding meetings in the big armory in Cleveland, Ohio, a theatrical manager called upon me at my hotel and said, "I demand the right to defend the stage from your platform."

I asked, "Why?"

He said, "Because you are doing a great profession a great wrong. I was in Philadelphia when you held your meetings there, and we theatrical managers got together while you were there, and we agreed together that your meetings cost the theaters of Philadelphia fifty thousand dollars."

I replied, "That is one of the best things I have ever heard about our meetings in Philadelphia. Now, what do you want to say?"

He said, "I want to defend the stage."

"Well," I said, "the Paris *Figaro* has said that it is wrong to judge actresses by the same moral canons that we judge other women; for what would be wrong in other women would be right in actresses, for it is a part of their art."

"Well," he said, "that is just what I believe."

"Well," I said, "that is worse than anything I have ever said about the theater."

While I was in that same city of Cleveland, one of the most highly respected actors was performing with his troupe in the city at that time. It was a famous troupe, known on both sides of the Atlantic, and of high repute. One of the leading ladies in the troupe came under the influence of our meetings, and in conversation with my private secretary, another woman told her what was practically required of any woman who hoped to become a star. When it was reported to me, I could not help but feel that I would rather see a daughter of my own in a coffin than to see her on the stage. Is God pleased when a child of His patronizes an institution like that, which has such an influence upon the women who perform on the stage?

When Mr. Alexander and I were holding meetings at the Royal Albert Hall in London, and I had said some pretty plain things about the stage, I received a letter from a man who at that time was managing more than thirty theaters in London. He wrote me saying, "I am the manager of more than thirty theaters in London at the present time, but I want to write you that every word you have said about the stage is true. I wish I were not in the business, but I am. Nevertheless, what you say is true." A number of people quite prominently connected with the stage gave up that work during our meetings in London.

How about dance? Should a Christian dance? The answer to this question is found in the other question, Will it please God? Is God better pleased when a child of His dances, or when His child refuses to dance? Now there are certain things that we all know about dance. First of all, we know that a familiarity of contact is permitted between the sexes in modern dance that is permitted nowhere else in decent society. How is it any better in dance than it is elsewhere?

When I was in Balarat, Australia, I said some pretty plain things about dancing, which led to a good many of the dancers giving up dance, and to the breaking up of a prominent dance club in the city. Some months afterward, I was crossing over from Tasmania to Australia, and a fellow passenger on the boat was a lawyer from Balarat. This lawyer came to me and said, "Are you not Dr. Torrey?"

"Yes."

"Well, I do not think you were fair to the dancers of Balarat."

"What did I say that was not true?"

He replied, "I simply think you were not fair."

"Yes, but will you state one single thing that was not true?"

He said, "I simply think you were not fair."

"Now see here," I said, "do you dance?"

"Yes."

Can You Get What You Pray For?

"Are you a married man?"

"Yes."

"Does your wife dance?"

"Yes."

"Well, tell me, if you were to see your wife having the same attitude that she takes in the ballroom toward some other man than yourself, at any other place than the ballroom, what would you do?"

He replied, "There would be trouble."

I said, "Will you please tell me how it is any better in the ballroom, to the strains of seductive music, than anywhere else? Now tell me another thing. Do you not know that in every class of society, even the most select, there are some men who are moral lepers?"

He replied, "Of course we all know, Dr. Torrey, that in every class of society there are men who are corrupt."

"And your wife dances with those men?"

"Well," he said, "she does not know their character."

"You are willing," I said, "that your wife should be in the embrace of some other man who is a moral leper, simply because she does not know his character?"

He made no reply. What reply could be made?

Now I do not believe for one single moment that every woman who dances has evil thoughts. I think that some of the girls who dance are sweet, innocent, pure-minded girls; but if they knew the thoughts that were in the minds of the men with whom they dance, they would never go on the floor again.

Three young men came to me in an Eastern college town and said to me. "Dr. Torrey, what have you got against dancing?"

I replied, "Do you dance?"

"Yes."

"Are you Christians?"

"Yes."

"Will you please tell me what your thoughts are when you dance?"

They said, "Our thoughts are all right if we dance with a pure girl."

241

The Power of Prayer

I said, "Do you dance with any other kind of girl?"

"Well," they said, "you know, Dr. Torrey, that there are some girls who are not what they ought to be."

"And," I said, "you dance with them?"

"Yes."

"Well, you have answered your own question."

It is a well-known fact, proven over and over again, that dancing is the greatest feeder of, and auxiliary to, the most awful institution that exists in civilized society today. Oh, if pure women could only know where many of the young men who dance with them go immediately after the dance is over! If I could only tell you things that I know personally—not things that I have read in books, but things that have come under my own personal observation—regarding the effect of dancing, among what are called the better classes of society, there is not a self-respecting woman who would go on the floor again.

But what about cards? Should a Christian play cards? Now I frankly admit that I do not think the case against playing cards is as clear as the case against the theater or dancing, but it is clear enough. Everyone who has studied the matter knows that cards are the gambler's darling weapon. We also know that pretty much every gambler's first lessons that led him to the gaming table took place at the quiet family card table. I have never known a single reformed gambler in my life (and I have known many of them) who did not hate cards as he hated poison. Why? Because he knew that cards were the secret of his own downfall.

When we were holding meetings in Nashville, Tennessee, my wife went out to one of the prisons near Nashville. There she learned of a man who was serving a life sentence for murder, because he had shot a man at the gaming table. He said that he took his first step in that direction by tallying for his mother as she played cards with her friends.

Some years ago a YMCA secretary in Ohio was going to the state penitentiary to visit some of the prisoners. Before he left, a lady came to him and asked, "Are you going to visit the prisoners?"

He said, "Yes."

Can You Get What You Pray For?

She said, "I have a son in that prison. Will you take him this Bible for me, and say that his mother sent it to him?"

The YMCA secretary consented. When he reached the prison he asked for this young man. The young man was brought in. He started to hand him the Bible saying, "Your mother sent you this Bible."

The prisoner looked at him and said, "Did my mother send me that Bible?"

"Yes."

"Well," he said, "you can take it right back to my mother. I do not want my mother's Bible. If my mother had not taught me to play cards, I would not be here today. I do not want my mother's Bible. Take it back to her."

I knew of a family where the father and mother tried to make home so pleasant for their three sons that they would not wish to go anywhere else at night. They did make their home pleasant—the pleasantest place in the whole community, and the sons were perfectly content to spend their nights at home. Among other things, to amuse their children, this father and mother played cards with them. Of the three sons, one did not have a taste for playing cards. He was not better than the other two; his tastes simply ran in another direction. The other two played cards at home. Now this theory of making the home pleasant would have been all right if young men were always to stay at home, but the time comes for these young men to leave home. They left home, and the two who had learned to play cards at home, with their Christian father and mother, both became gamblers.

Major Cole, the evangelist, was once holding meetings in an Arkansas city. At one of the meetings in the Presbyterian church, a disreputable looking man came in and took a seat over on the right-hand side of the church. When the meeting was opened for testimonies, this moral derelict rose in his place, looked around the church, and said, "All this looks very familiar to me. When I was a boy I attended this church. My father was an elder in this church. This is our old pew, where I am standing. There were seven of us boys who were in a Sunday school class. Our teacher was a very kind lady. She not only taught us the Bible on Sundays, but she also invited us to her house on Saturday afternoons to teach us the Bible and to play games with us. One day after we had been going there a while, she brought out a pack of cards and showed us tricks with the cards. Later we played games with the cards. We soon wanted more cards and asked the teacher if she would give us less Bible and more cards. But we did not get enough cards there, so we left Sunday school and spent our Sunday afternoons in a cotton press, playing cards.

"There were seven members in the class. Two of those members have already been hanged; two are in state prisons at the present time. I have lost track of one. The sixth member of the class is at present a fugitive from justice, and if the authorities knew where he was he would be under arrest. I am the seventh member of that class, and if the authorities knew where I was I would be under arrest." Just then a lady dressed in black, in the back of the church, sprang to her feet, came running down the aisle with her hands flung in the air, and crying, "Oh, my God, and I am that teacher," she fell at his feet as though she were dead. They thought for a while that she was dead. I would not like to have been that teacher.

Oh, fathers and mothers, happy is the young man or young woman who goes out into the world not knowing one card from another, and fully instructed in the peril there is in cards. And if any of you parents have a pack of cards in your home, I advise you to burn it up as soon as you get home.

What about the movies? I do not need to dwell upon that. The movies are worse than the theater ever dreamed of being—immeasurably worse. The stage, at its worst, was never so occupied with the most open depiction of degrading sin as are the movies today, and the character of movie actors and actresses is notorious. I do not mean to say for one single moment that every movie actress is immoral. I know better. One of the most modest and sweetest Christian young women I ever knew, who is now a minister's wife and a beautiful Christian mother, was, when I first became acquainted with her, a movie actress. And I do not question that there are others like her. But the lives of movie actors and actresses, taken as a whole, are full of the most terrible temptations, and many have yielded to those temptations. Movies as they exist today (I am not talking about educational movies, although some that are paraded as educational are among the vilest there are) are, for the most part, one of the greatest menaces that exist to the young life of our country, and also to pure family life. Is God pleased when a child of His patronizes a movie, when it is what we all know it is today?

There are many other things that I might mention, but this is enough to illustrate the principle. But someone will ask, "Dr. Torrey, do you mean to say that dancing, theatergoing, card playing, and going to the movies are sins in the sense that stealing, adultery, murder, gossiping, and slandering your neighbors are sins?" No, I do not say that. "Then," you ask, "where is the harm in it?" The harm is right here: our indulging in these things does not please God, and therefore they rob our prayers of power. I want every ounce of power in prayer that I can have, and if there is anything, no matter how innocent it may be in itself, or however much can be said in defense of it, that robs prayer of power, I am going to give it up.

Remember, in all that I am saying, I am not legislating for the world. If it were in my power to pass a law that there should be no more dancing, no more card playing, no more theaters, no more movies, I would not pass it. I would not believe in it. No, I am not legislating at all for the unsaved about these matters, or other matters. I am simply trying to tell men and women who profess to be Christians how to get the most out of your Christian life, and, in particular, how to have power in prayer. Beyond a doubt, these things rob prayer of power. The Christian who dances, goes to the theater, plays cards, attends the movies, or does many other things that are not pleasing to God, cannot be a man or woman of power in prayer.

In summary, the ones who can pray so that God will hear their prayers, and give them whatever they ask, are those who study the Word of God every day of their lives to find out what the will of God is, and do it every time they find it. Furthermore, these are the people who make it their study to get thoroughly acquainted with God, so that they know instinctively what will please God and what will displease God. Then, in every action of their lives, they seek to do the thing that pleases God, whether it pleases men or not, and not to do the thing that displeases God, no matter who else may do it. Oh, that we all might enter into the wonderful place of privilege described in our text: *"Whatsoever we ask, we receive of him, because we keep his commandments, and do those things that are pleasing in his sight."*

6

Praying in the Name of Jesus Christ

Whatsoever ye shall ask in my name, that will I do,
that the Father may be glorified in the Son.
If ye shall ask any thing in my name, I will do it.
—John 14:13–14

This is one of the most familiar, most wonderful, and at the same time most commonly misunderstood promises in the Bible regarding God's willingness to answer prayer.

Here our Lord Jesus Christ Himself tells us that if a certain class of people pray in a certain way, He will give them the very thing that they ask. Look at the promise again. *"Whatsoever ye shall ask in my name, that will I do, that the Father may be glorified in the Son. If ye shall ask any thing in my name, I will do it."* These words are plain, simple, positive, very precious, and cheering. They tell us that there are certain people who can get from God anything that they ask for, if only they will ask for it in a certain way.

There is a doctrine regarding prayer that is very common in our day. It is this: "If we pray, our praying will do much good in many ways. We may not get the very thing that we ask, but we will get something, something just as good as what we ask, or perhaps something far better than what we ask." I do not doubt that there is a measure of truth in this doctrine. It is a good thing sometimes that some of us do not get what we ask for; we are so careless, thoughtless, hasty, and so little under the control of the Holy Spirit when we pray, that it is oftentimes a good thing for us, and a good thing for others, that we do not get the very thing that we ask. It would be a great misfortune if some of us got some

247

of the things that we ask of God. But while there is a certain measure of truth in that doctrine, it is not the doctrine of prayer taught in the Bible.

The doctrine of prayer taught in the Bible is that there are certain people who can pray in a certain way and who will get not merely some good thing, or something just as good as what they ask, or something even better than what they ask, but the very thing that they ask. *"Whatsoever ye shall ask in my name, that will I do, that the Father may be glorified in the Son. If ye shall ask any thing in my name, I will do it."* There are two things to notice about this promise: first, to whom the promise is made, and who can ask in the name of the Lord Jesus and get the very thing they ask; second, how these persons must pray in order to get what they ask.

To Whom the Promise Is Made

First of all, notice to whom this promise is made. One of the most common sources of misinterpretation of the Bible is the applying of promises that are made to a certain clearly defined class of people to whom the promises were never made. God does not promise to answer the prayers of everyone; indeed, He tells us plainly that there are people to whose prayers He will pay no attention whatsoever. In the case of the present promise, we are told very definitely in the context just whose prayers God will answer, if they are offered in a certain way. Who are the people to whom God says through His Son Jesus Christ, *"Whatsoever ye shall ask in my name, that will I do"*? They are clearly described in verse twelve, the verse that immediately precedes, and verses fifteen and seventeen, the verses that follow the promise.

THOSE WHO BELIEVE ON JESUS CHRIST

First of all, then, look at verse twelve: *"Verily, verily, I say unto you, He that believeth on me, the works that I do shall he do also; and greater works than these shall he do; because I go unto my Father."* And then our Lord goes on to say, *"Whatsoever ye* [that is, you who believe on the Son, as just defined] *shall ask in my name, that will I do.*" The promise is therefore made, first of all, to those who believe on Jesus Christ. Notice that it is not made to those who believe *about* Jesus Christ, but those who believe *on* Jesus Christ. People are constantly confusing in their own minds two entirely different things—believing about Jesus Christ and believing on Jesus Christ. God does not promise to answer the prayers of those who merely believe about Jesus Christ even though their faith is perfectly and rigidly orthodox. He does promise to answer the prayers of those who believe on Jesus Christ. A person may believe perfectly correctly about Jesus Christ, and yet not believe on Him at all. The Devil himself believes about Jesus Christ, and is undoubtedly perfectly orthodox; he knows more about Jesus Christ as He really is than we do, but the devil certainly does not believe on Jesus Christ. There are many today who, because their view of Jesus Christ is perfectly orthodox, imagine that they believe on Jesus Christ. But that does not logically follow at all.

What does it mean to believe on Jesus Christ? To believe on Jesus Christ means to put our personal confidence in Jesus Christ as what He claims to be, and to accept Him to be to us what He offers Himself to be. It means that we accept Him as our Savior, as the One who *"bare our sins in his own body on the tree"* (1 Pet. 2:24). It means that we trust God to forgive us because Jesus Christ died in our place, and also that we accept Him as our Lord and Master to whom we surrender the absolute control of our lives. This we are told in so many words in John 1:12: *"But as many as received him, to them gave he power to become the sons of God, even to them that believe on his name."*

Nowhere in the entire Bible does God promise to hear the prayers of people who do not believe on Jesus Christ; that is, the prayers of people who are not united with Jesus Christ by a living faith in Himself as their Savior and Lord. I do not say that God never answers the prayers of those who are not believers on Jesus Christ. I believe that He sometimes does. He answered some of my prayers before I was, in the Bible sense, a believer on Him, but He does not promise to do it. His doing it belongs to what the

249

old theologians used to call so aptly "the uncovenanted mercies of God." He promises most plainly and most positively to answer the prayers of those who believe on Jesus Christ, but never does He promise to answer the prayers of those who do not believe on Jesus Christ. Anyone who does not believe on Jesus Christ has no right whatsoever to expect God to answer his prayers, and he has no cause whatsoever to complain that the promises of God are not true because He does not answer his prayers. There are many people who say they know that God does not answer prayer because He has never answered their prayers, and they have tried praying time and time again. But that is no proof that God does not answer prayer, for God has never promised to answer their prayers.

One of the many good things about believing on Jesus Christ is that it puts us on praying ground; it puts us in the place where we may go to God in every time of need and get from Him the very thing that we need and ask for. I would rather be on praying ground, in such a relationship with God that He can and will answer my prayers, than to have the combined wealth of a hundred Rockefellers. Times will come in the life of every one of us, sooner or later, when no earthly friend can help us, and no amount of wealth can help us; but the time will never come when God cannot help us and deliver us completely. This important question, therefore, confronts every one of us: "Do I believe on Jesus Christ?" Not do I believe about Him, but do I believe on Him? If you do not, there is but one wise thing to do that has even the slightest semblance of intelligence, and that is to believe on Jesus Christ right now. Put your confidence in Him as your Savior right now, and look to God to forgive your sins right now because Jesus Christ died in your place. Put your confidence in Him right now as your Lord and Master to whom you surrender the entire control of your thoughts and your life and your conduct.

THOSE WHO DO THE LORD'S WILL

But this is not all of the description of those whose prayers God promises to answer. The rest of the description of this fortunate class we find in the verse that follows the promise: *"If ye love me, keep my commandments"* (John 14:15). The promise, therefore, is made to those who believe on Jesus Christ and who love Him with that genuine love that leads them to keep His commandments. Of course, to keep His commandments we must know them, and to know them we must study His Word, in which He has revealed His will to us. Thus we see that the promise is made to those who study the Word of God each day of their lives so that they may know what God's will is regarding their conduct, and who, when they discover it, do it every time. This brings us to just where we were when we were studying 1 John 3:22: *"Whatsoever we ask, we receive of him, because we keep his commandments, and do those things that are pleasing in his sight."*

There is not a promise in the whole Book of God that God will hear and answer the prayers of a disobedient child. If we are to expect God to listen to us when we pray to Him, we must first of all listen to God when He speaks to us in His Word. We must obey God every time He commands; then, and only then, will He hear us every time we pray. We must study His Word each day of our lives so that we may find out what His will is, and when we find it we must do it every time. Then, and only then, are we on praying ground.

To sum it all up, then, the promise of God to give to a certain class of people whatever they ask in a certain way is made to those who are united to Him by a living faith and an obedient love—to them and to them alone. Someone may ask, "Which is more important in the prayer life, that we have a living faith in Jesus Christ or an obedient love for Jesus Christ?" The answer is simple. You cannot have one without the other. If you have a living faith in Jesus Christ, it will lead inevitably to an obedient love for Jesus Christ. Paul stated this point clearly in Galatians 5:6: *"For in Jesus Christ neither circumcision availeth any thing, nor uncircumcision; but faith which worketh by love."* On the other hand, you will never love Jesus Christ until you begin by believing in His love for you. We begin by believing in His love for us, and we end by loving Him. Or, as John put it in 1 John 4:19: *"We love him, because he first loved us."*

The Power of Prayer

Many people are trying to love God as a matter of duty, but no one ever succeeds in that attempt. Of course, we ought to love God, for He is infinitely worthy of our love. We ought to love Him because of His moral perfection, and because He is the infinite One and our Creator; but no one ever did love Him for these reasons, nor ever will or ever can. Here is where the Unitarians made their mistake. They tried to love God as a matter of duty. We never can and never will. But if we will first of all just put our trust in His wonderful love for us, vile and worthless sinners that we are, we will soon find ourselves loving Him without effort. Love for God is the inevitable outcome of our believing in His love for us.

One day in London a little girl came to Mark Guy Pearse (1842–1930), the great English preacher, looked up wistfully into his face, and said, "Mr. Pearse, I don't love Jesus. I wish I did love Jesus, but I don't love Jesus. Won't you please tell me how to love Jesus?" And the great preacher looked down into those eager eyes and said to her, "Little girl, as you go home today, keep saying to yourself, 'Jesus loves me. Jesus loves me. Jesus loves me.' And when you come back next Sunday I think you will be able to say, 'I love Jesus.'"

The following Sunday the little girl came up to him again. With happy eyes and a radiant face, she exclaimed, "Oh, Mr. Pearse, I do love Jesus! Last Sunday as I went home I kept saying to myself, 'Jesus loves me. Jesus loves me. Jesus loves me.' I began to think about His love, and I began to think how He died upon the cross in my place, and I found my cold heart growing warm, and the first I knew, it was full of love for Jesus."

That is the only way anyone will ever learn to love the Lord Jesus—by first of all believing what the Bible tells us about His love for us even when we are the vilest of sinners (Rom. 5:8); how He died in our place; how *"he was wounded for our transgressions, he was bruised for our iniquities: the chastisement of our peace was upon him; and with his stripes we are healed"* (Isa. 53:5). We begin by believing on Him; we begin by believing in His great love for us, and we wind up loving Him and showing our love to Him by studying His Word daily to find out His will, and doing it every time we find it. Then we are on praying ground.

Praying in the Name of Jesus Christ

Some years ago a great Scottish teacher delivered an address at Northfield on the subject of whether it was better to have faith in Jesus Christ without love, or to have love for Jesus Christ without faith. He came to the conclusion that it was better to have love without faith, than it was to have faith without love. But the whole address, though a great address in many ways, was built upon a misunderstanding and a false assumption. He had assumed that we could have love without faith, but we cannot. Love for Christ is the outcome of faith in Christ, and faith in Christ is the root out of which love for Christ grows. To discuss whether it is better to have faith without love, or love without faith, is like discussing whether it would be better to have an apple orchard in which the trees had good roots but bore no apples, or to have an orchard in which the trees had no roots but bore good apples. Of course, an orchard where the trees had no roots would bear no apples at all. Likewise, a life that is not rooted in faith in the love of Jesus Christ for us has no roots and cannot bear the fruit of love, and the obedience that comes out of love. So, then, this promise that we are considering is made to those who have a living faith in Jesus Christ that manifests itself in an obedient love.

How a Person Must Pray

But how must those who are united with Jesus Christ by a living faith that reveals itself in an obedient love pray if they are to get the very thing that they ask? Let us read the verse again: *"Whatsoever ye shall ask in my name, that will I do, that the Father may be glorified in the Son. If ye shall ask any thing in my name, I will do it."* If we are to get what we ask from God, we must ask it in the name of the Lord Jesus. Prayer in the name of Jesus Christ prevails with God. No other prayer does. There is no other approach to God for any man or woman except through Jesus Christ, as the Lord Himself tells us in John 14:6: *"I am the way, the truth, and the life: no man cometh unto the Father, but by me."*

But just what does it mean to pray in the name of Jesus? I have heard many explanations of this. Some of them were so profound, so mysterious, so mixed, or so obscure that when I finished reading them or listening to them, I knew less about it than when I started. I have heard two great Bible teachers, two of the most renowned Bible teachers in the world, say that to "pray in the name of Jesus means to pray in the person of Jesus." Now I do not question that these two Bible teachers had some definite thought in their own minds, but it certainly conveyed no clear and definite thought to my mind. The truth is, there is nothing mysterious about this matter. It is as simple as anything possibly can be, so simple that any intelligent child can understand it.

I am always suspicious of profound explanations of the Scriptures, explanations that require a scholar or philosopher to understand them. The Bible is the plain man's Book. The Lord Jesus Himself said in Matthew 11:25, *"I thank thee, O Father, Lord of heaven and earth, because thou hast hid these things from the wise and prudent, and hast revealed them unto babes."* In at least ninety-nine cases out of a hundred, the meaning of Scripture that lies on the surface, the meaning that any simple-minded man, woman, or child who really wants to know the truth and to obey it would see in it, is what it really means.

I have great sympathy with the little child who, when she once heard an educated attempt to explain away the plain meaning of Scripture, exclaimed, "If God did not mean what He said, why didn't He say what He meant?" Well, God always does say just what He means, just what you and I would understand by it if our wills were really surrendered to God, if we really desired to know exactly what God wished to tell us and not to read our own opinions into the Bible. By this expression, *"in my name,"* He means exactly what the words would indicate to any earnest and intelligent seeker of the truth who was willing to take God's words at their exact face value.

When you come across a word or a phrase in the Bible and do not know what it means, the thing to do is not to run off to a dictionary, a commentary, or some book of theology, but to take your concordance, go through the Bible, and look up every place where that word or phrase, or synonymous words or phrases, are used. Then you will know just what the word or phrase means. The meaning of words and phrases in the Bible is to be determined just as it is in all other books—by usage. I have done this with the phrase *"in my name"* and with the synonymous phrases *"in his name"* and *"in the name of Jesus Christ."* I have looked up every passage in the Bible where they are found, and I have discovered what I suspected at the outset—that these phrases mean exactly the same in the Bible as they do in ordinary, everyday speech.

What does it mean in ordinary, everyday speech to ask something in another person's name? Let me illustrate what it means. Suppose I were to walk into a bank at which I do not have an account. I write out a check, "Pay to the order of R. A. Torrey the sum of five dollars." Then I sign my own name at the bottom of the check, go to the teller's window, and ask to cash that check. What would I be doing? I would be asking that bank to give me five dollars. And in whose name would I be asking it? In my own name. And what would happen? The teller would take the check and look at it, and then look at me, and then he would say, "Dr. Torrey, do you have an account at this bank?"

"No."

Then what would the teller say? Something like this: "We would like to accommodate you, but that is not good business. You have no claim whatsoever on this bank, and we cannot honor your check even though it is for only five dollars." But suppose, instead of that, some man who had a hundred thousand dollars in that bank were to call me and say, "Dr. Torrey, I am greatly interested in the work of the Bible Institute. I have wanted to give some money toward it, and I am going to hand it to you." And then he makes out a check, "Pay to the order of R. A. Torrey the sum of five thousand dollars," and signs his name at the bottom of the check. So I go to the bank again. In presenting that check, what would I be doing? I would be asking that bank to give me five thousand dollars. And in whose name would I be asking it? Not in my own name, but in the name of the man whose name is signed at the bottom of the check, and who has claims of a hundred thousand dollars on that bank.

What would happen? The teller would look at the check, and he would not ask me whether I had any money in that bank. He would not care whether I had a penny in that bank or in any bank. If the check were properly written, and properly endorsed, he would count me out five thousand dollars; for I would be asking it in the other man's name, asking it on the ground of his claims on that bank.

Now that is exactly what praying in the name of Jesus Christ means. It means that we go to the Bank of Heaven, on which neither you nor I nor any other man on earth has any claim of his own, but upon which Jesus Christ has infinite claims. In Jesus' name, which He has given us a right to put on our checks, if we are united with Him by a living faith that reveals itself in an obedient love, we may ask whatever we need. Or, to put it another way, to pray in the name of Jesus Christ is to recognize that we have no claims on God whatsoever, that God owes us nothing whatsoever, that we deserve nothing from God; but, believing what God Himself tells us about Jesus Christ's claims upon Him, we ask God for things on the ground of Jesus Christ's claims upon God. And when we draw near to God in that way, we can get *"whatsoever we ask,"* no matter how great it may be.

Praying in the name of Christ means more than merely attaching the phrase "in Jesus' name" or "for Jesus' sake" to your prayers. Many people ask for things and attach those phrases to their prayers, while all the while they are really approaching God on the ground of some claim that they only imagine they have on God. In reality, though they use the phrase, they are not praying in the name of Jesus Christ but praying in their own name. A man who realizes that he has no claims on God might not put that phrase in his prayer at all, but he can believe that Jesus Christ has claims on God and can approach God on the ground of Jesus Christ's claims.

Here is where many people fail in getting an answer to prayer. Such people may ask things of God on the ground of some claim they imagine they have on God. They think that because they are such good Christians, so consistent in their lives and so active in their service, God is under obligation to grant their prayers.

In Melbourne, Australia, as I went on the platform one day at a businessmen's meeting, a note was put in my hands. This note read as follows:

Praying in the Name of Jesus Christ

Dear Dr. Torrey:

I am in great perplexity. I have been praying for a long time for something that I am confident is according to God's will, but I do not get it. I have been a member of the Presbyterian Church for thirty years, and have tried to be a consistent one all the time. I have been superintendent in the Sunday school for twenty-five years, and an elder in the church for twenty years; and yet God does not answer my prayer, and I cannot understand it. Can you explain it to me?

I took the note with me on to the platform and read it and said, "It is perfectly easy to explain. This man thinks that because he has been a consistent church member for thirty years, a faithful Sunday school superintendent for twenty-five years, and an elder in the church for twenty years, God is under obligation to answer his prayer. He is really praying in his own name, and God will not hear our prayers when we approach Him in that way. We must, if we want God to answer our prayers, give up any thought that we have any claims on God. Not one of us deserves anything from God. If we got what we deserved, every last one of us would spend eternity in hell. But Jesus Christ has great claims on God, and we should go to God in our prayers, not on the ground of any goodness in ourselves, but on the ground of Jesus Christ's claims."

At the close of the meeting, a gentleman stepped up to me and said, "I wrote that note. You have hit the nail square on the head. I did think that because I had been a consistent church member for thirty years, a Sunday school superintendent for twenty-five years, and an elder in the church for twenty years, God was under obligation to answer my prayers. I see my mistake."

Multitudes are making the same mistake. They imagine that because they are faithful church members, and active in Christian service, God is under obligation to answer their prayers, and they have some claim on God. Not one of us has any claim on God. We are all miserable sinners. But Jesus Christ has claims on God, and He has given us the right to draw near to God in His name, that is, on the ground of His claims on God.

Therefore, to pray in the name of Jesus Christ means simply this: that we recognize that we have no claims whatsoever on God; that we have no merit whatsoever in His sight; and furthermore, that Jesus Christ has immeasurable claims on God, and has given us the right to draw near to God, not on the ground of our claims, but on the ground of His claims. When we thus draw near to God in prayer, God will give us what we ask.

What a precious privilege it is to pray in the name of Jesus Christ! How rich we are if we only realize that Jesus Christ has given us the privilege of drawing near to the heavenly Father in His name, on the ground of His claims on God. When I was a boy, my father had put my brother, next older than me, in charge of the expenditures of the home, because my oldest brother was away from home. The bank account was in the name of my next-older brother. But he, too, was called away from home, and so he turned over the matter of paying bills and the conduct of the business to me. He gave me a checkbook full of blank checks with his signature on them and said, "Whenever you want any money, just fill out one of these checks for the amount that you want, and go and present it at the bank."

How rich I felt with that checkbook full of blank checks! I could fill one out at any time and go to the bank and get what I asked for. But what is that compared with what the Lord Jesus Christ has done for us? He has put His entire bank account at our disposal. He has given us the right to draw near to the Father in His name, and to ask anything of God on the ground not of our claims on God, but on the ground of His claims on God.

Even before D. L. Moody gave up business, he was active in Christian work and often went out from Chicago to some of the country towns and held short series of meetings. At one time he was holding a series of meetings in a town in Illinois some distance from Chicago. The wife of the judge of that district came to him and said, "Mr. Moody, won't you go and talk to my husband?"

Mr. Moody replied, "I cannot talk to your husband. Your husband is an educated man; I am nothing but an ignorant shoe clerk from Chicago."

Praying in the Name of Jesus Christ

But the judge's wife was very insistent that he should go and talk with him, and finally Mr. Moody consented to go. When he entered the outer office of the judge, the law clerks snickered audibly as they thought of how quickly the clever judge would dispose of this ignorant young worker from Chicago. Mr. Moody went into the judge's inner office and said to him, "Judge, I cannot talk with you. You are an educated man, and I am nothing but an uneducated shoe salesman from Chicago. But I want to ask you one thing. When you are converted, will you let me know?"

The judge answered with a contemptuous laugh, "Yes, young man, when I am converted I will let you know. Yes, when I am converted I will let you know. Good day."

As Mr. Moody passed out of the inner office to the outer office, the judge raised his voice higher so that the clerks in the outer office might hear, "Yes, young man, when I am converted I will let you know," and the law clerks snickered louder than before.

But the judge was converted within a year. Mr. Moody went back to the town and called on the judge.

He said, "Judge, do you mind telling me how you were converted?"

"No, Mr. Moody," he replied, "I will be very glad to tell you. One night after you were here, my wife went to the prayer meeting as she always did, and I stayed home as I always did and read the evening paper. After a while, as I sat there reading, I began to feel very miserable. I began to feel that I was a great sinner. Before my wife got home, I was so miserable that I did not dare face my wife, and I went to bed before she reached the house. She came up to my room and asked, 'Are you ill?' I replied, 'No, I wasn't feeling well and thought I would go to bed. Good night.' I was miserable all night, and when morning came I felt so badly that I did not dare face my wife at the breakfast table. I simply looked into the breakfast room and said, 'Wife, I am not feeling well. I'll not eat any breakfast this morning. Good-bye, I am going down to the office.' When I got to the office, I felt so miserable that I told my clerks that they could take a holiday. When they had left, I locked the outer door, went into my inner office, locked that door, and sat down. I felt more and more miserable as I thought of my sins, until at last I knelt down and said, 'Oh, God, forgive my sins.' There was no answer. And I cried more earnestly, 'Oh, God, forgive my sins.' There was still no answer. I would not say, 'Oh, God, for Jesus Christ's sake forgive my sins,' for I was a Unitarian and did not believe in the Atonement. Again I cried, 'Oh, God, forgive my sins.' But there was no answer. At last I was so perfectly miserable at the thought of my sins that I cried, 'Oh, God, for Jesus Christ's sake forgive my sins.' And I found instant peace."

There is no use in our trying to approach God in any other way than in the name of Jesus Christ, on the ground of His claims upon God, and on the ground of His atoning death, by which He took our sins upon Himself and made it possible for us to approach God on the ground of His claims upon God.

While we have no claims upon God because of any goodness or service of our own, Jesus Christ, as I have said, has infinite claims upon God and has given us the right to approach God in His name. Thus, we ought to go boldly to God and ask great things of God. Oftentimes when we pray and ask something that seems to be pretty big, the devil will come and say to us, "You ought not to pray for anything so great as that. You are such a poor Christian, and that is more than you deserve." Yes, it is more than we deserve, but it is not as much as Jesus Christ deserves. Time and again Satan has said to me when I have dared to ask something of God that seemed very large, "Oh, don't dare to ask as great a thing as that. You are not worthy of anything as great as that." I have replied, "I know that I am not worthy of anything as great as that. I am not worthy of anything at all, but Jesus Christ is worthy of that, and I am asking not on the ground of my claims upon God, but on the ground of His." Sometimes as I think of how precious the name of Jesus Christ is to God, how He delights to honor the name of His Son, I grow very bold and ask God for great things.

Do you realize that we honor the name of Christ by asking great things in His name? Do you realize that we dishonor that name by not daring to ask great things in His name? Oh, have faith in the power of Jesus' name, and dare to ask great things in His name!

During the Civil War, there was a father and mother in Columbus, Ohio, who had an only son, the joy of their hearts. Soon after the outbreak of the war, he came home one day and said to his father and mother, "I have enlisted in the army." Of course, they felt badly to have their son leave home, but they loved their country and were willing to make the sacrifice of giving their son to go to the war and fight for his country. After he had gone to the front, he wrote home regularly, telling his father and mother about his experiences in camp and elsewhere. His letters were full of brightness and good cheer, and they brought joy to the father's and mother's lonely hearts. But one day at the regular time, no letter came.

Days passed, and no letter. Weeks passed, and they wondered what might have happened to their boy. One day a letter came from the United States government, and in it they were told that there had been a great battle, that many had been killed, and that their son was among those who had been killed in battle. The light went out of that home. Days and weeks, months and years passed by. The war came to an end. One morning as they were sitting at the breakfast table, the maid came in and said, "There is a poor, ragged fellow at the door, and he wants to speak to you. But I knew you did not wish to speak to a man like him, and he handed me this note and asked me to put it in your hand." And she put a soiled and crumpled piece of paper in the hands of the father. The father opened it, and when he glanced at it his eyes fell upon the writing. Then he was startled, for he recognized the writing of his son. The note said:

> Dear Father and Mother:
> I have been shot and have only a short time to live, and I am writing you this last farewell note. As I write, there is kneeling beside me my most intimate friend in the company, and when the war is over he will bring you this note. When he does, be kind to him for Charlie's sake.
>
> Your son, Charles

There was nothing in that house that was too good for that poor tramp "for Charlie's sake," and there is nothing in heaven or on earth too good, or too great, for you and me in Jesus' name. Oh, be bold and ask great things of God in Jesus' name!

7

The Prayer of Faith

*And this is the boldness ["confidence," KJV] which we have toward
him, that, if we ask anything according to his will, he heareth us:
and if we know that he heareth us whatsoever we ask, we know
that we have the petitions which we have asked of him.*
—1 John 5:14–15 RV

This is one of the most remarkable statements found in the
whole Bible. It deals with God answering prayer, and our
knowing that God has heard our prayer and granted the
thing we have asked of Him. Look at it again:

*And this is the boldness which we have toward him, that, if we ask
anything according to his will, he heareth us: and if we know that
he heareth us whatsoever we ask, we know that we have the petitions
which we have asked of him.*

Please note carefully exactly what God tells us in this passage. We are told that there is a way in which certain people can
pray so as not only to get the very thing that they ask, but also to
know before they actually get it that God has heard their prayer
and has granted the thing that they have asked of Him. Certainly that is an astonishing statement: it gives to us the plain and
positive assurance that there are some people who can pray in
such a way that they will not only get whatever they ask, but furthermore they may know before they get it that God has heard
their prayers and granted the thing they have asked. It is certainly a great joy to be able to know that the prayers we have
offered have been heard and the thing for which we have asked

has been granted, and to be just as sure that it is ours as we will be afterward when we actually have it in our hands.

Is God's Promise Made to Everyone?

Please note, first of all, just who it is to whom God makes this promise. As I have said so often before, when you try to understand and apply the promises of God that you find in the Bible, you must always be very careful to note just exactly who the people are to whom the promise is made. In the verse that immediately precedes our text verse, we are told just who the persons are to whom this promise is made: *"These things have I written unto you, that ye may know that ye have eternal life, even unto you that believe on the name of the Son of God"* (1 John 5:13 RV). Then immediately follows the promise that we are studying, so it is clear that the promise is made to those who *"believe on the name of the Son of God,"* to them and to no one else. Anyone who does not believe on the name of the Son of God has no right whatsoever to take this promise for himself, or to think that if he does take the promise for himself and it is not fulfilled that God's Word has failed. The fault is with himself, and not with God's Word. He has taken for himself a promise that was made to someone else. Just what it means to believe on the Son of God we are told in John 1:12: *"But as many as received him* [that is, received Jesus Christ], *to them gave he the right to become children of God, even to them that believe on his name"* (RV).

So John himself interpreted "believing on the name of the Son of God" to mean receiving the Son of God, that is, receiving Him to be to us what He offers to be to all who put their trust in Him—our personal Savior who bore our sins in His own body on the cross (1 Pet. 2:24), and our Lord and Master to whom we surrender the absolute control of our thoughts, our wills, and our conduct. So then, this promise is made to those who have received Jesus Christ as their personal Savior, who have trusted God to forgive them because Jesus Christ died on the cross in their place, and who have also received Him as their Lord and Master to whom they have surrendered the absolute control of their thoughts, their wills, and their conduct. They have made an absolute surrender to Jesus Christ, the Son of God. The promise is made to them and to no one else, and no one else has the least right to claim it.

Here is where many go astray. They do not really believe on the name of the Son of God; they have not really received Him, yet they take for themselves this promise that was never made to them.

How We Must Pray

Now we come to the question, "How must those who *'believe on the name of the Son of God'* pray in order to know that God has heard their prayers and that He has granted the thing that they asked?" Read 1 John 5:14 again: *"And this is the boldness which we have toward him, that, if we ask anything according to his will, he heareth us."* To know that God has heard our prayer and granted us the thing we asked, we must pray according to His will. When we who believe on the name of the Son of God pray for anything that we know to be according to His will, then we may know, for the all-sufficient reason that God says so in His Word, that God has heard the prayer and granted us the thing that we ask. We may know it not because we feel it, not because of any inward illumination of the Holy Spirit, but we may know it for the very best of all reasons—because God says so in His Word, and God *"cannot lie"* (Titus 1:2).

But is it possible for us to know what the will of God is, so that we can be sure even while we are praying that we are asking something that is *"according to his will"*? We certainly can know the will of God with absolute certainty in many cases when we pray. How can we know the will of God?

By His Promises

In the first place, we may know the will of God by the promises in His Word. The Bible was given to us for the specific purpose of revealing to us the will of God. When we find that anything is definitely promised in the Word of God, we know that that is His will, for He has said so in so many words. And when we who believe on the name of the Son of God go to God and ask Him for anything that is definitely promised in His Word, we may know with absolute certainty that God has heard our prayers and that the thing we have asked of God is granted. We do not have to feel it—God says so, and that is enough.

For example, God says in James 1:5, *"If any of you lacketh wisdom, let him ask of God, who giveth to all liberally and upbraideth not; and it shall be given him"* (RV). So when I go to God and ask for wisdom, if I am a believer on the name of the Son of God, I know with absolute certainty that God has heard my prayer and that wisdom will be granted.

Some years ago I was speaking on the subject of prayer at a YMCA Bible Conference at Mahtomede, White Bear Lake, Minnesota. I had to hurry immediately from the amphitheater to the train. As I went out of the amphitheater, I saw another minister from Minneapolis. He was to immediately follow me on the program and was greatly excited. He stopped me and said, "Mr. Torrey, I am going to tear to pieces everything that you have said to these young men this morning."

I replied, "If I have not spoken according to the Bible, I hope you will tear it to pieces. But if I have spoken according to the Book, you had better be careful how you try to tear it to pieces."

"But," he exclaimed, "you have produced upon these young men the impression that they can pray for things and get the very thing that they ask for."

I replied, "I do not know whether that is the impression that I have produced or not, but it certainly is the impression I intended to produce."

"But," he said, "that is not right; you must say, 'If it is according to God's will.'"

I replied, "If you do not know that the thing you have asked for is according to God's will, then it is all right to say, 'If it is according to Your will.' But if you know God's will, what is the need of saying, 'If it is according to Your will'?"

"But," he said, "we cannot know God's will."

The Prayer of Faith

I answered, "What was the Bible given to us for if it was not to reveal God's will? Now when you find a definite promise in the Bible and take that promise to God, don't you know that you have asked something according to His will? For example, we read in James 1:5, *'If any of you lacketh wisdom, let him ask of God, who giveth to all liberally and upbraideth not; and it shall be given him'* (RV). Now when you ask for wisdom, do you not know that God is going to give it?"

"But," he said, "I do not know what wisdom is."

I said, "If you did you would not need to ask for it, but whatever it may be, do you not know that God is going to give it?" He made no reply. I never heard that he tried to tear what I said to pieces, but I know that he later spoke boldly on the subject of confidently asking God for the things that we need of Him, and that are according to His will.

When you have a definite promise in God's Word, you do not need to put any *ifs* before it. All the promises of God are *"yea, and...Amen"* in Christ Jesus (2 Cor. 1:20). They are absolutely sure, and if you plead any plain promise in God's Word, you do not need to put any *ifs* in your petition. You may know that you are asking something that is according to God's will, and it is your privilege to know that God has heard you. It is your privilege to know that you have the thing you have asked; for it is your privilege to get up from prayer with the same absolute certainty that that thing is yours that you will have afterward when you actually see it in your hands.

Suppose some cold winter morning when I lived in Chicago I had gone down to South Clark Street. It was then teeming with poor men. Suppose some shivering tramp came up to me and said, "Mr. Torrey, it is very cold, and I need an overcoat. Will you give me an overcoat?" I might have replied, "If you will come over to my house this afternoon at 39 East Pearson Street, at two o'clock, I'll give you an overcoat." Promptly at two o'clock, the tramp makes his appearance. I meet him at the door and bring him into the house. Then he says to me, "Mr. Torrey, you said to me this morning on South Clark Street that if I would come to your house at two o'clock this afternoon, you would give me an overcoat. Now if you will, please give me that overcoat." What would I say? I'd say, "Man, what did you say?" "I said, if you will, please give me that overcoat." "But why do you put any *if* in? Did I not say I would?" "Yes." "Do you doubt my word?" "No." "Then why do you put in an *if*?"

Why should we put any *if*s in when we take to God any promise of His own? Does God ever lie? There are many cases in which we do not know the will of God, and in such cases it is all right to put in "if it is Your will." And even in cases where we do know His will, our prayers should always be in submission to His will, for the dearest thing to the true child of God is God's will. But there is no need to put any *if*s in when He has revealed His will. To include an *if* in such a case as that is to doubt God, to doubt His Word, and really to make God a liar.

Our text verse is one of the most abused passages in the Bible. God put it into His Word to give us *"confidence"* (KJV) when we pray. It is constantly misused to make us uncertain when we pray. Often when some young and enthusiastic believer is asking for something with great confidence, some cautious brother will go to him after the meeting is over and say to him, "Now, my young brother, you must not be so confident as that in your prayers. It may not be God's will, and we ought to be submissive to the will of God. You should say, 'If it is Your will.'" And so some people always have an element of uncertainty in their prayers, and one would think that 1 John 5:14–15 reads, "This is the uncertainty that we have in Him, that we can never know God's will, and therefore can never be sure that our prayers are heard." But that is not the way the verses read. They read,

> *And this is the boldness* ["*confidence,*" KJV—not uncertainty, but absolute confidence] *which we have toward him, that, if we ask anything according to his will, he heareth us: and if we know that he heareth us whatsoever we ask, we know that we have the petitions which we have asked of him.* (RV)

Oh, how subtle the devil is to take a passage of Scripture that God has put into His Word to fill us with confidence when we pray, and use it to make us uncertain when we pray!

The Prayer of Faith

By the Holy Spirit

But can we know the will of God when we pray, even when there is no definite promise in regard to the matter about which we are praying? Yes, in many cases we can. How? Paul answered this question for us:

> *And in like manner the Spirit also helpeth our infirmity: for we know not how to pray as we ought; but the Spirit himself maketh intercession for us with groanings which cannot be uttered; and he that searcheth the hearts knoweth what is the mind of the Spirit, because he maketh intercession for the saints according to the will of God.* (Rom. 8:26–27 RV)

It is the work of the Holy Spirit when we pray to make known to us what is the will of God in the matter about which we are praying, and to show us (if the thing is according to His will) that it is according to His will. We need many things that are not definitely promised in the Word, and it doesn't logically follow at all that because they are not definitely promised in the Word, they are not *"according to the will of God."* It is the will of God to give us many things that He has not definitely promised in His Word; and it is the method of God, when we pray, to allow us, by the direct illumination of the Holy Spirit, to know His will even regarding things about which He has given us no definite promise.

For example, while I was pastor of the Moody Church in Chicago, the little daughter of a man and woman who were both members of our church was taken very ill. She first had the measles, and the measles were followed by meningitis. She sank very low, and the doctor said to her mother, "I can do no more for your child. She cannot live." The mother immediately hurried down to my house to get me to come to their house and pray for her child. But I was out of town holding meetings in Pittsburgh. So she sent for the assistant pastor, Rev. W. S. Jacoby, and he went up to the house with one of my colleagues and prayed for the child. That night when I got home from Pittsburgh, he came to my house to tell me about it, and he said, "Mr. Torrey, if I ever had an answer to my prayers in my life, it was today when I was praying for the Duff child." He was confident that God had heard his prayer and that the child would be healed. And the child was healed right away. This occurred on a Saturday.

The next morning the doctor visited the home again, and there was such a remarkable change in the child that he said to Mrs. Duff, "What have you done for your child?" She told him just what she had done.

Then he said, "Well, I will give her some more medicine."

"No," she said, "you will not. You said you could do no more for her, that she must die, so we went to God in prayer and God has healed her. You are not going to take the honor to yourself by giving her some more medicine." Indeed, the girl was not only improved that morning, but she was completely well.

Now neither Mr. Jacoby nor I could pray for every sick child in that way, for it is not the will of God to heal every sick child, nor every sick adult. It is God's general will in regard to His children that they be well in body, but there are cases when God, for wise purposes of His own, does not see fit to heal the sick. In those cases, if we are living near to God and listening for the voice of His Spirit, and are entirely surrendered to the Spirit in our praying, the Spirit of God will make clear to us the will of God.

Here is another illustration along an entirely different line. The healing of the body is only one of the lines along which God answers prayer, and not by any means the most important. In my first pastorate we had a series of meetings of all the churches of the town. In the course of the meetings, we had a day of fasting and prayer. During the morning meeting, as we were praying, God led me to pray that one of the most unlikely men in the town might be saved that night. He had led a wild life; few of his family were Christians; but as we knelt in prayer that morning, God put a great burden on my heart for that man's salvation, and I prayed that he might come to the meeting and be saved that night. As I prayed, God gave me a great confidence that he would come and be saved that night. And come he did, and he was saved. There was not a man in that whole town who was more unlikely to be saved than he.

The Prayer of Faith

That was more than forty years ago, but when I was in Chattanooga, Tennessee, a few years ago, I met another man whose mother was saved about the same time. He told me that this man was then living in Tennessee and was still living a Christian life. Now I cannot pray for the salvation of every unsaved person in that way, but God by His Spirit revealed to me His will regarding that man, and in many cases He has thus revealed His will.

Take an illustration along still another line. One day in Northfield, Massachusetts, I received word from Chicago from Mr. Fitt, Mr. Moody's son-in-law, that we needed $5,000 at once for the work in Chicago, and he asked me to pray for it. Another member of the faculty of the Bible Institute was in Northfield at that time, and that night we prayed and asked God to send that money. God gave my friend great confidence that He had heard the prayer, and he said to me, "God has heard the prayer, and the $5,000 will come." Mr. Fitt and Mr. Gaylord also prayed in Chicago, and God gave Mr. Gaylord a great confidence that the money would come. We knew it was ours; we knew that God had heard the prayer and that we had received the $5,000.

A telegram came the next day (I think it was from Indianapolis) saying $5,000 had been deposited in a bank in Indianapolis to our account. Though we had prayed and expected, Mr. Fitt could hardly believe it when he heard it. So he inquired at our bank in Chicago, and they asked the bank in Indianapolis if it were true. They found out that it was. As far as I know, the man who put that money in the bank in Indianapolis had never given a penny to the Bible Institute before. I did not know there was such a man in the world, and as far as I know, he has never given a penny to the Bible Institute since. Now I cannot go to God every time I think I need money and ask God for it with that same confidence, but there are times when I can. There have been many such times in my life, and God has never failed, and He never will. Banks sometimes fail; God never fails.

To sum it all up, when God makes His will known, either by a specific promise of His Word or by His Holy Spirit while we are praying, that the thing that we ask for is *according to his will*," it is our privilege to know—if we really believe on the name of the

Son of God—that the thing we have asked is granted, and that it is ours. It is just as truly ours as it will be afterward when we actually have it in our hands.

Praying in Faith

The passage we have been studying is closely related to another passage in the gospel of Mark that contains a promise of our Lord Himself in regard to God answering prayer. It is a familiar passage; you will find it in Mark 11:24: *"Therefore I say unto you, What things soever ye desire, when ye pray, believe that ye receive them, and ye shall have them."* I will not stop to call your attention to whom this promise is made, except to say that it is made (as are all the other promises of God) to those who believe on Jesus Christ, those who are united to Jesus Christ by a living faith that manifests itself in an obedient love. This is evident from the context, as you can find out for yourself if you will read the promise in its context.

And how must we pray in order to get the thing that we ask? We must pray in faith; that is, we must pray with a confident expectation of getting the very thing that we ask. There are those who say that any prayer that is in submission to the will of God, and in faith in Him and dependence on God, is a prayer of faith. But it is not "the prayer of faith" in the Bible sense of *"the prayer of faith"* (James 5:15). *"The prayer of faith"* in the Bible sense is the prayer that has no doubt whatsoever that God has heard the prayer and granted the specific thing *"which we have asked of him"* (1 John 5:15 RV). This is evident from James 1:5–7:

> But if any of you lacketh wisdom, let him ask of God, who giveth to all liberally and upbraideth not; and it shall be given him. But let him ask in faith, nothing doubting: for he that doubteth is like the surge of the sea driven by the wind and tossed. For let not that man think that he shall receive anything of the Lord. (RV)

No matter how positive the promises of God may be, we will never receive them in our own experience until we absolutely believe them. The prayer that gets what it asks is *"the prayer of faith"* (James 5:15), that is, the prayer that has no doubt whatsoever of getting the very thing that is asked.

This comes out more clearly in the Revised Version of Mark 11:24 than in the King James Version: *"Therefore I say unto you, All things whatsoever ye pray and ask for, believe that ye have received them, and ye shall have them"* (RV). When we pray to God, and pray according to His will as known by the promises in His Word, or as known by the Holy Spirit revealing His will to us, we should confidently believe that the very thing we have asked is granted us. We should believe that we have received, and what we thus believe we have received we will afterward have in actual personal experience.

Take, for example, the matter of praying for the baptism in the Holy Spirit. When anyone prays for the Holy Spirit—anyone who is united to Jesus Christ by a living faith that reveals itself in an obedient love, anyone who has received Jesus Christ as his Savior and is trusting God to forgive him on the sole ground that Jesus Christ died in his place, anyone who has received Jesus Christ as his Lord and Master and has surrendered all his thoughts and purposes and conduct to His control—he may know that he has prayed for something according to His will. This is because Jesus Christ definitely said in Luke 11:13, *"If ye then, being evil, know how to give good gifts unto your children: how much more shall your heavenly Father give the Holy Spirit to them that ask him?"* And as he knows that he has asked something that is according to God's will as He has clearly revealed it in His Word, it is his privilege to say, "I have what I asked. I have the Holy Spirit."

It is not a question at all of whether he feels that he has received the Holy Spirit or not; it is not a question of some remarkable experience; it is simply a question of taking God at His Word, and believing that he has received simply because God says so. What he has taken by naked faith on the Word of God, simply believing he has received, because God says so, he will afterward have in actual experiential possession. There is no need for him to work himself up into a frenzy of emotion, no need for him to fall into a trance, or into unconsciousness, an experience utterly foreign to anything described in the New Testament. He has a far better ground for his assurance that he has received what he asked than any feeling or any ecstasy; he has the immutable Word of God, *"that cannot lie"* (Titus 1:2).

Praying in faith, that is, praying with an unquestioning belief that you will receive just exactly what you ask—yes, believing as you pray that God has heard your prayer and that you have received the thing that you ask—is one of the most important factors in obtaining what we ask when we pray. As James put it, *"Let him ask in faith, nothing doubting: for he that doubteth is like the surge of the sea driven by the wind and tossed. For let not that man think that he shall receive anything of the Lord"* (James 1:6–7 RV). That is, let not the man who has any doubts that God has heard his prayer, think that he will receive anything of the Lord.

So the tremendously important question arises, How can we pray the prayer of faith? How can we pray with a confident, unquestioning certainty in our minds that God has heard our prayer and granted the thing that we ask? This has been partly answered in what I have already said, but in order that it may be perfectly clear, let me repeat the substance of it again.

STUDY THE WORD

To pray the prayer of faith, we must, first of all, study the Word of God, especially the promises of God, and find out what the will of God is. We must build our prayers on the written promises of God. Intelligent faith—the only kind of faith that counts with God—must have a sure foundation. We cannot believe by just trying to make ourselves believe. Such belief as that is not faith but credulity; it is "make believe."

The great foundation for intelligent faith is God's Word. As Paul put it in Romans 10:17, *"Faith cometh by hearing, and hearing by the word of God."* The faith that is built upon the sure Word of God is an intelligent faith; it has something to rest upon. So if we desire to pray the prayer of faith, we must study the Word of

God and find out what God has definitely promised. Then, with God's promise in mind, we may approach God and ask Him for the thing that He has promised.

Here is the point at which many go astray. Here is the point at which I went astray in my early prayer life. Not long after my conversion, I got hold of this promise of our Lord Jesus in Mark 11:24, *"Therefore I say unto you, What things soever ye desire, when ye pray, believe that ye receive them, and ye shall have them."* I said to myself, "All I need to do if I want anything is to ask God for it and then make myself believe that I am going to get it, and I'll have it." So whenever I wanted anything, I asked God for it and tried to make myself believe I was going to get it, but I didn't get it, for it was only "make-believe," and I did not really believe at all. But I later learned that *"faith cometh by hearing, and hearing by the word of God"* (Rom. 10:17), and that if I wished to pray *"the prayer of faith"* (James 5:15), I must have some basis for my faith, some ground upon which to rest my faith, and that the surest of all grounds for faith was the Word of God. So when I desired anything of God, I would search the Scriptures to find if there was some promise that covered that case, and then go to God and plead His own promise. Thus, resting upon that promise, I would believe that God had heard. He had heard, and I got what I asked.

One of the mightiest men of prayer of the last generation was George Müller of Bristol, England, who in the last sixty years of his life (he lived to be ninety-two) obtained the English equivalent of $7,200,000 by prayer. But George Müller never prayed for a thing just because he wanted it, or even just because he felt it was greatly needed for God's work. When it was laid upon George Müller's heart to pray for anything, he would search the Scriptures to find if there was some promise that covered the case. Sometimes he would search the Scriptures for days before he presented his petition to God. Then, when he found the promise, with his Bible open before him and his finger upon that promise, he would plead that promise, and so he received what he asked. He always prayed with a Bible open before him.

The Power of Prayer

THE SPIRIT'S HELP

But this is not all that is to be said about how to pray the prayer of faith. It is possible for us to have faith in many instances when there is no definite promise covering the case, and to pray with the absolute assurance that God has heard our prayer. It is possible to believe, with a faith that has not a shadow of a doubt in it, that we have received what we have asked for. In Romans we are plainly told how this comes to pass:

> In like manner the Spirit also helpeth our infirmity: for we know not how to pray as we ought; but the Spirit himself maketh intercession for us with groanings which cannot be uttered; and he that searcheth the hearts knoweth what is the mind of the Spirit, because he maketh intercession for the saints according to the will of God.
>
> (Rom. 8:26–27 RV)

In other words, the Holy Spirit, as I have already said, often makes clear to us as we pray what the will of God is, so that as we listen to His voice we can pray with absolute confidence, with a confidence that has not a shadow of doubt, that God has heard our prayer and granted the thing that we asked.

My first experience, at least the first that I recall, of this wonderful privilege of knowing the will of God, and of praying with confident faith even when I had no definite promise in the written Word that God would hear the prayer, came early in my ministry. There was a young dentist in my congregation whose father was a member of our church. This dentist was taken very ill with typhoid fever; he went down to the very gates of death. I went to see him and found him unconscious. The doctor and his father were by the bedside, and the doctor said to me, "He cannot live. The crisis is past, and it has turned the wrong way. There is no possibility of his recovery." I knelt down to pray, and as I prayed a great confidence came into my heart, an absolutely unshakable confidence that God had heard my prayer and that the young man was to be raised up. As I got up from my knees, I said to the father and the doctor, "The young man will get well. He will not die at this time."

276

The Prayer of Faith

The doctor smiled and said, "That is all right, Mr. Torrey, from your standpoint, but he cannot live. He will die."

I replied, "Doctor, that is all right from your standpoint, but he cannot die; he will live." I went to my home. Not long after, word was brought to me that the young man was dying. They told me what he was doing, and said that no one ever did that except just when they were dying. I calmly replied, "He is not dying. He will not die. He will get well." I knew he would, and he did. The last I knew, he was alive, and his healing took place between forty and forty-five years ago.

But I cannot pray for every sick man in that way, even though he may be an earnest Christian, which this man was not at that time. Sometimes it is God's will to heal; usually it is God's will to heal, if the conditions are met; but it is not always God's will to heal. *The prayer of faith shall save the sick,"* God tells us in James 5:15; but it is not always possible to pray *"the prayer of faith"*—it is only when God makes it possible by the leading of His Holy Spirit.

But not only will *"the prayer of faith"* heal the sick, it will also bring many other blessings—blessings of far more importance than physical healing. It will bring salvation to the lost; it will bring power to our Christian service; it will bring money into the treasury of the Lord; it will bring great revivals of religion.

In my first pastorate, one of the first persons to accept Christ was a woman who had been a backslider for many years. But she not only came back to the Lord, she came back in a very thorough way. Not long after her conversion, God gave her a great spirit of prayer for a revival in our church and community. When I had been there about a year, she was called to go out to California with a sick friend. Before going she came to the prayer meeting on her last night there and said, "God has heard my prayer for a revival. You are going to have a great revival here in the church." And we did have a revival, not only in the church, but also in the whole community—a revival that transformed every church in the community, and brought many souls to Christ. The revival went on again the next year, and the next, and the next until I left that field. It even went on under the pastor who followed me, and the pastor who followed him.

Oh, yes, *"the prayer of faith"* is the great secret of getting what we need in our personal lives, what we need in our service, what we need in our work, what we need in our church, what we need everywhere. There is no limit to what *"the prayer of faith"* can do; and if we would pray more, pray more intelligently, and pray *"the prayer of faith,"* there is no telling what God could do. But as I have said, to pray *"the prayer of faith,"* we must first of all study our Bibles intensely so that we may know the promises of God, what they are, how large they are, how definite they are, and just exactly what is promised. In addition to that, we must live so near to God, be so fully surrendered to the will of God, have such a delight in God, and so feel our utter dependence upon the Spirit of God, that the Holy Spirit Himself can guide us in our prayers and indicate clearly to us what the will of God is. He will make us sure while we pray that we have asked for something that is according to God's will, and thus enable us to pray with the absolute confidence that God has heard our prayers, and that we have received the thing that we asked of Him.

Here is where many of us fail in our prayer lives: we either do not know that it is our privilege to pray in the Spirit, that is, to pray under the Spirit's guidance; or else we do not realize our utter dependence upon the Holy Spirit, and do not cast ourselves upon Him to lead us when we pray. Therefore, we pray for the things that our own hearts prompt us to pray for, our own selfish desires; or else we are not in such an attitude toward God that the Spirit of God can make His voice heard in our hearts.

Oh, that we might all be made to realize the immeasurable blessings for ourselves, for our friends, for the church, and for the world, that lie within the reach of *"the prayer of faith"*; that we might all determine that we will pray the prayer of faith; that we might study the Word of God so that we can know God's will and what to pray for; and that we might be in such a relationship with God, be fully surrendered to His will and delight in Himself, and in utter, constant dependence upon the Holy Spirit, looking to the Holy Spirit, that as we pray it might not be so much we who pray as the Holy Spirit praying through us. Then we would soon see our spiritually dead cities and our spiritually dead churches *"blossom as the rose"* (Isa. 35:1).

8

Praying through and
Praying in the Holy Spirit

Men ought always to pray, and not to faint.
—Luke 18:1

Though he will not rise and give him, because he is his friend, yet
because of his importunity he will rise and give him as many as he
needeth. And I say unto you, Ask, and it shall be given you; seek,
and ye shall find; knock, and it shall be opened unto you.
—Luke 11:8–9

With all prayer and supplication praying at all seasons in the
Spirit, and watching thereunto in all perseverance and
supplication for all the saints.
—Ephesians 6:18 RV

There are two passages in the gospel of Luke that throw a flood of light upon the questions, "What sort of praying is it that prevails with God and obtains what it seeks from Him?" and, "Why do many prayers of God's own children come short of obtaining what we seek of God?" The first of these two passages you will find in Luke 11:5–10, where our Lord Himself is the speaker:

And he said unto them, Which of you shall have a friend, and shall
go unto him at midnight, and say unto him, Friend, lend me three
loaves; for a friend of mine in his journey is come to me, and I have
nothing to set before him? And he from within shall answer and say,
Trouble me not: the door is now shut, and my children are with me
in bed; I cannot rise and give thee. I say unto you, Though he will

280

not rise and give him, because he is his friend, yet because of his importunity he will rise and give him as many as he needeth. And I say unto you, Ask, and it shall be given you; seek, and ye shall find; knock, and it shall be opened unto you. For every one that asketh receiveth; and he that seeketh findeth; and to him that knocketh it shall be opened.

Praying Through

The central lesson in this parable of our Lord's is that, when we pray, if we do not obtain the thing the first time we ask for it, we should pray again; and if we do not obtain it the second time, we should pray a third time; and if we do not obtain it the hundredth time we pray, we should go on praying until we do get it. We should do much thinking before we ask anything of God and be clear that the thing that we ask is according to His will; we should not rush heedlessly into God's presence and ask for the first thing that comes into our minds without giving proper thought to the question of whether it is really a thing that we ought to have or not. But when we have decided that we should pray for the thing, we should keep on praying until we get it.

The word translated *"importunity"* in the eighth verse is a deeply significant word. Its primary meaning is "shameless-ness"—that is, it sets forth the persistent determination in prayer to God that will not be put to shame by any apparent refusal on God's part to grant the thing that we ask. This is a very startling way that our Lord Jesus sets forth the necessity of *"importunity"* and persistence in prayer. It is as if the Lord Jesus wants us to understand that God desires us to draw near to Him with a resolute determination to obtain the things that we seek, a determination that will not be put to shame by any seeming refusal or delay on God's part.

Our heavenly Father delights in the holy boldness on our part that will not take no for an answer. The reason He delights in it is that it is an expression of great faith, and nothing pleases God more than holy boldness in faith. We have an illustration of this in the Syrophenician woman in Matthew 15:21–28. She came to Jesus for the healing of her daughter. She cried, *"Have mercy on me, O Lord, thou son of David; my daughter is grievously vexed with a devil"* (v. 22). But our Lord seemed to pay no attention to her; as Matthew put it, *"He answered her not a word. And his disciples came [to Him] and besought him, saying, Send her away; for she crieth after us"* (v. 23). In spite of His apparent deafness to her appeal, she kept right on crying. Then He turned to her with an apparently more positive rebuff, saying, *"I am not sent but unto the lost sheep of the house of Israel"* (v. 24), and she was not of the house of Israel. Then she worshipped Him and kept on calling to Him, saying, *"Lord, help me"* (v. 25). Then came what almost appears like a cruel rebuff, when our Lord said, *"It is not meet to take the children's bread, and cast it to dogs"* (v. 26).

The word He used for *"dogs"* meant a little pet dog and was not at all as harsh as it seems, although it was an apparent refusal to hear her prayer. But as we will see, our Lord was simply putting her faith to the test so that she might receive an even larger blessing. Then she said, *"Truth, Lord: yet the dogs eat of the crumbs which fall from their masters' table"* (v. 27). She would not take no for an answer. And then came one of the most wonderful words of commendation that ever fell from the lips of our Lord. This is the way Matthew put it: *"Then Jesus answered and said unto her, O woman, great is thy faith: be it unto thee even as thou wilt. And her daughter was made whole from that very hour"* (v. 28). That sort of thing pleases God. He desires that we have the faith in His loving-kindness and in Himself that, even when He seems not to hear, will trust Him still to hear.

God does not always give us the things we ask the first time we ask them, but then we should not give up; no, we should keep on praying until we do receive. We should not only pray, but we should pray through.

It is deeply significant that this parable to persist in prayer comes almost immediately after the request on the part of the disciples of our Lord, in which they say, *"Lord, teach us to pray"* (Luke 11:1). Then follows Luke's version of the so-called Lord's Prayer (really the disciples' prayer), and then comes this parable.

Praying through and Praying in the Holy Spirit

The same lesson is taught in a striking way in Luke 18:1–8:

> *And he spake a parable unto them to the end that they ought always to pray, and not to faint; saying, There was in a city a judge, which feared not God, and regarded not man: and there was a widow in that city; and she came oft unto him, saying, Avenge me of mine adversary. And he would not for a while: but afterward he said within himself, Though I fear not God, nor regard man; yet because this widow troubleth me, I will avenge her, lest she wear me out by her continual coming. And the Lord said, Hear what the unrighteous judge saith. And shall not God avenge his elect, which cry to him day and night, and he is longsuffering over them? I say unto you, that he will avenge them speedily. Howbeit* ["nevertheless," KJV] *when the Son of man cometh, shall he find faith* [literally, "the faith," margin] *on the earth?*   (RV)

We find the central lesson of this parable in the words with which our Lord Jesus opens the parable, which are really the text of the whole parable. These words are, *"Men ought always to pray, and not to faint"* (Luke 18:1), the clear meaning of which is that when we begin to pray, we ought to pray on and on until we get the thing that we desire of God. The exact meaning of the parable is that if even an unrighteous judge will yield to persistent prayer and grant the thing that he did not wish to grant, how much more will a loving God yield to the persistent cries of His children? God will give the things that He longs to give, but which it would not be wise to give—would not be for the person's own good to give—until His children are trained to persevere in faith that will not take no for an answer. So we see again that God does not always give us at the first asking what we desire of Him in prayer.

Why does God not give to us the things we ask of Him, the very first time we ask Him? The answer is plain: God wishes to do more for us, and better for us, than to give us merely that thing. He wants to do us the far greater good of training us in persistent faith. The things that we get by any other effort than prayer to God, do not always become ours the first time we make an effort to get them; for our own good, God compels us to be persistent in our efforts. Thus, He does not always give us what we ask in prayer the first time we pray. Just as He desires to train us to be strong men and women along the lines of other efforts, so also He wants to train us to be strong men and women of prayer by compelling us to pray hard for the best things. He compels us to pray through.

Many people these days tell us that we ought not to pray for the same thing a second time. Sometimes they tell us that the way to pray is to ask God for a thing and then "take it" by faith the first time we ask. That is often true: when we find a thing definitely promised in the Word, we ought to rest upon the revealed Word of God; and when we have prayed, we ought to know that we have asked something according to God's will and therefore that the prayer is heard and that we have received. Resting there, we should ask no more but claim the thing as ours.

But that is only one side of the truth. The other side of the truth is that there are times when it is not made clear the first time, or the second time, or the third time, that the thing we ask is according to His will, and that therefore the prayer is heard and the thing asked granted. In such a case, we ought to pray on and on and on. While there are undoubtedly times when we are able through faith in the Word, or through the clear leading of the Holy Spirit, to claim a thing the first time that we have asked it of God, nevertheless, there are other times when we must pray again and again and again for the same thing before we get our answer. Those who claim that they have gotten beyond praying twice for the same thing have either gotten beyond our Master, our Lord and Savior Jesus Christ, or else they have not gotten up to Him. We are told distinctly regarding Him in Matthew 26:44, *"And he left them again, and went away, and prayed a third time, saying again the same words"* (RV). The truth is they have not yet gotten up to the Master, not that they have gotten beyond Him.

There are those—and there are many of them—who, when they pray for a thing once or twice and do not get it, stop praying. They call it "submission to the will of God" to stop praying when God does not grant their request at the first or second

284

asking. They say, "Well, perhaps it is not God's will." But as a rule, this is not submission to the will of God: it is spiritual laziness and lack of determination in that all-important human effort, prayer. None of us ever thinks of calling it submission to the will of God when we give up after one or two efforts to obtain things by efforts other than prayer. In those cases, we call it lack of strength of character. When the strong man of action starts out to accomplish a thing, if he does not accomplish it the first, the second, or the hundredth time, he keeps hammering away until he does accomplish it. In the same way, the strong man of prayer, when he starts to pray for a thing, keeps on praying until he prays it through and obtains what he seeks.

How fond we are of calling bad things in our conduct by good names, calling our spiritual inertia and laziness and indifference "submission to the will of God." We should be careful about what we ask from God; but when we do begin to pray for a thing, we should never give up praying for it until we get it, or until God definitely makes it very clear to us that it is not His will to give it.

I am glad that God does not always give us the things that we seek from Him the first time we ask. There is no more blessed training in prayer than that which comes through being compelled to ask again and again and again, even through a long period of years, before one obtains what he seeks from God. Then when it does come, what a sense we have that God really exists, and that God really answers prayer.

I recall an experience of my own that was full of blessing to me, and full of encouragement to my faith. In my first pastorate, there were two individuals whom God put upon my heart and for whose salvation I prayed through my entire pastorate there. But I left that field of labor without seeing either one of them converted. I went to Germany for further study, and then took a new pastorate in Minneapolis, but I kept on praying every day for those two persons. I went back to the place where I began my ministry to hold a series of meetings, praying every day for the conversion of those two persons. Then one night in that series of meetings, when I gave the invitation for all who would accept the Lord Jesus Christ as their personal Savior, those two people arose side by side. There was no special reason why they were side by side, for they were not relatives. When I saw those two persons for whom I had prayed every day through all those years standing up side by side to accept the Lord Jesus Christ, what an overwhelming sense came over my soul that there is a God, and that He hears prayer if we meet the conditions of prevailing prayer, and follow the method of prevailing prayer taught in His own Word.

We find right here why it is that many prayers fail to accomplish what we seek from God. We pray and pray and pray, and are almost on the verge of attaining what we are praying for; and right then, when God is just about to answer the prayer, we stop praying and we miss the blessing. For example, in many churches and in many communities there are people who are praying for a revival, and the revival does not come at once. In fact, it does not come for some time, and they keep on praying. They have nearly prayed through; they are right on the verge of attaining what they sought, and if they had prayed a little longer, the revival would have broken upon them. But they get discouraged, throw up their hands, and quit. They are just on the border of the blessing, but they do not cross into the promised land.

One January, the faculty of the Bible Institute of Chicago started a prayer meeting on Saturday nights from nine to ten o'clock, to pray for a worldwide revival. After we had been praying for some time, the thing happened that I knew would happen when we began: people came to me, or to Mr. Alexander, who was most closely identified with me in the leadership of these meetings, and they asked, "Has the revival come?"

"No, not as far as we can see."

"When is it coming?"

"We don't know."

"How long are you going to pray?"

"Until it comes." And come it did, a revival that began there in that room of the Bible Institute in Chicago and then broke out in far-away China, Japan, Australia, New Zealand, Tasmania, and India, and swept around the world with marvelous manifestations of God's saving power. The revival came not merely through Mr. Alexander and me, but through a multitude of others in India and Wales and elsewhere. In Wales, for example, under Evan Roberts and others, the revival resulted in 100,000 professed conversions in twelve months. And I believe that God is looking to us today to pray through again.

I prayed fifteen long years for the conversion of my oldest brother. He seemed to be getting farther and farther away from any hope of conversion, but I prayed on. One morning, my first winter in Chicago, after fifteen years of praying, never missing a single day, God said to me as I knelt in prayer, "I have heard your prayer. You need not pray anymore; your brother is going to be converted." And within two weeks my brother was in my home, shut in for two weeks with sickness that made it impossible for him to leave my home, and then the day he left he accepted Christ over in the Bible Institute in Mr. Moody's office, where he and I went to talk and pray together.

I told this incident once when I was holding meetings in a certain city. An elderly woman came to me at the close of the meeting and she said, "For many years I have been praying for the conversion of my brother, who is sixty-three years old. A short time ago I gave up and stopped praying, but I am going to begin my prayers again." Within two weeks of that time, she came to me and said, "I have heard from my brother, and he has accepted Christ." Oh, men and women, pray through, *pray through*, PRAY THROUGH. Do not just begin to pray and pray a little while and throw up your hands and quit; but pray and pray and pray, until God bends the heavens and comes down.

Praying in the Holy Spirit

There is another passage closely connected with the two that we have just been studying, to which I will now call your attention. It is found in one of our text verses, Ephesians 6:18: *"With all prayer and supplication praying at all seasons in the Spirit, and watching thereunto in all perseverance and supplication for all the saints"* (RV).

The Power of Prayer

The three words to which I wish to call your attention are these: *"in the Spirit."* We find the same thought in Jude 20–21: *"But ye, beloved, building up yourselves on your most holy faith, praying in the Holy Ghost, keep yourselves in the love of God, looking for the mercy of our Lord Jesus Christ unto eternal life."* In those words, *"praying...in the Spirit"* (Eph. 6:18) and *"praying in the Holy Ghost"* (Jude 20), we find one of the two greatest secrets of prevailing prayer.

The other of the two greatest secrets of prevailing prayer is found in the words of our Lord Jesus in John 14:13–14: *"And whatsoever ye shall ask in my name, that will I do, that the Father may be glorified in the Son. If ye shall ask any thing in my name, I will do it."* Those words we studied before, "praying in the name of the Lord Jesus," and *"praying in the Holy Ghost"* (Jude 20), are the two great secrets of prevailing prayer. If anyone were to ask me, "What is the great secret of holy living?" I would say at once, "Living in the Holy Spirit." If anyone were to ask me, "What is the great secret of effective service for Jesus Christ?" I would reply at once, "Serving in the Holy Spirit." If anyone should ask me, "What is the one greatest secret of profitable Bible study?" I would reply, "Studying in the Holy Spirit." And if anyone were to ask me what is the one great all-inclusive secret of prevailing prayer, I would reply, "Praying in the Holy Spirit." It is the prayer that the Holy Spirit inspires that God the Father answers.

What does it mean to pray in the Holy Spirit? It means to pray as the Holy Spirit—our ever present, indwelling Friend, Counselor, and Guide, the *"Comforter"* (John 14:16) whom our Lord Jesus Himself promised us when He Himself left this world—inspires us and guides us to pray. Over and over again as we have studied together, we have seen our dependence on the Holy Spirit if we are to pray correctly. When we were studying Acts 12:5 in chapter four, we saw that the Holy Spirit's work is to lead us into the presence of God and to make God real to us, so that we may really pray *"unto God"* (v. 5). We also saw that it is the Spirit who gives us the intense earnestness in prayer that prevails with God. And when we were studying how to pray according to the will of God, and how to pray the prayer of faith, we saw that it is the Holy Spirit who reveals to us what God's will is as we pray. We saw that the Spirit leads us to pray according to His will, so that we might know as we pray that we have asked something that is according to God's will, and might know that the prayer is heard.

CHARACTERISTICS OF SPIRIT-INSPIRED PRAYER

What are the characteristics of the prayer that is *"in the Spirit"* (Eph. 6:18), the characteristics of prayer that the Holy Spirit inspires?

The first characteristic of the prayer that is in the Holy Spirit is intense earnestness. We see this in Romans 8:26: *"And in like manner the Spirit also helpeth our infirmity: for we know not how to pray as we ought; but the Spirit himself maketh intercession for us with groanings which cannot be uttered"* (RV).

As we saw in studying Acts 12:5, the prayer that prevails with God is the prayer into which we throw our whole hearts, the prayer of intense earnestness; and it is the Holy Spirit who inspires us to that intense earnestness in prayer. Oh, how cold and formal we are in many of our prayers! How little intense longing there is in our souls to obtain the thing that we ask! We pray even for the salvation of the lost with much indifference, though we ought to realize that if our prayers are not heard, they are going to spend eternity in hell. But men and women whose prayer lives are under the control of the Holy Spirit pray with intense earnestness; they cry mightily to God; there is a great burden of prayer in their hearts; they pray sometimes *"with groanings which cannot be uttered."*

Charles Finney has told us about a man named Abel Clary:

He had been licensed to preach, but he was so burdened with the souls of men, and his spirit of prayer was so powerful, that he was not able to preach much. His whole time and strength were being given to prayer. The burden of his soul would frequently be so great that he was unable to stand, and he would writhe and groan in agony. I was well acquainted with him and knew something of the wonderful spirit of prayer that was upon him. He was a very silent man, as almost all are who have this powerful spirit of prayer.[‡]

Abel Clary was of great assistance to Mr. Finney, simply by praying, in his work in Rochester, New York, where a revival sprang up. The report of this particular revival resulted in revivals all over the country, and it is said to have brought 100,000 souls to Christ in a year.

Of Mr. Clary's work in Rochester, Mr. Finney wrote,

> I first learned of his being in Rochester when a gentleman who lived about a mile west of the city called on me one day and asked me if I knew a Mr. Abel Clary, a minister. I told him that I knew him well. "Well," he said, "he is at my house and has been there for some time, and I don't know what to think of him." I said, "I have not seen him at any of our meetings." "No," he replied, "he says he cannot go to the meetings. He prays nearly all the time, day and night, and in such an agony of mind that I do not know what to make of it. Sometimes he cannot even get up on his knees but will lie prostrate on the floor and groan and pray in a manner that quite astonishes me." I said to the brother, "I understand it; please keep still. It will all come out right; he will surely prevail."

Mr. Finney said of Mr. Clary in another place,

> The second Sunday that I was in Auburn at this time, I saw the solemn face of my friend Mr. Clary in the congregation. He looked as if he was borne down with an agony of prayer. Being well acquainted with him and knowing the great gift of the spirit of prayer that was on him, I was very glad to see him there. He sat in the pew with his brother, the doctor, who claimed to be religious but knew nothing of his brother Abel's great power with God.
>
> At intermission, as soon as I came from behind the pulpit, Mr. Clary, with his brother, met me at the pulpit stairs. The

---

[‡] For the source of these quotation regarding Mr. Abel Clary, see *Holy Spirit Revivals* by Charles Finney, available from Whitaker House.

doctor invited me to go home with him and spend the intermission and get some refreshments. I did so.

After arriving at his house, we were soon summoned to the dinner table. We gathered around the table, and Dr. Clary turned to his brother and said, "Abel, will you ask a blessing?" Brother Abel bowed his head and began, audibly, to ask a blessing. He had uttered only a sentence or two when he broke down, moved suddenly back from the table, and fled to his bedroom. The doctor supposed he had been taken suddenly ill, and rose up and followed him. In a few moments he came down and said, "Mr. Finney, my brother wants to see you." "What ails him?" said I. "I do not know, but he says that you know. He appears to be in great distress, but I think it is the state of his mind." I understood it in a moment and went to his room. He lay groaning upon the bed, the Spirit making intercession for him and in him *"with groanings which cannot be uttered"* (Rom. 8:26). I had barely entered the room, when he said, "Pray, Brother Finney." I knelt down and helped him in prayer. I continued to pray until his distress passed away, and then I returned to the dinner table.

A wonderful revival broke out in Auburn; hundreds of souls were converted there in six weeks.

Oh, that we had people in our churches who knew how to pray like that! I believe that the greatest need of the church of Jesus Christ in America today, and the church of Jesus Christ throughout the world, is men and women who pray in the Holy Spirit, with the intense earnestness that He gives, and He alone gives.

The second characteristic of praying in the Holy Spirit is intelligent praying, perfect wisdom in our praying, praying for things that are according to the will of God. This comes out in the next verse, Romans 8:27: *"And he that searcheth the hearts knoweth what is the mind of the Spirit, because he maketh intercession for the saints according to the will of God."*

The third characteristic of prayer that is really prayed in the Holy Spirit is complete assurance that God has heard and answered our prayer. We saw this in studying Mark 11:24. It is the prayer that the Holy Spirit inspires that is really *"the prayer of faith"* (James 5:15). The one who prays in such a way knows that he is praying *"according to the will of God"* (Rom. 8:27) and has assurance without a shadow of a doubt that God has heard and answered his prayer.

The fourth characteristic of prayer that is really prayed in the Holy Spirit is determination in our praying—the determination to get what we ask from God, a persistence in asking until we do get it. This comes out clearly in Ephesians 6:18, *"With all prayer and supplication praying at all seasons in the Spirit, and watching thereunto in all perseverance and supplication for all the saints"* (RV). What a marvelous depiction of the determination and perseverance in prayer that comes from the Holy Spirit having control of our prayer lives! We do not need to dwell upon that now, for we have just been talking about it in the earlier part of this chapter. Such are the characteristics of prayer that is really in the Holy Spirit.

PRACTICAL STEPS TO TAKE

We come now to the intensely practical question, and the immediately important question, "How may we pray in the Holy Spirit?" That is, how can we make sure that the Spirit of God is guiding us in our prayer, make sure that our prayers are not merely the promptings of our own selfish desires but the sure leadings of the Spirit of God within us? The answer to this all-important question is plainly set forth in the Word of God.

First of all, if we are to pray in the Spirit, we must surrender our wills and ourselves absolutely and unreservedly to God. This is made clear in many places in Scripture. For example, in Acts 5:32 we read, *"And we are witnesses of these things; and so is the Holy Ghost, whom God hath given to them that obey him"* (RV). Here we are plainly taught that God gives the Holy Spirit *"to them that obey him,"* and to them alone. The heart of obedience is in the will, the surrender of the will and the surrender of oneself to God. Unless we make this absolute surrender, God cannot take control of our lives by His Holy Spirit, and He cannot take control of our prayer lives any more than any other part of our lives. Our surrender to

Praying through and Praying in the Holy Spirit

Him must extend to our praying as well as to the other spheres of our activities.

In the second place, if we wish to pray in the Holy Spirit, we must scrupulously obey God in every department of our lives. Disobedience at any point of our lives grieves the Holy Spirit and makes it impossible for Him to control us in our actions, and it is just as impossible for Him to take control of our prayer lives as it is to take charge of any other part of our lives.

To obey God we must study the Word of God every day of our lives to find out what the will of God is, and then whenever we find it, do it every time. If we refuse to do it at any point, the Holy Spirit cannot keep control of our prayer lives, and we cannot pray in the Holy Spirit. This comes out very clearly in John 14:13–14: *"And whatsoever ye shall ask in my name, that will I do, that the Father may be glorified in the Son. If ye shall ask any thing in my name, I will do it."* And then Jesus went on to say, and by saying it clearly showed the connection between daily obedience and the power in prayer that comes through praying in the Holy Spirit,

> *If ye love me, ye will keep my commandments. And I will pray the Father, and he shall give you another Comforter, that he may be with you for ever, even the Spirit of truth: whom the world cannot receive; for it beholdeth him not, neither knoweth him: ye know him; for he abideth with you, and shall be in you.* (John 14:15–17 RV)

In other words, the Lord Jesus says that if we have the love for Him that leads us to obey Him in everything, day by day, then He prays to the Father, and the Father sends His Holy Spirit to help us in all the emergencies of life, especially in our prayer lives. Thus, whatever we ask in His name is *"according to his will"* (1 John 5:14), and therefore, whatever we ask we get. Again and again in our study of all these wonderful promises, we come to the thought that there is no effective praying of any kind possible on our part unless we are studying the Word of God daily to find out the will of God and doing it every time we find it.

In the third place, if we desire to pray wisely and prevailingly in the Holy Spirit, we must realize and keep in mind our own utter inability to pray correctly, and our entire dependence upon the Holy Spirit. Oh, if there is any time when we need to feel our utter dependence upon the Comforter, the ever present Friend and Helper and Counselor, the Holy Spirit, it is when we pray. We need to feel deeply our dependence upon Him in our lives, in our daily warfare with the world, the flesh, and the devil. We need to feel our dependence upon Him in our service for Christ, realizing that it is *"not by might, nor by power,* [not by any natural gifts or abilities of our own] *but by* [His] *spirit"* (Zech. 4:6) that we are to accomplish anything for God in this world. We need to feel our dependence upon Him in our Bible study, realizing that He is the only perfect Interpreter of the Word, and that He is ready to interpret the Word to us as we study. But above all, we need to feel our dependence upon Him when we pray.

We will do well if we always bear in mind the inspired words of Paul as found in Romans 8:26, *"We know not how to pray as we ought"* (RV). If Paul, that mighty servant of Jesus Christ, that inspired apostle, that wonderful man of prayer, knew not how to pray as he ought, certainly we do not. But we should also constantly keep in mind the words that immediately follow in that same verse and the following verse,

> *But the Spirit himself maketh intercession for us with groanings which cannot be uttered; and he that searcheth the hearts knoweth what is the mind of the Spirit, because he maketh intercession for the saints according to the will of God.* (Rom. 8:26–27 RV)

When you go to God in prayer, realize that you do not know how to pray as you ought, and keep before yourself your utter dependence upon the Holy Spirit in every word of prayer.

In the fourth place, if we wish to pray in the Holy Spirit, we must definitely ask God to guide us by His Holy Spirit as we pray. Tell God that you do not know how to pray as you ought, and ask Him to guide you by His Spirit as you pray, and He will.

In the fifth place, if we wish to pray in the Holy Spirit, we must count upon God's answering our prayer to send His Holy Spirit to teach us to pray. We can unhesitatingly count upon God sending Him because in the passage just read, Romans 8:26–27, He has definitely promised to do so.

In the sixth place, if we wish to pray in the Holy Spirit, we must keep getting filled with the Holy Spirit. Paul's inspired exhortation in Ephesians 5:18, *"Be filled with the Spirit"* (RV), or to translate more literally, "Be getting filled with the Holy Spirit" (it is a continuous process, as is indicated by the tense of the Greek verb used here), has the most intimate connection with our prayer lives. If we are filled with the Spirit, we will be guided by the Spirit in our prayers as well as in everything else. A Spirit-filled man will always be a prayerful man, and his prayers will be in the Holy Spirit. The way to be getting continually filled with the Holy Spirit is indicated in what we have just studied under the four preceding headings. If we do the things indicated there, we will be continually getting filled with the Spirit of God.

Finally, if we desire to pray in the Spirit, we must study the Word of God daily and earnestly. The written Word of God is the visible instrument through which the invisible Spirit of God works. So if you wish to remain filled with that Spirit, you must keep full of the Word. This is clearly set forth in Ephesians 5:18–19: *"Be filled with the Spirit; speaking one to another in psalms and hymns and spiritual songs, singing and making melody with your heart to the Lord"* (RV). Now in comparison, note carefully Colossians 3:16: *"Let the word of Christ dwell in you richly in all wisdom; teaching and admonishing one another with psalms and hymns and spiritual songs, singing with grace in your hearts unto God"* (RV). We see here that in Colossians Paul attributed to being filled with the Word exactly the same thing that in Ephesians he attributed to being filled with the Spirit, and these two epistles were written at just about the same time. We must never lose sight of the tremendously important fact that the invisible Spirit of God does His work through the visible written Word of God. If we keep ourselves in harmony with the mind of God by a constant daily study of the Word of God, and by scrupulous obedience to the Word of God, the instrument through which the Holy Spirit constantly works, then the Holy Spirit will guide us in our prayers, and only then. If we keep ourselves full of the Holy Spirit's truth contained in the written Word, the Holy Spirit is far more likely to pray through us. From this point of view, then, there is deepest significance in our Lord's own words found in John 6:63: *"The words that I speak unto you, they are spirit, and they are life."*

Often in our study of the most significant and precious passages in the Bible concerning how to pray so as to obtain from God the things that we ask of Him in prayer, we have been brought face-to-face with a great truth: prevailing prayer always goes hand in hand with persistent and obedient study of the Word of God.

Allow me to sum up what we have discovered on the subject of prevailing prayer. If we are to pray the prayer that obtains from our heavenly Father the things that we ask of Him, then we must do the following:

First of all, we must be careful as to what we ask of God, and be sure that it is something that we ought to have, something that is according to His infinitely wise and absolutely holy will. Then, when we begin to pray for it, we ought to keep on praying for it for days and weeks and months, and if need be for years, until we get it. We *"ought always to pray, and not to faint"* (Luke 18:1). We ought to pray through.

In the second place, we must see to it that we pray not from our own selfish (and possibly foolish) desires, but under the impulse, inspiration, guidance, and control of the Holy Spirit. We must be sure that we pray in the Holy Spirit; that we let Him pray through us; and that we pray in the wisdom, earnestness, intensity, never-wearying persistence, and resistless power of prayer that He imparts.

Then our prayers will be the mightiest power on earth; for all God has, and all God is, is at the disposal of that kind of praying. That kind of praying can accomplish anything that God Himself can accomplish. That kind of praying partakes of the omnipotence of the God with whom that kind of praying puts us in perfect connection. I long to live in the Holy Spirit; I long to preach and witness in the Holy Spirit; I long to study and understand the Word of God in the Holy Spirit; but above all else I long to pray in the Holy Spirit. I also desire that the church as a body would learn to pray in the Holy Spirit. Then nothing will be able to stand against the church as it sweeps on and on, from victory to victory for God.

9

Hindrances to Prayer

Ye lust, and have not: ye kill, and covet, and cannot obtain: ye
fight and war; ye have not, because ye ask not. Ye ask, and receive
not, because ye ask amiss, that ye may spend it in your pleasures.
—James 4:2–3 RV

W hy it is that God sometimes does not answer the prayers
of His children? James 4:2–3 explains: *"Ye lust, and*
have not: ye kill, and covet, and cannot obtain: ye fight and
war; ye have not, because ye ask not. Ye ask, and receive not, because ye
ask amiss, that ye may spend it in your pleasures" (RV).

In the second verse we are told that the reason we do not
have the things that we earnestly desire and urgently need is
that we do not ask for them, because we do not pray. We are told,
"Ye have not, because ye ask not." The secret of our poverty and
powerlessness is neglect of prayer. We may put forth the most
strenuous activity to get things that we need—lust, kill, covet,
fight, and war—and yet fail to get them because we do not pray.
In studying this verse earlier, we saw clearly that the great secret
of the poverty and powerlessness of the average Christian, the
average minister, and the average church was neglect of prayer.
But in the third verse we are told that we may pray and still not
obtain, because we *"ask amiss,"* or, as the original Greek word for
"amiss" means, we ask "evilly, wrongly, or improperly." In other
words, there is something that hinders God from answering our
prayers.

As we have discussed the mighty power of prayer, and the
great and wonderful things prayer brings to pass, many may
have said to themselves, "Well, my prayers have no such power as

that. God doesn't hear and answer my prayers that way." Why is that? Is it because what the Bible teaches about prayer is not true? Is it because God does not answer prayer? Is it because God in former times answered prayer but does not answer it any longer? No, not at all. It is for none of those reasons. Why is it, then? It is because there is something in your own life, or in your heart, that makes it impossible for God to answer your prayers. It is because there is something in your case that hinders prayer.

In this chapter we will study what these hindrances to prayer are—what the things are in our hearts, or in our lives, that make it impossible for God to answer our prayers. I trust that when you see what the things are that prevent God's answering your prayers, you will give them up and thus get into a place where you can not only pray but also obtain.

A Wrong Motive in Our Prayers

You will find the first hindrance to prayer right in our text: *"Ye ask, and receive not, because ye ask amiss, that ye may consume it upon your lusts"* (James 4:3). The Revised Version reads a little differently and more correctly: *"Ye ask, and receive not, because ye ask amiss, that ye may spend it in your pleasures."* The first thing, then, that hinders prayers, the first thing that makes it impossible for God to answer our prayers, is a selfish purpose in our prayers. We ask for things we have a right to ask for, things that it is the will of God to give us, but we ask for them in a wrong way. In other words, we ask from a wrong motive; we ask for them for our own selfish gratification, so that (as the Bible puts it) we *"may spend it in* [our] *pleasures."*

What should be our motive in our prayers? The Bible answers this question plainly and explicitly in 1 Corinthians 10:31: *"Whether therefore ye eat, or drink, or whatsoever ye do, do all to the glory of God."* Here we are told distinctly that in everything we do, even in our eating and drinking, the glory of God should be our main goal in doing it. If this is true of the simplest duties of everyday life, it certainly must be true of our praying. Our supreme motive in our prayers should be that God may be glorified by answering our prayers; not that we may get some gratification, but that God may get glory to Himself.

This thought comes out again and again in the Bible. For example, the Lord Jesus said in John 14:13, in that wonderful promise we have quoted so often, *"And whatsoever ye shall ask in my name, that will I do, that the Father may be glorified in the Son."* Then in that prayer that our Lord Himself taught us, as recorded in the sixth chapter of Matthew, the prayer begins with these words, *"Our Father which art in heaven, hallowed be thy name"* (v. 9), clearly showing us that the first thing in our prayers should be the hallowing of God's name, the glorifying of God Himself. Then again in John 17:1, in that marvelous prayer that our Lord Jesus offered the night before His crucifixion, the real "Lord's prayer," our Lord began with these words: *"Father, the hour is come; glorify thy Son, that thy Son also may glorify thee."* Whatever we ask of God in prayer, the first great purpose we have in asking anything should be that God may be glorified in giving it. But this is far from the thought of many of us when we pray, as will be evident from a few simple illustrations.

For example, how many Christian women are praying for the conversion of their husbands? Now that certainly is a proper thing to pray for; indeed, I cannot see how any truly converted woman can rest, or give God rest day or night, until her husband is truly converted and born again. But as proper as that prayer is, it often fails because the wife who offers it is praying for the conversion of her husband from a purely selfish motive. She thinks to herself, "How much happier our married life would be if both my husband and I were Christians; then we would sympathize in the deepest interests in life, and we would know what real marriage means." Now that is all true. No two persons can know the deepest joys of married life, and the real meaning of true marriage, where one is saved and the other unsaved; where one is "a believer" and the other is "an unbeliever." But to pray for the conversion of your husband for that reason is pure selfishness; it is a refined selfishness, but nevertheless selfishness.

Or suppose a woman often prays for the conversion of her husband because she cannot bear the thought that her husband will be lost forever. That, too, is pure selfishness; refined selfishness, but nevertheless selfishness. Why should a wife pray for the conversion of her husband? First of all, and above all else, that God may be glorified in the conversion of her husband. Then she should pray because she cannot bear it that God should any longer be dishonored by the Christless, godless, God-disobeying life of her husband; she should pray that God may be glorified by her husband obeying God and doing the first thing that God demands of every man, to believe on His Son the Lord Jesus Christ; that God may be glorified in her husband, ceasing his rebellion against God and his wicked life, and giving himself up to Jesus Christ and His service. These things should be the supreme motives for which a Christian woman prays for the conversion of her husband. And when a woman gets to praying for the conversion of her husband along these lines, it will not be long before she sees him converted.

How far that is from the thoughts of many women who are praying most earnestly, and even agonizingly, for the conversion of their husbands! This is very evident from the way in which they speak to others about their husbands. They will come to you and say, "I wish you would pray for my husband, that he may be converted; he is such a good man. It is true he is not a Christian, but he is such a good man." Could any woman who had any proper idea of the infinite majesty and glory of God, or the divine majesty and dignity of His Son Jesus Christ, call a man "a good man" when he is disobeying God by not believing in His Son Jesus Christ, no matter how kind he might be to her and how just to others? When he is trampling under foot the glorious Son of God (Heb. 10:29), how can she call such a man "a good man" just because he is her husband? No, no, no, he may be your husband; he may be kind and generous and excellent in many ways, but if he is rejecting Jesus Christ, he is a wicked, stubborn rebel against God. You may love him, and you ought to love him, but do not dishonor God by calling him good. Rather, cry to God for His conversion, not merely so that you may have the joy of seeing him converted, and not merely that he may have the joy of being converted and be saved from an eternal hell, but in order that

God may be glorified in his conversion. Pray that way, and it will not be long before you see your husband converted.

Consider another illustration. Many ministers and professing Christians are praying for a true revival. That certainly is a proper prayer; that certainly is a prayer that is according to God's will; it is a Bible prayer, for we read in Psalm 85:6, *"Wilt thou not revive us again: that thy people may rejoice in thee?"* Yes, that is a perfectly proper prayer; indeed, I cannot see how anyone who is a real Christian can keep from praying that prayer with intense earnestness in days such as these. But one may, and people often do, offer that prayer from an entirely selfish motive.

Many ministers are praying for a revival in their churches from purely selfish motives. I received a letter once from a minister, the pastor of a church, asking me to come and hold a meeting with him, and he wrote, "I am losing my hold upon my people, and if I do not have a revival I will have to give up my church." In other words, he wanted a revival merely so that he might maintain his living. Perhaps that was an extreme case, but there are many cases that are essentially the same. Both ministers and members are praying for a revival so that there may be an increase of members in the church; so that the church may have a larger prestige in the community; so that some of the rich people in the community may be converted and the burden of supporting the church will not be so heavy upon them; or for many other purely selfish reasons.

Why should we pray for a revival? We should pray for revival for many reasons:

- so that God may be glorified by a revival
- because we can no longer bear it that God should be dishonored by the low level of living among professing Christians, and by the increase of wickedness and godlessness in the world
- because we can no longer endure it that God should be dishonored by the outspoken infidelity so common among men today, and by the even more dangerous

infidelity of many of our church members, and even of some alleged preachers of the Gospel today

• so that God may be glorified by the church being brought up to the level of Christian life that will glorify God

• so that God may be glorified by the conversion of sinners, by stopping the mouths of unbelievers, and by delivering some of our church members and our preachers from dangerous heresy and unbelief to a God-honoring faith in God's Word and the truth contained in His Word

So that God may be glorified—that is why we should pray for a revival. But how far that is from the thoughts of many who are praying for a revival today!

Take still another illustration. There are many ministers and members in our churches today who are praying that they may be baptized with the Holy Spirit. That is certainly a proper prayer, a prayer that pleases God, a prayer that has abundant warrant in the Word of God, for the Lord Jesus distinctly tells us in Luke 11:13, *"If ye then, being evil, know how to give good gifts unto your children: how much more shall your heavenly Father give the Holy Spirit to them that ask him?"* We also read in Acts 4:31, *"And when they had prayed, the place was shaken where they were assembled together; and they were all filled with the Holy Ghost, and they spake the word of God with boldness."* Yes, indeed, it is a proper prayer; and I cannot understand how any Christian can rest until he is baptized with the Holy Spirit, and knows it.

But there is much prayer for the baptism with the Holy Spirit, or the filling with the Holy Spirit, that is purely selfish. Men and women pray for the baptism with the Holy Spirit because they think they will be happier if they are thus baptized. They know men and women who have been baptized with the Holy Spirit, and such a new and radiant and glorious joy has come into their lives that they want it, too. Or it may be that they pray for the baptism with the Holy Spirit because they know someone else who has been baptized with the Holy Spirit and a new power has come into their service, and they want the baptism with the Holy Spirit so that they, too, may be more prominent and successful in their work for God. Now all this is pure selfishness, and one can pray for the baptism with the Holy Spirit in that way until doomsday and never obtain it.

Why should we desire the baptism with the Holy Spirit? Or why, if we have been baptized with the Holy Spirit, should we pray for a new filling with the Holy Spirit? We should pray for the filling with the Holy Spirit for many reasons:

- so that God may be glorified in our being baptized or filled with the Holy Spirit
- because we can no longer endure it that God should be any longer dishonored by the low level of our living, and by the ineffectiveness of our service
- so that God may be glorified by our being empowered to lead lives that honor Him
- so that God may be glorified by our having the power in His service that we ought to have
- so that God may be glorified by our being baptized or filled with the Holy Spirit

That is why we should pray for the filling with the Holy Spirit. And when we get to praying for the baptism with the Holy Spirit along this line, it will not be many hours before we are thus baptized with the Spirit of God. But how far this is from the thoughts of many who are praying for the baptism with the Holy Spirit is very evident from the way they talk and the way they pray.

A friend of mine was holding a meeting in a town in New York State, near the Hudson River. At one of his morning services, he spoke on the baptism with the Holy Spirit. As he went away from the meeting, one of the ministers of the town walked with him. They had not gone far when this minister said, "I greatly enjoyed your address this morning. The baptism of the Holy Spirit that you were talking about is just what I need, and that is what I am going to have." Now that sounded encouraging, but the minister went on to say, "I have a salary of $12,000 a year. I believe if I had that baptism of the Holy Spirit that you have been talking about, I could get $15,000 a year."

Now you might smile at that, but it is really shocking, indeed appalling. It may be an extreme case, but it illustrates a tendency of thought that is exceedingly common among professing Christians and among ministers today who are praying that they may be baptized with the Holy Spirit. Oh, brothers and sisters, when you and I come to see this thing in the light of the Bible, come to see how dishonoring our lives are to God, and come to long for the baptism with the Holy Spirit, or filling with the Holy Spirit—not that we may be blessed, but that God may be glorified—it will not be long before we are baptized with the Holy Spirit.

Sin in the Heart or Life

You will find a second hindrance to prayer set forth in Isaiah 59:1–2: *"Behold, the LORD's hand is not shortened, that it cannot save; neither his ear heavy, that it cannot hear: but your iniquities have separated between you and your God, and your sins have hid his face from you, that he will not hear."* Here we are distinctly told that in many instances, the reason why God does not answer prayer is that our iniquities and our sins have separated us from our God, and hidden His face from us, so that He will not hear. The people of Isaiah's time were saying, "God does not answer prayer any longer. He may have answered it in the days of Moses; He may have answered in the days of Elijah, but He does not answer any longer. Either His ear is heavy and He cannot hear, or His hand is shortened that He cannot save."

"No, no," said Isaiah, "'*the LORD's hand is not shortened, that it cannot save; neither his ear heavy, that it cannot hear*' (Isa. 59:1). The trouble is not with God; the trouble is with you. '*Your iniquities have separated between you and your God, and your sins have hid his face from you, that he will not hear*' (v. 2)." Sin in our hearts or lives makes it impossible for God to answer our prayer, even though the thing for which we are praying is entirely according to His will.

If you are praying for something and you do not get it, do not conclude that God does not answer prayer; do not conclude that God does not answer prayer today as He did in former times; do not conclude that this thing that you are asking for is not according to the will of God. Get alone with God, ask Him to search your heart, and ask Him to show you whether there is anything in your past life that you have done that was wrong that you have not set straight, any past sin that you have not judged, or whether there is anything in your life today that is displeasing to Him. And then wait silently before Him and give Him an opportunity to show you. If He shows you anything, confess it to Him as sin and give it up.

If you will not do this, then there is not the least use in your trying to pray; nothing will come of your prayers. It will not be because God does not hear prayer today just as much as in former days; it will not be because the arm of the Lord is shortened so that He cannot save, or that His ear is heavy so that He cannot hear. God's ear is just as sharp to hear the voice of true prayer as it ever was, and His hand is just as long and just as strong to save as it ever was. *"But your iniquities have separated between you and your God, and your sins have hid his face from you, that he will not hear"* (Isa. 59:2). Right at this point we find the full explanation of why it is that many of our prayers are not heard and bring nothing to pass.

I had a striking illustration of this in my own life some years ago, an experience that I have never forgotten. I had started out to carry on the work that God had given me to do in Minneapolis without any pledges for its support, and without taking up any contributions or collections of any kind, but simply looking to God by prayer to furnish the money for the work. I do not believe that God asks every man to do this, or even that He asks the same man always to do it, but I was entirely sure that God had told me to do it at that time, and I had stepped out in simple faith in God. Before this time, I had had a strong society behind me who paid me a generous salary, paid for the rent of the various halls, paid for the missionaries I employed, and paid for all the work that was done.

Hindrances to Prayer

But I saw that the time had come when I should step out in simple faith in Him, and so I asked the society that had been supporting me if they would turn the work over to me to carry it on in that way. I told them what they knew to be true, that there was a great deal of other work they ought to be doing and they needed their money for that other work. Somewhat reluctantly but very kindly they agreed to my request, and in a single day I cut off every source of income I had in the world. From that time every penny that came for the support of my wife, our four children, and me, every penny that came for rent of halls, lights, fuel, and everything else, every penny that came for my missionaries, came in answer to prayer. We took up no collections, had no subscriptions; no one was ever asked for money, no one but God. A great many people were watching the experiment, many of them very sympathetically, others possibly quite critically. However, I must say that for an experiment that must have seemed so crazy to an outsider, it was received, as far as I know, with kindness everywhere.

The money came in day after day, and week after week, and month after month, not from the old sources, but almost entirely from new sources. Sometimes it came in small amounts, sometimes in large amounts; sometimes it came in ways most ordinary, and sometimes in ways apparently very extraordinary. But it came. But one day it did not come; that is to say, I had obligations that I had to meet very soon and no money to meet them. When I went home that night, before I went to bed, I took the matter to God in prayer and asked Him to send me that money, not only so that the work might go on, but also so that His name might not be dishonored by an apparent failure on His part to answer prayer. But I went to bed, I am afraid, without much clear faith that the money would come.

I was all alone in the house. In the middle of the night I was awakened by great pain and physical distress; I was very sick. I looked up to God and cried to Him that He would touch my body and heal me, and that He would send that money; but there was no answer. Again I cried to God to touch my body and send that money. Still no answer. It seemed as though the heavens

307

above my head were brass; it seemed as if there were no God there, and the devil came and taunted me. He said, as he said to the psalmist, "*Where is thy God?*" (Ps. 42:3). There is no God, or if there is a God, He does not answer prayer in the way that you have been teaching people that He does."

I was in great distress of soul as well as body; it seemed as if the very billows of hell were going over my head; it seemed as if the cherished faith of years was now worthless. Have you ever been there? Have you ever been where it seemed the faith that you cherished for years, and that you thought was so well founded, was suddenly worth little or nothing? Well, that was where I was. And again I cried to God. "Touch my body, heal me, and send that money." No answer. Then I looked up and I said, "Heavenly Father, if there is anything wrong in my life anywhere, show me what it is, and I will give it up." Instantly God brought up something that had often come up before to trouble me, but every time it would come up I would say, "That's all right. I know it's all right. There is nothing wrong about that," but all the time in the bottom of my heart I knew it was wrong.

Do you have anything of that kind in your heart and life, something that always comes up to trouble you when you get near to God, and yet you try to persuade yourself it is right? You say to yourself, "That's all right. I know it's all right. I am sure it is all right; it is all nonsense to think that that is wrong." Well, so it was with me. It came up again vividly, and I looked up and said, "Oh, God, if this thing is wrong in Your sight, I will give it up now." No answer. In the depths of my heart I knew it was wrong, but I said, "Oh, God, if it is wrong in Your sight, I will give it up." There was no answer. Then I cried, "Oh, God, this thing is wrong; it is sin. I give it up now." Instantly God touched my body; immediately I was as well as I am this moment, the money came in, and the work went on.

When? When I judged my sin. Oh, men and women, if you are praying for something and not getting it, I beg you, do not think that God does not answer prayer; do not decide that the thing that you are praying for is not according to God's will! God may be dealing with you; He may be trying to bring you to your senses and to Himself. Get alone with God and honestly ask Him to show you if there is anything wrong in your heart or life, anything that is displeasing to Him. When He shows you, set it straight at once, and you will find an open heaven and a God who answers prayer—a God whose ear is not only quick to hear prayer in general, and whose hand is not only strong to save in general, but a God whose ear is quick to hear your prayer, and whose hand is long and strong to give immediate deliverance to you. Oh, how many things there are that we greatly need and that we might have at once if we would only judge and put away our sin!

Idols in the Heart

Now turn to Ezekiel 14:1–3, where we will find a third hindrance to prayer.

> *Then came certain of the elders of Israel unto me, and sat before me. And the word of the LORD came unto me, saying, Son of man, these men have set up their idols in their heart, and put the stumblingblock of their iniquity before their face: should I be inquired of at all by them?*

The elders of Israel had come to Ezekiel to pray for them; it was seemingly a day of great triumph for Ezekiel. For a long time, for days and months, perhaps for years, Ezekiel had been longing for the time when the elders of Israel would come to their senses and come to him and ask him to pray for them, and the time seemed to have come. With a glad heart Ezekiel was about to go to God in prayer for them, and for the people. But God suddenly stopped him and said, "Ezekiel, do not pray for these men. They *'have set up their idols in their heart, and put the stumblingblock of their iniquity before their face: should I be inquired of at all by them?'*" Here we are clearly told that idols in the heart make it impossible for God to attend to our prayers.

In Japan, China, India, and other non-Christian lands, they set up their idols in their temples and in their homes, but the

Jews, and we Christians also today, set up our idols in our hearts. There are no hideous images on our mantels or in other places in our homes, but there are idols in the hearts of many of us. These make it just as impossible for God to answer our prayers as if we had the most hideous images in our homes or in our churches.

What is an idol? An idol is anything that a man or woman puts before God. Many men make idols of their wives. No man can love his wife too much; the more truly a man loves God, the more deeply and tenderly he will love his wife. But a man may put his wife in the wrong place; he may put his wife before God. Many men, many professing Christian men, many active Christian men, do things to please their wives that they know do not please God. They are making idols of their wives; they are not on praying ground.

Many wives also make idols of their husbands. No wife can love her husband too much. The more truly a woman loves God, the more deeply and tenderly she will love her husband. But a wife can put her husband in the wrong place; she can put her husband before God, and she can do things to please her husband that she knows do not please God. Many wives are doing this in these days; many wives are doing things in the matter of dress, in the matter of social engagements, in the matter of amusements, and in other matters, to please their husbands—things that they know full well do not please God. They are making idols of their husbands, and they are not on praying ground.

We can make idols of our children. We must not love our children too much; the more truly we love God, the more deeply and tenderly we will love our children, but we can put our children in the wrong place. We can put our children before God, and we can do things to please our children that we know do not please God. How many Christians are doing that very thing today? How many Christian fathers and mothers are allowing forms of amusement, social entertainment, and other things in their homes that they know are displeasing to God, because their children want them? They are making idols of their children, and they are not on praying ground.

Hindrances to Prayer

Many individuals make idols of social position. Many professedly Christian men and women—quite earnest men and women in some respects—are doing things to secure or maintain a social position that they desire to occupy, which they know are not right in the sight of God. Major Whittle, the evangelist, was once holding meetings in the city of Washington, D.C. An old friend of his was at the time occupying a high position in the United States government. This friend invited Major Whittle to his beautiful Washington home. One day he was showing Major Whittle around the home, and as they went from room to room, they came into a very large and beautifully decorated room. Major Whittle glanced around it and then said to the man, "What is this room for?"

The man evaded an answer, but Major Whittle was not easily put off, and he repeated his question, "What is this room for?"

The man replied, "Well, Major, if you must know, it is a ballroom."

Major Whittle looked at him sternly and said, "Do you mean to tell me that you have fallen so low in the moral scale that you have a ballroom in your home?"

The man dropped his head and said, "Major, I did not think I would ever come to this, but here we are in Washington society, and my wife and daughter told me that we must do this to maintain our position in society, and I have yielded to them." He and his wife had made an idol of social position, and before he got through, he and his wife paid dearly for it.

The temptation to make an idol of our reputation is especially real with ministers of the Gospel. We ministers know perfectly well that in this day in which we are living, which puts such an extraordinary and absurd value upon what it calls advanced thought and original thinking, that if a minister is true to the old God-given doctrines, no matter how scholarly and how brilliant he may be, he will be rated by a great many persons as not scholarly and not up-to-date. Yet, on the other hand, no matter how unscholarly a man is, or how poor a thinker he may be, if he throws out views that are a little questionable, or a great deal questionable, he will at once be rated as a great scholar and thinker, fully abreast of the times.

So many ministers who are perfectly sound at heart in their own views will throw out a little suggestion now and then to make people realize that they are abreast of the times, and this will undermine the faith of the young men and young women in their congregations. They have made an idol of their reputation, and have lost their power in prayer.

Or again, we ministers often realize that if we use ornate rhetoric and theatrical modes of address, we will not win so many souls to Christ as we will by preaching the simple, straight Gospel, but we will get a far greater reputation as pulpit orators. Many men in the pulpit today have sacrificed their real power for God by cultivating an elaborate and highly polished rhetoric and oratorical methods of delivery that awakened the admiration and applause of shallow men and women, but robbed them of real power for God. Such men have made an idol of their reputation and are not on praying ground.

Oh, if you desire power in prayer, get alone with God and let Him search you. Ask Him to show you if there is any idol in your heart, and when He shows it to you, do away with it today.

> The dearest idol I have known,
> Whate'er that idol be,
> Help me to tear it from its throne
> And worship only Thee.

An Unforgiving Spirit

Our Lord Jesus Christ set forth a fourth hindrance to prayer in Mark 11:25: *"And when ye stand praying, forgive, if ye have ought against any: that your Father also which is in heaven may forgive you your trespasses."* Here we are distinctly told that an unforgiving spirit makes it impossible for God to answer our prayers. All of God's desire and ability to answer our prayers is based upon His dealing with us as forgiven sinners, and God cannot deal with us as forgiven sinners while we are not forgiving those who have wronged us. I believe that this touches on one of the most frequent causes of unanswered prayer: bitterness in our hearts toward those who have wronged us, or whom we imagine have wronged us.

How many wives are praying, praying earnestly, praying with almost breaking hearts, for the conversion of their husbands, but all the time they have bitterness in their hearts toward those who have wronged them, or whom they imagine have wronged them? Woman, are you willing that your husband should be eternally lost for the poor, miserable gratification of hating someone who has wronged you, or whom you only imagine has wronged you? How many mothers are praying, praying so earnestly, for the conversion of their sons or daughters, and all the time they are praying they have bitter hatred in their hearts toward some other woman who has wronged them, or whom they imagine has wronged them? Woman, are you willing that your son or daughter should go down to an eternal hell for the poor, miserable gratification of hating someone?

If we wish to have power in prayer, let us search our hearts today, and let us look to God to search our hearts and bring to light any enmity that there may be in our hearts toward anyone. If we find that there is such enmity, no matter how much that person may have wronged us, let us give it up and let the Spirit of God come into our hearts, the Spirit who makes us love everyone, even our cruelest enemies.

When Mr. Alexander and I were holding meetings in Launceston, Tasmania, we had a day of fasting and prayer. There was a Christian man in the community who had a son-in-law, and he and his wife had had some trouble with that son-in-law. They had forbidden him ever to come under their roof again. At the morning service I spoke, as I always did on the day of fasting and prayer, on hindrances to prayer. When I reached this part of my sermon, the man was deeply convicted of that sin. As he went away from the meeting to his home at the noon hour, he began thinking of it, and he wondered to himself whether he ought to write his son-in-law. Just as he was reaching home he was wondering whether he ought to speak to his wife about this matter. He went up the steps and reached out his hand to open the door, still thinking about this. Unknown to him, his wife had been at the meeting also, and as he reached out to open the door, his wife opened the door from the other side and instantly said, "Telegraph him to come at once." And they did. And power in prayer came into the life of that man and woman.

Some of you who are reading these words have had no power in prayer for days, or weeks, or months, or it may be for years, simply because of some bitterness that you have in your heart toward someone. There is no use whatsoever of your praying until you let God cast out that bitterness. Listen again to the words of Jesus Christ Himself: *"When ye stand praying, forgive, if ye have ought against any: that your Father also which is in heaven may forgive you your trespasses"* (Mark 11:25).

Stinginess in Our Giving

Now turn to Proverbs 21:13, a deeply significant passage of Scripture that throws great light on the subject that we are studying: *"Whoso stoppeth his ears at the cry of the poor, he also shall cry himself, but shall not be heard."* Here God distinctly tells us that if we block our ears to the cry of the poor when they cry unto us for help, He will block His ears to us when we cry unto Him for help. The one who is stingy in his giving cannot be a mighty man of prayer. This thought runs all through the Bible. Read, for example, Luke 6:38:

> *Give, and it shall be given unto you; good measure, pressed down, and shaken together, and running over, shall men give into your bosom. For with the same measure that ye mete withal it shall be measured to you again.*

Here God distinctly tells us that He measures out His benefits to us in exactly the same measure that we measure out our giving to others. Some of us use such tiny measures in our giving that God can only give us a small blessing. God puts His gifts into our lives in answer to our prayers through the same door that we give out our kindnesses to others, and some of us open the door of our kindnesses such a tiny crack that God can only get in the smallest blessing to us.

There is another passage, one of the most familiar promises in the Bible. It is a promise that one hears in almost every prayer meeting that he attends, and yet a promise that is constantly quoted without any reference whatsoever to the context and to the condition of fulfillment implied in the context: *But my God shall supply all your need according to his riches in glory by Christ Jesus"* (Phil. 4:19). What a wonderful promise it is, but the Revised Version makes it even more wonderful: *"And my God shall fulfil every need of yours according to his riches in glory in Christ Jesus."* Turn that word *"fulfil"* around, and you get exactly what the Greek word signifies: "fill full." Now read it that way: *"And my God shall* [fill full] *every need of yours according to his riches in glory in Christ Jesus."*

One of the elders of our church in Chicago stood up one night in our prayer meeting and said, "I thank God, fellow believers, that there is one promise in the Bible without any condition," and then he quoted this passage: *"But my God shall supply all your need according to his riches in glory by Christ Jesus."*

I stopped him and said, "Hold on a minute, Brother H———, there is a condition; it is exceedingly plain in the context. Look back at the fifteenth verse, and read from there." And so I read to him:

> *Now ye Philippians know also, that in the beginning of the gospel, when I departed from Macedonia, no church communicated with me as concerning giving and receiving, but ye only. For even in Thessalonica ye sent once and again unto my necessity.*
> (Phil. 4:15–16)

Paul went on to say how they had just sent to him again, and then he said, *"And my God shall fulfil every need of yours* [that is, every need of a generously giving church] *according to his riches in glory in Christ Jesus"* (v. 19 RV). There is absolutely nothing here that a stingy Christian has a right to claim. We are plainly told that the promise is made to large givers, and to them alone. Of course the gift may not be large in itself, but large in comparison with what a person has.

The Power of Prayer

There is another familiar promise that sounds much like this one that we have just noted. We read in 2 Corinthians 9:8, *"And God is able to make all grace abound toward you; that ye, always having all sufficiency in all things, may abound to every good work."* Just look at the *alls* and the *every* and the *abounds*. Read it again, *"And God is able to make all grace abound toward you; that ye, always having all sufficiency in all things, may abound to every good work."* Wonderful promise, isn't it? But read it in its context. Begin at verses 6 and 7:

> *He which soweth sparingly* [the context shows that Paul was speaking about the sowing of gifts, and sowing sparingly means giving sparingly] *shall reap also sparingly; and he which soweth bountifully shall reap also bountifully. Every man according as he purposeth in his heart, so let him give; not grudgingly, or of necessity: for God loveth a cheerful giver* [the Greek word here translated *"cheerful"* is *hilaros*, from which we get our word *hilarious*]. *And God is able to make all grace abound toward you* [that is, toward the hilarious giver]; *that ye* [that is, that you hilarious givers], *always having all sufficiency in all things, may abound to every good work.* (2 Cor. 9:6–8)

There is nothing here for the stingy Christian, only for the Christian who is a hilarious giver. Are you a hilarious giver? Do you love to find opportunities to give? When you see the collection basket coming, do you say to yourself, "I am so glad I have another opportunity to give"? Or do you say, "I wish they wouldn't constantly take up collections"?

Take one other passage of Scripture, that wonderful promise in 1 John 3:22: *"And whatsoever we ask, we receive of him, because we keep his commandments, and do those things that are pleasing in his sight."* What a wonderful promise that is. John here told us plainly that whatever he asked of God he received. But why? Read the context; begin back at the fifteenth verse:

> *Hereby perceive we the love of God, because he laid down his life for us: and we ought to lay down our lives for the brethren. But whoso hath this world's good, and seeth his brother have need, and shutteth up his bowels of compassion from him, how dwelleth the love of God in him?* (1 John 3:16–17)

Hindrances to Prayer

I can tell you how—it will not happen at all! But read on: *"My little children, let us not love in word, neither in tongue; but in deed and in truth"* (v. 18). That is to say, let us not love in mere profession of love, but in reality, by actually doing.

For example, it is a cold winter night. There are only a few people at the prayer meeting, but an enthusiastic brother enters. In a little while he gets up in the prayer meeting and says, "Brothers, I am so glad to be here tonight. I do so enjoy the society of Christian people. I know that I have passed from death unto life, because I love my fellow Christians (1 John 3:14). Oh, how I love my fellow Christians; how glad I am to be here tonight! I'd rather be here than to go to the theater or the circus or any entertainment. I do not see how anyone who calls himself a Christian can go to places like that. There is no place I enjoy as much as I enjoy the prayer meeting; no fellowship that I love as I love the fellowship of Christians. I know I have passed from death unto life, because I love my fellow Christians."

Immediately after the meeting is over, one goes to this enthusiastic, glowing brother and says to him, "Brother Smith, I was so glad to hear your testimony tonight; it just warmed my heart. But I want to speak to you about a little matter. You know Sister Johnson. She has been through some rough times. Her husband died a few months ago. He left her no insurance, and she is having a hard time paying her rent and keeping her family together. She lives in that little house of yours over on the other side of town, and she is afraid she cannot pay the rent this time. Can't you let her off on the rent?" And instantly this glowing Christian becomes cold, and he says, "Well, of course I sympathize with the poor sister, and I wish I could help her, but business is business. If she cannot pay the rent I suppose she will have to get out." How can the love of God dwell in that man? I will tell you how—it doesn't! He simply loves *"in word"* and *"in tongue,"* but not *"in deed and in truth"* (1 John 3:18).

Take another illustration. Another brother comes into a prayer meeting, and he gets up with the same glowing testimony—tells how glad he is to be there, how he loves his fellow believers, how he loves the society of Christian people, how he knows that he has passed from death unto life because he loves his fellow believers. When the meeting is over, one goes to him and says, "Brother Brown, I so enjoyed your testimony tonight; it warmed my heart. But Brother Brown, you know Sister Jones; you know what a hard time she is having. You remember how her husband was coming home from work a few weeks ago and was run over by a train and killed, and how he had no insurance and no money saved, and she has been unable to get any damages from the railroad. It is going to be a cold winter, and they have no coal over in Sister Jones' house. We are getting together a little money to stock the house with coal or wood, and to put in a barrel of flour, and potatoes, and other provisions, so that she can keep her family together and not suffer."

Suddenly this brother also becomes cold and says, "Well, I am sorry for her, and I'd like to help her, but charity must begin at home. And I've got to pay my income tax, and you know how heavy it is. And though I would like to help, I cannot." It does not seem to occur to the brother that unless he had plenty of money, he would not have a very heavy income tax.

"How dwelleth the love of God in him?" (1 John 3:17). It doesn't. He loves merely *"in word"* and *"in tongue,"* but not *"in deed and in truth"* (v. 18). But read on:

> *And hereby* [that is, by loving not merely in word and in tongue, but by our actual giving, *"in deed and in truth"*] *we know that we are of the truth, and shall assure our hearts before him* [that is, before God]. *For if our heart condemn us,* [that is, condemn us in the matter of our stingy giving], *God is greater than our heart, and knoweth all things. Beloved, if our heart condemn us not* [that is, does not condemn us because of our stingy giving], *then have we confidence toward God. And whatsoever we ask* [that is, we whose hearts do not condemn us because of our stinginess, we who are giving generously as we ought, we who love *"in deed and in truth"*], *we receive of him, because we keep his commandments, and do those things that are pleasing in his sight.*
> (1 John 3:19–22)

Hindrances to Prayer

You may go straight through your Bible, and you will find that every great promise on God's part to give in answer to our prayers, is dependent on our generous giving to others who need our help.

Right here we discover the secret of why individual believers, and the church of Christ as a whole, have so little power in prayer today. It is because of our downright stinginess in giving. Great men of prayer are all great givers, that is, great givers according to their abilities. George Müller, as I have already mentioned, was one of the greatest men of prayer. For about sixty years he carried on a most marvelous work in supporting and training the orphans of England, oftentimes housing 2,000 or more orphans at one time, feeding them three meals a day. Yet every penny that came for the support of the orphans, and for the support of the other work for which he felt responsible, came in answer to prayer. No appeal was ever made to anyone, no collections or offerings were ever taken, and yet the money never failed to come. Sometimes it seemed almost up to the last moment as if it would fail, but it always came. He would ask God for £100, and it would come, and he would pass it on. He would ask for £60,000, and it would come and he would pass it on. In all, as we have already stated, he asked for over $7,200,000, and it came, and he passed it on.

That was the reason why it kept coming, because he kept passing it on. None of it stuck to his fingers. And when he died, he had just enough left to pay his funeral expenses. We ask and we get and we keep, and so God ceases to give. We block our ears to the cry of the poor, the poor in our own land and the poor in other lands, the spiritually poor even more than the poor in purse, and so God blocks His ears to our cries, just as He told us in Proverbs 21:13 He would do.

The churches of America do not average ten cents a week per member for foreign missions, and yet we wonder why God does not hear our prayers. Many professedly Christian women, every year of their lives, spend more on single items of fancy clothing than they do upon foreign missions, and yet they wonder why God does not hear their prayers. I am not saying that women should not wear nice clothes, but I am saying that a Christian woman should certainly give more for the work of sending the Gospel to the perishing heathen than she does on a matter of personal adornment.

Many professing Christian men, every year of their lives, spend more on the unnecessary, not to say filthy and unwholesome, tobacco habit than they do upon sending the Gospel to the perishing in China, India, Africa, and elsewhere. Yet they wonder why God does not answer their prayers. Many men in our churches today, if you ask them for $100 for foreign missions, would almost faint away, and yet they spend more than fifty cents a day on cigars, and fifty cents a day would add up to more than $100 in a year. Many of them spend many times fifty cents a day on cigars or cigarettes, or tobacco in some form, and never dream of giving the same amount to foreign missions. Yet they wonder why God does not answer their prayers. There is no wonder about it; it is their stinginess, their downright penny-pinching in their giving.

A young lady once came into my office in Minneapolis. I was interested in the newsboys of Minneapolis, and so was she. I was vice president of the Newsboys' Home, and we needed something badly for that home. I have forgotten now what it was. This young woman was the daughter of a wealthy railway magnate. Standing by my table in my office, she rested her fingers upon the table and said to me, "Oh, Mr. Torrey, we must get that money for the newsboys. How shall we get it?" And as she said it, the value of one diamond alone that flashed on her finger would have met the need many times over.

At a great world missionary meeting in Rochester some years ago, an enthusiastic missionary advocate stretched out her hands to the audience in a pathetic appeal and said, "Sisters, we must have money for foreign missions." Yet as she said it, more than $7,000 worth of diamonds flashed on her fingers. Yet we wonder why God does not answer our prayers. Oh, there is no wonder at all about it; the explanation is simple. It is found in the Word of God; it is because of our stinginess, the smallness of our giving. Doesn't God say it in His Word, and is He not thundering it in our ears right now: *"Whoso stoppeth his ears at the cry of the poor, he also shall cry himself, but shall not be heard"* (Prov. 21:13)?

A Wrong Treatment of Husband or Wife

There is one more hindrance to prayer that I must mention. We find it plainly stated in 1 Peter 3:7: *"Likewise, ye husbands, dwell with [your wives] according to knowledge, giving honour unto the wife, as unto the weaker vessel, and as being heirs together of the grace of life; that your prayers be not hindered."* That is plain enough, is it not? God here distinctly tells us that a wrong treatment of a wife by a husband (and vice versa, of course), hinders prayer; and it makes it impossible for God to hear the prayer of the husband or wife, as the case may be.

Some of us are searching far and wide to discover what it is that hinders our prayers. We do not need to look so far away. Look into your home life. Husband, are you treating your wife as the Bible tells us a husband ought to treat his wife? Wives, are you treating your husbands as the Bible tells us wives ought to treat their husbands? If you are not, God will not hear your prayers. You may make all kinds of pretense of piety; you may be faithful in attending religious services and cooperating in Christian work, but God's eye is on your home life. The religion of our Lord Jesus Christ is a religion that enters right into the practicalities of everyday home life. That is one reason why I rejoice in it and am glad that I am a Christian.

Christianity magnifies the home. Our modern modes of living, even among believers, lessen the home, but God doesn't.

How many men are in our churches today who, if you heard them talk in the prayer meeting, or in the missionary meeting, you would think they were perfect saints of God? How soft and pleasing and earnest are their words! And many women who hear them think, "How pleasant it must be to live with a husband like that!" But in their homes these men are quite different; they are cross, harsh, domineering, and overbearing. They come down to breakfast, and if by some mischance the bacon isn't cooked just right—perhaps it is a little burnt—they fly into a rage and say to their wives, "Why can't we have a decent breakfast in this house? You are always burning the food. If I can't get a good breakfast at home, I am going to a restaurant." So they rise from the table, hurry out of the room, take their hats, and start for a restaurant. The poor brokenhearted wives then sit down and begin to sob. These men are actually shortening the lives of their wives, yet they wonder why God does not answer their prayers.

There is no wonder about it; it is because they are brutes, and God nowhere promises to answer the prayers of brutes—but of men, real 100 percent, Christian men.

I heard some years ago of a husband who did that very thing. He came to the breakfast table, the bacon was burned, he arose from the table cross and complaining, and he said to his wife, "Why can't we have decent bacon in this house? If we can't, I am going to the restaurant." He dashed out of the room, took his hat, and started for the restaurant. His wife, of course, sank down by the table, buried her face in her arms, and began to cry and sob. They had a darling little boy, a sweet sympathetic boy. He came up to his sobbing mother, and his arms went around her neck, and he cried with her and sobbed out, "Ma, I'm awfully sorry we married pa, ain't you?" There are many men today who act this way in their homes, though they claim to be earnest Christians, and make their children sorry that they "married pa." Yet these men wonder why their prayers are not answered.

Take another illustration on the other side. Many professedly Christian women today are sweet as a summer morn, as engaging and alluring as a June breeze, when they are at the missionary society, or the sewing circle, or any other public gathering of the church. But how different they are at home—cross, moody, nagging. A husband comes home tired from work. As he and his wife are about to sit down to the evening meal, his wife says to him, "John, did you mail that letter I gave you this morning?"

He looks at her aghast, puts his hand in his pocket, and finds the letter there, and begins to apologize and says, "Wife, I am so sorry I forgot to mail it."

Hindrances to Prayer

Then she storms, "Of course you forgot to mail it; you always forget to mail it; you never do what I ask you to do," and thus she goes on. At last he, in anger and disgust, rises from the table, takes his hat, and starts for the local bar. And that woman wonders how such a good Christian woman as she could have a drunkard for a husband. I'll tell you, woman, it is because you made him so. God forbid that I should justify a man for being a frequenter of places like that under any circumstances, but it is a simple matter of fact that many men frequent such places because their professedly Christian wives made their homes so hellish that they felt they could not stay there. Yet that woman wonders why her prayers are not answered.

Consider another illustration. How many women are there who, when a certain young man is coming to call on her, stand before the mirror and array themselves down to the smallest detail with the utmost care because "Charlie" is coming tonight? If it were anyone else but Charlie, she would not take such care, but it is Charlie. But then the months pass, and she and Charlie have been married, perhaps several months. If anyone, any other gentleman, is coming to dinner besides her husband, she is as careful as ever to make herself look attractive. But when "no one is coming tonight but Charlie," then any old dress is good enough, for "it is only Charlie." And yet she wonders why her prayers are not answered. Oh, men and women, if you and I are to expect God to answer our prayers, we must take our Christianity into our home lives, and we must be lovers always.

Some years ago in the *Ladies' Home Journal,* the question was, "How long should the honeymoon last?" I have forgotten what the answer given was, but I can tell you: forever. Every year of married life should be more loving and tender and thoughtful than the one that went before, and it must be if we are to have power in prayer.

Men and women, if we are to have power in prayer, we must look very carefully into our home lives. There are other things in married life that hinder prayer; other things that one cannot speak of in public, and yet how much they need to be spoken of in the day in which you and I are living. Many hideous abominations

323

are covered up under the sacred name of marriage. Oh, men and women, if you and I are to have power in prayer, we must spread our whole married life out before the all-seeing, all-searching, all-holy eye of God, and say to Him, "Heavenly Father, if there is anything in my married life anywhere that is displeasing in Your sight, show me what it is and I will put it away." Then let us wait before God and let Him search our married lives there in the white light of His Word, the white light of the indwelling Spirit of God. When He discloses any spot of any kind, as most likely He will, let us put it away. Then we will have an open door of access to God, and our prayers will no longer be hindered. We will call to God, and He will hear and give us what we seek from Him.

10
Prevailing Prayer and Real Revival

*It is time for thee, L*ORD*, to work: for they have made void thy law.*
—Psalm 119:126

Wilt thou not revive us again: that thy people may rejoice in thee?
—Psalm 85:6

*These all continued with one accord in prayer and supplication....
And when the day of Pentecost was fully come, they were all with
one accord in one place. And suddenly there came a sound from
heaven as of a rushing mighty wind, and it filled all the house
where they were sitting....And they were all filled with the Holy
Ghost, and began to speak with other tongues, as the Spirit gave
them utterance....Then they that gladly received his word were
baptized: and the same day there were added unto them about three
thousand souls. And they continued stedfastly in the apostles' doctrine and fellowship, and in breaking of bread, and in prayers.*
—Acts 1:14; 2:1–2, 4, 41–42

*Then said he unto me, Prophesy unto the wind, prophesy, son of
man, and say to the wind, Thus saith the Lord G*OD*; Come from
the four winds, O breath, and breathe upon these slain, that they
may live. So I prophesied as he commanded me, and the breath
came into them, and they lived, and stood up upon their feet,
an exceeding great army.*
—Ezekiel 37:9–10

*If ye then, being evil, know how to give good gifts unto your chil-
dren: how much more shall your heavenly Father give
the Holy Spirit to them that ask him?*
—Luke 11:13

The Power of Prayer

The great need of the church today is a general, widespread, deep, thorough, genuine revival. That is also the greatest need of business, the greatest need of human society, the greatest need of human government, the greatest need of international relations, the greatest need of missions. In every department of life today—business, relationships, politics, international relations, education, church—we are facing the most menacing problems and the most important crises that have confronted the human race in centuries, if not in human history. The only hope of the church is a great revival or revolution. It is a real and larger coming of the life of God into the church and through the church into society as a whole.

Of course, those of us who know our Bibles at all know well that the final revival—the revival to be followed by a universal and permanent reign of righteousness on earth as well as in heaven, when God's kingdom will come and His will is done *"in earth, as it is in heaven"* (Matt. 6:10), and when *"the earth shall be full of the knowledge of the LORD, as the waters cover the sea"* (Isa. 11:9)—will come only as the result of the return of our Lord Jesus Christ to this earth to take the reins of government. The time of that coming is God's concern and not ours (Acts 1:7), and is in His hands. For that coming we should pray (Rev. 22:20) and desire earnestly (2 Pet. 3:12 RV) and wait. But that does not mean that we should in the meantime sit down and let things go to the dogs, glorying in the fact that things are getting worse and worse all the time, and congratulating ourselves on what fine folks we are and what a tough crowd the rest are.

There is no Bible ground for being sure that the Lord may not tarry and that there may not be another revival, or perhaps many revivals, before that glad Day comes, and that most glorious of all revivals comes.

If Wesley had so reasoned in his day of widespread spiritual and theological darkness, or Martin Luther in his day, or John Knox in his day, or Jonathan Edwards in his day, or Charles Finney in his day, what would have become of the church, of the state, of human society, and of the faith of God?

Prevailing Prayer and Real Revival

Whether the Lord Jesus comes soon or whether He tarries, we need a revival, and we need it badly. If He were to come within a year and find us doing our best to bring about that greatly needed revival, He would say to us, *"Well done, thou good and faithful servant: thou hast been faithful over a few things, I will make thee ruler over many things: enter thou into the joy of thy lord"* (Matt. 25:21), and blessed will that servant be, *"whom his lord when he cometh shall find so doing"* (Matt. 24:46). But if, on the other hand, He were to come in this year and find us sitting in idle meditation on the glorious truth of His second coming and congratulating ourselves that we were "not as the rest of men are" (the men who supposedly do not know the truth), He would cut us into pieces and appoint us our portion with the rest of the hypocrites (v. 51).

So my first prayer is, *"Even so, come, Lord Jesus"* (Rev. 22:20). But I do not know and cannot know how soon that prayer will be answered, for God has seen fit to set the times and seasons within His own authority (Acts 1:7). Thus, my second prayer is (and it is getting to be a more and more intense and insistent prayer), "Lord, send a revival, and let it begin in me."

In this chapter, what I have to say will come under three headings: first, what a real revival is, and what the results of a real revival are; second, the need for a real revival; and third, the relationship of persistent prayer to a real revival.

What a Real Revival Is

First, then, let us consider what a real revival is and what its results are.

New Life Imparted

A real revival is a time of quickening or impartation of life. That is exactly what the word revival means according to its etymology, and also according to its usage today. That is exactly what the Hebrew word translated *"revive"* in our second text, *"Wilt thou not revive us again"* (Ps. 85:6) means, and it is so translated in the

Revised Version: *"Wilt thou not quicken us* [that is, impart life to us] *again?"* Since God alone can give life, a revival is a time when God visits His people, imparts new life to them by the power of His Spirit, and through them imparts life to sinners dead in trespasses and sins. We frequently have religious excitements aroused by the cunning methods and hypnotic influence of the mere professional evangelist or "revivalist," but these are not revivals and are not needed. They are, in fact, a curse and not a blessing; they are the devil's imitations of a revival.

New life from God—that is a revival. A general revival is a time when this new life from God is not confined to scattered localities, but is general throughout Christendom and the earth.

The reason why a general revival is needed is that spiritual dearth and desolation and death are general. They are not confined to any one country, though they may be more manifest in some countries than in others. They are found in our foreign mission fields as well as in our home fields. We have had, and are having, local revivals. The life-giving Spirit of God has breathed upon this minister and that, this church and that, this community and that; but what we need, and sorely need, is a revival that is widespread and general.

THE RESULTS OF REVIVAL

Now in order that we may have a more complete idea of what a revival really is, let us look at the results of a revival.

Upon Ministers

The first results are in ministers of the Gospel.

1. In times of revival, the minister has a new love for souls. We ministers, as a rule, do not have the love for souls that we ought to have, the love for souls that our Lord Jesus had, the love for souls that Paul had. But when God visits His people, the hearts of ministers are greatly burdened for the unsaved; their hearts go out in great longing for the salvation of their fellowmen. They forget their ambition to preach great sermons, and

their ambitions for fame; they long for one thing, and one thing only: to see men brought to Christ and thus saved.

2. When true revivals come, ministers get a new love for God's Word and a new faith in God's Word. They fling to the winds their doubts and their criticisms of the Bible and of the creeds, and go to preaching the Bible and, especially, Christ crucified. Revivals make ministers who are loose in their doctrines orthodox. A genuine, wide-sweeping revival would do more to get our ministers and theological professors right in their doctrine than all the heresy trials that were ever instituted.

3. Revivals bring to ministers new liberty, new joy, and new power in preaching. It is no weeklong grind to prepare a sermon, and no nerve-consuming effort to preach it after it has been prepared. Preaching becomes a joy and a refreshment, and there is real power in it in times of revival.

Upon Christians in General

Now let us look at the results of a revival in Christians generally. The results of a revival in Christians generally are as marked as its results upon the ministry.

1. In times of revival, Christians come out from the world and live separated lives. Christians who have been dallying with the world, who have been playing cards and dancing and going to the theaters and the movies, and indulging in similar unbecoming foolishness, give them up. They get a new spiritual vision, by which they see clearly that these things are incompatible with their increasing life and light.

2. In times of revival, Christians get a new spirit of prayer. Prayer meetings are no longer a mere duty but become the necessity of a hungry, importunate heart. Private prayer is followed with new zest. The voice of earnest prayer to God is heard day and night. People no longer ask, "Does God answer prayer?"; they know He does, and they besiege the throne of grace day and night.

3. In times of revival, Christians go to work for lost souls. They do not go to meetings simply to enjoy themselves and get

blessed. They go to meetings to watch for souls and bring them to Christ. They talk to men on the street and in the stores and in their homes. The cross of Christ, salvation, heaven, and hell become the subjects of constant conversation. Politics and the weather and Easter bonnets and the latest novels are forgotten. The things of God occupy the whole horizon of their thought.

4. In times of revival, Christians have new joy in the Lord Jesus (Acts 2:46; John 15:11). Life is always joy, and new life is new joy. Revival days are glad days, exceedingly glad days, *"days of heaven upon the earth"* (Deut. 11:21).

5. In times of revival, Christians get a new love for the Word of God; they want to study it day and night. Revivals are bad for bars and parties and theaters and movies, but they are good for bookstores and Bible agencies.

Upon the Unsaved World

Now let us look at the results of real revival on the unsaved world. Revivals have a most decided influence on the unsaved world.

1. First of all, real revivals bring a deep conviction of sin. Our Lord said that when the Spirit was come, He would *"convict the world...of sin"* (John 16:8 RV). Now, we have seen that a revival is a coming of the Holy Spirit, and therefore there must be a new conviction of sin, and there always is. If you see something that men call a revival and there is no conviction of sin, you may know at once that it is not a real revival, but a bogus revival. This is a sure mark of real revival: deep conviction of sin.

2. Real revivals also bring conversions and regenerations. When God refreshes His people, He always converts sinners also. The first result of Pentecost was new life and power to the 120 disciples in the Upper Room; the second result was 3,000 conversions in a single day. It is always so. I am constantly reading of revivals here and there, where Christians were greatly helped, but where there were no conversions. I have my doubts about all such revivals. If Christians are truly refreshed, they will get after the unsaved by prayer and

testimony and persuasion and preaching and personal work, and there will be, there must be, conversions, real conversions, regenerated lives, lives completely transformed: infidels becoming earnest believers in Jesus Christ; drunkards becoming sober; impure men and women becoming pure; thieves becoming honest men and industrious citizens; and lazy people getting down gladly to hard work. A true revival always begins in the hearts of those who are already Christians, but it never ends there. It goes out to the unsaved, and there are definite conversions.

The Need for Revival

Now let us look at the need for a revival at the present time. I think that the mere description of what a revival is and what a revival does shows that it is needed, sorely needed, but let us look at some specific conditions that exist today that show the need for a revival. If one dwells upon these conditions, he is likely to be called pessimistic. If facing the facts is to be called a pessimist, I am willing to be called a pessimist. I am in fact an optimist, an optimist of the optimists. But I am not a blind optimist, that is, one who shuts his eyes to facts that are as clear as day. If to be an optimist one must shut his eyes and call black white, and error truth, and sin righteousness, and death life, I have no desire to be an optimist. But I am an optimist all the same. Pointing out the real conditions that are very bad will lead to better conditions.

IN THE MINISTRY

Look first at the ministry.

Heretical Teaching

Many of us who are professedly orthodox ministers are practically infidels. That may be rather blunt, but it is also an indisputable fact. There is no essential difference between the

331

teachings of some famous infidels, on the one hand, and the teachings of some of our theological professors on the other.

Theological professors are not so blunt and honest about it as infidels are; they phrase it in more elegant and studied and honeyed sentences, but their teaching means the same thing and produces the same damnable results. Much of the so-called "New Learning" and "Higher Criticism" and "Modernism" is simply infidelity sugarcoated and flavored with a pretense of piety.

There is little new in "Higher Criticism," or in modernistic or liberal theology in general. Our future ministers oftentimes are being educated under infidel professors. Also, because so many of them are really only immature boys when they enter seminary, they naturally come out as infidels in many cases, and then go forth to poison the church.

Few Men of Prayer

Even when our ministers are orthodox, as, thank God, so large a number are today, nevertheless, they are oftentimes not men of prayer. How many modern ministers, do you suppose, know what it means to "agonize in prayer" (see Romans 15:30) and to wrestle in prayer, to spend a good share of a night in prayer? Of course, we do not know how many, but I do know that many do not.

No Love for Souls

Many of us who are ministers have no love for souls. How many of us preach because we must preach, preach because we feel that men everywhere are perishing, and by our preaching hope to save some? How many of us follow up our preaching as Paul did his, by beseeching men everywhere to be *"reconciled to God"* (2 Cor. 5:20)?

Perhaps I have said enough about ministers, but it is evident that a revival is needed for our sake, or some of us will have to stand before God overwhelmed with confusion in that awful Day of Reckoning that is surely coming (Rom. 14:12).

Prevailing Prayer and Real Revival

THE CHURCH IN GENERAL

Let us now look at the church.

Its Doctrinal State

Look at the doctrinal state of the church today. It is surely bad enough, and apparently getting worse all the time. Many of our church members do not believe in the whole Bible. To many, the book of Genesis is a myth, Jonah is an allegory, and even the miracles of the Son of God are questioned. They have been denied in an article in one of our most popular and widely circulated magazines by one of the most prominent Presbyterian ministers in this country, a member of the Board of Foreign Missions of the Presbyterian Church. With a great many people, the doctrine of prayer is old-fashioned, and the work of the Holy Spirit is sneered at. We are told that conversion and regeneration are unnecessary, and hell is no longer believed in. Then look at the fads and errors that have sprung up in consequence of this loss of faith and creedal chaos: Christian Science, Unitarianism, Spiritualism, Universalism, Russellism, Babism, Theosophy, Metaphysical Healing, and a perfect pandemonium of *"doctrines of devils"* (1 Tim. 4:1).

Its Spiritual State

Look at the spiritual state of the church.

1. Worldliness is rampant, if not reigning, among church members. Many church members are just as eager as any in the rush to get rich. They use the methods of the world in the accumulation of wealth, and they hold on to it just as tightly as any worldling when they get it.

2. Prayerlessness also abounds among church members on every hand. It is doubtful if one in ten of the church members of this country attend prayer meetings with any regularity, and secret prayer takes little of the time or attention of the average church member. Someone has said that Christians, on an average, do not spend more than five minutes a day in secret prayer.

Of course, none of us knows whether that is true or not, but I fear that it is far truer than most of us suspect.

3. Neglect of the Word of God goes hand in hand with neglect of prayer to God. Many professing Christians spend twice as much time every day of their lives in wallowing through the mire of the daily papers as they do bathing in the cleansing basin of God's Holy Word. How many Christians average an hour a day spent in Bible study?

4. Along with neglect of prayer and neglect of the Word of God goes a lack of generosity. The churches are rapidly increasing in wealth, but the treasuries of the missionary societies are empty. Evangelical church members do not average more than a few dollars a year for foreign missions. It is simply appalling.

5. Then there is an increasing disregard for the Lord's Day. The Sabbath has largely become a day of worldly pleasure, instead of a day of holy service. The Sunday newspaper, with its inane twaddle and filthy scandal, takes the place of the Sunday school and church service.

6. Church members mingle with the world in all forms of questionable amusements. In many places, the young man or young woman who does not believe in the dance, with its rank immodesties; the card table, with its strong drift toward gambling; and the theater and the movies, with their increasing appeal to lewdness, is counted an old fogy, a relic of a played-out Puritanism.

Then, what a small proportion of our membership has really entered into fellowship with Jesus Christ, with His burden for souls. But enough has been said of the spiritual state of the church.

THE STATE OF THE WORLD

Now look at the state of the world.

Few Conversions

Note, first of all, how few conversions there are. Many churches last year lost more members than they gained. Here and there a church has a large number of new members upon confession of faith, but these churches are rare exceptions. And even where there are many new members, in very few cases are the conversions deep, thorough, and satisfactory.

Lack of Deep Conviction

There is also, in most circles, an utter lack of deep conviction of sin. Seldom are men overwhelmed with a sense of their awful guilt in trampling underfoot the Son of God (Heb. 10:29). Sin is regarded as a mere "misfortune," as "infirmity," or even as "good in the making"; seldom is it regarded as an enormous wrong against a holy God, deserving of eternal damnation.

Increasing Unbelief

Unbelief is rampant. Many regard it as a mark of intellectual superiority to reject the Bible, and even faith in a personal God and a future life. In most cases they are all the more proud of this mark of intellectual superiority because it is the only mark of intellectual superiority that they possess.

Gross Immorality

Hand in hand with this widespread unbelief goes the grossest immorality, as has always been the case. Infidelity and immorality are Siamese twins: they always exist and always grow and always fatten together. This prevailing immorality is found everywhere. Look at the legalized adultery that we call divorce. Much so-called marriage is little more than legalized prostitution. Men marry one wife and then another, and are still admitted into good society, and women do likewise. Thousands of supposedly respectable men in America live with other men's wives, and thousands of supposedly respectable women live with other women's husbands.

The increasing immorality is seen in the state of the theater. The theater, at its best, is bad enough, but now plays reeking with evil suggestion seem to rule the day, and the women who debauch themselves by appearing in such plays are defended in the newspapers and welcomed by supposedly respectable people. The movies are even viler than the theater ever dared to be, and the rottenness of them is paraded before our eyes in the newspapers that we are urged to receive into our homes and let our children read.

Much of our literature is rotten, but people will read books that a few years ago would have been in danger of being banned as obscene literature. I say that even supposedly decent people read these books because they are all the rage.

Art is frequently a mere covering for shameless indecency. Women are induced to cast all modesty and decency to the wind so that the artist may perfect his art and defile his morals by employing them as "models."

Greed for money has become a mania with both the rich and the poor. The multi-millionaire will often sell his soul and trample the rights of his fellowmen underfoot in the mad hope of becoming a billionaire. And the laboring man will often commit murder to increase the power of the union and to keep up wages. Wars are waged and men shot down like dogs and subjected to all kinds of cruelty to improve commerce and to gain political prestige for unprincipled politicians who parade as statesmen.

The wild and almost incredible licentiousness of the day lifts its serpent head everywhere. You see it in the newspapers, you see it on the billboards, you see it in the advertisements. You see it on the streets at night. You see it just outside the church door. You find it not only in the awful cesspools set apart for it in the great cities, but it is also crowding into our hotels and apartments and into the residential areas. Alas! Now and then you find it, if you look sharply, in supposedly respectable homes; indeed it will be brought to your ears by the confessions of brokenhearted men and women. The moral condition of the world in our day is disgusting, reeking, sickening, appalling.

We need a revival—deep, widespread, general, in the power of the Holy Spirit. It is either going to be a general revival or a general dissolution of the church, the home, and the state. A revival, new life from God, is the cure, and the only cure, that will stem the awful tide of immorality and unbelief. Mere argument will not do it, but a wind from heaven, a new outpouring of the Holy Spirit, a true, God-sent revival will. Infidelity, higher criticism, liberalism, modernism, Christian Science, spiritualism, universalism, theosophy—all will go down before the outpouring of the Spirit of God. We need a new breath from God to relegate to the limbo of forgetfulness the destructive critics of our day, and the parrots that they have trained to occupy university chairs and evangelical pulpits, to keep them company.

The Place of Prayer in Revival

We now come to the place of prayer in revival. This is the most important point I have to make, and all that I have said thus far is simply a preparation for this and was intended to lead up to this.

The great need of today, as I have said, is a general revival; that is clear and allows for no honest difference of opinion. What, then, will we do? Pray. Take up the psalmist's prayer, *"Wilt thou not revive us again: that thy people may rejoice in thee?"* (Ps. 85:6). Take up Ezekiel's prayer, *"Come from the four winds, O breath* [the breath of God], *and breathe upon these slain, that they may live"* (Ezek. 37:9).

The first great revival of Christian history had its origin, on the human side, in a prayer meeting that lasted for ten days. We read of that handful of disciples, *"These all continued with one accord in prayer and supplication"* (Acts 1:14). The result of that prayer meeting was that *"they were all filled with the Holy Ghost, and began to speak with other tongues, as the Spirit gave them utterance"* (Acts 2:4). Further on in the same chapter we read, *"And the same day there were added unto them about three thousand souls"* (v. 41). In the next verse we read how real and lasting the revival proved to be, for these are the words there recorded: *"And they continued stedfastly in the apostles' doctrine and fellowship, and in breaking of bread, and in prayers"* (v. 42). The last verse of the chapter says, *"And the Lord added to the church daily such as should be saved"* (v. 47).

The Power of Prayer

The great revival in Acts 4 came in the same way. A time of great peril had come to the church that seemed to threaten its very existence. The two great leaders of the church, Peter and John, had been arrested, imprisoned, and threatened with death. What did the church do? We read, *"And being let go, they went to their own company, and reported all that the chief priests and elders had said unto them. And when they heard that, they lifted up their voice to God with one accord"* (Acts 4:23–24). Further on we read,

And when they had prayed, the place was shaken where they were assembled together; and they were all filled with the Holy Ghost, and they spake the word of God with boldness. And the multitude of them that believed were of one heart and of one soul: neither said any of them that ought of the things which he possessed was his own; but they had all things common. And with great power gave the apostles witness of the resurrection of the Lord Jesus: and great grace was upon them all. Neither was there any among them that lacked: for as many as were possessors of lands or houses sold them, and brought the prices of the things that were sold, and laid them down at the apostles' feet: and distribution was made unto every man according as he had need. (Acts 4:31–35)

Every true revival from that day to this has had its earthly origin in prayer. The Great Awakening under Jonathan Edwards in the eighteenth century began with his famous Call to Prayer, and he carried it forward by prayer. It has been recorded of Jonathan Edwards that he "so labored in prayer that he wore grooves into the hard wooden boards where his knees pressed so often and so long."

The marvelous work of grace among the North American Indians under David Brainerd, in 1743 and the following years, had its origin in the days and nights that Brainerd spent before God in prayer for an enduement of *"power from on high"* (Luke 24:49) for this work.

But we can go further back than that and see how a revival is always the result of prayer. In the early part of the seventeenth century there was a great religious awakening in Ulster, Ireland. The lands of the rebel chiefs, which had been forfeited to the

338

British crown, were settled by a class of colonists who for the most part were governed by a spirit of wild adventure. Real piety was rare. Seven ministers, five from Scotland and two from England, settled in that country, the earliest arrivals coming in 1613. Of one of these ministers, named Blair, it is recorded by a contemporary, "He spent many days and nights in prayer, alone and with others, and was granted great intimacy with God."

Mr. James Glendenning, a man of meager natural gifts, was also a man of prayer. The work began under this man Glendenning. As the historian of the times wrote,

> He was a man who never would have been chosen by a wise assembly of ministers, nor sent to begin a reformation in this land. Yet this was the Lord's choice to begin with him the admirable work of God, which I mention on purpose so that all may see how the glory is only the Lord's in making a holy nation in this profane land, and that it was not by might, nor by power, nor by man's wisdom, but by the Spirit. (See Zechariah 4:6)

By James Glendenning's preaching at Oldstone, multitudes of hearers experienced great anxiety and terror of conscience. They looked upon themselves as altogether lost and damned, and cried out, "What shall we do to be saved?" (See Acts 16:30.) They were made to faint by the power of God's Word. A dozen in one day were carried out of doors as dead. These were not women, but some of the boldest spirits of the neighborhood, "some who had formerly feared not with their swords to put a whole town into a fray." Concerning one of them, the historian wrote, "I have heard one of them, then a mighty strong man, now a mighty Christian, say that his purpose in coming into church was to consult with his companions about how to work some mischief."

This work spread throughout the whole country. By the year 1626, a monthly prayer meeting was held in Antrim. The work spread beyond the bounds of Down and Antrim to the churches of the neighboring counties. The religious interest became so great that Christians would come thirty or forty miles to the meetings, and continue without sleep from the time they came until they returned. Many of them neither ate nor drank, and yet some of them claimed that they "went away most fresh and vigorous, their souls so filled with the sense of God." This revival changed the whole character of Northern Ireland.

I have told you in other chapters of the great Ulster Revival, the marvelous work of God, in several of the northern counties of Ireland in 1859 and 1860. That revival, too, came by prayer. Around the spring of 1858, a work of power began to manifest itself. It spread from town to town and from county to county. The congregations became too large for the buildings, and the meetings were held in the open air, often attended by many thousands of people. Hundreds of people were frequently convicted of sin in a single meeting. In some places the criminal courts and jails were closed for lack of occupation. There were manifestations of the Holy Spirit's convicting and regenerating power of a most remarkable character, clearly proving that the Holy Spirit is as ready to work today as in the days of the apostles. The Spirit will work when ministers and Christians really believe in Him and begin to prepare the way by prayer for Him to work.

It was in answer to the prayers of Wesley and his associates that the Lord saved the church and the state in England in the early part of the eighteenth century. The little group met for prayer long before God so wonderfully used them in preaching, and even a historian so utterly rationalistic as William Lecky admits that it was the Wesleyan Revival that saved England politically and commercially and in every other way. Conditions were appalling when the group of believers whom God had aroused and endued with the spirit of supplication began to pray. One observer remarked of the English of that day that they were "the most lifeless people in Europe." It is said that "the greater part of the prominent statesmen of that time were unbelievers in any form of Christianity, and were known for the grossness and immorality of their lives." Yet in answer to the prayers of a company of godly men, the prayers that would not take no for an answer, there came such a religious revival that in a few years the whole character of English society was changed, and there came a period of great spiritual life and activity in the church.

The wonderful revival of 1857 and 1858 in America, which has been described as "the greatest revival known since the days of the apostles," was the result of prayer. First came the prayers of an obscure city missionary in New York, and then the prayers of those whom he succeeded in associating with him in his burden of a desire for a revival. It has been said of America, of the time immediately preceding this revival, that its moral and spiritual degradation was such that "the whole country was on the very verge of a volcanic eruption of vice and political disaster." But prayer prevailed with God, the spirit of prayer spread, and prayer meetings were held in New York in churches and theaters, attended by thousands. Prayer meetings were held every hour of the day and night, and a chain of prayer was formed that was two thousand miles in length. There was such an outpouring of the Spirit of God that countless thousands were born again, and the influence of that great work crossed the Atlantic Ocean and led to the prayers in Northern Ireland that resulted in the great Ulster Revival.

The great awakening under D. L. Moody in England, Scotland, Ireland, and America—the results of which were felt in all the missionary countries of the earth and in the distant islands of the sea—had its origin, on the human side, in prayer. Mr. Moody, though from the time of his conversion a most active worker, made no real impression until men and women began to cry to God. His going to England at all was in answer to the importunate cries of a bedridden saint, and while the spirit of prayer continued, that wonderful work of God went on in strength. But in the course of time, less and less was made of prayer, and the work of that mighty man of God fell off very perceptibly in power.

Beyond a doubt, one of the great secrets of the unsatisfactoriness, superficiality, unreality, and temporary character of many of our modern, so-called revivals is that so much dependence is put upon man's machinery and so little upon God's power. His power must be sought and obtained by the earnest, persistent, believing prayer that will not take no for an answer. We live in a day characterized by the multiplication of machinery and the diminution of God's power. The great cry of our day is work, work, work, organize, organize, organize, give us some new committee, tell us some new methods, devise some new machinery; but the great need of our day is prayer, more prayer, and better prayer.

Prayer could work as marvelous results today as it ever could, if the church would only give itself to praying, real praying, prevailing prayer. There seem to be increasing signs that the church is awakening to this fact. Here and there, God is laying upon individual ministers and churches a burden of prayer that they have never known before. Many are getting entirely disgusted with mere machinery and with man-made revivals, and are learning to depend more upon God.

Ministers are crying to God day and night for power. In a few places, perhaps many, churches or portions of churches are meeting together in the early morning hours and the late evening hours, crying to God for His power to come raining down. There are indications of the coming of a mighty and widespread revival.

What is needed is a general revival, but if we cannot have a general revival, sweeping over the whole earth, we can have local revivals and state revivals and national revivals. It is not necessary that the whole church get to praying to begin with. Great revivals always begin first in the hearts of a few men and women whom God arouses by His Spirit to believe in Him as a living God, as a God who answers prayer, and upon whose hearts He lays a burden from which no rest can be found except in importunate crying unto God. Oh, may He, by His Spirit, lay such a burden upon our hearts today! I believe He will.

God, the Bible, and You

Contents

1

Is the Bible Inspired by God?

For prophecy never came by the will of man, but holy men of God
spoke as they were moved by the Holy Spirit.
—2 Peter 1:21 NKJV

All Scripture is given by inspiration of God, and is profitable for
doctrine, for reproof, for correction, for instruction in
righteousness, that the man of God may be complete,
thoroughly equipped for every good work.
—2 Timothy 3:16–17 NKJV

To what extent is the Bible inspired by God? The answer to this question is of vital and fundamental importance. We must understand that the writers of the various books of the Bible were inspired by God in a sense that no other men were ever inspired by God. Indeed, they were so gifted and taught and led by the Holy Spirit in recording the words of the Bible that they taught the truth and nothing but the truth. Their teachings were absolutely without error. We have in the Bible a court of final appeal and of infallible wisdom to which we can go to settle every question of doctrine or duty.

However, many believe that the writers of the Bible were "inspired" only in the vague and uncertain sense that Shakespeare, Browning, and many other men of genius were inspired. In other words, they were inspired only to the extent that their minds were made more keen to see the truth than ordinary men, and they still made mistakes and chose the wrong words to express their thoughts. Those who believe this false but popular doctrine say that we must recast the Bible writers' thoughts by discovering, if we may, the inspired thoughts behind the uninspired words.

If this is the case, we are all lost at sea. We are in hopeless confusion, for each generation must then settle for itself what the Holy Spirit meant to say through the blundering Bible writers. However, since no generation can determine with any accuracy what the Spirit meant, no generation can arrive at the truth but must simply promote blunders for the next and wiser generation to correct, to be corrected in turn by the next generation. Thank God that this subtle doctrine can be proven to be utterly untrue!

There is a great need for crystal clear teaching on this subject. Our seminaries, pulpits, and Sunday schools, as well as our religious literature, are full of teaching that is vague, inaccurate, misleading, unscriptural, and often grossly false. Many people these days say, "I believe that the Bible is inspired," when by "inspired" they do not mean at all what we understand or what the mighty men of faith in the past meant by inspired. They often say that they "believe the Bible is the Word of God," when at the same time they believe it is full of errors.

But the Bible is as clear as crystal in its teachings and claims regarding itself. Either those claims are true, or the Bible is the biggest fraud in all the literature of the human race. The position held by so many today—that the Bible is a good book, perhaps the best book in the world, but at the same time is full of errors that must be corrected by the higher wisdom of our day—is utterly illogical and absolutely ridiculous. If the Bible is not what it claims to be, it is a fraud—an outrageous fraud.

What does the Bible teach and claim concerning itself? What does it teach and claim regarding the fact and extent of its own inspiration?

Previously Undiscovered Truth Was Revealed

The first thing taught in the Bible regarding the inspiration of the various authors of the books of the Bible is this: truth hidden from men for ages, which they had not discovered and could not have discovered by the unaided processes of human reasoning, was revealed to the Bible writers by the Holy Spirit. We find this very clearly taught in the Word of God:

Is the Bible Inspired by God?

If indeed you have heard of the dispensation of the grace of God which was given to me for you, how that by revelation He made known to me the mystery (as I have briefly written already, by which, when you read, you may understand my knowledge in the mystery of Christ), which in other ages was not made known to the sons of men, as it has now been revealed by the Spirit to His holy apostles and prophets. (Eph. 3:2–5 NKJV)

The meaning of these words is unmistakable. Here Paul declared very plainly that God *"by the Spirit"* had revealed *"the mystery of Christ...to His holy apostles and prophets."* This mystery had not been made known to the sons of men in former generations. Men had not discovered it and could not discover it, except by revelation from God. But Paul and the other apostles and prophets knew it by direct revelation from God Himself through the Holy Spirit.

The Bible contains truth that men never had discovered and never could have discovered if left to themselves. The Father, in great grace, has revealed this truth to His children through His servants, the prophets and apostles. This teaching is inescapable.

We see the foolishness, a foolishness so common in our day, of seeking to test the statements of Scripture by the conclusions of human reasoning. The revelation of God transcends human reasoning; therefore, human reasoning cannot be its test. Furthermore, Christian reasoning is the product of studying the truth of the Bible; it is not the test of the truth of the Bible. If our reasoning differs from the statements of the Bible, the thing for us to do is not to try to pull God's revelation down to the level of our reasoning, but to elevate our reasoning to the level of God's Word.

The Revelation to the Prophet Was Independent of His Own Thinking

A second thing about the inspiration of the Bible writers that the Bible makes perfectly clear is this: the revelation made by

God through His Holy Spirit to the prophets was independent of the prophets' own thinking. It was made to them by the Spirit of Christ, who was in them. They themselves often did not thoroughly understand the full meaning of what the Spirit was saying through them. In fact, they diligently searched and inquired in their own minds as to the meaning of what they themselves had said. This point comes out very plainly in 1 Peter:

> *Of this salvation the prophets have inquired and searched carefully, who prophesied of the grace that would come to you, searching what, or what manner of time, the Spirit of Christ who was in them was indicating when He testified beforehand the sufferings of Christ and the glories that would follow. To them it was revealed that, not to themselves, but to us they were ministering the things which now have been reported to you through those who have preached the gospel to you by the Holy Spirit sent from heaven; things which angels desire to look into.* (1 Pet. 1:10–12 NKJV)

Here, again, the meaning is clear; it is inescapable. We are told that the prophets had a revelation made to them by the Holy Spirit, the meaning of which they did not thoroughly comprehend. They themselves *"inquired and searched carefully"* as to the meaning of this revelation that they had received and recorded. Through them the Spirit testified beforehand about *"the sufferings of Christ and the glories that would follow."* (See, for example, Isaiah 53:3 and Psalm 22.) They recorded what the Spirit testified, but what it meant they did not thoroughly understand.

It was not merely that their minds were made keen to see things that they would not otherwise see and they therefore more or less accurately recorded them. No, there was a very definite revelation, arising not from their own minds at all, but from the Spirit of God. This they recorded. The revelation was not of themselves, for they themselves wondered about its meaning. What they recorded was not at all their own thoughts; it was the thoughts of the Holy Spirit who spoke through them. How utterly different this concept is from what is so persistently taught in many of our pulpits and theological seminaries!

Is the Bible Inspired by God?

Prophetic Utterances Were from God Himself

The third thing that the Bible makes perfectly clear is that not one single prophetic utterance was of the prophet's own will (that is, it was not in any sense merely what he wished to say). In every instance, the prophet's words were from God, and the prophet was "carried along" in the prophetic utterance by the Holy Spirit, regardless of his own will or thoughts. We find this stated in so many words in 2 Peter 1:21, where we read,

> *For prophecy never* [literally, "not a prophecy ever"] *came* [literally, "was brought"] *by the will of man, but holy men of God spoke as they were moved* [literally, "carried along" or "borne"] *by the Holy Spirit.* (NKJV)

There can be no honest mistaking of the meaning of this language. The prophet never thought that there was something that needed to be said and therefore said it, but God took possession of the prophet and carried him along in his utterance by the power of the Holy Spirit. The prophet did not speak by his own reasoning or by his own intuition; he spoke *"by the Holy Spirit."* As God's messenger, he spoke what God told him to say.

The Holy Spirit Was the Real Speaker

The fourth thing that the Bible teaches regarding the inspiration of the Bible writers and their utterances is that the Holy Spirit was the real speaker in the prophetic utterances. What was said or written was the Holy Spirit's words, not the words of the prophet. This truth is revealed repeatedly in various Scriptures.

For example, in Hebrews 3:7–8, we read, *"Therefore, as the Holy Spirit says: 'Today, if you will hear His voice, do not harden your hearts'"* (NKJV). The author of the epistle to the Hebrews was quoting Psalm 95:7–8; he said that what the psalmist is recorded as saying is actually what *"the Holy Spirit says."*

Again, in Hebrews 10:15–16, we read,

> *The Holy Spirit also witnesses to us; for...He had said before, "This is the covenant that I will make with them after those days, says the* Lord*: I will put My laws into their hearts, and in their minds I will write them."*
>
> (NKJV)

Now, the author of the epistle to the Hebrews is quoting Jeremiah 31:33, and he does not hesitate to say that the testimony that Jeremiah gave is *the testimony of the Holy Spirit*, that the Holy Spirit was the real speaker.

We read in Acts 28:25–27 that Paul said,

> *The Holy Spirit spoke rightly through Isaiah the prophet to our fathers, saying, "Go to this people and say: 'Hearing you will hear, and shall not understand; and seeing you will see, and not perceive; for the hearts of this people have grown dull. Their ears are hard of hearing, and their eyes they have closed, lest they should see with their eyes and hear with their ears, lest they should understand with their hearts and turn, so that I should heal them.'"*
>
> (NKJV)

Here Paul was quoting Isaiah's words as recorded in Isaiah 6:9–10, and he distinctly said that the real speaker was not Isaiah, but *"the Holy Spirit"* who spoke *"through Isaiah the prophet."*

Turning now to the Old Testament, we read in 2 Samuel 23:2 this assertion by David regarding the things that he said and wrote: *"The Spirit of the* Lord *spoke by me, and His word was on my tongue"* (NKJV). There can be no mistaking the meaning of these words on the part of anyone who goes to the Bible to find out what it really claims and teaches. The Holy Spirit was the real speaker in the prophetic utterances. It was the Holy Spirit's utterance that was upon the prophet's tongue. The prophet was simply the mouth by which the Holy Spirit spoke. Merely as a man, except as the Holy Spirit taught him and used him, the prophet was fallible as other men are fallible. But when the Spirit was upon him, when he was taken up and carried along by the Holy Spirit, he became infallible in his teachings; for his teachings were not his, but the teachings of the Holy Spirit. It was God who was then speaking, not the prophet.

Is the Bible Inspired by God?

For example, Paul, merely as a man, even as a Christian man, undoubtedly had mistaken notions on many things and was more or less subject to the ideas and opinions of his time. But when he taught as an apostle, under the power of the Holy Spirit, he was infallible; rather, the Spirit who taught through him was infallible, and the teachings that resulted from the Spirit's teaching through him were infallible, as infallible as God. Common sense demands that we carefully distinguish between what Paul may have thought as a man and what he actually taught as an apostle. In the Bible, we have the record of what he taught as an apostle.

Someone may cite as possible exceptions to this statement 1 Corinthians 7:6, 25, where Paul said,

> *But I say this as a concession, not as a commandment....Now concerning virgins: I have no commandment from the Lord; yet I give judgment as one whom the Lord in His mercy has made trustworthy.* (NKJV)

There are those who think that Paul does not seem to have been sure here that he had the word of the Lord in this particular matter, but that is not the meaning of the passage. The meaning of verse 6 is that his teaching that he had just given was by way of concession to their weakness, not a commandment as to what they must do. And the teaching of verse 25 is that the Lord, during His earthly life, had given no commandment on this subject, and that Paul was giving his judgment. But he said distinctly that he was giving it as *"one whom the Lord in His mercy has made trustworthy."* Furthermore, in the fortieth verse of the chapter, he distinctly said that he had the Spirit of God in his judgment.

But even if we said that the other interpretation of this passage is the correct one—that Paul was not absolutely sure in this case that he had the word of the Lord and the mind of the Lord—that would only show that where Paul was not absolutely sure that he was teaching in the Holy Spirit he was careful to note the fact. This interpretation would only give additional certainty to all other passages that he wrote.

351

It is sometimes said that Paul taught in his earlier epistles that the Lord would return during his lifetime, and that in this matter he certainly was mistaken. But Paul never taught this in his earlier epistles or any other epistles—he never taught this anywhere. This assertion is contrary to fact. He did say in 1 Thessalonians, which was his first epistle,

> *Then we who are alive and remain shall be caught up together with them* [that is, the believers who had already died] *in the clouds to meet the Lord in the air. And thus we shall always be with the Lord.* (1 Thess. 4:17 NKJV)

In this verse, Paul did put himself in the same class with those who were still alive when he wrote the words. He naturally and necessarily did not include himself with those who had already died. But in speaking of the Lord's return, he did not say or even hint that he would still be alive when the Lord returned. It is quite probable that Paul did believe at this time that he might be alive when the Lord returned, *but he never taught that he would be alive.* The attitude of expectancy is the true attitude in all ages for every believer. This was the attitude that Paul took until it was distinctly revealed to him that he would depart before the Lord came. I think it is very probable that Paul was inclined to believe in the earlier part of his ministry that he would live until the coming of the Lord, but the Holy Spirit kept him from teaching this and also kept him from all other errors in his teachings.

The Very Words Were Given by the Holy Spirit

The fifth thing that the Bible makes clear about the inspiration of the Bible writers is that the Holy Spirit in them not only gave the thought, but also gave the words in which the thought was to be expressed. We find this very clearly stated in 1 Corinthians 2:13:

> *These things we also speak, not in words which man's wisdom teaches but which the Holy Spirit teaches, comparing spiritual things with spiritual.* (NKJV)

Is the Bible Inspired by God?

One of the most popular of the false theories of inspiration in our day is that the Holy Spirit was the author of the thought but the Bible writers were left to their own choice of words in the expression of the thought. Therefore, according to this theory, we cannot emphasize the exact meaning of the Bible's words, but we must try to find the thought of God that was behind the words, which the writer more or less inaccurately expressed.

Many teachers in our pulpits and theological seminaries today speak very sneeringly and arrogantly of those who believe in verbal inspiration—that is, the doctrine that the Holy Spirit chose the very words in which the thought He was teaching was to be expressed. But regardless of how contemptuously they may speak of those who believe in verbal inspiration, certainly the Bible claims for itself that it was verbally inspired. The passage that I previously quoted makes it as plain as language can possibly make it that the *"words"* in which the apostle Paul spoke were not *"words which man's wisdom teaches but which the Holy Spirit teaches"* (1 Cor. 2:13 NKJV).

Now, if this were not the fact, if only the thought that was given to Paul was from God and Paul clothed the thought in his own words, then Paul was thoroughly deceived on a fundamental point. In this case, we cannot depend on any point of his teachings. Or, Paul was a deliberate fraud, in which case the quicker we burn up his books, the better for us and all concerned.

Attempts to find a compromise between the two positions have landed those who have tried it in all kinds of absurdities. There is no possibility of finding any middle ground. If you have an exact and logical mind, you must make your choice between verbal inspiration and blatant unbelief. I, for one, must choose verbal inspiration, for Paul distinctly stated that the words in which he conveyed to others the truth that was revealed to him were the words that the Holy Spirit taught him.

The Holy Spirit Himself has anticipated all these ingenious but wholly unbiblical, utterly illogical, and entirely false theories regarding His own work in the Bible writers. The theory that "the concept" was inspired but the words in which the concept was expressed were not was anticipated by the Holy Spirit. He discredited it many centuries before our supposedly wise theological teachers conceived it and attempted to foist it upon an unsuspecting public.

Furthermore, the theory is absurd in itself. The only way thought can be conveyed from one mind to another—from one man's mind to another man's mind, or from the mind of God to the mind of man—is by words; therefore, if the words are imperfect, the thought expressed by those words is also imperfect. The theory is an absurdity on its very surface, and it is difficult to see how intelligent men could ever have deceived themselves into believing such a thoroughly illogical theory. If the words are not inspired, the Bible is not inspired. Let us not deceive ourselves; let us face facts.

In addition, the more carefully and minutely one studies *the wording* of the statements of this wonderful Book—the Bible—the more he will become convinced of the marvelous accuracy of *the very words* used to express the thought. To a superficial thinker, the doctrine of verbal inspiration may appear questionable or even absurd. But any regenerate and Spirit-taught individual who ponders the words of Scripture day by day, and year after year, will become thoroughly and immovably convinced that the wisdom of God is in *the very words* used as well as in the thought that is expressed in the words.

It is a significant and deeply impressive fact that our difficulties with the Bible rapidly disappear as we note the precise language used. The changing of a word or letter, or a tense, case, or number, would often land us in contradiction or untruth. But as we take the words *exactly as written in the original manuscripts*, difficulties disappear and truth shines forth. Countless times people have come to me with apparent difficulties and supposed contradictions in the Bible and have asked for a solution. I have pointed them to the exact words used, and the solution was found in taking the words exactly as written. It was because they changed in a slight degree the very words that God spoke that a difficulty had seemed to arise.

The divine origin of nature shines forth more clearly the closer we examine it under a microscope. By the use of a powerful microscope, we see the perfection of form in the minutest particles of matter. We are overwhelmingly convinced that God, a God of infinite wisdom and power, a wisdom extending down to the minutest parts of matter, is the author of the material universe. Likewise, the divine origin of the Bible shines forth more and more clearly under close inspection. The more intently we study the Bible, the more we note the perfection with which the turn of a word reveals the absolute thought of God.

An important question—and a question that has puzzled many writers at this point—is this: If the Holy Spirit is the author of the very words of Scripture, how do we account for the variations in style and wording? How is it, for example, that Paul always used Pauline language, that John always used Johannine language, and so on? The answer to this question is very simple and is twofold.

First, even if we could not account at all for this fact, it would have little weight against the explicit statements of God's Word. Anyone who is humble and wise will recognize that there are a great many things that he cannot account for at all that could be easily accounted for if he knew a little more. It is only the man who has such amazing and astounding conceit that he thinks he knows as much as God—in other words, that he is infinite in wisdom—who will reject an explicit statement of God's Word simply because he sees a difficulty within it that he, in his limited knowledge, cannot solve.

But there is a second answer, and an all-sufficient one, and it is this: these variations in style and wording are easily accounted for because the Holy Spirit is infinitely wise. He Himself is the creator of man and of man's power of speech; therefore, He is wise enough and has quite enough skill in the use of language that, when revealing truth to and through any individual, He uses words, phrases, and forms of expression that are in that person's ordinary vocabulary and forms of thought. He is also quite wise enough to make use of that person's individuality in revealing the truth through him. It is one of the marks of the divine wisdom of this Book that the same divine truth is expressed with absolute accuracy in such widely different forms of expression.

Every Scripture Is Inspired by God

The sixth thing that the Bible makes plain regarding the work of the Holy Spirit in the various writers of Scripture, is that all Scripture—that is, everything contained in all the books of the Old and New Testaments—is inspired by God. We are distinctly taught this truth in 2 Timothy 3:16–17. Here we read,

> *All Scripture* [more exactly, "every Scripture"] *is given by inspiration of God* [more literally, "is God-breathed"], *and is profitable for doctrine* [or teaching], *for reproof, for correction, for instruction in righteousness* [rather, instruction that is in righteousness], *that the man of God may be complete, thoroughly equipped* [better, "equipped completely"] *for every good work.*
>
> (NKJV)

In the Revised Version, an attempt has been made to obscure the full force of these words. In this translation, the words are rendered as follows:

> *Every Scripture inspired of God is also profitable for teaching, for reproof, for correction, for instruction which is in righteousness: that the man of God may be complete, furnished completely unto every good work.*

There is absolutely no warrant in the Greek text for changing "[Every] *Scripture is given by inspiration of God, and is profitable for* [teaching]" to *"Every Scripture inspired of God is also profitable for teaching."* "Every" is in the Greek. There is no "is" in the Greek. It must be supplied, as is often the case in translating from Greek into English. "Is" must be supplied somewhere, either before *"given by inspiration"* or after it. But if the "is" is placed after it, "and" must be changed to "also" (a change that is possible but very uncommon). Furthermore, there is not a single instance in the New Testament outside of this one in which two adjectives coupled by "and" are ripped apart and the "is" is placed between them and the "and" is changed to "also." On the other hand, the other construction, "[Every] *Scripture is given by inspiration of God, and is profitable for* [teaching]," is not at all uncommon. So we see that the translation of the Revised Version does violence to all customary usage of the Greek language.

But we do not need to dwell on that, for, even if we accept the changes given in the Revised Version, the thought is not essentially changed. If Paul had said what the Revised Version makes him say, that *"Every Scripture inspired of God is also profitable for teaching,"* there can be no question that by *"every Scripture inspired of God"* he referred to every Scripture contained in the Old Testament. Here, then, taking whichever translation you will, we have the plain teaching that every Scripture of the Old Testament is "God-breathed" or *"inspired of God."* Certainly, if we can believe this about the Old Testament, there is no difficulty in believing it about the New.

Furthermore, there can be no question that Paul claimed for his own teaching an authority equal to that of Old Testament teaching. This we will see clearly in the next section of this chapter. And not only did Paul claim this, but the apostle Peter also classified the teaching of Paul with Old Testament teaching as being Scripture. Peter said in 2 Peter 3:15–16,

> *As also our beloved brother Paul, according to the wisdom given to him, has written to you, as also in all his epistles, speaking in them of these things, in which are some things hard to understand, which untaught and unstable people twist to their own destruction, as they do also the rest of the Scriptures.* (NKJV)

Here Peter clearly spoke of Paul's epistles as being Scripture.

The Bible Is God's Inerrant Word

The seventh thing that the Bible teaches concerning the extent of the inspiration of its writings is that, because of this inspiration of the writers of the Bible, the whole Bible as originally given is the absolutely inerrant Word of God. In the Old Testament, David said of his own writings, in a passage already referred to, *"The Spirit of the L*ORD *spoke by me, and His word was on my tongue"* (2 Sam. 23:2 NKJV). In Mark 7:13, our Lord Jesus Himself called the Law of Moses *"the word of God."* He said, *"making the word of God of no effect through your tradition which you have handed down"* (NKJV). In the verses immediately preceding, He had been drawing a contrast between the teachings of the Mosaic Law (not merely the teachings of the Ten Commandments, but other parts of the Mosaic Law as well) and the traditions of the scribes and Pharisees. He had shown how the traditions of the scribes and Pharisees flatly contradicted the requirements of the Law as given through Moses. In summing up the matter, He said in the verse just quoted that the scribes and Pharisees invalidated *"the word of God"* by their traditions, thus calling the Law of Moses *"the word of God."*

When I was in England, a high dignitary and scholar in the Church of England wrote me a private letter in which he tried to reprimand me by saying that the Bible nowhere claims to be the Word of God. I replied to him by showing him that not only does the Bible claim it, but the Lord Jesus Himself said in so many words that the Law given through Moses was *"the word of God."*

In 1 Thessalonians 2:13, the apostle Paul claimed that his own epistles and teachings are *"the word of God."* He said,

> *For this reason we also thank God without ceasing, because when you received the word of God which you heard from us, you welcomed it not as the word of men, but as it is in truth, the word of God, which also effectively works in you who believe.* (NKJV)

Here the apostle Paul claimed in the most absolute way that his own teachings are *"the word of God."*

When we read the words of Jeremiah, Isaiah, Paul, John, James, Jude, and the other Bible writers, we are reading what God says. We are not listening to the voice of man, but we are listening to the voice of God. The Word of God, which we have in the Old and New Testaments, is absolutely inerrant as originally given—down to the smallest word and smallest letter or part of a letter. In Matthew 5:18, our Lord Jesus Himself said of the Pentateuch (the first five books of the Bible), *"For assuredly, I say to you, till heaven and earth pass away, one jot or one tittle will by no means pass from the law till all is fulfilled"* (NKJV). Now, a *"jot"* is the Hebrew character *yodh*, the smallest character in the Hebrew alphabet, less than half the size of any other letter in the Hebrew alphabet. A *"tittle"* is a part of a letter, the little horn put on some of the Hebrew consonants, less than the cross we put on a "t." Here our Lord said that the Law given through Moses is absolutely inerrant, down to its smallest letter or part of a letter. That certainly is verbal inspiration with a vengeance.

Again, Jesus said, as recorded in John 10:35, after having quoted from Psalm 82:6 as conclusive proof of a point, *"The Scripture **cannot be broken"*** (NKJV, emphasis added). Thus He asserted the absolute inerrancy and finality of the Scriptures. If the Scriptures as originally given are not the inerrant Word of God, then not only is the Bible a fraud, but Jesus Christ Himself was utterly misled and is therefore utterly unreliable as a teacher.

I have said that the Scriptures of the Old and New Testaments *as originally given* were absolutely inerrant. Of course, the following question arises: To what extent are the modern translations the inerrant Word of God? The answer is simple: they are the inerrant Word of God just to the extent that they are an accurate rendering of the Scriptures of the Old and New Testaments as originally given. There are, it is true, many variations in the many manuscripts we possess—thousands of variations. But by a careful study of these variations, we are able to find with marvelous accuracy what the original manuscripts said. A very large share of the variations are of no importance whatsoever, since it is evident from a comparison of different manuscripts that they are the mistakes of a transcriber. Many other variations simply concern the order of the words used, and in translating into English, in which the order of words is often different from what it is in the Greek, the variation is not translatable. Many other variations are of small Greek particles, many of which are not translatable into English anyway. When all the variations of any significance have been reduced to the minimum to which it is possible to reduce them by a careful study of manuscripts, not one single variation is left that affects any doctrine held by the evangelical churches.

2
Who Is the God of the Bible?

God is Spirit.
—John 4:24 NKJV

God is light.
—1 John 1:5 NKJV

God is love.
—1 John 4:8, 16 NKJV

The texts above give three of the most remarkable statements that were ever uttered. In the clearest possible way, they set before us the Christian understanding of God as distinguished from every other understanding of God.

Many wrong ideas about God are being promoted today. The Christian Scientists are one group that is spreading falsehood. They constantly quote one of our texts: *"God is love"*; in fact, they quote it more than almost any other passage in the Bible. But by *"God is love"* they do not mean at all what 1 John 4:8 or 1 John 4:16 clearly mean when taken in their context. By *"love"* the Christian Scientists do not mean a personal attribute of God; they mean an impersonal, abstract quality that is itself God. Mary Baker Eddy, the founder of Christian Science, frankly and flatly denied that God is a person.

Not only do the Christian Scientists say, *"God is love,"* but they also say, "Love is God." Not only do they say, *"God is good"* (Ps. 73:1 NKJV), but they also say, "Good is God." Saying "Love is God" is entirely different from saying *"God is love."* You might as well say, "Spirit is God," because the Bible says, *"God is Spirit."* However, we know that all spirit is not God. Or you might as well say, "Light is God," because the Bible says, *"God is light."* However, we know that light is not God. In the same way, love is not God, though *"God is love."*

What is meant by *"love"* in the inspired statement *"God is love"*? The answer is shown by the definition or description of love given in the context and in a passage in the immediately preceding chapter—1 John 3:13–18. These verses clearly show that the statement in 1 John 4:8 and 1 John 4:16, *"God is love,"* does not mean that God is an abstract quality called love and that the abstract quality of love is God. It means that God is a person whose whole being and conduct are dominated by the quality of love, that is, by a desire for and delight in the highest welfare of others. This fact will be evident to you if you read the passage from 1 John:

> *Do not marvel, my brethren, if the world hates you. We know that we have passed from death to life, because we love the brethren. He who does not love his brother abides in death. Whoever hates his brother is a murderer, and you know that no murderer has eternal life abiding in him. By this we know love, because He laid down His life for us. And we also ought to lay down our lives for the brethren. But whoever has this world's goods, and sees his brother in need, and shuts up his heart from him, how does the love of God abide in him? My little children, let us not love in word or in tongue, but in deed and in truth.* (1 John 3:13–18 NKJV)

This fact is also evident from the context of the chapter of our text—1 John 4:

> *Beloved, let us love one another, for love is of God; and everyone who loves is born of God and knows God. He who does not love does not know God, for God is love. In this the love of God was manifested toward us, that God has sent His only begotten Son into the world, that we might live through Him. In this is love, not that we loved God, but that He loved us and sent His Son to be the propitiation for our sins. Beloved, if God so loved us, we also ought to love one another. No one has seen God at any time. If we love one another, God abides in us, and His love has been perfected in us. By this we know that we abide in Him, and He in us, because He*

has given us of His Spirit. And we have seen and testify that the Father has sent the Son as Savior of the world. Whoever confesses that Jesus is the Son of God, God abides in him, and he in God. And we have known and believed the love that God has for us. God is love, and he who abides in love abides in God, and God in him. Love has been perfected among us in this: that we may have boldness in the day of judgment; because as He is, so are we in this world.　　　　　　　　　　　　　　　　　　　(1 John 4:7–17 NKJV)

Along with Christian Science, modern philosophy also spreads false ideas about God. The God of modern philosophy is sometimes called "The Absolute." What is generally meant by "The Absolute" is a cold, abstract thing, not a dear, definite, warm Person who loves others and grieves, suffers, and works intelligently for them. Modern philosophy often teaches that not only is God *in* all things but God *is* all things and all things are God. Such a God is no God at all. However, the God of the Bible, as we will see as we proceed, is a divine Person who exists apart from the world that He created and who existed before the world that He created. The God of the Bible is actively involved in the world He has made, and He works along definite and clearly revealed lines.

In addition, many political leaders are fond of talking about God, but if anyone will carefully study their words, it often becomes plain that by "God" they do not mean the God and Father of our Lord Jesus Christ.

So we come face to face with the question, What sort of a being is the God of the Bible, the one true God, the only God whom we should worship, love, and obey?

God Is Spirit

First of all, *"God is Spirit"* (John 4:24 NKJV). This we read in our first text. Notice that the King James Version says, *"God is a Spirit."* However, there is no indefinite article in the Greek language. Wherever an indefinite article is necessary in an English translation to fit the English idiom, it has to be supplied, and it is supplied in this case. But there is no more reason for supplying it here than for supplying it in 1 John 4:8 and saying "God is a love," or in 1 John 1:5 and saying "God is a light." The preferable translation is as I have given it: *"God is Spirit."*

WHAT IS MEANT BY "SPIRIT"?

"God is Spirit" is a definition of the essential nature of God. What does it mean? Our Lord Jesus Himself defined what is meant by *"spirit"* in Luke 24:39, where He is recorded as saying after His resurrection, *"Behold My hands and My feet, that it is I Myself. Handle Me and see, for a spirit does not have flesh and bones as you see I have"* (NKJV). It is evident from these words of our Lord that *"spirit"* is that which is contrasted with body. That is to say, *"spirit"* is invisible reality. To say that *"God is Spirit"* (John 4:24 NKJV) is to say that God is essentially incorporeal (without a material body) and invisible (see 1 Timothy 6:16), that God in His essential nature is not material but immaterial and invisible, but nevertheless real.

This thought is also found in the very heart of the revelation that God made of Himself to Moses in the Old Testament. We read in the book of Deuteronomy,

> *Take careful heed to yourselves, for you saw no form when the LORD spoke to you at Horeb out of the midst of the fire, lest you act corruptly and make for yourselves a carved image in the form of any figure: the likeness of male or female, the likeness of any animal that is on the earth or the likeness of any winged bird that flies in the air, the likeness of anything that creeps on the ground or the likeness of any fish that is in the water beneath the earth.* (Deut. 4:15–18 NKJV)

Fifteen centuries before Christ, this is a plain declaration of the spirituality of God in His essential nature. God is essentially invisible spirit.

CAN GOD BE SEEN WITH THE HUMAN EYE?

Spirit, however, may be manifested in visible, bodily form. This fact is clearly revealed in the Word of God. We read in John

Who Is the God of the Bible?

1:32 these words of John the Baptist about what his own eyes had seen: *"And John bare witness, saying, I have beheld the Spirit descending as a dove out of heaven; and it abode upon him* [Jesus]" (RV). Here, then, we see God the Holy Spirit, who is essentially spirit, manifesting Himself in a bodily, visible form.

Furthermore, we are told in the Bible that God the Father has manifested Himself in visible form. We read in Exodus,

> *Then Moses went up, also Aaron, Nadab, and Abihu, and seventy of the elders of Israel, and they saw the God of Israel. And there was under His feet as it were a paved work of sapphire stone, and it was like the very heavens in its clarity.* (Exod. 24:9–10 NKJV)

What they saw was not God in His essential nature as spiritual being. Indeed, what we see when we see one another is not our essential selves, but the houses we live in. Therefore, John could say, as he did in John 1:18: *"No one has seen God at any time"* (NKJV). Similarly, I could say that no one has ever seen me. Nevertheless, it was a real manifestation of God Himself that they saw. It could be said, and said truthfully, that they had seen God, even as it could be said truthfully that people have seen me.

Furthermore, though God is essentially spirit, He has a visible form. This is taught in the most unmistakable terms in Philippians 2:6, where we are told that our Lord Jesus existed originally *"in the form of God"* (NKJV). The Greek word that is translated *"form"* in this passage means "visible form," "the form by which a person or thing strikes the vision," "the external appearance." It cannot mean anything else. This is the definition given in the best Greek-English lexicon of the New Testament. Now, since Jesus existed originally *"in the form of God,"* it is evident that God Himself must have a form, this form in which our Lord Jesus is said to have existed originally.

The fact that God in His external form, though not in His invisible essence, is *seeable,* is also clear from Acts 7:55–56, where we read,

But he [Stephen], *being full of the Holy Spirit, gazed into heaven and saw the glory of God, and Jesus standing at the right hand of God, and said, "Look! I see the heavens opened and the Son of Man standing at the right hand of God!"* (NKJV)

Now, if God does not have a form that can be seen, then, of course, the Lord Jesus could not be seen standing at His right hand. As we will see later, God is everywhere, but God is not everywhere *in the same sense*. There is a place where God is visibly and clearly present in a way in which He is not present anywhere else.

Does God Live in Heaven?

Although in His spiritual presence God pervades the universe, the place of God's visible presence and full manifestation of Himself is heaven. This fact is evident from many passages in the Scriptures. For example, it is clear from the prayer that our Lord taught us—a portion of Scripture accepted by many who reject most of the Bible. Our Lord began the prayer that He taught His disciples with these words: *"Our Father which art in heaven"* (Matt. 6:9). If these words mean anything, they certainly mean that God our Father is in heaven in a way in which He is not elsewhere. That was where God was when Jesus was addressing Him. We read in Matthew 3:17, *"Suddenly a voice came from heaven, saying, 'This is My beloved Son, in whom I am well pleased'"* (NKJV). If these words mean anything, they mean that God is in heaven and that His voice came out of the heavens to the Lord Jesus who was here on earth.

Again, in John 14:28, Jesus is recorded as saying,

You have heard Me say to you, "I am going away and coming back to you." If you loved Me, you would rejoice because I said, "I am going to the Father," for My Father is greater than I. (NKJV)

Taken in the light of the events that were to follow, these words, if they mean anything, mean that Jesus was going away from the place where He was then—earth—to another place—heaven.

Furthermore, in going to heaven, He was going to where God is, and He was leaving earth, where God is not present in the sense in which He is in heaven.

We read in Acts 11:9: *"But the voice answered me again from heaven, 'What God has cleansed you must not call common'"* (NKJV). Here, again, God is represented as speaking from heaven, where He was.

Again, our Lord Jesus Christ is recorded in John 20:17 as saying to Mary Magdalene after His resurrection,

> *Do not cling to Me, for I have not yet ascended to My Father; but go to My brethren and say to them, "I am ascending to My Father and your Father, and to My God and your God."* (NKJV)

From this it is unmistakably evident that there is a place where God is, a place to which Jesus was going after His resurrection. That place is heaven. There is no possibility of explaining this away by saying that Jesus was using a figure of speech. The whole passage loses its meaning by any such interpretation, and to attempt to so explain it is a trick and a deception that will not bear close examination.

Moreover, the apostle Paul told us regarding our Lord Jesus Christ that God the Father *"raised Him from the dead and seated Him at His right hand in the heavenly places"* (Eph. 1:20 NKJV). This verse makes it as clear as language can make anything that there is a place called heaven where God is in a sense that He is nowhere else, and where one can be placed at His right hand.

The same thing is evident from the verses that I already quoted when talking about God in His external form—Acts 7:55–56. Here we are told that Stephen,

> *being full of the Holy Spirit, gazed into heaven and saw the glory of God, and Jesus standing at the right hand of God, and said, "Look! I see the heavens opened and the Son of Man standing at the right hand of God!"* (NKJV)

The meaning of these words—to anybody who wishes to know what words are intended to convey and does not merely wish to distort them to fit his own theories—is that God is, in a special sense, present in heaven. There is no escaping this truth by any fair, honest interpretation.

Men who are skillful in the art of discrediting truth by assigning it improper names—names that sound very scholarly—may call this precious truth found in Acts 7:55–56 *anthropomorphism* (which means "attributing qualities of personhood to something that is not a person"). That sounds very learned. Nevertheless, whether it is anthropomorphism or what not, this truth is the clear teaching of the Word of God, in spite of frightful terms used to scare immature college students. There is no mistaking that this truth that God is in heaven is the teaching of the Bible, and we have already proven that the Bible is God's Word. As such, it is to be taken at its face value, in spite of all the attempts to explain it away—attempts made by men and women who profess to be wise but have become fools (Rom. 1:22).

God Is a Person

The next thing that the Bible teaches about God is that God is a person. That is to say, He is a being who knows, feels, loves, speaks, acts, and hears. He is a being who interacts intelligently with us and with whom we can interact.

While God is in all things, He is a person distinct from the persons and things in which He is. He has created these persons and things. The Bible, both in the Old and New Testaments, is full of this vital teaching of "a living God" as distinguished from the mere cold ideas of "The Absolute" or "The Infinite" or "The Supreme Being" or "The Great First Cause," all of which modern philosophy loves to promote.

For example, we read in Jeremiah,

> But the LORD is the true God; He is the living God and the everlasting King. At His wrath the earth will tremble, and the nations will not be able to endure His indignation. Thus you shall say to them: "The gods that have not made the heavens and the earth shall perish from the earth and from under these heavens." He has made the earth by His power, He has established the world by His wisdom,

and has stretched out the heavens at His discretion. When He utters His voice, there is a multitude of waters in the heavens: "and He causes the vapors to ascend from the ends of the earth. He makes lightning for the rain, He brings the wind out of His treasuries." Everyone is dull-hearted, without knowledge; every metalsmith is put to shame by an image; for his molded image is falsehood, and there is no breath in them. They are futile, a work of errors; in the time of their punishment they shall perish. The Portion of Jacob is not like them, for He is the Maker of all things, and Israel is the tribe of His inheritance; the LORD of hosts is His name.

(Jer. 10:10–16 NKJV)

In this passage, God is distinguished from idols, which are things and not persons—things that *"cannot speak," "cannot go," "cannot do evil, nor can they do any good"* (Jer. 10:5 NKJV). We are also told that Jehovah is wiser than *"all the wise men"* (v. 7 NKJV). Is *"the living God," "the everlasting King,"* who has *"wrath"* and *"indignation"* (v. 10 NKJV), separate from His creatures? The answer is found in the same verse: *"At His wrath the earth will tremble, and the nations will not be able to endure His indignation"* (v. 10 NKJV).

In the New Testament, we find another example of the wonderful truth that God is a person. In the fourteenth chapter of Acts, the people of Lystra observed a miracle performed by Paul and supposed that he and Barnabas were gods. As the people were about to sacrifice to Paul and Barnabas, the two men cried out,

Men, why are you doing these things? We also are men with the same nature as you, and preach to you that you should turn from these useless things [false gods, idols] *to the living God, who made the heaven, the earth, the sea, and all things that are in them.*

(Acts 14:15 NKJV)

Here, also, we have the representation of God as a personal being distinct from His created work, and also clearly distinct from idols, which are not living gods. In addition, in 1 Thessalonians 1:9, the converts at Thessalonica are represented as turning from *"idols* [dead gods] *to serve the **living** and true God"* (NKJV emphasis added).

God, the Bible, and You

In 2 Chronicles 16:9, we are told that *"the eyes of the LORD run to and fro throughout the whole earth, to show Himself strong on behalf of those whose heart is loyal to Him"* (NKJV). In Psalm 94:9–10, we read, *"He who planted the ear, shall He not hear? He who formed the eye, shall He not see? He who instructs the nations, shall He not correct?"* (NKJV). These are clearly descriptions of a personal God, not a mere abstract idea, such as "The Absolute" or "The Infinite" or "The Supreme Being."

The distinction between God, who is present in all things and dwells in all believers, and the things and persons in which He dwells, is brought out very clearly by our Lord Himself in John 14:10. Here Jesus revealed that He is one with the Father, but that the Father works within Him independently as a separate person:

> *Do you not believe that I am in the Father, and the Father in Me? The words that I speak to you I do not speak on My own authority; but the Father who dwells in Me does the works.* (NKJV)

In the twenty-fourth verse of the same chapter, our Lord Jesus again distinguished between His own personhood and that of the Father, who dwelt in Him, in these words: *"He who does not love Me does not keep My words; and the word which you hear is not Mine but the Father's who sent Me"* (NKJV).

This understanding of God pervades the entire Bible. The view of God presented in the Bible is entirely different from the view of God presented in pantheism, Buddhism, Theosophy,* and Christian Science. The correct understanding of God is found in the opening words of the Bible: *"In the beginning God created the heavens and the earth"* (Gen. 1:1 NKJV). Here the God of the Bible is clearly differentiated from the so-called God of pantheism and the so-called God of Christian Science. The proper understanding of God is also found in the last

---

* Theosophy is the teaching of a movement that originated in the U.S. in 1875 and that follows primarily Buddhistic and Hindu theories, especially of pantheistic evolution and reincarnation.

chapter of the Bible, and it is found in every chapter of the Bible between the first and the last. The God of the Bible is a personal being who, while He created all things and is in all things, is a distinct person, separate from the persons and things He has created.

God Is Actively Involved in the World

We turn now to a consideration of the present relationship of this personal God to the world that He has created and to the people whom He has created.

In the first place, we find that God sustains, governs, and cares for the world He has created. He shapes the whole present history of the world. This comes out in the Bible again and again. A few illustrations must suffice. We read in the book of Psalms,

> *These all wait for You, that You may give them their food in due season. What You give them they gather in; You open Your hand, they are filled with good. You hide Your face, they are troubled; You take away their breath, they die and return to their dust. You send forth Your Spirit, they are created; and You renew the face of the earth.* (Ps. 104:27–30 NKJV)

We read in Psalm 75:6–7, "*For exaltation comes neither from the east nor from the west nor from the south. But God is the Judge: He puts down one, and exalts another*" (NKJV). These passages, along with others that could be cited, set forth God's present relationship to the world that He has created.

Now let us look at God's relationship to the concerns of people. We will find that God has a present, personal interest and an active hand in the concerns of people. He makes a path for His own people and leads them. He delivers, saves, and punishes.

To prove this point, four illustrations from the Bible will suffice. First of all, we read in Joshua,

> *And Joshua said, "By this you shall know that the living God is among you, and that He will without fail drive out from before you*

the Canaanites and the Hittites and the Hivites and the Perizzites and the Girgashites and the Amorites and the Jebusites."

(Josh. 3:10 NKJV)

Now we will look at a passage in Daniel:

And when he [the king] came to the den, he cried out with a lamenting voice to Daniel. The king spoke, saying to Daniel, "Daniel, servant of the living God, has your God, whom you serve continually, been able to deliver you from the lions?" Then Daniel said to the king, "O king, live forever! My God sent His angel and shut the lions' mouths, so that they have not hurt me, because I was found innocent before Him; and also, O king, I have done no wrong before you."...Then King Darius wrote:...I make a decree that in every dominion of my kingdom men must tremble and fear before the God of Daniel. For He is the living God, and steadfast forever; His kingdom is the one which shall not be destroyed, and His dominion shall endure to the end. He delivers and rescues, and He works signs and wonders in heaven and on earth, who has delivered Daniel from the power of the lions. (Dan. 6:20–22, 25–27 NKJV)

First Timothy 4:10 provides the third illustration: *"For to this end we both labor and suffer reproach, because we trust in the living God, who is the Savior of all men, especially of those who believe."* Now we will look at some verses in Hebrews:

Anyone who has rejected Moses' law dies without mercy on the testimony of two or three witnesses. Of how much worse punishment, do you suppose, will he be thought worthy who has trampled the Son of God underfoot, counted the blood of the covenant by which he was sanctified a common thing, and insulted the Spirit of grace? For we know Him who said, "Vengeance is Mine, I will repay," says the Lord. And again, "The Lord will judge His people." It is a fearful thing to fall into the hands of the living God. (Heb. 10:28–31 NKJV)

In all these passages, we have this same concept of God in His relationship to man, namely, that God has a personal interest and an active hand in the concerns of people. He makes a path for His own people and leads them. He delivers, saves, and punishes.

The God of the Bible is to be clearly distinguished, not merely from the God of the pantheists, who has no existence separate from His creation, but also from the God of the deists, who has created the world, put into it all the necessary powers of self-government and development, set it going, and left it to go by itself. The God of the Bible is a God who is personally and actively present in the affairs of the universe today. He sustains, governs, and cares for the world He has created; He shapes the whole present history of the world. He has a present, personal interest and an active hand in the concerns of people, and it is He who is behind all the events that are occurring today. He reigns and makes even the wrath of men to praise Him, and the remainder of wrath He restrains (Ps. 76:10).

Armies may clash, force and violence and outrage may seem victorious for the passing hour, but God stands triumphant over all. Through all the confusion and the discord and the turmoil and the agony and the ruin, through all the outrageous atrocities that are making men's hearts stand still with horror, He is carrying out His own purposes of love and making all things work together for good to those who love Him (Rom. 8:28).

3

Is God Perfect, and Is He One?

God is light and in Him is no darkness at all.
—1 John 1:5 NKJV

God is love.
—1 John 4:8, 16 NKJV

With God all things are possible.
—Matt. 19:26 NKJV

His understanding is infinite.
—Ps. 147:5 NKJV

In this chapter, we will continue to consider the Christian understanding of God. We saw in the previous chapter that God is spirit, that God is a person, and that God has a personal interest and an active hand in the concerns of people today. He sustains, governs, and cares for the world He has created, and He shapes the whole present history of the world.

The Infinite Perfection of God

The next thing to be observed about the Christian understanding of God is that God is perfect and infinite in power and in all His intellectual and moral attributes.

GOD IS LIGHT

First of all, fix your attention on the first part of our first text: *"God is light"* (1 John 1:5 NKJV). These three words form a marvelously beautiful and overwhelmingly impressive statement of the truth. They set forth the absolute holiness and perfect wisdom of God. These three words need to be meditated on rather than expounded upon. *"In Him is no darkness at all"* (v. 5 NKJV). That is to say, in God is no darkness of error, no darkness of ignorance, no darkness of sin, no darkness of moral imperfection or intellectual imperfection of any kind. The three words *"God is light"* form one of the most beautiful, one of the most striking, and one of the most stupendous statements of truth that has ever been penned.

GOD IS OMNIPOTENT

Second, the God of the Bible is omnipotent, or all-powerful. This wonderful fact comes out again and again in the Word of God. One direct statement of this great truth, which is especially striking because of the context in which it is found, is in Jeremiah 32:17:

> *Ah, Lord GOD! Behold, You have made the heavens and the earth by Your great power and outstretched arm. There is nothing too hard for You.* (NKJV)

Here Jeremiah said that there is nothing too difficult for God, but in the twenty-seventh verse, Jehovah Himself said, *"Behold, I am the LORD, the God of all flesh. Is there anything too hard for Me?"* (NKJV).

When at last Job had been brought to see and to recognize the true nature of Jehovah, he said, *"I know that You can do everything, and that no purpose of Yours can be withheld from You"* (Job 42:2 NKJV). In Matthew 19:26, our Lord Jesus said, *"With God all things are possible"* (NKJV).

So we are plainly taught by our Lord Himself and by others that God can do all things, that nothing is too hard for Him, that all things are possible with Him—in a word, that God is omnipotent.

Here is a very impressive passage from the book of Psalms that sets forth this same great truth:

By the word of the LORD the heavens were made, and all the host of them by the breath of His mouth. He gathers the waters of the sea together as a heap; He lays up the deep in storehouses. Let all the earth fear the LORD; let all the inhabitants of the world stand in awe of Him. For He spoke, and it was done; He commanded, and it stood fast. (Ps. 33:6–9 NKJV)

Here we see God, by the mere utterance of His voice, bringing to pass anything that He desires to be brought to pass.

We find this same majestic portrayal of God in the very first chapter of the Bible. So many people who imagine themselves to be scholarly are telling us this chapter is out-of-date, yet it contains some of the sublimest words that were ever written, unmatched by anything that any philosopher, scientist, or orator is saying today. The very first words of this chapter read, *"In the beginning God created the heavens and the earth"* (Gen. 1:1 NKJV). This description of the origin of things has never been matched for simplicity, sublimity, and profundity. In the third verse, we read, *"Then God said, 'Let there be light'; and there was light"* (NKJV). These words need no comment. In this verse, there is a sublime thought about the omnipotence of God's mere word, before which any truly intelligent and alert soul will stand in wonder and awe. Nothing in poetry or in philosophical dissertation, ancient or modern, can for one moment compare with these sublime words.

Over and over again, the thought is brought out in the Word of God that all nature is absolutely subject to God's will and word. We see this, for example, in the book of Psalms:

For He commands and raises the stormy wind, which lifts up the waves of the sea. They [the sailors] *mount up to the heavens, they go down again to the depths; their soul melts because of trouble. They reel to and fro, and stagger like a drunken man, and are at their wits' end. Then they cry out to the LORD in their trouble, and He brings them out of their distresses. He calms the storm, so that its waves are still.* (Ps. 107:25–29 NKJV)

A similar description is found in the book of Nahum:

Is God Perfect, and Is He One?

The LORD is slow to anger and great in power, and will not at all acquit the wicked. The LORD has His way in the whirlwind and in the storm, and the clouds are the dust of His feet. He rebukes the sea and makes it dry, and dries up all the rivers. Bashan and Carmel wither, and the flower of Lebanon wilts. The mountains quake before Him, the hills melt, and the earth heaves at His presence, yes, the world and all who dwell in it. Who can stand before His indignation? And who can endure the fierceness of His anger? His fury is poured out like fire, and the rocks are thrown down by Him.

(Nah. 1:3–6 NKJV)

What a picture we have here of the omnipotence and awe-inspiring majesty of God!

Not only is nature shown to be absolutely subject to God's will and word, but men also are shown to be absolutely subject to His will and word. For example, we read in the book of James,

There is one Lawgiver, who is able to save and to destroy. Who are you to judge another? Come now, you who say, "Today or tomorrow we will go to such and such a city, spend a year there, buy and sell, and make a profit"; whereas you do not know what will happen tomorrow. For what is your life? It is even a vapor that appears for a little time and then vanishes away. Instead you ought to say, "If the Lord wills, we shall live and do this or that."

(James 4:12–15 NKJV)

Happy is the man who voluntarily subjects himself to God's will and word. But whether we voluntarily subject ourselves or not, we are subject. The angels are also subject to His will and word (Heb. 1:13–14). Even Satan himself, though entirely against his own will, is absolutely subject to the will and word of God, as is evident from Job 1:12 and Job 2:6.

The exercise of God's omnipotence is limited by His own wise and holy and loving will. God *can* do anything but *will* do only what infinite wisdom, holiness, and love dictate. This comes out, for example, in Isaiah 59:1–2:

Behold, the Lord's hand is not shortened, that it cannot save; nor His ear heavy, that it cannot hear. But your iniquities have separated you

from your God; and your sins have hidden His face from you, so
that He will not hear. (NKJV)

GOD IS OMNISCIENT

The God of the Bible is also omniscient, or all-knowing. In 1 John 3:20, we read, *"God...knows all things"* (NKJV). Turning to the Old Testament, we read, *"Great is our Lord, and mighty in power; His understanding is infinite"* (Ps. 147:5 NKJV). The literal translation of the last clause of this passage is "of His understanding there is no number." In these passages, it is plainly declared that God knows everything and that His understanding is inexhaustible.

In Job 37:16, Elihu, the messenger of God, said that Jehovah is *"perfect in knowledge"* (NKJV). Along the same lines, in Acts 15:18, we read, *"Known to God from eternity are all His works"* (NKJV). In Psalm 147:4, we are told that *"He counts the number of the stars; He calls them all by name"* (NKJV), while in Matthew 10:29, we are told that *"not one* [sparrow] *falls to the ground apart from your Father's will"* (NKJV). The stars in all their magnitude and the sparrows in all their insignificance are equally in His mind.

We are further told that everything has a part in God's purpose and plan. In Acts 3:17–18, the apostle Peter said of the crucifixion of our Lord, the wickedest act in all the history of the human race,

Yet now, brethren, I know that you did it in ignorance, as did also your rulers. But those things which God foretold by the mouth of all His prophets, that the Christ would suffer, He has thus fulfilled.
(NKJV)

In addition, Peter had declared on the Day of Pentecost that the Lord Jesus was *"delivered* [up] *by the determined purpose and foreknowledge of God"* (Acts 2:23 NKJV). According to the words of the psalmist, God takes the acts of the wickedest men into His plans and causes the wrath of men to praise Him, and the remainder of wrath He restrains (Ps. 76:10).

Is God Perfect, and Is He One?

For example, even war with all its horrors, with all its atrocities, with all its abominations, is foreknown by God and taken into His own gracious plan of the ages. He will make every event, even the most horrible things designed by the vilest conspiracy of Devil-inspired men, work together for the good of those who love God and are called according to His purpose (Rom. 8:28).

The whole plan of the ages—not merely of the centuries, but of the immeasurable ages of God—and every man's part in it, has been known to God from all eternity. This is made very clear in the book of Ephesians, where we read,

> [God] *made known to us the mystery of His will, according to His good pleasure which He purposed in Himself, that in the dispensation of the fullness of the times He might gather together in one all things in Christ, both which are in heaven and which are on earth; in Him. In Him also we have obtained an inheritance, being predestined according to the purpose of Him who works all things according to the counsel of His will, that we who first trusted in Christ should be to the praise of His glory.* (Eph. 1:9–12 NKJV)

And later in the book of Ephesians, we are told,

> *(When you read, you may understand my knowledge in the mystery of Christ), which in other ages was not made known to the sons of men, as it has now been revealed by the Spirit to His holy apostles and prophets: that the Gentiles should be fellow heirs, of the same body, and partakers of His promise in Christ through the gospel, of which I became a minister according to the gift of the grace of God given to me by the effective working of His power. To me, who am less than the least of all the saints, this grace was given, that I should preach among the Gentiles the unsearchable riches of Christ, and to make all see what is the fellowship of the mystery, which from the beginning of the ages has been hidden in God who created all things through Jesus Christ.* (Eph. 3:4–9 NKJV)

There are no afterthoughts with God. Everything is seen, known, purposed, and planned from the outset. We may well exclaim, *"Oh, the depth of the riches both of the wisdom and knowledge of God! How unsearchable are His judgments and His ways past finding out!"* (Rom. 11:33 NKJV). God knows from all eternity what He will do for all eternity.

GOD IS OMNIPRESENT

Furthermore, not only is God perfect in His intellectual and moral attributes and in power, but He is also omnipresent, or all-present. In Chapter 2 of this book, we saw that God has a particular habitation, that there is a place where He exists and manifests Himself in a way in which He does not manifest Himself everywhere. But while we insist on this clearly revealed truth, we must also never lose sight of the fact that God is everywhere. We find this truth set forth by Paul in his sermon to the Epicurean and Stoic philosophers on Mars Hill:

> *God, who made the world and everything in it, since He is Lord of heaven and earth, does not dwell in temples made with hands. Nor is He worshiped with men's hands, as though He needed anything, since He gives to all life, breath, and all things. And He has made from one blood every nation of men to dwell on all the face of the earth, and has determined their preappointed times and the boundaries of their dwellings, so that they should seek the Lord, in the hope that they might grope for Him and find Him, though He is not far from each one of us; for in Him we live and move and have our being, as also some of your own poets have said, "For we are also His offspring."* (Acts 17:24–28 NKJV)

This thought about God also comes out in the Old Testament. In the book of Psalms, we read,

> *Where can I go from Your Spirit? Or where can I flee from Your presence? If I ascend into heaven, You are there; if I make my bed in hell, behold, You are there. If I take the wings of the morning, and dwell in the uttermost parts of the sea, even there Your hand shall lead me, and Your right hand shall hold me.* (Ps. 139:7–10 NKJV)

There is no place where one can flee from God's presence, for God is everywhere. This great truth is set forth in a remarkable way in the book of Jeremiah:

Is God Perfect, and Is He One?

"Am I a God near at hand," says the Lord, "and not a God afar off?
Can anyone hide himself in secret places, so I shall not see him?"
says the Lord; "do I not fill heaven and earth?" says the Lord.
(Jer. 23:23–24 NKJV)

From these passages, we see that God is all-present. He is in all parts of the universe, and He is near to each individual. In Him each individual lives and moves and has his being (Acts 17:28). God is in every rose and lily and blade of grass.

God Is Eternal

There is one thought in the Christian understanding of God that needs to be placed alongside of His omnipresence, and that is His eternity. God is eternal. His existence had no beginning and will have no ending. He always was, always is, and always will be. God is not only everywhere present in space, but also everywhere present in time. This teaching about God appears constantly in the Bible. We are told in Genesis 21:33 that Abraham *"called on the name of the Lord, the Everlasting God"* (NKJV). In Isaiah 40:28, we read this description of Jehovah:

Have you not known? Have you not heard? The everlasting God,
the Lord, the Creator of the ends of the earth, neither faints nor is
weary. His understanding is unsearchable.   (NKJV)

Here, again, He is called *"the everlasting God."*

Habakkuk set forth the same picture of God. He said, *"Are You not from everlasting, O Lord my God, my Holy One?"* (Hab. 1:12 NKJV). The psalmist also gave us the same description of God:

Before the mountains were brought forth, or ever You had formed
the earth and the world, even from everlasting to everlasting, You
are God....For a thousand years in Your sight are like yesterday
when it is past, and like a watch in the night.   (Ps. 90:2, 4 NKJV)

We have the same description of God later in the book of Psalms:

> *O my God, do not take me away in the midst of my days; Your years are throughout all generations. Of old You laid the foundation of the earth, and the heavens are the work of Your hands. They will perish, but You will endure; yes, they will all grow old like a garment; like a cloak You will change them, and they will be changed. But You are the same, and Your years will have no end.*
>
> (Ps. 102:24–27 NKJV)

The very name of God—His covenant name, *Jehovah*—sets forth His eternity. He is the eternal *"I Am"* (Exod. 3:14), the One who is, was, and ever will be (Rev. 1:8).

God Is Holy

God is also absolutely and infinitely holy. This is a point of central and fundamental importance in the biblical understanding of God. It comes out in our first text: *"God is light and in Him is no darkness at all"* (1 John 1:5 NKJV). When John wrote these words, he gave them as the summary of *"the message which we have heard from* [God]" (v. 5 NKJV).

In the vision of Jehovah that was given to Isaiah in the year that King Uzziah died, the *"seraphim"* (Isa. 6:2 NKJV), or "burning ones," burning in their own intense holiness, are shown standing before Jehovah with covered faces and covered feet and constantly crying, *"Holy, holy, holy is the Lord of hosts"* (v. 3 NKJV). And in 1 Peter 1:16, God cries to us, *"Be holy, for I am holy"* (NKJV).

This thought of the infinite and awe-inspiring holiness of God pervades the entire Bible. It underlies everything in it. The entire Mosaic system is built on and is about this fundamental and central truth. The instructions given to Moses, as well as the punishment of those who disobeyed, were intended to teach, emphasize, and burn into the minds and hearts of the Israelites the fundamental truth that God is holy, unapproachably holy. These instructions and punishments included the following: the system of washings; the divisions of the tabernacle; the divisions of the people into ordinary Israelites, Levites, priests, and high priests, who were all permitted different degrees of approach to God under strictly defined conditions; insistence on blood sacrifices as the necessary medium of approach to God; the strict orders to Israel in regard to approaching Mount Sinai when Jehovah came down upon it; God's directions to Moses in Exodus 3:5 and to Joshua in Joshua 5:15 to remove their shoes; the doom of Korah, Dathan, and Abiram in Numbers 16:1–34; the destruction of Nadab and Abihu in Leviticus 10:1–3; and the punishment of King Uzziah in 2 Chronicles 26:16–21.

The truth that God is holy is the fundamental truth of the Bible—of the Old Testament and the New Testament—and of the Jewish religion and the Christian religion. It is the preeminent factor in the Christian understanding of God. No fact in the Christian understanding of God needs to be more emphasized in our day than the fact of the absolute, unqualified, and uncompromising holiness of God. This is the chief note that is lacking in Christian Science, Theosophy, occultism, Buddhism, New Thought,* and all the base but boasted cults of the day. The great truth of God's holiness underlies the fundamental doctrines of the Bible—atonement by shed blood and justification by faith. The doctrine of the holiness of God is the keystone in the arch of Christian truth.

GOD IS LOVE

God is also love. This truth is declared in one of our texts for this chapter: *"God is love."* These words are found twice in the same chapter of the Bible (1 John 4:8, 16). This truth is essentially the same truth as *"God is light"* (1 John 1:5) and *"God is holy"* (Ps. 99:9), for the very essence of true holiness is love. Light is love, and love is light.

The Unity of God

One more fact about the Christian understanding of God remains to be mentioned, and it is this: There is but one God. The

---

* New Thought teaches that the power of the mind can achieve health and happiness. Its teachings are similar to those of Christian Science.

unity of God comes out again and again in both the Old Testament and the New. For example, we read in Deuteronomy 4:35, *"The Lord Himself is God; there is none other besides Him"* (NKJV). And in Deuteronomy 6:4, we read, *"Hear, O Israel: the Lord our God, the Lord is one!"* (NKJV). Turning to the New Testament, we read, *"There is one God and one Mediator between God and men, the Man Christ Jesus"* (1 Tim. 2:5 NKJV). And in Mark 12:29, our Lord Jesus Himself said, *"Hear, O Israel, the Lord our God, the Lord is one"* (NKJV).

But we must bear in mind the character of the divine unity. It is clearly revealed in the Bible that in this divine unity, in this one Godhead, there are three persons. This reality is expressed in a variety of ways.

In the first place, the Hebrew word translated *"one"* in the various passages given denotes a compound unity, not a simple unity. (See also John 17:22–23; 1 Corinthians 3:6–8; 1 Corinthians 12:13; and Galatians 3:28.)

In the second place, the Old Testament word most frequently used for God is a plural noun. The Hebrew grammarians and lexicographers tried to explain this by saying that it was the "pluralis majestatis" (*we* in place of *I* in the speech of royalty). But the very simple explanation is that the Hebrews, in spite of their intense monotheism, used a plural name for God because there is a plurality of persons in the one Godhead.

More striking yet, as a proof of the plurality of persons in the one Godhead, is the fact that God Himself uses plural pronouns in speaking of Himself. For example, in the first chapter of the Bible, we read that God said, *"Let Us make man in Our image, according to Our likeness"* (Gen. 1:26 NKJV). And in Genesis 11:7, He is further recorded as saying, *"Come, let Us go down and there confuse their language, that they may not understand one another's speech"* (NKJV). In Genesis 3:22, we read, *"Then the Lord God said, 'Behold, the man has become like one of Us, to know good and evil'"* (NKJV). And in that wonderful vision to which I have already referred, in which Isaiah saw Jehovah, we read this statement of Isaiah: *"Also I heard the voice of the Lord, saying: 'Whom shall I send, and who will go for Us?' Then I said, 'Here am I! Send me'"* (Isa. 6:8 NKJV).

Is God Perfect, and Is He One?

Another illustration of the plurality of persons in the one Godhead in the Old Testament understanding of God is found in Zechariah 2:10–11. Here Jehovah spoke of Himself as sent *by Jehovah* in these words:

> *"Sing and rejoice, O daughter of Zion! For behold, I am coming and I will dwell in your midst," says the LORD. "Many nations shall be joined to the LORD in that day, and they shall become My people. And I will dwell in your midst. Then you will know that the LORD of hosts has sent Me to you."* (NKJV)

Here Jehovah clearly spoke of Himself as sent *by Jehovah*, thus clearly indicating two persons of the Deity.

This same thought of the plurality of persons in the one Godhead is brought out in John 1:1, where we reach the very climax of this thought. Here we are told, *"In the beginning was the Word, and the Word was with God, and the Word was God"* (NKJV). We will see later, when we come to study the deity of Christ and the personhood and deity of the Holy Spirit, that the Lord Jesus and the Holy Spirit are clearly designated as divine beings and, at the same time, are distinguished from one another and from God the Father. So it is clear that in the Christian understanding of God, while there is but one God, there are three persons in the one Godhead.

In these two chapters on the Christian understanding of God, I have inadequately stated this understanding. This understanding of God runs throughout the whole Bible, from the first chapter of the book of Genesis to the last chapter of the book of Revelation. This is one of the many marvelous illustrations of the divine unity of the Bible. How wonderful is that Book! There is unity of thought on this very profound doctrine pervading the whole Book! This is a clear indication that the Bible is the Word of God.

In the Bible, there is a philosophy that is profounder than any human philosophy, ancient or modern. The only way to account for it is that God Himself is the author of this incomparable philosophy. What a wondrous God we have! How we ought to meditate on His person! With what awe and, at the same time, with what delight we should come into His presence and bow before Him, adoringly contemplating the wonder, beauty, majesty, and glory of His being.

4

Is Jesus Christ God?

While the Pharisees were gathered together, Jesus asked them, say-
ing, "What do you think about the Christ? Whose Son is He?"
—Matt. 22:41–42 NKJV

This question that our Lord Jesus asked the Pharisees is the most fundamental question concerning Christian thought and faith that can be asked of anybody in any age. Jesus Christ Himself is the center of Christianity, so the most fundamental questions of faith are those that concern the person of Christ. If a man holds right views concerning the person of Jesus Christ, he will sooner or later get right views on every other question. If he holds wrong views concerning the person of Jesus Christ, he is pretty sure to go wrong on everything else sooner or later. *"What do you think about the Christ?"* That is the great central question; that is the vital question.

The most fundamental question concerning the person of Christ is, "Is Jesus Christ really God?" Not merely, "Is He divine?" but, "Is He actually God?" When I was a boy, for a person to say that he believed in the divinity of Christ meant that he believed in the real deity of Christ, that he believed that Jesus is actually a divine person, that He is God. It no longer means that. The Devil is shrewd and subtle, and he knows that the most effective way to instill error into the minds of the uninformed and unwary is to take old and precious words and give them new meanings.

So when Satan's messengers, who masquerade as *"ministers of righteousness"* (2 Cor. 11:15 NKJV), seek to lead, if possible, the elect astray (Matt. 24:24), they use the old precious words but with entirely new and entirely false meanings. They talk about

Is Jesus Christ God?

"the divinity of Christ," but by this they do not mean at all what was meant in former days. In the same way, they talk about "the Atonement," but by the Atonement they do not mean at all the substitutionary death of Jesus Christ by which eternal life is secured for us. And often, when they talk about Christ, they do not mean at all our Lord and Savior Jesus Christ, the actual historical Jesus of the four gospels. They mean an "ideal Christ" or a "Christ principle."

Therefore, our subject in this chapter is not the divinity of Christ, but the deity of Christ. Our question is not, "Is Jesus Christ divine?" but, "Is Jesus Christ God?" Who was that person who was born at Bethlehem many centuries ago; who lived thirty-three or thirty-four years here on earth as recorded in the four gospels of Matthew, Mark, Luke, and John; who was crucified on Calvary's cross; who rose from the dead the third day; and who was exalted from earth to the right hand of the Father in heaven? Was He God manifested in the flesh? Was He God embodied in a human being? Was He and is He a being worthy of our absolute faith, our supreme love, our unhesitating obedience, and our wholehearted worship, just as God the Father is worthy of our absolute faith, supreme love, unhesitating obedience, and wholehearted worship? Should all men honor Jesus Christ even as they honor God the Father (John 5:23)? The question is not merely whether He is an example that we can wisely follow or a master whom we can wisely serve, but whether He is a God whom we can rightly worship.

I presume that most of you, my readers, do believe that Jesus was God manifested in the flesh and that He is God today at the right hand of the Father. But why do you believe this? Are you so well-informed in your faith, and therefore so well-grounded, that no silver-tongued talker, no Unitarian* or Jehovah's Witness or Christian Scientist or Theosophist or other errorist, can confuse you and upset you and lead you astray? It is important that we be thoroughly sound in our faith on this point, and thoroughly well-informed, wherever else we may be in ignorance or error.

* Unitarianism denies the Christian doctrine of the Trinity and the Christian doctrine of the deity of Jesus Christ.

For we are distinctly told in John 20:31 that *"these* [things] *are written that you may believe that Jesus is the Christ, the Son of God, and that believing you may have life in His name"* (NKJV). It is evident from these words of the inspired apostle John that this question is not merely a matter of theoretical opinion, but a matter that concerns our salvation. I am writing this chapter to strengthen and instruct you in your blessed faith, your saving faith in Jesus Christ as a divine person.

When I studied the subject of the deity of Christ in a theological seminary, I got the impression that there are a few proof texts in the Bible that conclusively prove that He is God. Years later, I found that there are not merely a few proof texts that prove this fact, but that the Bible in many ways and in countless passages clearly teaches that Jesus Christ was God manifest in the flesh. Indeed, I found that the doctrine of the deity of Jesus Christ forms the very foundation of the Bible.

Jesus' Divine Names Prove His Deity

The first proof of the absolute deity of our Lord Jesus is that many names and titles clearly implying deity are used of Jesus Christ in the Bible, some of them repeatedly. In fact, the total number of passages reaches far into the hundreds. Of course, I can give you only a few illustrations. First of all, look at Revelation 1:17:

> *And when I saw Him* [Jesus], *I fell at His feet as dead. But He laid His right hand on me, saying to me, "Do not be afraid; I am the First and the Last."* (NKJV)

The context clearly shows that our Lord Jesus is the speaker, and here our Lord Jesus distinctly called Himself *"the First and the Last."* Now, beyond a question, this is a divine name, for we read in Isaiah 44:6,

> *Thus says the LORD, the King of Israel, and his Redeemer, the LORD of hosts: "I am the First and I am the Last; besides Me there is no God."* (NKJV)

Is Jesus Christ God?

In Revelation 22:12–13, our Lord Jesus said that He is "the Alpha and the Omega." His words are,

Behold, I am coming quickly, and My reward is with Me, to give to every one according to his work. I am the Alpha and the Omega, the Beginning and the End, the First and the Last. (NKJV)

Now, in Revelation 1:8, *"the Lord God"* declared that *He* is *"the Alpha and the Omega."* His words are, *"I am the Alpha and the Omega, saith the Lord God, which is and which was and which is to come, the Almighty"* (RV).

In 1 Corinthians 2:8, the apostle Paul spoke of our crucified Lord Jesus as *"the Lord of glory."* His exact words are, *"Which none of the rulers of this age knew; for had they known, they would not have crucified the Lord of glory"* (NKJV). There can be no question that *"the Lord of glory"* is Jehovah God, for we read in Psalm 24:8–10,

Who is this King of glory? The LORD strong and mighty, the LORD mighty in battle. Lift up your heads, O you gates! Lift up, you everlasting doors! And the King of glory shall come in. Who is this King of glory? The LORD of hosts, He is the King of glory. (NKJV)

We are told in the passage already referred to that our crucified Lord Jesus is *"the Lord* [the King] *of glory"*; therefore, He must be Jehovah.

In John 20:28, Thomas addressed the Lord Jesus as his Lord and his God: *"And Thomas answered and said to Him, 'My Lord and my God!'"* (NKJV). Unitarians have endeavored to get around the force of this statement of Thomas by saying that Thomas was excited and that he was not addressing the Lord Jesus at all, but was saying, *"My Lord and my God!"* as an exclamation of astonishment, just in the way that the ungodly sometimes use these exclamations today. This interpretation is impossible, and it shows to what desperate measures the Unitarians are driven, for Jesus Himself commended Thomas for seeing the truth and saying it. Our Lord Jesus' words immediately following those of Thomas are, *"Thomas, because you have seen Me, you have believed. Blessed are those who have not seen and yet have believed"* (v. 29 NKJV).

In Titus 2:13, our Lord Jesus is spoken of as *"God"*: *"Looking for the blessed hope and glorious appearing of our great God and Savior Jesus Christ"* (NKJV). In Romans 9:5, Paul told us that *"Christ... is over all, the eternally blessed God"* (NKJV). Unitarians have desperately tried to overcome the force of these words, but the only fair translation and interpretation of the words that Paul wrote in Greek are the translation and interpretation just given.

To the person who goes to the Bible to find out what it actually teaches—not to read his own thoughts into it—there can be no honest doubt that Jesus is spoken of by various names and titles that beyond a question imply deity, and that He is in so many words called God. In Hebrews 1:8, it is said of the Son, *"But to the Son He* [God] *says: 'Your throne, O God, is forever and ever; a scepter of righteousness is the scepter of Your Kingdom'"* (NKJV). If we were to go no further, it is clearly the plain and often repeated teaching of the Bible that Jesus Christ is truly God.

Jesus' Divine Attributes Prove His Deity

But there is a second proof that Jesus Christ is God, one that is equally convincing. It is this: all the distinctively divine attributes are ascribed to Jesus Christ, and in Him is said to dwell *"all the fullness of the Godhead"* (Col. 2:9 NKJV). There are five distinctively divine attributes, that is, five attributes that God alone possesses. These are omnipotence, omniscience, omnipresence, eternity, and immutability. Each one of these distinctively divine attributes is ascribed to Jesus Christ.

First of all, omnipotence is ascribed to Jesus Christ. We are taught that Jesus had power over disease, death, winds, the sea, and demons; they were all subject to His word. In fact, He is *"far above all principality and power and might and dominion, and every name that is named, not only in this age but also in that which is to come"* (Eph. 1:21 NKJV). In addition, the Bible says that He upholds *"all things by the word of His power"* (Heb. 1:3 NKJV).

Omniscience is also ascribed to Jesus Christ. We are taught in the Bible that Jesus knew men's lives, even their secret histories (see John 4:16–19), that He knew the secret thoughts of men,

Is Jesus Christ God?

knew all men, and knew what was in man (Mark 2:8; Luke 5:22; John 2:24–25). Significantly, we are distinctly told in 2 Chronicles 6:30 and Jeremiah 17:9–10 that only God possesses this knowledge. In addition, we are told in so many words in John 16:30 that Jesus knew *"all things,"* and in Colossians 2:3 that in Him *"are hid all the treasures of wisdom and knowledge."*

Omnipresence is also ascribed to Jesus Christ. We read in Matthew 18:20 that *"where two or three are gathered together in* [His] *name,"* He is *"in the midst of them."* And in Matthew 28:20, we are told that wherever His obedient disciples would go, He would be with them, *"even to the end of the age"* (NKJV). In John 14:20 and 2 Corinthians 13:5, we see that He dwells in each believer, in all the millions of believers scattered over the earth. In Ephesians 1:23, we are told that He *"fills all in all"* (NKJV).

Eternity is also ascribed to Jesus Christ. John 1:1 states that *"in the beginning was the Word, and the Word was with God, and the Word was God"* (NKJV). In John 8:58, Jesus Himself said, *"Most assuredly, I say to you, before Abraham was, I Am"* (NKJV). Note that the Lord Jesus did not merely say that "before Abraham was, I *was,"* but *"before Abraham was, I Am,"* thus declaring Himself to be the eternal *"I Am."* (See Exodus 3:14.) Even in the Old Testament, we have a declaration of the eternity of the Christ who was to be born in Bethlehem. In Micah 5:2, we read,

But you, Bethlehem Ephrathah, though you are little among the thousands of Judah, yet out of you shall come forth to Me the One to be Ruler in Israel, whose goings forth are from of old, from everlasting.　　　　　　　　　　　　　　　　　　　　　　(NKJV)

And in Isaiah 9:6, we learn of the Child who was to be born,

Unto us a Child is born, unto us a Son is given; and the government will be upon His shoulder. And His name will be called Wonderful, Counselor, Mighty God, Everlasting Father, Prince of Peace.　　　　　　　　　　　　　　　　　　　　(NKJV)

In Hebrews 13:8, we are told that *"Jesus Christ is the same yesterday, today, and forever"* (NKJV).

His immutability is also taught in the passage just quoted from Hebrews. In addition, in Hebrews 1:11–12, we see that while even the heavens change, the Lord Jesus does not change. The exact words are,

They [the heavens] *will perish, but You remain; and they will all grow old like a garment; like a cloak You will fold them up, and they will be changed. But You are the same, and Your years will not fail.* (NKJV)

So we see that each one of the five distinctly divine attributes is ascribed to our Lord Jesus Christ. And in Colossians 2:9, we are told, *"In Him dwells all the fullness of the Godhead bodily* [that is, in a bodily form]" (NKJV). Here, again, we might rest our case, for what has been said about His divine attributes, even if taken alone, clearly proves the absolute deity of our Lord Jesus Christ. It shows that He possesses every perfection of nature and character that God the Father possesses.

Jesus' Divine Offices Prove His Deity

But we do not need to rest the case here. There is a third indisputable proof that Jesus Christ is God; namely, all the distinctively divine offices are attributed to Jesus Christ. The seven distinctively divine offices—seven things that God alone can do—are creation, preservation, forgiveness of sin, the raising of the dead, the transformation of bodies, judgment, and the bestowal of eternal life. Each of these distinctly divine offices is ascribed to Jesus Christ.

Creation is ascribed to Him. In Hebrews 1:10, these words are spoken to our Lord: *"You, LORD, in the beginning laid the foundation of the earth, and the heavens are the work of Your hands"* (NKJV). The context clearly shows that the Lord addressed here is the Lord Jesus. In John 1:3, we are told that *"all things were made through Him* [Jesus Christ], *and without Him nothing was made that was made"* (NKJV).

Preservation of the universe and of everything in it is also ascribed to Him in Hebrews 1:3, where it is said of the Lord Jesus,

Is Jesus Christ God?

Who being the brightness of His [God's] glory and the express image of His [God's] person, and **upholding all things by the word of His power,** *when He had by Himself purged our sins, sat down at the right hand of the Majesty on high.* (NKJV, emphasis added)

The forgiveness of sin is ascribed to Jesus Christ as well. Jesus Himself said in Mark 2:10, when His power to forgive sins was questioned because that was recognized as a divine power, *"The Son of Man has power on earth to forgive sins"* (NKJV).

The future raising of the dead is distinctly ascribed to Him in John 6:39, 44, where Jesus said,

This is the will of the Father who sent Me, that of all He has given Me I should lose nothing, but should raise it up at the last day....No one can come to Me unless the Father who sent Me draws him; and I will raise him up at the last day. (NKJV)

The transformation of our bodies is ascribed to Him in Philippians 3:20–21: *"The Lord Jesus Christ...will transform our lowly body that it may be conformed to His glorious body"* (NKJV).

In 2 Timothy 4:1, judgment is ascribed to Him. We are told that He *"will judge the living and the dead"* (NKJV). Jesus Himself declared that He would be the judge of all mankind and emphasized the fact of the divine character of that office. In John 5:22–23, He said,

For the Father judges no one, but has committed all judgment to the Son, that all should honor the Son just as they honor the Father. He who does not honor the Son does not honor the Father who sent Him. (NKJV)

The bestowal of eternal life is ascribed to Jesus Christ again and again. In John 10:28, He Himself said, *"I give them eternal life, and they shall never perish; neither shall anyone snatch them out of My hand"* (NKJV). And in John 17:1–2, Jesus said,

Father, the hour has come. Glorify Your Son, that Your Son also may glorify You, as You have given Him authority over all flesh, that He should give eternal life to as many as You have given Him. (NKJV)

Here, then, we have the seven distinctively divine offices all attributed to Jesus Christ. This evidence alone would prove that He is God, and we could rest the case here. But there are even more proofs of His absolute deity.

A Comparison of Old Testament and New Testament Verses Proves His Deity

The fourth proof of the absolute deity of Jesus Christ is found in the fact that over and over again statements in the Old Testament that are made distinctly of Jehovah are taken in the New Testament to refer to Jesus Christ. Many illustrations could be given, but I will give only one illustration here. In Jeremiah 11:20, the prophet said,

O LORD of hosts, You who judge righteously, testing the mind and the heart, let me see Your vengeance on them, for to You I have revealed my cause. (NKJV)

Here the prophet Jeremiah distinctly said that it is Jehovah of Hosts who "*judge*[s]" and "*test*[s] *the mind and the heart.*" And in Jeremiah 17:10, the prophet represented Jehovah Himself as saying the same thing in these words: "*I, the LORD, search the heart, I test the mind, even to give every man according to his ways, according to the fruit of his doings*" (NKJV).

But in the New Testament, the Lord Jesus said, "*I am He who searches the minds and hearts. And I will give to each one of you according to your works*" (Rev. 2:23 NKJV). We are distinctly told in the context that it is "*the Son of God*" (v. 18 NKJV) who is speaking here. So Jesus claimed for Himself in the New Testament what Jehovah in the Old Testament said is true of Himself and of Himself alone.

In many other instances, statements that in the Old Testament are made distinctly of Jehovah are taken in the New Testament to refer to Jesus Christ. This is to say, Jesus Christ occupies the place in New Testament thought and doctrine that Jehovah occupies in Old Testament thought and doctrine.

The Names of the Father and the Son Coupled Together Prove Christ's Deity

The fifth proof of the absolute deity of our Lord is found in the way in which the name of Jesus Christ is coupled with that of God the Father. In numerous passages, His name is coupled with the name of God the Father in a way in which it would be impossible to couple the name of any finite being with that of Deity. I will give only a few of the many illustrations that could be given.

A striking instance is in the words of our Lord Himself in John 14:23, where we read,

> *Jesus answered and said to him, "If anyone loves Me, he will keep My word; and My Father will love him, and We will come to him and make Our home with him."* (NKJV)

Here our Lord Jesus did not hesitate to couple Himself with the Father in such a way as to say *"We"*—that is, "God the Father and I"—*"will come...and make Our home with him."*

In John 14:1, Jesus said, *"Let not your heart be troubled; you believe in God, believe also in Me"* (NKJV). If Jesus Christ is not God, this is shocking blasphemy. There is absolutely no middle ground between admitting the deity of Jesus Christ and charging Christ with the most daring and appalling blasphemy of which any man in all history was ever guilty.

Christ's Acceptance of Worship Proves His Deity

There is a sixth proof of the absolute deity of our Lord Jesus. The proofs already given have been decisive—each one of the five has been decisive—but this, if possible, is the most decisive of them all. It is this: we are taught that Jesus Christ should be worshipped as God, both by angels and men. In numerous places in the Gospels, we see Jesus Christ accepting without hesitation a worship that good men and angels declined with fear and that He Himself taught should be rendered only to God. (See Matthew 14:33; Matthew 28:9; and Luke 24:52. Compare Matthew 4:9–10; Acts 10:25–26; and Revelation 22:8–9.)

A curious and very misleading comment is made in the margin of the American Standard Revision on the meaning of the word translated *"worship"* in these passages. It says, "The Greek word translated 'worship' denotes an act of reverence, *whether paid to a creature* or to the Creator" (emphasis added). Now, this is true, but it is utterly misleading. While this word is used to denote an act of reverence paid to a creature by *idolaters,* our Lord Jesus Himself distinctly said, using exactly the same Greek word, *"You shall worship the LORD your God, and Him only you shall serve"* (Matt. 4:10 NKJV).

Furthermore, Jesus said in John 5:23 that *"all should honor the Son just as they honor the Father"* (NKJV). And in Revelation 5:8–9, 12–13, the four living creatures and the twenty-four elders are shown falling down before the Lamb and offering worship to Him just as worship is offered to Him who sits on the throne, that is, God the Father. In Hebrews 1:6, we are told, *"When He* [God] *again brings the firstborn* [Jesus] *into the world, He says: 'Let all the angels of God worship Him'"* (NKJV).

One night, in a church in Chicago, I stepped up to an intelligent-looking man and asked him, "Are you a Christian?" He replied, "I do not suppose you would consider me a Christian." "Why not?" I asked. He said, "I am a Unitarian." I said, "What you mean, then, is that you do not think that Jesus Christ is a person who should be worshipped." He replied, "That is exactly what I think," and added, "The Bible nowhere says we ought to worship Him." I said, "Who told you that?" He replied, "My pastor," mentioning a prominent Unitarian minister in the city of Boston. I said, "Let me show you something," and I opened my Bible to Hebrews 1:6 and read, *"When He* [God] *again brings the firstborn* [Jesus] *into the world, He says: 'Let all the angels of God worship Him'"* (NKJV).

The Unitarian man said, "Does it say that?" I handed him the Bible and said, "Read it for yourself." He read it and said, "I did not know that was in the Bible." I said, "Well, it is there, isn't it?" "Yes, it is there." Language could not make it any plainer. The Bible clearly teaches that Jesus, the Son of God, is to be worshipped as God by angels and men, even as God the Father is worshipped.

Additional Verses Amazingly Prove Christ's Deity

The six proofs of the deity of Jesus Christ that I have given leave no possibility of doubting that Jesus Christ is God, that Jesus of Nazareth is God manifest in a human person, that He is a being to be worshipped, even as God the Father is worshipped. But there are also incidental proofs of His absolute deity that, if possible, are in some ways even more convincing than the direct assertions of His deity.

First, our Lord Jesus said in Matthew 11:28, *"Come to Me, all you who labor and are heavy laden, and I will give you rest"* (NKJV). Now, anyone who makes a promise like that must either be God, a lunatic, or an impostor. No one can give rest to all the weary and burdened who come to him unless he is God, yet Jesus Christ offers to do it. If He offers to do it and fails to do it when men come to Him, then He is either a lunatic or an impostor. If He actually does it, then beyond a question He is God. And thousands can testify that He actually does it. Thousands and tens of thousands who were weary and burdened and crushed, and for whom there was no help in man, have come to Jesus Christ, and He has given them rest. Surely, then, He is not merely a great man—He is God.

Second, in John 14:1, Jesus Christ demanded that we put the same faith in Him that we put in God the Father, and He promised that in such faith we will find a cure for all troubles and anxieties. His words are, *"Let not your heart be troubled; you believe in God, believe also in Me"* (NKJV). It is clear that He demanded that the same absolute faith be put in Him that is to be put in God Almighty. Now, in Jeremiah 17:5, a Scripture with which our Lord Jesus was perfectly familiar, we read, *"Thus says the LORD: 'Cursed is the man who trusts in man'"* (NKJV). Yet regardless of this clear curse pronounced upon all who trust in man, Jesus Christ demanded that we put trust in Him just as we put trust in God. It is the strongest possible assertion of deity on His part. No one but God has a right to make such a demand, and Jesus Christ, when He made this demand, must either have been God or an impostor. Furthermore, thousands and tens of thousands have found that when they have believed in Him just as they believe in God, their hearts have been delivered from trouble no matter what their bereavement or circumstances have been.

Third, the Lord Jesus demanded supreme and absolute love for Himself. It is as clear as day that no one but God has a right to demand such a love, but there can be no question that Jesus did demand it. In Matthew 10:37, He said to His disciples, *"He who loves father or mother more than Me is not worthy of Me. And he who loves son or daughter more than Me is not worthy of Me"* (NKJV). And in Luke 14:26, 33, He said,

> *If anyone comes to Me and does not hate his father and mother, wife and children, brothers and sisters, yes, and his own life also, he cannot be My disciple....So likewise, whoever of you does not forsake all that he has cannot be My disciple.* (NKJV)

There can be no question that this is a demand on Jesus' part of supreme and absolute love for Himself, a love that puts even the dearest loved ones in an entirely secondary place. No one but God has a right to make such a demand, but our Lord Jesus made it; therefore, He is God.

Fourth, the Lord Jesus claimed absolute equality with the Father. He said, *"I and My Father are one"* (John 10:30 NKJV).

Fifth, our Lord Jesus went so far as to say, *"He who has seen Me has seen the Father"* (John 14:9 NKJV). He claimed here to be so absolutely God that to see Him is to see the Father who dwells in Him.

Sixth, Jesus said, *"And this is eternal life, that they may know You, the only true God, and Jesus Christ whom You have sent"* (John 17:3 NKJV). In other words, He claimed that knowledge of Himself is as essential a part of eternal life as knowledge of God the Father.

Is Jesus Christ God?

Christ's Deity: A Glorious Truth

There is no room left to doubt the absolute deity of Jesus Christ. It is a glorious truth. The Savior in whom we believe is God—a Savior for whom nothing is too hard, a Savior who can save *from* the uttermost and *to* the uttermost (Heb. 7:25). Oh, how we should rejoice that we have no merely human Savior, but a Savior who is absolutely God.

On the other hand, how black is the guilt of rejecting such a Savior as this! Whoever refuses to accept Jesus as his divine Savior and Lord is guilty of the enormous sin of rejecting a Savior who is God. Many a man thinks he is good because he has never stolen or committed murder or cheated. "Of what great sin am I guilty?" he complacently asks. Have you ever accepted Jesus Christ? "No." Well, then, you are guilty of the awful and damning sin of rejecting a Savior who is God. "But," he answers, "I do not believe that He is God." That does not change the fact or lessen your guilt. Questioning a fact or denying a fact never changes it, regardless of what anyone may say to the contrary.

Suppose a man has a wife who is one of the noblest, purest, and truest women who has ever lived. Would her husband's bringing baseless charges against her, questioning her purity and loyalty, change the fact? It would not. It would simply make that husband guilty of awful slander; it would simply prove that man to be an outrageous scoundrel. Likewise, denying the deity of Jesus Christ does not make His deity any less a fact, but it does make the denier of His deity guilty of awful, incredible, blasphemous slander.

5

Is Jesus Christ Truly Man?

And the Word [Jesus Christ] *became flesh and dwelt among us,*
and we beheld His glory, the glory as of the only begotten of the
Father, full of grace and truth.
—John 1:14 NKJV

[Jesus], *being in the form of God, did not consider it robbery to*
be equal with God, but made Himself of no reputation, taking the
form of a bondservant, and coming in the likeness of men. And
being found in appearance as a man, He humbled Himself and
became obedient to the point of death,
even the death of the cross.
—Phil. 2:6–8 NKJV

There is one God and one Mediator between God
and men, the Man Christ Jesus.
—1 Tim. 2:5 NKJV

In the preceding chapter, we saw many things about Jesus
Christ. First, we saw that *"in Him dwells all the fullness of the*
Godhead bodily" (Col. 2:9 NKJV). He possesses all the distinctively
divine attributes and exercises all the distinctively divine offices.
He occupies the position in New Testament thought that Jehovah occupies in Old Testament thought. He is a being worthy
of our absolute faith, supreme love, unhesitating obedience, and
wholehearted worship. In summary, we saw that He was God and
is God.

But in this chapter's three texts, we are told that this Divine
One, who had existed from all eternity with God the Father and
who was God, became a man. In becoming a man, He did not

400

cease to be God; however, the Word, the Eternal Word, which was *"with God"* and *"was God"* (John 1:1 NKJV), took human nature upon Himself. While Jesus was very God of very God, He was also a real man, as truly and completely a man as any man who has ever walked on this earth.

The doctrine of the real humanity of Christ is as essential a part of the Christian faith as the doctrine of His real deity. There is a very large group of people who do not accept the real deity of Jesus Christ. They are in fundamental error. Another large group of people accept only His deity and do not accept the reality of His humanity. They also are in error. A doctrine of a Savior who is only man is a false doctrine, and a doctrine of a Savior who is only God is an equally false doctrine. The doctrine of the Bible is that One who from all eternity was God became man in the person of Jesus of Nazareth. There are many passages in the Bible that set forth the deity of our Lord Jesus in a way that is unmistakable and inescapable. Many other passages in the Bible set forth the complete humanity of our Lord Jesus in a way that is equally unmistakable and inescapable. It is with the doctrine of His real humanity that we are concerned in this chapter.

The Human Parentage of Jesus Christ

First of all, the Bible teaches that Jesus Christ had a human parentage. We read in Luke 2:7,

> *And she* [Mary] *brought forth her firstborn Son, and wrapped Him in swaddling cloths, and laid Him in a manger, because there was no room for them in the inn.* (NKJV)

Here we are told that our Lord Jesus Christ, though supernaturally conceived, was Mary's son. Mary was as truly His mother as God was His Father. He had a human parentage as truly as He had a divine parentage.

In Luke 1:35, we read,

> *And the angel answered and said to her* [Mary], *"The Holy Spirit will come upon you, and the power of the Highest will overshadow*

*you; therefore, also, that Holy One who is to be born will be called
the Son of God."* (NKJV)

He was called *"the Son of God"* because He was begotten
directly by the power of the Holy Spirit. But the Holy Spirit came
upon Mary, and she became the mother of this One who was to
be called *"the Son of God."*

Jesus' human parentage was not only reflected in the fact
that He descended from Mary; we are also clearly told in Romans
1:3 that God's Son *"was born of the seed of David according to the
flesh"* (NKJV). In Acts 2:30, we are told that He was *"the fruit of his
[David's] body, according to the flesh"* (NKJV). And in Hebrews 7:14,
we are told that *"our Lord arose from Judah"* (NKJV). While we read
in Galatians 4:4 that *"when the fullness of the time had come, God
sent forth His Son"* (NKJV), we are also told with equal plainness in
the same verse that this Son of God was *"born of a woman."* The
human parentage of our Lord and Savior Jesus Christ is just as
real and just as essential a part of Him as His divine parentage.

The Human Physical Nature of Jesus Christ

Not only did Jesus Christ have a human parentage, but He
had a human physical nature, a human body. This comes out in
the first of our texts: *"The Word became flesh"* (John 1:14 NKJV). In
Hebrews 2:14, we are taught that

> *inasmuch then as the children have partaken of flesh and blood, He
> [our Lord Jesus] Himself likewise shared in the same, that through
> death He might destroy him who had the power of death, that is, the
> devil.* (NKJV)

Words could not make it any plainer that our Lord Jesus had
a real human body, a real human physical nature. Indeed, the
apostle John taught us that not to believe in the actuality of His
human body is a mark of the Antichrist. He said,

> *By this you know the Spirit of God: Every spirit that confesses that
> Jesus Christ has come in the flesh is of God, and every spirit that*

Is Jesus Christ Truly Man?

does not confess that Jesus Christ has come in the flesh is not of God. And this is the spirit of the Antichrist, which you have heard was coming, and is now already in the world.   (1 John 4:2–3 NKJV)

There were those in John's day who denied the reality of Jesus' human nature, who asserted that His body was only a seeming or apparent body, that it was an illusion, or, as the Christian Scientists now put it, "mortal thought." John, speaking in the wisdom and power of the Holy Spirit, asserted that this doctrine is a mark of the Antichrist. It is the one supreme mark today that Christian Science is of the Antichrist.

Not only did Jesus Christ have a human body during His life here on earth, but He still had a human body after His resurrection. The Millennial Dawnists* tell us that this is not so. They say that before His incarnation He was wholly a spiritual being, at His incarnation He became wholly a human being, and after His death and resurrection He became wholly a divine being. All of this is unscriptural and is therefore untrue. Jesus Himself said to His disciples after His resurrection,

> *"Behold My hands and My feet, that it is I Myself. Handle Me and see, for a spirit does not have flesh and bones as you see I have."* *When He had said this, He showed them His hands and His feet.* (Luke 24:39–40 NKJV)

And Jesus said to Thomas, after Thomas had doubted the reality of His resurrection, *"Reach your finger here, and look at My hands; and reach your hand here, and put it into My side. Do not be unbelieving, but believing"* (John 20:27 NKJV).

Not only did Jesus have a real human body after His resurrection while He was still here on earth, but He retains His human body in heaven. Of that wonderful view into heaven that was given to Stephen at the time he was stoned and killed, we read,

---

* Also known as the Dawn Bible Students, this cult sprang from the teachings of Charles Taze Russell, whose teachings also led to the formation of the cult known as the Jehovah's Witnesses.

> *But he, being full of the Holy Spirit, gazed into heaven and saw the glory of God, and Jesus standing at the right hand of God, and said, "Look! I see the heavens opened and the Son of Man standing at the right hand of God!"* (Acts 7:55–56 NKJV)

Furthermore, when Christ comes again to take His rightful authority on this earth, He will come with a human body. He will come as *"the Son of Man."* He Himself said to the high priest when He stood before him on trial, *"Hereafter you will see the Son of Man sitting at the right hand of the Power, and coming on the clouds of heaven"* (Matt. 26:64 NKJV). In these words of our Lord, we have both a clear declaration of His deity and an equally clear declaration that He was a real man and will come again as a real man with a human, though glorified, body. Indeed, we are told in Philippians 3:20–21 that when He does come in this way, He is going to transform our present human bodies into the likeness of His own *"glorious body"* (v. 21 NKJV)—His glorified human body.

The Human Limitations of Jesus Christ

The reality and completeness of our Lord's human nature come out in the fact that He had a human parentage and a human body, but that is not all. We are also clearly taught that, while as God He possessed all the attributes and exercised all the offices of Deity, as a man He was subject to human limitations.

His Physical Limitations

Jesus was subject to the physical limitations that are inherent to humanity. In John 4:6, we read that Jesus Christ was weary. The words are, *"Jesus therefore, being wearied from His journey, sat thus by the well. It was about the sixth hour"* (NKJV). But God is never weary. We read explicitly in Isaiah 40:28,

> *Have you not known? Have you not heard? The everlasting God, the LORD, the Creator of the ends of the earth, neither faints nor is weary.* (NKJV)

Is Jesus Christ Truly Man?

We are told in Matthew 8:24 that Jesus Christ slept. But God never sleeps. Psalm 121:4–5 says, *"Behold, He who keeps Israel shall neither slumber nor sleep. The LORD is your keeper; the LORD is your shade at your right hand"* (NKJV). By comparing these two verses, we see distinctly that Jehovah never sleeps, yet Jesus did sleep. So Jesus was Jehovah, but He was not Jehovah only. He was man as truly as He was God.

In Matthew 21:18 and John 19:28, we read that Jesus Christ was hungry and thirsty. In Luke 22:44, we see that Jesus Christ suffered physical agony. His agony was so great that He was on the point of dying with agony.

In 1 Corinthians 15:3, we read that Christ died. First Corinthians 15:1–3 reveals that Jesus' death is an essential part of the Gospel. Paul said,

> Moreover, brethren, I declare to you the gospel which I preached to you, which also you received and in which you stand, by which also you are saved, if you hold fast that word which I preached to you; unless you believed in vain. For I delivered to you first of all that which I also received: that Christ died for our sins according to the Scriptures. (NKJV)

Christ's death was not merely an "apparent" death; it was a real death. It was no illusion. Our salvation depends on the reality of His death.

Christian Science cuts the very heart out of the Gospel by denying the reality of His death. I am often asked, "Was it the human nature of Jesus Christ that died, or was it the divine nature that died?" It was neither the one nor the other. Natures do not die; persons die. It was *Jesus* who died, the Person who was at once God and man. We are told in 1 Corinthians 2:8 that they *"crucified the Lord of glory"* (NKJV), and we saw in the last chapter that *"the Lord of glory"* is unquestionably a divine title. It was the one person Jesus, at once human and divine, who died on the cross of Calvary.

HIS INTELLECTUAL AND MORAL LIMITATIONS

Jesus Christ was also, as a man, subject to intellectual and moral limitations. We read in Luke 2:52, *"Jesus increased in wisdom and stature, and in favor with God and men"* (NKJV). Since we are told here that He grew in wisdom, He must have been more perfect in wisdom after He grew than before He grew. And since He grew in favor with God and man, He must have attained a higher type of moral perfection when He grew than He had attained before He grew. God was incarnate in the Babe of Bethlehem; nevertheless, Jesus was a real babe and grew not only in stature, but in wisdom and in favor with God and man.

As a man, Jesus was limited in knowledge. He Himself said in Mark 13:32,

> *But of that day and hour* [that is, the day and the hour of His own return] *no one knows, not even the angels in heaven, nor the Son, but only the Father.* (NKJV)

Of course, His knowledge was *self-limited.* To set an example for you and me to follow, He voluntarily *as a man* put away His knowledge of the time of His own return.

Furthermore, we are definitely and explicitly taught in Hebrews 4:15 that Jesus Christ was *"in all points tempted as we are"* (NKJV). We should bear in mind that this is a clear and complete proof of the reality of His humanity—not only physical but mental and moral. We should also bear in mind what is stated in the same verse, that He was *"without sin"*; that is, there was not the slightest taint or tinge of sin in Him as a result of His temptations, not one moment's yielding to them in thought or desire or act. He was tempted and overcame temptation in the same way that we may overcome it—by the Word of God and prayer. He Himself voluntarily placed Himself under the basic moral limitations that man is under, in order to redeem man.

HIS LIMITATIONS IN OBTAINING AND EXERCISING POWER

As a man, Jesus was also subject to limitations in the ways in which He obtained power and exercised power. Jesus Christ obtained power for the divine work that He did while here on earth, not by His incarnate deity, but by prayer. We read in Mark

Is Jesus Christ Truly Man?

1:35, *"Now in the morning, having risen a long while before daylight, He went out and departed to a solitary place; and there He prayed"* (NKJV). And we read also that before He raised Lazarus from the dead—before He called him forth from the tomb by His word—He lifted up His eyes to God and said, *"Father, I thank You that You have heard Me"* (John 11:41 NKJV). By this He showed conclusively that the power by which He raised Lazarus from the dead was not His inherent, inborn, divine power, but was power obtained by prayer. It is mentioned not less than twenty-five times in the New Testament that Jesus prayed. He obtained power for work and for moral victory as other men do—by prayer.

Again, Jesus was subject to human conditions for obtaining what He desired. He obtained power for the divine works and miracles that he did by the anointing of the Holy Spirit as well as by prayer. We read in Acts 10:38,

> God anointed Jesus of Nazareth with the Holy Spirit and with power, who went about doing good and healing all who were oppressed by the devil, for God was with Him. (NKJV)

We are taught, furthermore, that Jesus was subject, during His earthly life, to limitations in the exercise of power. He Himself said just before His crucifixion and subsequent glorification,

> Most assuredly, I say to you, he who believes in Me, the works that I do he will do also; and greater works than these he will do, because I go to My Father. (John 14:12 NKJV)

The evident meaning of this Scripture is that during the days of His earthly existence there was a limitation to His exercise of power. But then He was glorified with the Father with the glory that He had with Him before the world was (John 17:5). After His glorification, there were no more limitations to the exercise of His power. Therefore, we, being united to our Lord Jesus, not as He was on earth but as He is in His exaltation and restoration to divine glory, will do greater works than He did during the days of His earthly existence.

The Human Relationship That Jesus Had with God

The completeness of the humanity of Jesus Christ comes out in still another matter, that is, the relationship that He had with God. God was His God. He Himself said to Mary in John 20:17,

> Do not cling to Me, for I have not yet ascended to My Father; but go to My brethren and say to them, "I am ascending to My Father and your Father, and to My God and your God." (NKJV)

The evident meaning of this verse is that Jesus Christ's relationship to God the Father was the relationship between a man and God. He spoke of God the Father as *"My God."* Though possessing all the attributes and exercising all the functions of Deity, Jesus Christ the Son was subordinate to the Father.

This truth explains statements of our Lord that have puzzled many who believe in His deity. One example of a puzzling statement is in John 14:28, where Jesus said,

> You have heard Me say to you, "I am going away and coming back to you." If you loved Me, you would rejoice because I said, "I am going to the Father," for My Father is greater than I. (NKJV)

The question is often asked, "If Jesus Christ is God, how could the Father be greater than He?" The very simple answer to this is that He, *as the Son,* is subordinate to the Father. He is equal to the Father in the possession of all the distinctively divine attributes, in the exercise of all the divine offices, and as an object of our wholehearted worship, but He is subordinate to the Father in His position as Son. Jesus Christ's relationship to the Father is like the relationship of the wife to the husband in this respect. The wife may be fully the equal of the husband; nevertheless, *"the head of woman is man"* (1 Cor. 11:3 NKJV). This means that she is subordinate to the man. We are told in the same verse that *"the head of Christ is God."* This means that Jesus Christ the Son is subordinate to the Father.

Is Jesus Christ Truly Man?

Jesus Christ: A Real Man in Every Way

It is evident from what we have read from God's Word that Jesus Christ was in every respect a true man, a real man, a complete man. He was made *"in all things...like His brethren"* (Heb. 2:17 NKJV). He was subject to all the physical, mental, and moral conditions of existence inherent to human nature. He was in every respect a real man. He became this way voluntarily in order to redeem men. From all eternity He had existed *"in the form of God"* (Phil. 2:6 NKJV) and could have remained *"in the form of God,"* but if He had remained that way, we would have been lost. Therefore, out of love for us, the fallen race, He

> *did not consider it robbery to be equal with God, but made Himself of no reputation, taking the form of a bondservant, and coming in the likeness of men. And being found in appearance as a man, He humbled Himself and became obedient to the point of death, even the death of the cross.* (Phil. 2:6–8 NKJV)

Oh, wondrous love! Out of love for us, He took our nature upon Himself, turning His back on the glory that had been His from all eternity. He took upon Himself all the shame and suffering that was involved in our redemption and became one of us so that He could die for us and redeem us. Oh, the wondrous grace of our Lord Jesus Christ! *"Though He was rich, yet for your sakes He became poor, that you through His poverty might become rich"* (2 Cor. 8:9 NKJV). He partook of human nature so that we might become partakers of the divine nature (2 Pet. 1:4). The philosophy of the divine and human natures of Christ, which is the philosophy of the New Testament, is a most wonderful philosophy—the most wonderful philosophy the world has ever heard. And, thank God, it is true.

Reconciling Two Apparently Contradictory Doctrines

Someone may ask, "How can we reconcile the biblical doctrine of the true deity of Jesus Christ with the biblical doctrine of the true humanity of Jesus Christ? How can we reconcile the doctrine that He was truly God with the doctrine that He was equally truly man?" The answer to this question is very simple. Reconciling doctrines is not our main business. Our first business is to find out what the various passages in the Bible mean, taken in their natural, grammatical interpretation. Then, if we can reconcile them, well and good. If not, we should still believe them. We should leave the reconciliation of the two apparently conflicting doctrines to our increasing knowledge, as we go on communing with God and studying His Word. It is an utterly foolish and wrong idea that we must interpret every passage of the Bible in such a way that we can readily reconcile it with every other passage. It is this idea of interpretation that gives rise to one-sided, and therefore untrue, theology.

One man, for example, takes the passages in the Bible concerning the sovereignty of God, which Calvinists emphasize, and believes them. Then he twists and distorts the other passages that teach the freedom of man to make them fit with those that teach the sovereignty of God. In this way, he becomes a one-sided Calvinist. Another man sees only the passages that clearly teach man's power of self-determination, which Arminians emphasize. Then he seeks to twist all the passages that teach the sovereignty of God and the foreordaining wisdom and will of God. In this way, he becomes a one-sided Arminian. And so it is with the whole gamut of doctrine.

It is utter foolishness, to say nothing of presumption, to thus handle the Word of God deceitfully. Our business is to find out the plainly intended sense of a passage that we are studying, as determined by the usage of words, grammatical construction, and context. When we have discovered the plainly intended meaning, we are to believe it whether we can reconcile it with something else that we have found out and believe or not.

Two truths that seem to be utterly irreconcilable or flat contradictions often, with increased knowledge, are seen to harmonize beautifully. We should always remember this point. Then we will have no difficulty in recognizing the fact that truths that still seem to be contradictory to us do perfectly harmonize in the infinite wisdom of God. Moreover, they will perfectly harmonize in our minds when we more closely approach God's omniscience.

Setting Christ's Deity and His Humanity Side by Side

The Bible, in the most fearless way, puts the absolute deity of Jesus Christ in closest juxtaposition with the true humanity of Jesus Christ. For example, we read in Matthew 8:24, *"And suddenly a great tempest arose on the sea, so that the boat was covered with the waves. But He [Jesus] was asleep"* (NKJV). Here we have a plain statement of the real humanity of our Lord. But two verses later, in the twenty-sixth verse, we read,

> *But He said to them, "Why are you fearful, O you of little faith?" Then He arose and rebuked the winds and the sea, and there was a great calm.* (NKJV)

Here we have a clear shining forth of His deity, even the winds and the waves being subject to His word. No wonder the disciples asked one another, *"Who can this be, that even the winds and the sea obey Him?"* (v. 27 NKJV). The answer is plain: a divine Man.

Again, we read in Luke 3:21, *"When all the people were baptized, it came to pass that Jesus also was baptized; and while He prayed, the heaven was opened"* (NKJV). Here we see Jesus in His humanity, baptized and praying. Surely this is a man. But in the next verse we read,

> *And the Holy Spirit descended in bodily form like a dove upon Him, and a voice came from heaven which said, "You are My beloved Son; in You I am well pleased."* (Luke 3:22 NKJV)

Here, with an audible voice, God declared Him to be divine, to be His Son.

In John 11:38 we read, *"Then Jesus, again groaning in Himself, came to the tomb. It was a cave, and a stone lay against it"* (NKJV). Here we see Jesus in His humanity, but five verses further down, we read, *"Now when He had said these things, He cried with a loud voice, 'Lazarus, come forth!' And he who had died came out"* (vv. 43–44 NKJV). Here His deity shines forth.

In Luke 9:28, we read, *"Now it came to pass, about eight days after these sayings, that He took Peter, John, and James and went up on the mountain to pray"* (NKJV). Here we very clearly see Jesus' humanity, His limitation, His dependence on God. But in the very next verse, we read, *"As He prayed, the appearance of His face was altered, and His robe became white and glistening"* (NKJV). Here we see His divinity shining forth. Then, again, in the thirty-fifth verse, we read of the voice coming out of the cloud, saying, *"This is My beloved Son. Hear Him!"* (NKJV). Jesus' deity is unmistakably revealed again.

In Matthew 16:16–17, we read,

Simon Peter answered and said, "You are the Christ, the Son of the living God." Jesus answered and said to him, "Blessed are you, Simon Bar-Jonah, for flesh and blood has not revealed this to you, but My Father who is in heaven." (NKJV)

Here is a clear declaration by Jesus Himself of His deity. But four verses further down, we read,

From that time Jesus began to show to His disciples that He must go to Jerusalem, and suffer many things from the elders and chief priests and scribes, and be killed, and be raised the third day. (Matt. 16:21 NKJV)

Here we have the clear declaration of the reality and completeness of His humanity.

In Hebrews 1:6, we read of our Lord Jesus, *"When He* [God the Father] *again brings the firstborn* [Jesus] *into the world, He says: 'Let all the angels of God worship Him'"* (NKJV). Here is a most unmistakable and inescapable declaration that Jesus Christ is a divine person, to be worshiped as God by angels as well as by men. In verse 8, we read this further declaration of His absolute deity: *"But to the Son He* [God] *says: 'Your throne, O God, is forever and ever'"* (NKJV). Here, again, the Son is declared to be God. But in the very next chapter, we read, *"For in that He Himself has suffered, being tempted, He is able to aid those who are tempted"* (Heb. 2:18 NKJV). Here we have the clearest possible declaration of the reality of His human nature.

In Hebrews 4:14, we read, *"Seeing then that we have a great High Priest who has passed through the heavens, Jesus the Son of God, let us hold fast our confession"* (NKJV). Here we have a plain declaration of His deity. But in the very next verse, we read, *"For we do not have a High Priest who cannot sympathize with our weaknesses, but was in all points tempted as we are, yet without sin"* (NKJV)—one of the Bible's plainest declarations of the fullness and completeness of His humanity.

The doctrine of the deity of Jesus Christ and the doctrine of the humanity of Jesus Christ go hand in hand in the Bible. What kind of a Savior, what kind of a Lord Jesus, do you believe in? Do you believe in a Savior who is man and man only? Then you do not believe in the Savior who is presented in the Bible. On the other hand, do you believe in a Savior who is God and God only? Then you do not believe in the Savior of the Bible. The Lord Jesus, our Lord and Savior, presented to us in the Bible, is very God of very God and, at the same time, is our brother, our fellowman, and is not ashamed to call us fellow believers (Heb. 2:11).

Oh, I thank God that I have a Savior who is God, possessing all the attributes and powers of Deity, all the perfections of Deity—a Savior for whom nothing is too hard. I thank God that my Savior is One who made the heavens and the earth, and who holds all the powers of nature and of history in His control. But I equally thank God that my Savior is my brother man, One who was tempted in all points as I am (Heb. 4:15). I truly thank God that my Savior was in a position to bear my sins (Heb. 9:28), on the one hand because He is God, on the other hand because He is man. A merely divine Savior could not be a Savior for me. A merely human Savior could not be a Savior for me. But a Savior in whom Deity and humanity meet, a Savior who is at once God and man, is just the Savior I need, and just the Savior you need. He is a Savior who is *"able to save to the uttermost"* all who come to God through Him (Heb. 7:25 NKJV).

6

Is the Holy Spirit a Person?

The communion of the Holy Spirit be with you.
—2 Cor. 13:14 NKJV

The doctrine of the personhood of the Holy Spirit is both fundamental and vital. Anyone who does not know the Holy Spirit as a person has not arrived at a complete and well-rounded Christian experience. Anyone who knows God the Father and God the Son but does not know God the Holy Spirit has not arrived at the Christian understanding of God. At first glance, it may seem to you that the doctrine of the personhood of the Holy Spirit is a purely technical and apparently impractical doctrine, but it is not. As we will see shortly, the doctrine of the personhood of the Holy Spirit is a doctrine of the utmost practical importance.

The Importance of the Doctrine of the Personhood of the Holy Spirit

FROM THE STANDPOINT OF WORSHIP

This doctrine is vital from the standpoint of worship. If we do not know the Holy Spirit as a divine person, if we think of Him as only an impersonal influence or power, then we are robbing a divine person of the worship that is His due, and the love that is His due, and the trust and surrender and obedience that are His due.

May I stop at this point to ask you, "Do you worship the Holy Spirit?" Theoretically, we all do, every time we sing the doxology,

Is the Holy Spirit a Person?

Praise God from whom all blessings flow,
Praise Him all creatures here below.
Praise Him above, ye heavenly hosts,
Praise Father, Son, *and Holy Ghost.*

Theoretically, we all do, every time we sing the Gloria Patri: "Glory be to the Father and to the Son *and to the Holy Ghost,* as it was in the beginning, is now, and ever shall be, world without end. Amen." But it is one thing to do a thing theoretically and quite another thing to do it in actuality. It is one thing to sing words and quite another thing to realize the meaning and the force of the words that we sing.

I had a striking illustration of this some years ago. I was going to a Bible conference in New York State. I had to pass through a city four miles from the place where the conference was being held. A relative of mine lived in that city, and on the way to the conference I stopped to see my relative, who went with me to the conference. This relative was much older than I and had been a Christian much longer than I. She was a member of the Presbyterian Church and was thoroughly orthodox. That morning at the conference, I spoke on the personhood of the Holy Spirit. After the meeting was over, we were standing on the veranda of the hotel when she turned to me and said, "Archie, I never thought of *it* before as a person." Well, I had never thought of *it* as a person, but thank God I had come to know *Him* as a person.

From a Practical Standpoint

In the second place, it is of the highest importance from a practical standpoint that we know the Holy Spirit as a person. If you think of the Holy Spirit, as even so many Christians do, as a mere influence or power, then your thought will be, "How can I get hold of the Holy Spirit and use it?" But if you think of Him in the biblical way, as a divine person, your thought will be, "How can the Holy Spirit get hold of me and use me?" There is a great difference between man—the worm—using God to thresh the mountain, and God using man—the worm—to thresh the mountain. (See Isaiah 41:14–15.) The former concept is heathenish; essentially, it is no different from the concept of primitive tribes in Africa using magical charms and trying to control their gods. On the other hand, the concept of God the Holy Spirit getting hold of and using us is sublime and Christian.

Again, if you think of the Holy Spirit merely as an influence or power, your thought will be, "How can I get more of the Holy Spirit?" But if you think of Him in the biblical way as a person, your thought will be, "How can the Holy Spirit get more of me?"

The concept of the Holy Spirit as a mere influence or power inevitably leads to self-confidence, self-exaltation, and the parade of self. If you think of the Holy Spirit as an influence or power, and then fancy that you have received the Holy Spirit, the inevitable result will be that you will strut around as if you belonged to a superior order of Christians. I remember a woman who came to me one afternoon at the Northfield Bible Conference and said to me, "Brother Torrey, I want to ask you a question. But before I do, I want you to understand that I am a Holy Spirit woman." Her words made me shudder.

On the other hand, if you think of the Holy Spirit in the biblical way, as a divine person of infinite majesty who comes to dwell in our hearts and take possession of us and use us, you are led to self-renunciation, self-denial, and deep humility. I know of no thought that is more calculated to induce meekness than this great biblical truth about the Holy Spirit.

FROM THE STANDPOINT OF EXPERIENCE

The doctrine of the personhood of the Holy Spirit is of the highest importance from the standpoint of experience. Thousands and tens of thousands of Christian men and women can testify to an entire transformation in their lives through coming to know the Holy Spirit as a person. In fact, this subject of the personhood of the Holy Spirit, which I have covered in almost every city in which I have held a series of meetings, is in some respects the deepest and most technical subject that I have ever attempted to handle before a public audience. Yet, notwithstanding that fact, more men and women have come to me or written to me at the close of the meetings, testifying to personal blessing received, than after covering any other subject that God has permitted me to speak on.

Four Proofs of the Personhood of the Holy Spirit

There are four separate and distinct proofs of the personhood of the Holy Spirit.

THE HOLY SPIRIT HAS CHARACTERISTICS THAT ONLY A PERSON COULD HAVE

The first proof of the personhood of the Holy Spirit is that all the distinctive marks or characteristics of personhood are ascribed to the Holy Spirit in the Bible. What are the distinctive characteristics of personhood? Knowledge, will, and feeling. Any being who knows and wills and feels is a person. Often, when I say that the Holy Spirit is a person, people think that I mean that the Holy Spirit has hands and feet and fingers and toes and eyes and ears and so on. But these are not the marks of personhood; these are the marks of bodily existence. Any being who knows, wills, and feels is a person, whether he has a body or not. Now, all three characteristics of personhood are ascribed to the Holy Spirit in the Bible.

Knowledge

Read, for instance, 1 Corinthians 2:11:

For what man knows the things of a man except the spirit of the man which is in him? Even so no one knows the things of God except the Spirit of God. (NKJV)

Here knowledge is ascribed to the Holy Spirit. In other words, the Holy Spirit is not a mere illumination that comes to our minds whereby our minds are cleared and strengthened to see truth that they would not otherwise discover. The Holy Spirit is a person who Himself knows the things of God and reveals to us what He knows.

Will

We read in 1 Corinthians 12:11, *"But one and the same Spirit works all these things, distributing to each one individually as He wills"* (NKJV). In this verse, will is ascribed to the Holy Spirit. Clearly the thought is not that the Holy Spirit is a divine power that we get hold of and use according to our will, but that the Holy Spirit is a person who gets hold of us and uses us according to His will. This is one of the most fundamental facts about the Holy Spirit that we must bear in mind if we are to get into a right relationship with Him.

More people are going astray at this point than almost any other. They are trying to acquire some divine power that they can use according to their own will. I thank God that there is no divine power that I can possess and use according to my will. What could I, in my foolishness and ignorance, do with a divine power? What evil I might work! On the other hand, I am even gladder that while there is no divine power that I can get hold of and use according to my foolish will, there is a divine person who can get hold of me and use me according to His infinitely wise and loving will.

Romans 8:27 tells us, *"Now He who searches the hearts knows what the mind of the Spirit is, because He makes intercession for the saints according to the will of God"* (NKJV). What I wish you to notice here is the expression *"the mind of the Spirit."* The Greek word here translated *"mind"* is a comprehensive word that has in it the ideas of both thought and purpose. It is the same word that is used in the seventh verse of the chapter, where we read, *"The carnal mind is enmity against God."* This does not mean merely that the thought of the flesh is against God, but that the whole moral and intellectual life of the flesh is against God.

Is the Holy Spirit a Person?

Feeling

Now let us look at a most remarkable passage:

Now I beg you, brethren, through the Lord Jesus Christ, and through the love of the Spirit, that you strive together with me in prayers to God for me. (Rom. 15:30 NKJV)

What I wish you to notice in this verse are the words *"the love of the Spirit."* That the Holy Spirit loves us is a wonderful thought. It teaches us that the Holy Spirit is not a mere blind influence or power that comes into our hearts and lives. He is a divine person, loving us with the tenderest love.

I wonder how many believers have ever thought much about *"the love of the Spirit."* I wonder how many ministers have ever preached a sermon on *"the love of the Spirit."* Every day of your life you kneel down before God the Father, at least I hope you do, and say, "Heavenly Father, I thank You for Your great love that led You to give Your Son to come down to this world and die on the cross of Calvary in my place." Every day of your life you kneel down before Jesus Christ the Son and say, "Blessed Son of God, I thank You for that great love of Yours that led You to come down to this world in obedience to the Father and die in my place on the cross of Calvary." But have you ever knelt down and looked to the Holy Spirit and said to Him, "Holy Spirit, I thank You for that great love of Yours"?

We owe our salvation as much to the love of the Holy Spirit as we do to the love of the Father and of the Son. If it had not been for the love of God the Father looking down on me in my lost state, yes, anticipating my fall and ruin and sending His Son down to this world to die on the cross, to die in my place, I would be in hell today. If it had not been for the love of Jesus Christ the Son, who came down to this world in obedience to the Father to lay down His life as a perfect atoning sacrifice on the cross of Cavalry in my place, I would be in hell today. But if it had not been for the love of the Holy Spirit, who came down to this world in obedience to the Father and the Son and sought me out in my lost condition, I would be in hell today.

The Holy Spirit continued to follow me when I would not listen to Him, when I deliberately turned my back on Him, when I insulted Him. He followed me into places where it must have been agony for One so holy to go. He followed me day after day, week after week, month after month, year after year, until at last He succeeded in bringing me to my senses. He brought me to realize my utterly lost condition and revealed the Lord Jesus to me as just the Savior I needed. He induced me and enabled me to receive the Lord Jesus as my Savior and my Lord. I repeat: if it had not been for this patient, long-suffering, never-wearying love of the Spirit of God for me, I would be in hell today.

Now let us consider Ephesians 4:30: *"And do not grieve the Holy Spirit of God, by whom you were sealed for the day of redemption"* (NKJV). Here grief is ascribed to the Holy Spirit. In other words, the Holy Spirit is not a mere blind impersonal influence or power that comes to dwell in your heart and mine. He is a person—a person who loves us, a person who is holy and intensely sensitive toward sin, a person who recoils from sin in what we call its slightest forms as the holiest person on earth never recoiled from sin in its grossest and most repulsive forms.

The Holy Spirit sees whatever we do; He hears whatever we say; He knows our very thoughts. Not a wandering thought is allowed a moment's lodging in our minds without His knowing it. If there is anything impure, unholy, immodest, untrue, harsh, or unChristlike in any way, He is grieved beyond expression. This truth about the Holy Spirit is a wonderful thought. It is the strongest incentive of which I know to walk a Christian walk.

How many a young man is kept back from doing things that he would otherwise do by the thought that, if he did do them, his mother might hear about his actions and be grieved beyond expression? Many a young man has come to the big city and, in some hour of temptation, has been about to go into a place that no self-respecting man ought ever to enter. But just as his hand has been on the doorknob and he has been about to open the door, the thought has come to him, "If I go in, Mother might hear about it. If she did, it would nearly kill her," and he has turned away without entering.

Is the Holy Spirit a Person?

There is One holier than the holiest mother that any of us has ever known, One who loves us with a tenderer love than the love with which our own mothers love us, One who sees everything we do, not only in the daylight but under the cover of night. He hears every word we utter, every careless word that escapes our lips. He knows our every thought; yes, He knows every fleeting notion that we allow a moment's entertainment in our minds. If there is anything unholy, impure, immodest, improper, unkind, harsh, or unChristlike in any way, in act or word or thought, He sees it and is grieved beyond expression.

Oh, how often there has come into my mind some thought or imagination—I do not know from what source—that I ought not to entertain. Just as I have been about to dwell on it, the thought has come, "The Holy Spirit sees that and will be grieved by it," and the improper thought has left.

Keeping this truth about the Holy Spirit in our minds will help us to solve all the questions that perplex the young believer today. Take, for example, the question, "Should I as a Christian go to the movies?" Well, if you go, the Holy Spirit will go, for He dwells in the heart of every believer and goes wherever the believer goes. Would the atmosphere of the place be congenial to the Holy Spirit? If not, do not go. "Should I as a Christian go to a dance?" Well, here again, if you go, the Holy Spirit will surely go. Would the atmosphere of the place be congenial to the Holy Spirit? If not, do not go. "Should I as a Christian go somewhere with my friends to play cards?" Would the atmosphere of the place be congenial to the Holy Spirit? If not, do not go. With the questions that come up and that some of us find so hard to settle, this thought of the Holy Spirit will help you to settle them all, and to settle them right—if you really desire to settle them right and not merely to do the thing that pleases you.

Characteristics Revealed in the Old Testament

Now let us look at a passage in the Old Testament:

You also gave Your good Spirit to instruct them, and did not with-hold Your manna from their mouth, and gave them water for their thirst. (Neh. 9:20 NKJV)

In this verse, both intelligence and goodness are ascribed to the Holy Spirit. This passage does not add anything to what I have already said on this matter; I include it simply because it is from the Old Testament. There are those who say that the doctrine of the personhood of the Holy Spirit is in the New Testament but is not in the Old Testament. But here we find it as clearly in the Old Testament as in the New. Of course, we do not find it as frequently in the Old Testament, for the dispensation of the Holy Spirit began in the New Testament. But the doctrine of the personhood of the Holy Spirit is most certainly in the Old Testament.

THE HOLY SPIRIT PERFORMS ACTIONS THAT ONLY A PERSON COULD PERFORM

The second proof of the personhood of the Holy Spirit is this: many actions are ascribed to the Holy Spirit that only a person could perform. Many biblical examples illustrate this point, but I will limit our consideration to three instances.

The Holy Spirit Searches the Deep Things of God

We will first consider 1 Corinthians 2:10: *"But God has revealed them to us through His Spirit. For the Spirit searches all things, yes, the deep things of God"* (NKJV). Here the Holy Spirit is represented as searching the deep things of God. In other words, as I have already said, the Holy Spirit is not a mere illumination whereby our minds are made clear and strong to comprehend truth that we would not otherwise discover. The Holy Spirit is a person who searches the deep things of God and reveals to us the things that He discovers. Such words could only be spoken of a person.

The Holy Spirit Prays

In Romans 8:26, we read,

Is the Holy Spirit a Person?

Likewise the Spirit also helps in our weaknesses. For we do not know what we should pray for as we ought, but the Spirit Himself makes intercession for us with groanings which cannot be uttered.

(NKJV)

Here the Holy Spirit is represented as doing what only a person could do—praying. The Holy Spirit is not a mere influence that compels us to pray. He is not a mere guidance to us in offering our prayers. He is a person who Himself prays. Every believer in Christ has two divine Persons praying for him. First, the Son, our Advocate with the Father, who always lives to make intercession for us at the right hand of God in the place of power (1 John 2:1; Heb. 7:25). Second, the Holy Spirit, who prays through us on earth. Oh, what a wonderful thought, that we have these two divine Persons praying for us every day! What a sense it gives us of our security.

The Holy Spirit Teaches

Now let us consider two other closely related passages. First, John 14:26:

But the Helper, the Holy Spirit, whom the Father will send in My name, He will teach you all things, and bring to your remembrance all things that I said to you. (NKJV)

Here the Holy Spirit is represented as doing what only a person could do, namely, teaching. The same thought occurs again in John 16:12–14:

I still have many things to say to you, but you cannot bear them now. However, when He, the Spirit of truth, has come, He will guide you into all truth; for He will not speak on His own authority, but whatever He hears He will speak; and He will tell you things to come. He will glorify Me, for He will take of what is Mine and declare it to you. (NKJV)

Here, again, the Holy Spirit is represented as a living, personal teacher. It is our privilege to have the living person of the

Holy Spirit today as our Teacher. Every time a person studies his Bible, it is possible for him to have this divine Person, the author of the Book, interpret it for him and teach him its meaning.

This truth about the Holy Spirit is a precious thought. When we have heard some great human teacher whom God has made a special blessing to us, many of us have thought, "Oh, if I could only hear that person every day, then I might make some progress in my Christian life." But every day we can have a teacher far more competent than the greatest human teacher who has ever spoken—the Holy Spirit.

THE HOLY SPIRIT IS TREATED IN WAYS THAT ONLY A PERSON COULD BE TREATED

There is another proof of the personhood of the Holy Spirit: the Bible describes the Holy Spirit as being treated in ways that only a person could be treated. In Isaiah 63:10, we are taught that the Holy Spirit is "*rebelled* [against]" and "*grieved*" (NKJV). You cannot rebel against or grieve a mere influence or power. Only a person can be rebelled against and grieved. In Hebrews 10:29, we are taught that the Holy Spirit is "*insulted*" (NKJV). One cannot insult an influence or power, only a person. In Acts 5:3, we are taught that people can "*lie to the Holy Spirit*" (NKJV). One can only lie to a person. In Matthew 12:31, we are taught that the Holy Spirit is "*blasphem*[ed] *against*" (NKJV). We are told that blasphemy against the Holy Spirit is more serious than blasphemy against the Lord Jesus (v. 32), and this certainly could only be said of a person—a divine person.

THE HOLY SPIRIT FILLS AN OFFICE THAT ONLY A PERSON COULD FILL

The fourth proof of the personhood of the Holy Spirit is that an office is attributed to the Holy Spirit that could only be attributed to a person. Look, for example, at John 14:16–17. Here we read,

> *And I will pray the Father, and He will give you another Helper,*
> *that He may abide with you forever; the Spirit of truth, whom the*

Is the Holy Spirit a Person?

world cannot receive, because it neither sees Him nor knows Him;
but you know Him, for He dwells with you and will be in you.
(NKJV)

Here the Holy Spirit is represented as *"another Helper"* who was coming to take the place of our Lord Jesus. Up to this time, our Lord Jesus had always been the Friend at hand to help the disciples in every emergency that arose. But now He was leaving, and their hearts were filled with consternation. He told them that although He was going, Another was coming to take His place. Can you imagine our Lord Jesus saying this if the One who was coming to take His place had been a mere impersonal influence or power? If the One who was coming to take His place had not been another person but a mere influence or power, I could not imagine our Lord Jesus saying what He said in John 16:7,

Nevertheless I tell you the truth. It is to your advantage that I go
away; for if I do not go away, the Helper will not come to you; but if
I depart, I will send Him to you. (NKJV)

Is it conceivable for one moment for our Lord to say that it was to their advantage for Him, a divine person, to leave and for a mere influence or power, no matter how divine, to come to take His place? No! What our Lord said was that He, one divine Person, was going, but that another Person, just as divine, was coming to take His place.

To me, this promise is one of the most precious promises in the whole Word of God. During the absence of my Lord, until that glad day when He will come back again, another Person, just as divine as He, is by my side—yes, dwells in my heart every moment to commune with me and to help me in every emergency that can possibly arise.

The Meaning of the Word "Helper"

I suppose you know that the Greek word translated *"Helper"* in these verses means helper plus a whole lot more. The Greek word so translated is *parakletos*. This word is a compound word, made up of the word *para,* which means "alongside," and *kletos,* which means "one called." So *parakletos* means "one called to stand alongside another"—to take his part and help him in every emergency that arises.

Parakletos is the word that is translated *"Advocate"* in 1 John 2:1: *"If anyone sins, we have an Advocate with the Father, Jesus Christ the righteous"* (NKJV). But the word *"Advocate"* does not give the full force of the word *parakletos.* Etymologically, it means about the same. *Advocate* is a Latin word transliterated into English. The word is a compound word made up of *ad,* meaning "to," and *vocatus,* meaning "one called," that is to say, "one called to another to take his part, to help him." But in our English usage, the word *advocate* has obtained a restricted sense. The Greek word, as I have already said, means "one called alongside another," and the thought is of a helper always at hand with his counsel and his strength and any form of help needed.

Up to this time, the Lord Jesus Himself had been the disciples' Paraclete, or their Friend always at hand to help. Whenever they got into any trouble, they simply turned to Jesus. For example, on one occasion they were perplexed about the subject of prayer. They said to Him, *"Lord, teach us to pray"* (Luke 11:1 NKJV), and He taught them to pray. On another occasion, Jesus was coming to them by walking on the water. When their first fear was over and He had said, *"It is I; do not be afraid"* (Matt. 14:27 NKJV), Peter said to Him, *"Lord, if it is You, command me to come to You on the water"* (v. 28 NKJV). The Lord said to him, *"Come"* (v. 29 NKJV). Then Peter clambered over the side of the fishing boat and started to go to Jesus by walking on the water. Seemingly, he turned around, took his eyes off the Lord, and looked at the fishing boat to see if the other disciples were noticing how well he was doing. But no sooner had he taken his eyes off the Lord and focused on his fears than he began to sink. He cried out, *"Lord, save me!"* (v. 30 NKJV), and Jesus reached out His hand and held him up.

In the same way, when the disciples got into any other emergency, they turned to the Lord, and He delivered them. Now He was leaving, and, as I said, consternation filled their hearts.

Is the Holy Spirit a Person?

But the Lord said to them, "Yes, I am going, but Another just as divine, just as able to help, is coming to take my place." This other Paraclete is with us wherever we go, every hour of the day or night. He is always by our side.

The Cure for Fear

If this thought gets into your heart and stays there, you will never have another moment of fear no matter how long you live. How can we fear in any circumstance if He is by our side? You may be surrounded by a howling mob, but what of it if He walks between you and the mob? This thought will banish all fear.

I had a striking illustration of this truth in my own experience some years ago. I was speaking at a Bible conference at Lake Kenka in New York State. A cousin of mine had a cottage four miles up the lake, and I went there and spent my day off with him. The next day he brought me down in his boat to where the conference was being held. As I stepped off the boat onto the pier, he said to me, "Come back again tonight and spend the night with us," and I promised him that I would. But I did not realize what I was promising.

That night, after the meeting, as I left the hotel and started on my walk, I found that I had undertaken a very difficult task. The cottage was four miles away, and a four-mile walk or an eight-mile walk was nothing under ordinary circumstances. But a storm was brewing; the whole sky was overcast. The path led along a cliff bordering the lake, and the path was near the edge of the cliff. Sometimes the lake was perhaps not more than ten or twelve feet below; at other times it was some thirty or forty feet below. I had never traveled on the path before, and since there was no starlight, I could not see the path at all. Furthermore, there had already been a storm that had torn out deep ditches across the path into which one might fall and break his leg. I could not see these ditches except when there was a sudden flash of lightning. I would see one, and then my surroundings would be darker and I would be blinder than ever.

As I walked along this path with all its furrows, so near the edge of the cliff, I felt it was perilous to make the trip and thought of going back. Then the thought came to me, "You promised that you would come tonight, and they might be sitting up waiting for you." So I felt that I must go on. But it seemed creepy and uncanny to walk along the edge of that cliff on a path that I could not see. I could only hear the sobbing and wailing and moaning of the lake at the foot of the cliff. Then the thought came to me, "What was it that you told the people there at the conference about the Holy Spirit being a person always by our side?" At once I realized that the Holy Spirit walked between me and the edge of the cliff, and that four miles through the dark was four miles without a fear—a cheerful instead of a fearful walk.

I once explained this thought in the Royal Albert Hall in London one dark, dismal February afternoon. There was a young lady in the audience who was very much afraid of the dark. It simply seemed impossible for her to go into a dark room alone. After the meeting was over, she hurried home and rushed into the room where her mother was sitting and cried, "Oh, Mother, I have heard the most wonderful message this afternoon about the Holy Spirit always being by our side as our ever present Helper and Protector. I will never be afraid of the dark again." Her mother was a practical Englishwoman and said to her, "Well, let us see how real this is. Go upstairs to the top floor, into the dark room; shut the door, and stay in there alone in the dark." The daughter went bounding up the stairs, went into the dark room, and closed the door. It was pitch dark. "Oh," she wrote me the next day, "it was dark, utterly dark, but that room was bright and glorious with the presence of the Holy Spirit."

The Cure for Insomnia

In this thought is also the cure for insomnia. Have you ever had insomnia? I have. For two dark, awful years. Night after night, I would go to bed, almost dead, as it seemed to me, for lack of sleep, and I thought I would certainly sleep since I could hardly stay awake. But scarcely had my head touched the pillow when I knew I would not sleep. I would hear the clock strike twelve, one, two, three, four, five, six, and then it was time to get up. It seemed as though I did not sleep at all, though I have no doubt I did, for I believe that people who suffer from insomnia sleep more than they think they do, or else they would die. But it seemed as if I did not sleep at all, and this went on for two whole years, until I thought that if I could not get sleep I would lose my mind.

Then I received deliverance. For years after being delivered, I would retire and fall asleep about as soon as my head touched the pillow. But one night I went to bed in the Bible Institute in Chicago, where I was then staying. I expected to fall asleep almost immediately, as had become my custom, but scarcely had my head touched the pillow when I knew I was not going to sleep. Insomnia was back. If you have ever had it, you will always recognize it. It seemed as if Insomnia were sitting on the foot of my bed looking like an imp, grinning at me and saying, "I'm back for two more years."

"Oh," I thought, "two more years of this awful insomnia." But that very morning I had been teaching the students in the lecture room on the floor below about the personhood of the Holy Spirit, and the thought came to me almost immediately, "What was that you were telling the students downstairs this morning about the Holy Spirit always being with us?" And I said, "Why don't you practice what you preach?" I looked up and said, "O blessed Holy Spirit of God, You are here. If You have anything to say to me, I will listen." And He opened to me some of the sweet and precious things about Jesus Christ, filling my soul with calm and peace and joy. The next thing I knew I was asleep, and then it was the next morning. Whenever Insomnia has come around since and sat on the foot of my bed, I have done the same thing, and relying on the Holy Spirit has never failed.

The Cure for Loneliness

Also in this thought of the Holy Spirit as our Helper is a cure for all loneliness. If the thought of the Holy Spirit as an ever present friend once enters your heart and stays there, you will never have another lonely moment as long as you live. For the majority of the last sixteen years, my life has been a lonely life. I have often been separated from my whole family for months at a time. Sometimes I have not seen my wife for two or three months, and for eighteen months I was with my wife but did not see any other member of my family.

One night I was walking the deck of a ship in the South Seas between New Zealand and Tasmania. It was a stormy night. Most of the other passengers were below, sick; none of the officers or sailors could walk with me because they had their hands full looking after the boat. I walked the deck alone. Four of the five other members of my family were on the other side of the globe, seventeen thousand miles away by the nearest route that I could get to them. And the one member of my family who was nearer was not with me that night. As I walked the deck alone, I got to thinking about my four children seventeen thousand miles away and was about to get lonesome when the thought came to me of the Holy Spirit by my side. I knew that as I walked He took every step with me, and all loneliness was gone.

I expressed this thought some years ago in the city of Saint Paul. At the close of the meeting, a physician came to me and said, "I wish to thank you for that thought. I am often called to go out alone at night, through darkness and storm, to attend to a sick patient, and I have been very lonely. But I will never be lonely again, for I will know that every mile of the way the Holy Spirit is beside me."

The Cure for a Broken Heart

In this same precious truth there is a cure for a broken heart. Oh, how many brokenhearted people there are in the world today! Many of us have lost loved ones. But we need not have a moment's heartache if we only know *"the communion of the Holy Spirit"* (2 Cor. 13:14 NKJV). There is perhaps some woman who a year ago, or a few months ago, or a few weeks ago, or a few days ago, had by her side a man whom she dearly loved, a man so strong and wise that she was freed from all sense of responsibility and care, for all the burdens were on him. How bright and happy life was in his companionship. But the dark day came when that loved one was taken away, and how lonely, empty, barren, and full of burden and care her life is today! Listen! There is One who walks right by your side, wiser and stronger and more loving than the wisest and strongest and most loving husband who has ever lived, ready to bear all the burdens and responsibilities of life. Yes, He is ready to do far more. He is ready to come and dwell in your heart and fill every nook and corner of your empty, aching heart, and thus banish all loneliness and heartache forever.

I made this statement one afternoon in Saint Andrews Hall in Glasgow. At the close of the meeting, when I went to the reception room, a lady who had hurried along to meet me approached me. She wore the customary clothing of a widow, her face bore the marks of deep sorrow, but now there was a happy look in her face. She hurried to me and said, "Doctor Torrey, this is the anniversary of my dear husband's death," (her husband was one of the most highly esteemed Christian men in Glasgow) "and I came to Saint Andrews Hall today saying to myself, 'Doctor Torrey will have something to say that will help me.' Oh," she continued, "you have said just the right thing! I will never be lonesome again, never have a heartache again. I will let the Holy Spirit come in and fill every aching corner of my heart."

Eighteen months passed. I was in Scotland again, taking a short vacation on the Clyde River on the private yacht of a friend. One day, when we stopped, a little boat came alongside the yacht. The first one who clambered up the side of the yacht and onto the deck was this widow. Seeing me standing on the deck, she hurried across and took my hand in both of hers, and with a radiant smile on her face she said, "Oh, Doctor Torrey, the thought you gave me in Saint Andrews Hall that afternoon stays with me still, and I have not had a lonely or sad hour from that day to this."

Help in Our Christian Work

It is in our Christian work that this thought comes to us with the greatest power and helpfulness. Take my own experience as an example. I became a minister simply because I had to or be forever lost. I do not mean that I am saved by preaching the Gospel. I am saved simply on the ground of Christ's atoning blood and that alone, but my becoming a Christian and accepting Him as my Savior depended on my preaching the Gospel. For six years I refused to become a Christian because I was unwilling to preach, and I felt that if I became a Christian I must preach. The night that I was converted I did not say, "I will accept Christ" or "I will give up my sins." I said, "I will preach."

But if there was ever a man who by natural temperament was unfit to preach, it was I. I was an abnormally bashful boy. A stranger could scarcely speak to me without my blushing to the roots of my hair. Of all the tortures I endured at school, none was so great as that of reciting in front of the class. To stand up on the platform and have all the other students looking at me—I could scarcely endure it. When I had to recite and my own mother and father asked me to recite to them before I went to school, I simply could not recite in front of my own parents. Think of a man like that going into the ministry!

Even after I started attending Yale College, when I would go home on a vacation and my mother would have visitors and send for me to come in and meet them, I could not say a word. After they were gone, my mother would say to me, "Archie, why didn't you say something to Mrs. So-and-So," and I would say, "Why, Mother, I did!" She would reply, "You didn't utter a sound." I thought I had, but the sound would come no farther than my throat and would be smothered there.

I was so bashful that I would never even speak in a church prayer meeting until after I entered the theological seminary. Then I thought that if I was to be a preacher, I must at least be able to speak in my own church prayer meeting. Making up my mind that I would, I learned a little message by heart. I remember some of it now, but I think I forgot much of it when I got up to speak that night. As soon as the meeting started, I grasped the back of the seat in front of me, pulled myself up to my feet, and held on to that seat so that I would not fall. I tremblingly repeated as much of my little message as I could remember and then dropped back into my seat. At the close of the meeting, a dear old lady, a lovely Christian woman, came to me and encouragingly said, "Oh, Mr. Torrey, I want to thank you for what you said tonight. It did me so much good. You spoke with so much feeling." Feeling! The only feeling I had was that I was scared nearly to death. Think of a man like that going into the ministry!

My first years in the ministry were torture. I would preach three times each Sunday. I would commit my sermons to memory, and then I would stand up and twist the top button of my coat until I had twisted the sermon out. Then, when the third sermon was preached and finished, I would drop back into my seat with a great sense of relief that that was over for another week. Then the thought would take hold of me, "Well, you have to begin tomorrow morning to get ready for next Sunday!"

But a glad day came when the truth I am trying to teach you took possession of me. That truth is this: when I stood up to preach, though people saw me, there was Another who stood by my side whom they did not see, but upon whom was all the responsibility for the meeting. All that I had to do was to get as far back out of sight as possible and let Him do the preaching. From that day, preaching has been the joy of my life. I would rather preach than eat. Sometimes, when I rise to preach, before I have uttered a word, the thought of Him standing beside me, able and willing to take charge of the whole meeting and do whatever needs to be done, has so filled my heart with exultant joy that I have felt like shouting.

The same thought applies to Sunday school teaching. Perhaps you worry about your Sunday school class for fear that you will say something that ought not to be said, or leave unsaid something that ought to be said. The thought of the burden and responsibility almost crushes you. Listen! Always remember this as you teach your class: there is One right beside you who knows just what ought to be said and just what ought to be done. Instead of carrying the responsibility of the class, let Him carry it; let Him do the teaching.

One Monday morning I met one of the most faithful laymen I have ever known, who was also a very gifted Bible teacher.

He was deep in the blues over his failure with his class the day before—at least, what he regarded as failure. He unburdened his heart to me. I said to him, "Mr. Dyer, did you not ask God to give you wisdom as you went before that class?" He said, "I did." I said, "Did you not expect Him to give it?" He said, "I did." Then I said, "What right have you to doubt that He did?" He replied, "I never thought of that before. I will never worry about my class again."

The same thought applies to personal ministry. At the close of a meeting, when the pastor urges those who are saved to go and speak to someone about his soul's salvation, oh, how many of you want to go, but you do not stir. You think to yourself, "I might say the wrong thing." You will if *you* say it. You will certainly say the wrong thing. But trust the Holy Spirit—He will say the right thing. Let Him have your lips to speak through. It may not appear the right thing at the time, but sometime you will find out that it was just the right thing.

One night in Launceston, Tasmania, as Mrs. Torrey and I left the meeting, my wife said to me, "Archie, I wasted my whole evening. I have been talking to the most frivolous girl. I don't think that she has a serious thought in her head." I replied, "Clara, how do you know? Did you not trust God to guide you?" "Yes." "Well, leave it with Him." The very next night at the close of the meeting, the same seemingly frivolous girl came up to Mrs. Torrey, leading her mother by the hand, and said, "Mrs. Torrey, won't you speak to my mother? You led me to Christ last night; now please lead my mother to Christ."

Conclusion

So we see by these many examples that the Holy Spirit is a person. Theoretically, you probably believed this before, but do you, in your real thoughts of Him, in your practical attitude toward Him, treat Him as a person? Do you really regard Him as just as real a person as Jesus Christ is—as loving, as wise, as strong, as worthy of our confidence and love and surrender? Do you see Him as a divine person always by your side?

Is the Holy Spirit a Person?

After our Lord's departure, the Holy Spirit came into this world to be to the disciples, and to be to us, what Jesus Christ had been to them during the days of His personal companionship with them. Is He that to you today? Do you know *"the communion of the Holy Spirit"* (2 Cor. 13:14 NKJV)—the companionship of the Holy Spirit, the partnership of the Holy Spirit, the fellowship of the Holy Spirit, the comradeship of the Holy Spirit? To put it simply, the whole purpose of this chapter—I say it reverently—is to introduce you to my Friend, the Holy Spirit.

7

Is the Holy Spirit God, and Is He Separate from the Father and Son?

The grace of the Lord Jesus Christ, and the love
of God, and the communion of the
Holy Spirit be with you all.
—2 Cor. 13:14 NKJV

In the previous chapter, I wrote about the personhood of the Holy Spirit. We saw clearly that the Holy Spirit is a person. I referred to His deity in passing but did not dwell on it; so the question remains, "Is the Holy Spirit a divine person?" And still another question remains: "If the Holy Spirit is a divine person, is He separate and distinct from the Father and the Son?" In this chapter, we will consider what the Bible teaches on these subjects.

Proofs of the Deity of the Holy Spirit

First, let us examine the question of the deity of the Holy Spirit. The fact that the Holy Spirit is a person does not prove that He is divine. There are spirits who are persons but are not God. However, there are five distinct proofs of the deity of the Holy Spirit.

THE HOLY SPIRIT'S DIVINE ATTRIBUTES PROVE HIS DEITY

The first proof that the Holy Spirit is God is that four distinctively divine attributes are ascribed to the Holy Spirit in the Bible. As I mentioned in the chapter on the deity of Christ, when I speak of distinctively divine attributes, I am speaking of attributes that God alone possesses. Any person who has these attributes must therefore be God. These four distinctively divine attributes are omnipotence, omniscience, omnipresence, and eternity.

Omnipotence

First of all, omnipotence is ascribed to the Holy Spirit. Take, for example, Luke 1:35:

> And the angel answered and said to her, "The Holy Spirit will come upon you, and the power of the Highest will overshadow you; therefore, also, that Holy One who is to be born will be called the Son of God." (NKJV)

This passage plainly declares that the Holy Spirit has the power of the Highest, that He is omnipotent.

Omniscience

In the second place, omniscience is ascribed to the Holy Spirit. This is done, for example, in 1 Corinthians 2:10–11:

> But God has revealed them to us through His Spirit. For the Spirit searches all things, yes, the deep things of God. For what man knows the things of a man except the spirit of the man which is in him? Even so no one knows the things of God except the Spirit of God. (NKJV)

Here we are distinctly told that the Holy Spirit searches all things and knows all things, even the deep things of God.
We find the same thought again in John 14:26:

> But the Helper, the Holy Spirit, whom the Father will send in My name, He will teach you all things, and bring to your remembrance all things that I said to you. (NKJV)

Here we are distinctly told that the Holy Spirit teaches all things; therefore, He must know all things.

This truth is stated even more explicitly in John 16:12–13:

I still have many things to say to you, but you cannot bear them now. However, when He, the Spirit of truth, has come, He will guide you into all truth; for He will not speak on His own authority, but whatever He hears He will speak; and He will tell you things to come.

(NKJV)

In all these passages, it is either directly declared or unmistakably implied that the Holy Spirit knows all things, that He is omniscient.

Omnipresence

In the third place, omnipresence is ascribed to the Holy Spirit. We find this in Psalm 139:7–10:

Where can I go from Your Spirit? Or where can I flee from Your presence? If I ascend into heaven, You are there; if I make my bed in hell, behold, You are there. If I take the wings of the morning, and dwell in the uttermost parts of the sea, even there Your hand shall lead me, and Your right hand shall hold me.

(NKJV)

Here we are told in the most explicit and unmistakable way that the Spirit of God, the Holy Spirit, is everywhere. There is no place in heaven, earth, or hades where we can go from His presence.

Eternity

Eternity is also ascribed to the Holy Spirit. This we find in Hebrews 9:14, where we read,

How much more shall the blood of Christ, who through the eternal Spirit offered Himself without spot to God, cleanse your conscience from dead works to serve the living God?

(NKJV)

438

Here we find the words *"the eternal Spirit"* just as elsewhere we find the words *"the eternal God"* (Deut. 33:27 NKJV).

Putting these different passages together, we see clearly that each of four distinctively divine attributes, four attributes that no one but God possesses, is ascribed to the Holy Spirit.

THE HOLY SPIRIT'S DIVINE WORKS PROVE HIS DEITY

The second proof of the true deity of the Holy Spirit is found in the fact that three distinctively divine works are ascribed to the Holy Spirit. That is to say, the Holy Spirit is said to do three things that God alone can do.

Creation

The first of these distinctively divine works is the one that we always think of first when we think of God's work—the work of creation. We find creation ascribed to the Holy Spirit in Job 33:4: *"The Spirit of God has made me, and the breath of the Almighty gives me life"* (NKJV). We find the same thing implied in Psalm 104:30: *"You send forth Your Spirit, they are created; and You renew the face of the earth"* (NKJV). In these two passages, the most distinctively divine of all works—the work of creation—is ascribed to the Holy Spirit.

Impartation of Life

The impartation of life is also ascribed to the Holy Spirit. This we find, for example, in John 6:63: *"It is the Spirit who gives life; the flesh profits nothing"* (NKJV). We find the same thing again in Romans 8:11:

> But if the Spirit of Him who raised Jesus from the dead dwells in you, He who raised Christ from the dead will also give life to your mortal bodies through His Spirit who dwells in you. (NKJV)

In this passage, we do not have merely the impartation of life to the spirit of man, but the impartation of life to the body of man in the resurrection.

Man's creation and the impartation of life to man are ascribed to the operation of the Holy Spirit in the first book in the Bible, where we read,

And the LORD *God formed man of the dust of the ground, and breathed into his nostrils the breath of life; and man became a living being.* (Gen. 2:7 NKJV)

Here we are told that man was created and became a living soul through God's breathing into him the breath of life. These words clearly imply that man's creation was through the instrumentality of the Holy Spirit, for the Holy Spirit is the breath of God going out in a personal way.

Authorship of Divine Prophecies

The third divine work ascribed to the Holy Spirit is the authorship of divine prophecies. We find this, for example, in 2 Peter 1:21: *"For prophecy never came by the will of man, but holy men of God spoke as they were moved by the Holy Spirit"* (NKJV). Here we are distinctly told that it was through the operation of the Holy Spirit that men were made the mouthpiece of God and uttered God's truth. We find this same thought in the Old Testament in 2 Samuel 23:2–3: *"The Spirit of the* LORD *spoke by me, and His word was on my tongue. The God of Israel said, the Rock of Israel spoke to me"* (NKJV). In this passage, the authorship of God's prophecies is ascribed to the Holy Spirit.

Putting all these passages together, we see that three distinctively divine works are ascribed to the Holy Spirit.

A COMPARISON OF OLD TESTAMENT AND NEW TESTAMENT VERSES PROVES HIS DEITY

The third proof of the deity of the Holy Spirit is found in the fact that passages that refer to Jehovah in the Old Testament are taken to refer to the Holy Spirit in the New Testament. There are numerous instances of this—not as numerous as in the case of Jesus Christ the Son, yet enough to make it perfectly clear that the Holy Spirit occupies the same place in New Testament thought that Jehovah occupies in Old Testament thought.

Isaiah 6:8–10 and Acts 28:25–27

A striking illustration of this is found in Isaiah 6:8–10, where we read,

> *Also I heard the voice of the Lord, saying: "Whom shall I send, and who will go for Us?" Then I said, "Here am I! Send me." And He said, "Go, and tell this people: 'Keep on hearing, but do not understand; keep on seeing, but do not perceive.' Make the heart of this people dull, and their ears heavy, and shut their eyes; lest they see with their eyes, and hear with their ears, and understand with their heart, and return and be healed."* (NKJV)

Here we are distinctly told it is *"the Lord"*—and the context shows that *"the Lord"* is the Lord Jehovah—who is speaking. But when we turn to Acts 28:25–27, we read these words:

> *So when they did not agree among themselves, they departed after Paul had said one word: "The Holy Spirit spoke rightly through Isaiah the prophet to our fathers* [notice that in the passage in Isaiah we are told it is the Lord Jehovah who spoke, and here we are told by Paul that it is the Holy Spirit who spoke through the prophet], *saying, 'Go to this people and say: "Hearing you will hear, and shall not understand; and seeing you will see, and not perceive; for the hearts of this people have grown dull. Their ears are hard of hearing, and their eyes they have closed, lest they should see with their eyes and hear with their ears, lest they should understand with their hearts and turn, so that I should heal them."'"* (NKJV)

In the Old Testament, we are told that the Lord Jehovah is the speaker; in the New Testament, we read that the Holy Spirit is the speaker. The Holy Spirit occupies the place in New Testament thought that the Lord Jehovah occupies in Old Testament thought.

It is notable that this same passage is applied to Jesus Christ in John 12:39–41. In the same chapter of Isaiah, in the threefold *"holy"* (Isa. 6:3 NKJV) in the seraphic cry, do we not have a hint of the tri-personhood of Jehovah of Hosts? Is it then not proper to have a threefold application of Isaiah's vision?

Exodus 16:7 and Hebrews 3:7–9

Another illustration of a statement that in the Old Testament refers to Jehovah but in the New Testament refers to the Holy Spirit, is found by a comparison of Exodus 16:7 with Hebrews 3:7–9. In Exodus 16:7, we read,

> *And in the morning you shall see the glory of the* LORD; *for He hears your complaints against the* LORD. *But what are we, that you complain against us?* (NKJV)

Here we are told that the murmuring and provocation of the children of Israel in the wilderness were against Jehovah. But in Hebrews 3:7–9, we read,

> *Therefore, as the Holy Spirit says: "Today, if you will hear His voice, do not harden your hearts as in the rebellion, in the day of trial in the wilderness, where your fathers tested Me, tried Me, and saw My works forty years."* (NKJV)

In this New Testament passage, we are told that it was the Holy Spirit whom they provoked in the wilderness. It is clear that the Holy Spirit occupies here in New Testament thought the position Jehovah occupies in Exodus 16:7 in Old Testament thought.

To sum up the passages in this section, we see that statements that in the Old Testament distinctly name the Lord, God, or Jehovah as their subject are applied to the Holy Spirit in the New Testament. That is to say, the Holy Spirit occupies the position of Deity in New Testament thought.

Is the Holy Spirit God, and Is He Separate...?

THE NAME OF THE HOLY SPIRIT COUPLED WITH THAT OF THE FATHER AND OF THE SON PROVES HIS DEITY

The fourth way that the deity of the Holy Spirit is clearly taught in the New Testament is that the name of the Holy Spirit is coupled with that of the Father and of the Son in a way in which it would be impossible for a reverent and thoughtful mind to couple the name of any finite being with that of Deity. There are numerous illustrations of this point. Three will suffice for our present purpose.

We read, for example, in 1 Corinthians 12:4–6:

There are diversities of gifts, but the same Spirit. There are differences of ministries, but the same Lord. And there are diversities of activities, but it is the same God who works all in all. (NKJV)

In this passage, we see the name of the Holy Spirit coupled with that of God and of the Lord on a ground of equality.

We see the same thing again in Matthew 28:19: *"Go therefore and make disciples of all the nations, baptizing them in the name of the Father and of the Son and of the Holy Spirit"* (NKJV). If the Holy Spirit were not God, it would be shocking to couple His name in this way with that of God the Father and of the Lord Jesus His Son.

Another striking illustration is found in 2 Corinthians 13:14: *"The grace of the Lord Jesus Christ, and the love of God, and the communion of the Holy Spirit be with you all"* (NKJV). Here the name of the Holy Spirit is coupled on a ground of equality with that of the Father and of the Son.

In all these passages, as we have seen, the name of the Holy Spirit is coupled with that of God in a way in which it would be impossible for an intelligent worshiper of the Lord to couple the name of any finite being with that of Deity.

THE FACT THAT THE HOLY SPIRIT IS CALLED GOD PROVES HIS DEITY

The fifth way, and perhaps the most decisive way, in which the deity of the Holy Spirit is taught in the Bible, is that the

Holy Spirit in so many words is called God. This we find in Acts 5:3–4:

> But Peter said, *"Ananias, why has Satan filled your heart to lie to the Holy Spirit and keep back part of the price of the land for yourself? While it remained, was it not your own? And after it was sold, was it not in your own control? Why have you conceived this thing in your heart? You have not lied to men but to God."* (NKJV)

In the third verse, we are distinctly told that it was the Holy Spirit to whom Ananias had lied, while in the fourth verse, we are told that it was God to whom Ananias had lied. Putting the two statements together, we clearly see that the Holy Spirit is God.

ALL THESE FACTS ABOUT THE HOLY SPIRIT COMBINED PROVE HIS DEITY

Allow me to sum up all that I have said about the deity of the Holy Spirit. We see that the Holy Spirit is a divine person by the following: several distinctively divine attributes are ascribed to the Holy Spirit; several distinctively divine works are ascribed to the Holy Spirit; statements that in the Old Testament distinctly name Jehovah, the Lord, or God as their subject distinctly name the Holy Spirit in the New Testament; the name of the Holy Spirit is coupled with that of God in a way in which it would be impossible to couple the name of any finite being with that of Deity; and the Holy Spirit is called God.

In all these unmistakable ways, God distinctly proclaims in His Word that the Holy Spirit is a divine person. It is absolutely impossible for anyone who goes to the Bible to find out what it actually teaches—and not merely to twist and distort it to fit into his own preconceived notions—to come to any other conclusion than that the Holy Spirit is God.

Is the Holy Spirit God, and Is He Separate...?

Proofs of the Distinction between the Father, the Son, and the Holy Spirit

But now we come to the question, Is the Holy Spirit a person who is distinct from the Father and from the Son? He might be a person, as we have clearly seen that He is, and He might be a divine person, as we have just seen that He is. But at the same time, He might be only the same person who manifested Himself at times as the Father and at other times as the Son. In this case, there would not be three divine Persons in the Godhead, but one divine Person who variously manifested Himself as Father, Son, and Holy Spirit. So, again, the question that confronts us is, "Is the Holy Spirit a person who is separate and distinct from the Father and from the Son?" This question is plainly answered in various passages in the New Testament.

VERSES THAT PROVE THE DISTINCTIVENESS OF THE PERSON OF THE HOLY SPIRIT

In the first place, we find this question answered in John 14:26 and John 15:26. In John 14:26, we read,

But the Helper, the Holy Spirit, whom the Father will send in My name, He will teach you all things, and bring to your remembrance all things that I said to you. (NKJV)

In John 15:26, we read,

But when the Helper comes, whom I shall send to you from the Father, the Spirit of truth who proceeds from the Father, He will testify of Me. (NKJV)

In both of these passages, we are told that the Holy Spirit is a person entirely distinct from the Father and the Son, that He is sent from the Father by the Son. Elsewhere we are taught that Jesus Christ was sent by the Father. (See John 6:29; 8:29, 42.) In these passages, it is as clear as language can make it that Father, Son, and Holy Spirit are not one and the same Person manifesting Himself in three different forms, but that they are three distinct Persons.

We find clear proof that the Father, Son, and Holy Spirit are three distinct Persons in John 16:13, where we read,

> *However, when He, the Spirit of truth, has come, He will guide you into all truth; for He will not speak on His own authority, but whatever He hears He will speak; and He will tell you things to come.*
> (NKJV)

In this passage, the clearest possible distinction is drawn between the Holy Spirit who speaks and the One from whom He speaks. We are told in so many words that this One from whom the Spirit speaks is not Himself, but Another.

In the next verse, the same thought is brought out in still another way. In this verse, Jesus said, *"He will glorify Me, for He will take of what is Mine and declare it to you"* (John 16:14 NKJV). Here the clearest distinction is drawn between *"He,"* the Holy Spirit, and *"Me,"* Jesus Christ. It is the work of the Holy Spirit not to glorify Himself, but Another, and this Other is Jesus Christ. The Holy Spirit takes what belongs to Another—that is, to Christ— and declares it to believers. It would be impossible to express in human language a distinction between two persons more plainly than the distinction between the Son and the Holy Spirit that is expressed in this verse.

The distinction between the Father and the Son and the Holy Spirit is very clearly brought out in Luke 3:21–22:

> *Now it came to pass, when all the people were baptized, that, Jesus also having been baptized, and praying, the heaven was opened, and the Holy Ghost descended in a bodily form, as a dove, upon him, and a voice came out of heaven, Thou art my beloved Son; in thee I am well pleased.* (RV)

Here a clear distinction is drawn between Jesus Christ, who was on the earth; the Father, who spoke to Him from heaven;

and the Holy Spirit, who descended from the Father upon the Son in bodily form as a dove.

Still another striking illustration is found in Matthew 28:19: *"Go therefore and make disciples of all the nations, baptizing them in the name of the Father and of the Son and of the Holy Spirit"* (NKJV). Here a clear distinction is drawn between the name of *"the Father"* and the name of *"the Son"* and the name of *"the Holy Spirit."*

A very clear distinction between the Father, Son, and Holy Spirit is found in John 14:16–17: *"And I will pray the Father, and He will give you another Helper, that He may abide with you forever; the Spirit of truth"* (NKJV). Here the clearest possible distinction is drawn between the Son who prays, the Father to whom He prays, and *"another Helper"* who is given in response to the Son's prayer. Nothing could possibly be plainer than the distinction that Jesus Christ made in this passage between Himself and the Father and the Holy Spirit.

We find the same thing again in John 16:7:

> *Nevertheless I tell you the truth. It is to your advantage that I go away; for if I do not go away, the Helper will not come to you; but if I depart, I will send Him to you.* (NKJV)

Here, once more, the Lord Jesus Himself made a clear distinction between Himself, who was about to go away, and the Holy Spirit, the other Helper who was coming to take His place after He had gone away.

The same thing is brought out again in Acts 2:33 in Peter's sermon on the Day of Pentecost, in which Peter is recorded as saying about Jesus,

> *Therefore being exalted to the right hand of God, and having received from the Father the promise of the Holy Spirit, He poured out this which you now see and hear.* (NKJV)

Here a clear distinction is drawn between the Son, who was exalted to the right hand of the Father, the Father Himself, and the Holy Spirit, whom the Son received from the Father and poured out on the church.

THE DOCTRINE OF THE TRINITY

In summary, let me say that again and again the Bible draws the clearest possible distinction between the Holy Spirit, the Father, and the Son. They are three separate Persons who have mutual relationships with one another, who speak of or to one another, and who apply the pronouns of the second and third persons to one another.

We have seen that the Bible makes it plain that the Holy Spirit is a divine person and that He is an entirely separate person from the Father and from the Son. In other words, there are three divine Persons in the Godhead. It has often been said that the doctrine of the Trinity is not taught in the Bible. It is true that the doctrine of the Trinity is not directly taught in the Bible in so many words, but this doctrine is simply the putting together of truths that are distinctly and unmistakably taught in the Bible. The Bible clearly states that there is but one God (Deut. 6:4). But it teaches with equal clearness, as we have seen in this chapter, that there are three divine Persons—the Father, the Son, and the Holy Spirit. The doctrine of the Trinity, therefore, is the putting together of these truths, which are taught with equal plainness.

Many people say that the doctrine of the Trinity is in the New Testament but not in the Old Testament. But it is in the very first chapter of the Bible. In Genesis 1:26, we read, *"Then God said, 'Let Us make man in Our image, according to Our likeness'"* (NKJV). Here the plurality of the persons in the Godhead comes out clearly. God did not say, "I will" or "Let Me make man in My image." He said, *"Let Us make man in Our image, according to Our likeness."*

Moreover, the three persons of the Trinity are found in the first three verses of the Bible. *"In the beginning God created the heavens and the earth"* (Gen. 1:1 NKJV). There you have God the Father. *"The earth was without form, and void; and darkness was on the face of the deep. And the Spirit of God was hovering over the face of the waters"* (v. 2 NKJV). There you have the Holy Spirit. *"Then God said"*—there you have the Word—*"'Let there be light'; and there was light"* (v. 3 NKJV). Here we have the three persons of the Trinity in the first three verses of the Bible.

In fact, the doctrine of the Trinity is found hundreds of times in the Old Testament. In the Hebrew Bible, it is found every place where you find the word *God* in your English Bible, for the Hebrew word for *God* is a plural noun. Literally translated, it would be "Gods," not "God."

The Unitarians and the Jews reject the deity of Christ. They often refer to Deuteronomy 6:4 as conclusive proof that the deity of Christ cannot be true: *"Hear, O Israel: the LORD our God, the LORD is one!"* (NKJV). But the very doctrine that they are seeking to disprove is found in Deuteronomy 6:4, for the literal translation of the verse is, "Hear, O Israel: Jehovah our Gods is one Jehovah."

Why did the Hebrews, with their intense monotheism, use a plural name for God? This question puzzled the Hebrew grammarians and lexicographers. The best explanation they could find was that the plural for God used in the Bible was the "pluralis majestatis" (*we* in place of *I* in the speech of royalty). This explanation is entirely inadequate, to say nothing of the fact that its validity is very doubtful. Another explanation is far nearer at hand, and far more adequate and satisfactory: the inspired Hebrew writers used a plural name for God in spite of their intense monotheism because there is a plurality of persons in the one Godhead.

Someone may ask, "How can God be three and one at the same time?" The answer to this question is very simple and easily understandable. He cannot be three and one in the same sense, nor does the Bible teach that He is. In what sense can He be one and three? A perfectly satisfactory answer to this question is clearly impossible from the very nature of the case. In the first place, *"God is Spirit"* (John 4:24), and numbers belong primarily to the physical world. Difficulty always arises when we attempt to conceive of a spiritual being in the forms of physical thought.

In the second place, a perfectly satisfactory answer is impossible because God is infinite and we are finite. God dwells *"in the light which no man can approach unto"* (1 Tim. 6:16). Our attempts at a philosophical explanation of the triune nature of God are attempts to put the facts of infinite being into the forms of finite thought, and of necessity such attempts can at the very best be only partially successful.

This much we know, that God is essentially one, and also that there are three Persons in this one Godhead. There is but one God, but this one God makes Himself known to us as three distinct Persons—Father, Son, and Holy Spirit. There is one God, eternally existing, and manifesting Himself in three Persons.

If we were to go into the realm of philosophy, it could be shown from the very necessities of the case that, if God was to be God, He had to exist as more than one person. Before the creation of finite beings, there had to be a multiplicity of persons in the eternal Godhead. Otherwise, God could not love, for there would be no one to love, and therefore, God could not be God.

The ease with which one can grasp the Unitarian concept of God is not in its favor but against it.* Any God who could be thoroughly comprehended by a finite mind would not be an infinite God. It would be impossible for a thoroughly intelligent mind to really worship a God whom he could thoroughly understand. If God is to be truly God, He must be beyond our complete understanding.

The doctrine of the Trinity is not merely a speculative doctrine. It is a doctrine of tremendous daily practical importance. It enters into the very foundation of our experience, if our experience is a truly Christian one. For example, in our prayers, we need God the Father, to whom we pray; we need God the Son, through whom we pray; and we need God the Holy Spirit, in whom we pray. Also, in our worship, we need God the Father, the very center of our worship; we need the Son, through whom we approach the Father in our worship; and we need the Holy

---

* Unitarianism denies the Christian doctrine of the Trinity and instead teaches that God exists in only one person.

Spirit, by whom we worship. But all three—Father, Son, and Holy Spirit—are the objects of our worship. The following doxology is thoroughly Christian in its worship:

> Praise God from whom all blessings flow,
>   Praise Him all creatures here below.
> Praise Him above, ye heavenly hosts,
>   Praise Father, Son, and Holy Ghost.

So, also, is the Gloria Patri, the words of which we so often sing, but the thought of which we so seldom grasp: "Glory be to the Father and to the Son and to the Holy Ghost, as it was in the beginning, is now, and ever shall be, world without end. Amen."

The Bible Answer Book

Contents

Introduction

Seasoned believers, new Christians, and those who are seeking God or exploring Christianity all have questions about the Bible and how to live the Christian life. In this book, renowned evangelist and Bible expert R. A. Torrey delves into some of the most perplexing questions people ask, such as "Why does God allow evil?"; "Is there an afterlife?"; "How can I get to heaven?"; "Why aren't all our prayers answered?"; "Who or what is the Antichrist?"; and "Are all religions the same?" He also provides practical advice for living the Christian life, addressing such issues as how to return to God if you've fallen away from Him, how to receive the Holy Spirit, how to have daily victory over sin, and how to study the Bible effectively.

This book is fascinating to read from cover to cover; it is also an extremely useful reference book to have on hand to answer questions that will come up as you grow in your faith and face new life situations.

Some topics are addressed in several different sections. In these instances, you will be referred to corresponding sections in the book. You may also find that some of the same material is covered in more than one question. This has been done to make each individual answer as complete as possible. In addition, Torrey includes biblical texts in many of his responses to give you a Scriptural basis for his answers and to enable you to do further study of these important topics on your own. Additional Scriptures have been included for further clarification.

Reuben Archer Torrey is respected as one of the greatest evangelists of modern times. Torrey was a Congregational minister who joined Dwight L. Moody in his evangelistic work in Chicago. Under Torrey's direction, Moody Institute became a pattern for Bible institutes around the world. At the turn of the twentieth century, Torrey began his evangelistic tours and campaigns, conducting a worldwide revival campaign from 1903–05. He and his team ministered in many parts of the world and reportedly brought nearly one hundred thousand people to Jesus Christ. Torrey continued worldwide crusades for the next fifteen years, reaching as far as Japan and China. During these years, he also served as Dean of the Bible Institute of Los Angeles and was pastor of the Church of the Open Door in that city.

Torrey's straightforward style of evangelism has led many people to Christ and has shown thousands of Christians how to present the Gospel clearly and effectively. In this book, you will discover how to address many important issues and challenges in your Christian faith so that you may draw closer to Christ, live a victorious Christian life, and be a credible witness to the Gospel.

The Bible Answer Book

The Afterlife

Q: What becomes of our spirits when we die? Upon death, does one's soul pass directly to heaven or hell, or is there an intermediate state?

A: Immediately at death, the spirit of the believer departs to be with Christ in a state that is far better than the one in which it existed here on earth (Philippians 1:23). It is *"absent from the body and...at home with the Lord"* (2 Cor. 5:8 NAS). But this is not the final state of blessedness of the redeemed. In our final state of blessedness, the spirit is not merely unclothed from its present mortal body but is clothed with its resurrection body. (See verses 1–4.) We will obtain this resurrection body at the second coming of Christ, when the bodies of those who sleep in Christ are raised from the dead and the bodies of believers then living are transformed in the twinkling of an eye—when our perishable bodies become imperishable. (See 1 Thessalonians 4:15–17; 1 Corinthians 15:51–53.)

On the other hand, immediately at death, the spirits of the wicked depart into that portion of hades reserved for the wicked dead, where they consciously exist in great torment. (See Luke 16:19–31.) But this is not their final condition of torment. At the close of the Millennium—the thousand-year reign of Christ on earth after His second coming—those who have died in sin will be raised again to stand before the Great White Throne of God, to be judged and assigned to their final condition of torment. (See Revelation 20:11–15; 21:8.) It is then that they will enter into their final and fullest suffering. Just as the redeemed spirits will be clothed at the coming of Christ with their glorious resurrection bodies, which will be perfect counterparts of the redeemed spirits that inhabit them and partakers with them in all their joy, the wicked are to be clothed with bodies that will be perfect counterparts of the lost spirits that inhabit them and will be partakers with them in all their misery.

Alcohol

Q: Should a Christian drink alcohol, or should he abstain from it?

A: One of the most common and destructive sins of our time is that of excessive drinking. I urge Christians to practice total abstinence for their own sake and for the sake of others. I make it a point that if a person can do just as well without intoxicating beverages, then he ought to do without them for the sake of his brother (see 1 Corinthians 8:4–13). However, if he cannot do just as well without them, then he ought to do without them for his own sake.

Q: What should a person do whose spouse continually drinks?

A: If your spouse continually drinks, you should first go to God in prayer. God will reveal to you if there is anything in you that causes your spouse to drink. If you are angry and totally disagreeable in the home, while in a prayer meeting seem totally sweet and angelic, you should first get thoroughly right with God and then filled with the Holy Spirit. In this way, you may show, through the Spirit-filled life, the beauty of holiness. Your spouse will be attracted and won by this. Then pray and watch for an opportunity to speak to your spouse— to move heaven and earth and never quit until your spouse is converted.

Annihilation of the Wicked

Q: What is meant by the theory of the annihilation of the wicked?

A: It means the annihilation of the existence of those who die without having accepted Jesus Christ as their Savior.

Q: Why is the theory of the annihilation of the wicked, supposedly indicated by Revelation 20:14–15, unscriptural and a reprehensible doctrine?

A: The annihilation of the wicked is not indicated in Revelation 20:14–15 to anyone who reads the whole passage and parallel passages in the Scriptures. The passage reads: *"Then Death and Hades were cast into the lake of fire. This is the second death. And anyone not found written in the Book of Life was cast into the lake of fire"* (NKJV). The fate of those cast into the lake of fire is not annihilation. There is no Scripture to support such a theory. The Bible clearly teaches that the future destiny of the wicked is a condition of unresting, unending, conscious torment and anguish. (Please refer to the section "Eternal Punishment" in this book.)

As to its being a "reprehensible doctrine," I would say that I have never known anyone who accepted this doctrine who did not lose power in serving God. I could give examples of men whom God greatly used who have been led to accept this doctrine and who, in consequence, have been in part or altogether set aside as soulwinners. If one really believes the doctrine of the endless, conscious torment of the unrepentant, he will work as never before for their salvation before it is too late.

The Antichrist

Q: Who is the Antichrist, and when will he appear?

A: The Antichrist will be a person in whom Satan's resistance to Christ and His kingdom will culminate. He will be a man, but a man whom Satan will fill to such an extent that he will be Satan incarnate. The Devil always seeks to mimic God's work, and his mimicking of God's work will culminate in his mimicking of the incarnation of God in Jesus Christ. The Antichrist's coming will be *"according to the working of Satan, with all power, signs, and lying wonders, and with all unrighteous deception"* (2 Thess. 2:9–10 NKJV).

The Antichrist will appear just prior to the second coming of Jesus Christ, and our Lord will *"consume [him] with the breath of His mouth and destroy [him] with the brightness of His coming"* (v. 8 NKJV).

There are already many antichrists preparing the way for the final and consummate Antichrist (1 John 2:18). Indeed, everyone who denies the Father and the Son is an antichrist (v. 22), but there seems to be a special preparation for *the* Antichrist, in whom all the forces of evil will coalesce. These forces of evil will join and be headed by one man whom the devil will especially gift and in whom he will dwell, and that man will be the Antichrist.

Assurance of Salvation

Q: Is it right for a person to say that he is saved? In other words, may I know that I am saved, and if so, on what authority?

A: If you really are saved, you may know it on the authority of God's Word. God says in John 3:36, *"He who believes in the Son has everlasting life"* (NKJV, emphasis added). You know whether you believe in the Son or not. If you do believe in the Son, you know you have everlasting life because God says so here in so many words.

This is also emphasized in 1 John 5:11–12: *"And this is the testimony: that God has given us eternal life, and this life is in His Son.*

He who has the Son has life; he who does not have the Son of God does not have life" (NKJV). When one who believes in the Son doubts that he has life, he makes God a liar. This is indicated in the preceding verse, where we read: *"He who does not believe God has made Him a liar, because he has not believed the testimony that God has given of His Son"* (v. 10 NKJV).

Furthermore, anyone who has received Jesus as his Savior and Lord and King may know that he is a child of God. God says so in so many words in John 1:12: *"But as many as received Him, to them He gave the right to become children of God"* (NKJV). If you have received Jesus, you have a right to call yourself a child of God. You have no right to doubt that you are a child of God.

Again, everyone who believes in Jesus has a right to know that he is justified, that his sins are all forgiven, and that God regards him as righteous in Christ. He has a right to know it on the very best authority, namely, because God says so. We read in Acts 13:38–39: *"Therefore let it be known to you, brethren, that through this Man is preached to you the forgiveness of sins; and by Him everyone who believes is justified from all things."* Notice that it says, *"Everyone who believes is justified"* (NKJV). You know whether you believe or not. If you do believe in Jesus, God says you are justified. Many people doubt their salvation because they rely on their feelings instead of looking at the Word of God. It is not at all a question of whether you *feel* that you are a child of God; it is simply a question of what God says. If you rely on your feelings instead of the Word of God, you make God a liar for the sake of your own feelings.

God caused the book of 1 John to be written for the very purpose that everyone who believes in the Son of God might know that he has eternal life: *"These things [are] written to you who believe in the name of the Son of God, that you may **know** that you have eternal life"* (1 John 5:13 NKJV, emphasis added). If God caused a book of the Bible to be written so that we might know this, then certainly we may know it. The above verse teaches us that the way to know it is from what is *"written."* The first thing to be sure of is that you really do believe in Jesus—that you really have received Him as your Savior, surrendered to Him as your Lord and Master, and confessed Him as such publicly. When you are sure of this, you may be absolutely sure that you are saved, that you have eternal life, that your sins are totally forgiven, and that you are a child of God.

The Atonement

Q: What theory of atonement does the Bible teach?

A: The Bible does not teach a theory of atonement. It teaches a fact, the glorious fact that every one of our sins was laid upon Jesus Christ. (See Isaiah 53:6; 2 Corinthians 5:21; Galatians 3:13; 1 Peter 2:24.) As a result of Jesus Christ having borne our sins, there is not only pardon for every sin but also justification, which is more than pardon. The Bible teaches that because Jesus Christ took our place on the cross, the moment we accept Jesus Christ, we step into His place, the place of perfect acceptance before God. We become *"the righteousness of God in Him"* (2 Cor. 5:21 NKJV). We no longer have our own poor, pitiable, unsatisfactory righteousness but a perfect righteousness, the righteousness of God in Christ (Philippians 3:9).

Q: How could God punish His innocent Son for the guilt of man?

A: The doctrine of the Bible is not that God, a holy first person, takes the sins of man, a guilty second person, and lays them upon His own holy Son, an innocent third person. That is the way the doctrine is often misrepresented. In fact, it is the depiction usually made by those who reject the Bible doctrine of substitution—that Christ, as our Substitute, suffered and died for our sins in our place.

The real teaching of the Bible is that Jesus Christ is not a third person, but that He is indeed the first person—*"that God was in Christ reconciling the world to Himself"* (2 Cor. 5:19 NKJV). In the atoning death of His Son, instead of laying the punishment of guilty man upon an innocent third person, God took the shame and suffering due to man upon Himself. That is the complete opposite of being unjust and cruel—it is amazing grace!

Furthermore, Jesus Christ was also the second person. He was not merely *a* man, He was the Son of Man, the representative Man, the Head of the race. No ordinary man could bear the guilt of other men, but the Son of Man, the representative Man, could.

If we take the teaching of the Bible as a complete whole and not in a fragmentary way, it is the most wonderful philosophy the world has ever known. We will ponder and admire its inexhaustible depths throughout eternity. But if we take any one doctrine out of the Bible, the other doctrines become absurd. If we give up the doctrine of the deity of Jesus Christ, then the doctrine of the Atonement becomes an absurdity, and the difficulty suggested by this question naturally arises. Or if we give up the doctrine of the real humanity of Christ, the doctrine of the Atonement loses its profound significance. But if we take all that the Bible says, namely, that Jesus was really divine, *"God... manifested in the flesh"* (1 Tim. 3:16 NKJV), and that He was truly man, not merely *a* man but the Son of Man, the representative Man, then the doctrine of the Atonement does not present any difficulties. Rather, it presents an amazing depth of truth.

It is strange how little the average objector to the doctrine of substitution knows about the real doctrine of the Bible on this point. Instead of fighting what the Bible really teaches, he is fighting a figment of his own uninstructed imagination.

Backsliding

Q: How would you deal with a backslider? Is there hope for him, and how?

A: Everywhere I go, I find many people who tell me that they were once Christians, but who confess that they have gone back into the world. I am persuaded that many of these people were never truly saved. They have gone forward in revival meetings, have joined the church, or have done something of that sort, but they have never really fully accepted Jesus Christ as their Savior and Lord. Having failed in their first attempt, they hesitate to make another.

This hesitation is unreasonable. The fact that one has attempted to do something and has done it in the wrong way is no reason for not doing it in the right way. If people would begin the Christian life correctly, they would not be so likely to go back into the world. Also, if they have begun it in the wrong way, they had better begin it over again in the right way. As God's own Word shows us, this is the right way to begin:

♦ First, accept Jesus Christ as Savior. That is, believe God's testimony concerning Him—that He bore all your sins in His own body on the cross—and trust God to forgive you, not because of anything that you have done but because of what Christ did when He made full atonement for your sins. (See 1 Peter 2:24; Galatians 3:13.)

♦ Second, accept Jesus Christ as your Lord and King (Acts 2:36). This involves the utter surrender of your mind to Him, so that it may be renewed by Him, and of your life to Him, so that it may be governed by Him. You must put yourself completely at His disposal. You must not only sing "I surrender all" with your lips, but you must also make it a fact in your life. This lack of absolute surrender at the time of starting the Christian life is the cause of a large measure of backsliding.

♦ Third, accept Christ as the risen Son of God who has all power in heaven and on earth (see Matthew 28:18), and trust Him day by day to keep you from falling and from all the power of sin and temptation. (See Hebrews 7:25; Jude 24.)

When you have begun right, most of the battle is won, but you must continue in obedience to Christ. Continuance in the Christian life is not at all a question of your strength, but of Christ's. If you have begun the Christian life once and failed, begin it again and succeed. Many of the strongest Christians today are those who were once backsliders. The apostle Peter himself was once a backslider, but after Pentecost, he was one of the mightiest servants of Christ that the world ever saw. Pentecost is possible for you.

No one can be more miserable than the backslider. Jeremiah was certainly right when he said to backsliding Israel, *"It is an evil and bitter thing that you have forsaken the* Lord *your God"* (Jer. 2:19 NKJV). The one who forsakes Christ forsakes the *"fountain of living waters, and* [digs himself] *cisterns; broken cisterns that can hold no water"* (v. 13 NKJV). Let him leave the broken cisterns of the world and come back to Christ, the Fountain of Living Water.

Baptism

Q: Is baptism necessary for salvation?

A: It depends upon what you mean by the words *salvation* and *baptism*. Certainly, some have found forgiveness of sins and have entered into eternal life without water baptism, such as the thief on the cross. (See Luke 23:39–43.) There is a body of believers who do not practice water baptism at all, namely the Friends, who are also called Quakers. Many of the Friends have the consciousness of having their sins forgiven, and God has set His seal upon their acceptance by giving them the gift of the Holy Spirit.

However, the term *salvation* is used in Scripture not merely in regard to forgiveness of sins and eternal life, but also in a larger sense of all the fullness of blessing that is to be found in Christ. Certainly, one cannot enter into all the fullness of blessing that there is in Christ without absolute obedience to Him (Acts 5:32). If there is any commandment of Christ that we know we do not obey, we certainly cannot enjoy the fullness of fellowship with Him. Jesus Christ Himself commanded water baptism

(Matt. 28:19). He also commanded it through His disciples (Acts 2:38). As an act of obedience to Christ, therefore, water baptism certainly is, in the larger sense, a saving ordinance for those who believe that Jesus Christ commands it. Submitting to baptism has been the turning point in the experience of many men and women. It has been done as an act of conscious obedience to Jesus Christ, and has been accompanied by great blessing.

There are earnest followers of Christ who do not see in such passages as the above a command to baptize or be baptized with water, and in not being baptized, they are not consciously disobeying Jesus Christ. It is difficult for me to see how anyone can study the New Testament with the single-minded purpose of discovering what it actually teaches and not see the necessity of water baptism. Yet from my contact with those believers known as Friends, I must conclude that many of them are perfectly conscientious Christians, even though they have not been baptized with water, and that they are true children of God.

Q: What is the explanation of 1 Corinthians 15:29: *"What will they do who are baptized for the dead, if the dead do not rise at all? Why then are they baptized for the dead?"* (NKJV).

A: In Paul's time, there seems to have been a custom in which people were baptized on behalf of those who, for one reason or another, had died without baptism. The above verse is the only reference in Scripture to this custom. It evidently was not a custom that the Bible commanded or sanctioned. Paul was not sanctioning it here. He simply referred to it as existing, and he referred to those who practiced it as showing that they believed in the resurrection, for otherwise this baptism for the dead would have no significance.

The custom of baptism for the dead was practiced for a time, but only among heretics. It was repudiated by the church. Many customs crept into the church very early on that were not of God, that the apostles did not endorse, and that ought not to be followed by us. The Mormons practice the custom today, and this verse, which they use as a warrant for it, does not support the custom. Certainly, if Paul had wanted us to follow this custom, he would have said something more about it than he did in this Scripture verse. He would at least have endorsed it, and he did not. When we look at the verse carefully, we see that Paul not only did not endorse it but also by implication rejected it, for he separated himself from the custom by saying, *"What will **they** do who are baptized for the dead?"* By this word *"they,"* he not only separated himself from this third party who were baptized for the dead, but he also separated those to whom he wrote.

The Bible

Q: Do you believe in the verbal inspiration of the Bible?

A: I do. That is, I believe that the writers of the various books of the Bible were guided by the Holy Spirit, not only in the thoughts to which they gave expression but also in the choice of the words in which they expressed the thoughts. They *"spoke from God as they were carried along by the Holy Spirit"* (2 Pet. 1:21 NIV). It was the Holy Spirit who spoke. The words that were uttered were His words. (See 2 Samuel 23:2; Hebrews 3:7–8; 10:15–16; Acts 28:25.) The very words that were used were the words that the Holy Spirit taught. Nothing could be plainer than Paul's statement: *"These things we also speak, not in words which man's wisdom teaches but which the Holy Spirit teaches"* (1 Cor. 2:13 NKJV).

The Holy Spirit Himself anticipated all these modern, ingenious but unbiblical and false theories regarding His own work in the apostles. The more carefully and minutely one studies the wording of the statements made in the Bible, the more he will become convinced of the marvelous accuracy of the words that were used to produce the thoughts. To a superficial student, the doctrine of verbal inspiration may appear questionable or even absurd, but any regenerated and Spirit-taught person who ponders the words of Scripture day after day and year after year will become increasingly convinced that the wisdom of God is in the very words used as well as in the thoughts that are expressed in the words.

It is a very significant fact that our difficulties with the Bible rapidly disappear when we come to notice the precise language that is used. The change of a word or a letter, of a tense, case, or number, often lands a person in contradiction or untruth. However, by taking the words just as they were written, difficulties disappear, and the truth shines forth. The more microscopically we study the Bible, the more clearly its divine origin shines forth as we see its perfection of form as well as of substance.

Q: Are all parts of the Bible equally inspired by God?

A: *"**All** Scripture is given by inspiration of God* [is God-breathed]" (2 Tim. 3:16 NKJV, emphasis added). There is no warrant for the change that the Revised Version makes in this passage: *"Every scripture inspired of God…."* As originally written, the entire Bible was infallible truth, and in our English versions, we have the original writings translated with substantial accuracy. But not all parts of the Bible are equally important. For example, the genealogies given in the first nine chapters of 1 Chronicles are important, far more important than the average student of the Bible realizes, but they certainly are not as important to the believer today as the teachings of Christ and the apostles.

Q: If the Holy Spirit is the author of the words of Scripture, how do we account for variations in style and wording? For example, how do we account for the fact that Paul always uses Pauline language, and John Johannine language, and so on?

A: Even if we could not account at all for this fact, it would have little weight against the explicit statements of God's Word. Anyone who is humble enough and wise enough to recognize that there are a great many things that we cannot account for at all that could be easily accounted for if we knew a little more, is never staggered by an apparent difficulty of this kind. But in point of fact, it is easy enough to account for these variations. The simple explanation is this: the Holy Spirit is wise enough and has facility enough in the use of language in revealing truth, to and through any individual, to use words, phrases, and forms of expression that are in that person's vocabulary and forms of thought to which that person is accustomed, and in every way to make use of that person's particular individuality. It is one of the many signs of the divine wisdom of this Book that the same divine truth is expressed with absolute accuracy in such widely varying forms of expression.

Q: If the Bible is verbally inspired, why did the gospel writers not give Jesus' and other people's words exactly? I can understand how their accounts of events may differ, but Jesus' words cannot properly be rendered one way by Matthew and another way by Luke if verbal inspiration is correct. Note that Galatians 3:16 stresses the importance of accurate wording in Scripture: *"Now to Abraham and his Seed were the promises made. He does not say, 'And to seeds,' as of many, but as of one, 'And to your Seed,' who is Christ"* (NKJV).

A: The gospel writers did give people's words exactly when they claimed to give them exactly. When they only claimed to give the substance of what people said, the words may not be given exactly as they were spoken. But even when the gospel writers gave Jesus' words exactly, they did not always claim to record everything that He said, so that the book of Matthew may give part of what He said, and Luke another part of what He said. To get all that He said, both accounts must be taken together. Matthew gave the part that was adapted to the purpose of his book, and Luke gave the part that was adapted to his. It is well that they were given in just this way, for it is one of the many incidental proofs that the Gospels are independent of one another and were not composed by writers who were in collusion with one another.

Furthermore, it must be kept in mind that the words of Jesus recorded by Matthew and Luke were spoken in Aramaic and were translated by Matthew and Luke into Greek. There is reason to suppose that the utterances recorded by Matthew, Mark, and Luke were largely utterances that Jesus gave in Aramaic, while those recorded by John were largely those that Jesus spoke in Greek. It must be remembered that in the time of Jesus, the people in Palestine were a bilingual people.

Q: How would you endeavor to interest an indifferent person in the study of the Bible?

A: First of all, I would have to get him to accept Jesus Christ as his Savior. Then I would show him that the Bible is God's Word to him and that the only way to be strong and to grow in grace is to study the Word. I would then explain to him some simple method of Bible study and have him begin doing it. The best way for a converted person to become interested in the study of the Bible is to actually start studying it. The more one studies it, the more his taste for Bible study increases.

Q: What books of the Bible should a young convert read or study first?

A: First of all, he should read the gospel of John. It is one of the most profound books of the Bible, and yet there is much in it for the youngest believer. It was written for the specific purpose of bringing people to believe that *"Jesus is the Christ, the Son of God, and that believing* [they might] *have life in His name"* (John 20:31 NKJV). There is nothing that the young believer needs more than to come to an intelligent, fixed faith in Jesus as the Christ, the Son of God.

After the gospel of John, I would have the young disciple read the gospel of Mark, then Luke, then Matthew. After that, I would urge him to study the Acts of the Apostles and then the epistle to the Romans. I think that, after that, I would have him read through the whole New Testament starting from the beginning.

Q: There are some verses in the Bible that are not translated in the way you know they were intended to be. When a person takes up those points with you, what do you tell him?

A: I tell him that we know now what the correct translation is, and I show him what it is. Not one fundamental doctrine has been affected by the variations in manuscripts or in translations.

The Christian Life

Q: What advice do you give for having a consistent and abundant Christian life?

A: The Bible gives us seven steps to an abundant Christian life:

♦ First, begin right. John 1:12 tells us what a right beginning is: *"But as many as received Him, to them He gave the right to become children of God, to those who believe in His name"* (NKJV). Receive Christ as your Savior who died for your sin. Trust the whole matter of your forgiveness to Him. Rest upon the fact that He has paid the full penalty for your sin. *"For He made Him who knew no sin to be sin for us, that we might become the righteousness of God in Him"* (2 Cor. 5:21 NKJV). Take Him as your Deliverer who will save you from the power of sin, who will give life to those who are dead in trespasses and sins. Don't try to save yourself from the power of sin; trust Him to do it. Take Him as your Master. Don't seek to guide your own life. Surrender unconditionally to His lordship over you. The life of entire surrender is a joyous life all along the way. If you have never before received Christ as your Savior and surrendered your life to Him, and if you wish to make a success of the Christian life, get alone with God and say, "All for Jesus."

♦ Second, confess Christ openly before men. *"Therefore whoever confesses Me before men, him I will also confess before My Father who is in heaven"* (Matt. 10:32 NKJV). *"For with the heart one believes unto righteousness, and with the mouth confession is made unto salvation"* (Rom. 10:10 NKJV). The life of confession is the life of full salvation.

♦ Third, study the Word. *"As newborn babes, desire the pure milk of the word, that you may grow thereby"* (1 Pet. 2:2 NKJV). The

Word of God is the soul's food. It is the nourishment of the new life. A person who neglects the Word cannot make much of a success of the Christian life. All who do well in the Christian life are great feeders on the Word of God.

◆ Fourth, *"pray without ceasing"* (1 Thess. 5:17). The one who wants to succeed in the Christian life must lead a life of prayer. This is easy enough if you just begin to do it.

Have set times for prayer. The rule of David and Daniel, three times a day, is a good rule. David wrote, *"Evening and morning and at noon I will pray, and cry aloud, and He shall hear my voice"* (Ps. 55:17 NKJV). The book of Daniel records, *"Now when Daniel knew that the writing was signed* [which decreed that no one could pray to any god or man except the king of Persia], *he went home. And in his upper room, with his windows open toward Jerusalem, he knelt down on his knees three times that day, and prayed and gave thanks before his God, as was his custom since early days"* (Dan. 6:10 NKJV). Begin the day with thanksgiving and prayer—thanksgiving for the definite mercies of the past, and prayer for the definite needs of the present day. Stop in the midst of the bustle and worry and temptation of the day for thanksgiving and prayer. Close the day with thanksgiving and prayer.

Then there should be special prayer in special temptation—when we see the temptation approaching. Keep looking to God. It is not necessary that we be on our knees all the time. However, the *heart* should be on its knees all the time.

There are three things for which the person who wants to make a success of the Christian life must especially pray. First, he must pray for wisdom: *"If any of you lacks wisdom, let him ask of God"* (James 1:5 NKJV). Second, he must pray for strength: *"Those who wait on the LORD shall renew their strength"* (Isa. 40:31 NKJV). Third, he must pray for the Holy Spirit: *"Your heavenly Father* [will] *give the Holy Spirit to those who ask Him"* (Luke 11:13 NKJV). If you have not yet received the baptism with the Holy Spirit, you should offer definite prayer for this definite blessing and definitely expect to receive it. If you have already received the baptism with the

Holy Spirit, you should, with each new emergency that you encounter in your Christian life and ministry, pray to God for a new filling with the Holy Spirit. (See Acts 4:18–31.)

♦ Fifth, go to work for Christ. *"For to everyone who has, more will be given, and he will have abundance; but from him who does not have, even what he has will be taken away"* (Matt. 25:29 NKJV). The context of this verse is that those who use what they have will get more, and those who let what they have lie idle will lose even that. The working Christian—the one who uses his talents, whether few or many, in Christ's service—is the one who does well in the Christian life here, and who will hereafter hear, *"Well done, good and faithful servant; you were faithful over a few things, I will make you ruler over many things. Enter into the joy of your lord"* (v. 21 NKJV). Find some work to do for Christ, and do it. Look for work. If it is nothing more than distributing tracts, do it. Always be looking for something more to do for Christ, and you will always be receiving something more from Christ.

♦ Sixth, give generously. *"The generous soul will be made rich"* (Prov. 11:25 NKJV). *"He who sows sparingly will also reap sparingly, and he who sows bountifully will also reap bountifully.... And God is able to make all grace abound toward you, that you, always having all sufficiency in all things, may have an abundance for every good work"* (2 Cor. 9:6, 8 NKJV). Success and growth in the Christian life depend most on generous giving. A stingy Christian cannot be a growing Christian. It is wonderful how a Christian begins to grow when he begins to give.

♦ Seventh, keep pushing on. *"Brothers, I do not consider myself yet to have taken hold of it. But one thing I do: forgetting what is behind and straining toward what is ahead, I press on toward the goal to win the prize for which God has called me heavenward in Christ Jesus"* (Phil. 3:13–14 NIV).

Forget the sins that lie behind you. If you fail anywhere, if you fall, don't be discouraged, don't give up, don't brood over the sin. Confess it instantly. Believe God's Word: *"If we confess our sins, He is faithful and just to forgive us our sins and to cleanse us from all unrighteousness"* (1 John 1:9 NKJV). Believe that the sin is forgiven, forget it, and press on. Satan deceives many of us in regard to this. He keeps us brooding over our failures and sins.

In addition, forget the achievements and victories of the past, and press on to greater ones. Here, too, Satan cheats many of us out of the abundant life. He keeps us thinking so much about what we have already obtained, and he makes us so contented with it and so puffed up over it, that we come to a standstill or even backslide. Our only safety is in forgetting the things that are behind and pressing on. There is always something better ahead, until we *"come...to a perfect man, to the measure of the stature of the fullness of Christ"* (Eph. 4:13 NKJV).

Christian Science

Q: How would you prove the error of Christian Science?

A: Many are being led astray into Christian Science. Most Christian Scientists claim to believe the Bible. Take them, therefore, to 1 John 4:1–3: *"Beloved, do not believe every spirit, but test the spirits, whether they are of God; because many false prophets have gone out into the world. By this you know the Spirit of God: every spirit that confesses that Jesus Christ has come in the flesh is of God, and every spirit that does not confess that Jesus Christ has come in the flesh is not of God. And this is the spirit of the Antichrist, which you have heard was coming, and is now already in the world"* (NKJV).

This passage strikes at the very foundation of Christian Science. As one of its fundamental doctrines, Christian Science denies the reality of matter, the reality of the body, and (of necessity) the reality of the Incarnation. Show them by this passage that the Bible says that every spirit that does not confess that Jesus Christ came in the flesh is not of God, but of antichrist, and therefore any doctrine that denies the Incarnation is not Christian.

Q: Why do you believe that Christian Science founder Mary Baker Eddy's claim that she received the tenets of Christian Science by divine inspiration is false?

A: First of all, I know that her claim is false because it has been proven that she got her theories from a man by whom she was treated.* When she wrote her first book in its original form, she did not claim that it was her original work or that she had received it from God; she truly acknowledged that she was writing down the views of this person by whom she had been treated and under whom she had studied.

In the second place, I know that her claim is false because the tenets themselves are false. Mrs. Eddy denies the reality of the Incarnation, and this is one of the primary tests of the truth or falsehood of any system or doctrine. This is the decisive question to ask of any spirit and any system of doctrines, as shown in the previous answer. Mrs. Eddy also denies the Atonement, the fundamental truth of the Gospel. Her view of the Atonement is not the one taught in the Bible, namely, that Jesus Christ Himself bore our sins in His own body on the cross. (See 2 Corinthians 5:21; Galatians 3:13; 1 Peter 2:24.) These are only some of the many great errors in the teaching of Mrs. Eddy.

There are, it is true, some elements of truth in the teachings of Christian Science. Every false system must have some true teachings in it; otherwise, it could not have any success at all. Every dangerous system of error takes some truth and distorts and perverts it and covers it up with a large amount of error. That the mind has a tremendous influence over the body and that much disease can be overcome through the mind is unquestionably true. That God answers prayer and, in answer to prayer, heals the sick, is taught in the Bible and taught by experience. That Jesus Christ had a mission for the body as well as for the soul is clearly taught in Scripture. That a great deal of harm has been done by the use of drugs, every wise physician admits. Mrs. Eddy has taken these truths, which the church has often lost sight of, and has opened the door for the introduction of a vast amount of

---

*Phineas Parkhurst Quimby, a well-known and influential mental healer. *Editor's note.*

destructive and damning error. If the church had been truer to its own mission and had given people a real and full and satisfying Gospel, the great majority of those who have fallen prey to Mrs. Eddy's teaching would have escaped the snare.

The Church

Q: What are the conditions of entrance into the church?

A: The word *church* in the New Testament is used, first, of the whole body of believers in Jesus Christ. (See Matthew 16:18; Acts 2:47; 20:28; Ephesians 5:24–25; Colossians 1:18, 24.) Second, it is used of the body of believers in any one place—for example, the church of the Thessalonians (1 Thess. 1:1). Third, it is used of the local congregations meeting regularly for worship, teaching, and the breaking of bread—for example, the church that met in Rome in the home of Priscilla and Aquila (Rom. 16:3–5).

The conditions of entrance into the church in its first and deepest meaning are acceptance of Jesus Christ as one's personal Savior, surrender to Him as Lord and Master, and open confession of Him before the world (Rom. 10:9–10). The conditions of entrance into local churches are determined by the churches themselves. Most churches receive members upon satisfactory evidence that they have really forsaken sin, accepted Christ as their personal Savior, and surrendered their lives to Him. Some churches require subscription to a creed, more or less detailed. For example, it might include general affirmations of faith or also more detailed beliefs of the church's denomination. Some evangelical denominations require water baptism on the part of the applicant for membership. (See Acts 2:38, 41, 47.)

Q: What does Matthew 16:18 mean: *"You are Peter, and on this rock I will build My church"* (NKJV)? Does this verse teach that Peter was the rock upon which Christ would build His church, and does it prove that the Roman Catholic Church, as built upon Peter, is the only true church?

A: The passage does not teach that Peter was the rock upon which Christ would build His church. Peter's name in Greek is *Petros*, meaning "a piece of rock." The word translated *"rock"* in the above verse is *petra*, which means "a rock." Peter had just made a confession of Jesus as *"the Christ, the Son of the living God"* (v. 16 NKJV). Jesus, as the Christ, the Son of the living God, is the Rock upon which the church is built. *"No other foundation can anyone lay than that which is laid, which is Jesus Christ"* (1 Cor. 3:11 NKJV). Peter, by his faith in Jesus as the Christ, the Son of God, and by his confession of Him as such, became a piece of the Rock. Every believer, by believing in Jesus as the Christ, the Son of the living God, and by confessing Him as such, becomes a piece of the Rock and, in this sense, a part of the foundation upon which the church is built, *"Jesus Christ Himself being the chief corner stone"* (Eph. 2:20 NKJV; see also verses 21–22).

Furthermore, the Roman Catholic Church is not built upon Peter. There is no real evidence that Peter was the first bishop of the church of Rome. Even if he were, that would not prove that those who followed him in the office were his true successors. The true successors of Peter are those who build on the same Christ that Peter built upon, who teach the same doctrine, and who exhibit the same life.

Q: Was Peter the first pope?

A: No, he was not. There was no pope until long after Peter was dead and buried. The papacy was a later outgrowth of the church of which there was not even an apparent seed in the days of Peter. Peter was far from being a pope. Consider the fact that the apostle Paul rebuked him openly (Gal. 2:11–14).

As I explained in the previous answer, there is no proof that Peter was ever bishop of the church in Rome; there is no decisive proof that he was ever in Rome. However, even if he was, he certainly was not a pope in any sense that the word now carries. There is nothing in the Bible that warrants such an office as that of pope. In fact, Jesus Christ expressly forbids any man from holding such an office. He said in Matthew 23:8–10, *"Do not be called 'Rabbi'; for One is your Teacher, the Christ, and you are all brethren. Do not call anyone on earth your father; for One is your Father, He who is in heaven. And do not be called teachers; for One is your Teacher, the Christ"* (NKJV). Now, the pope claims to be a "father" in the very sense used here, in the very sense that Jesus forbids any man to be called father.

Q: What does Matthew 16:19 mean: *"I will give you the keys of the kingdom of heaven, and whatever you bind on earth will be bound in heaven, and whatever you loose on earth will be loosed in heaven"* (NKJV)? Does this teach that Peter had the power to admit anyone to the kingdom of heaven or shut him out, and that therefore the Roman Catholic Church, built upon Peter, is the true church?

A: No, it does not teach anything of the kind. When anyone studied under a Jewish rabbi, it was the custom of the rabbi to give him a key when he had become perfect in the doctrine, signifying that he was now able to unlock the secrets of the kingdom. Christ's words refer to this custom. Peter, by his confession of Jesus as the Christ, the Son of God, had proven that the Father was revealing the truth to him (v. 17), and Jesus looked forward to the day when, filled with the Holy Spirit, Peter would be guided into all the truth (John 16:12–14) and thus be competent to unlock the kingdom to men. Every Spirit-filled person, everyone taught by the Holy Spirit, has the keys of the kingdom of heaven. He has spiritual discernment and is competent to unlock the kingdom to men.

"Binding" and "loosing" were common expressions in Jesus' day for forbidding and permitting. What a rabbi forbade, he was said to "bind." What he permitted, he was said to "loose." Peter and the other disciples, as Spirit-filled men, would have discernment to know what God permitted and what God forbade. Whatever Peter, as a Spirit-filled man, forbade on earth would be forbidden in heaven, and whatever he permitted would be permitted in heaven.

We see Peter, on the Day of Pentecost, using the keys to unlock the kingdom to the Jews, and three thousand people entered into the kingdom that day. In Acts 10, we see Peter now using the keys to unlock the kingdom to the Gentiles, and a whole household entered into the kingdom that day.

Every time anyone preaches the Gospel in the power of the Holy Spirit, he is using the keys. Not only did Peter have the keys, but we may have them today. Since we are taught by the Spirit, we may have discernment as to what God permits and what God forbids. Then, what we forbid here on earth will be the thing that God forbids in heaven and what we permit will be the thing that God permits in heaven.

Q: What should an earnest Christian do in a day when the churches are so full of worldliness and error as they are today? Should he join the church?

A: Yes. I fully recognize the worldliness that is in many churches today and the error that is taught from many pulpits. But after all is said, the church is the best organization there is in the world. What would the world be today if it were not for the churches that are in it? The churches, even with all their present imperfections, are the institutions that are saving society from utter corruption.

Any Christian can accomplish more for the salvation of souls and the upbuilding of Christian character and the good of the community by uniting with some church than he can by trying to live a Christian life all by himself. There may be times when a person has to voice his protest against sins of a glaring nature in some individual church, and, if his protest will not be heard, it may be necessary for him to withdraw as a testimony against that church. But these occasions are comparatively rare.

Great corruption—unspeakable immorality, in fact—had crept into the church in Corinth, and yet Paul did not hint for a moment to any of the members of that church that they should withdraw from it. He did write to them that they should judge the person who had committed sexual immorality with his own father's wife, and to put him out of the church, but he never suggested that they should withdraw from the church. (See 1 Corinthians 5:1–13.) Even Jesus did not withdraw from the synagogues of His day until He was put out of them. (See Luke

4:15–30.) Synagogue worship had become full of formality and error, and yet it was the custom of our Lord to attend the synagogue on the Sabbath day (v. 16). The apostle Paul followed His example in this matter (Acts 17:2). There are many earnest Christian men and women today who have lost all power and influence for God and good in the community by abandoning their fellowship with other believers who were not as well instructed as they, and by giving themselves up to harsh and condemning criticism.

Some Christians justify their actions by saying that the book of Revelation tells us to "come out of Babylon." (See Revelation 18:1–4.) The word *Babylon* is used in this context to symbolize the spirit of immorality and idolatry that will culminate in the Antichrist. While it is true that the Bible says to "come out of Babylon," Babylon, in this ultimate sense, has not yet been formed. Everything in the book of Revelation after the first verse of the fourth chapter describes the time after the Rapture of the church, not the present time. To apply this command to "come out of Babylon" to the present time and the present state of the churches is to handle the Word of God deceitfully and not rightly divide the Word of Truth (2 Tim. 2:15).

Of course, if the pastor of a church persistently preaches glaring and pernicious error, one should protest against it and should not allow his children to sit under that kind of false doctrine. But again, these occasions are comparatively rare.

Q: Do you believe in having different denominations? Do sects do more harm than good in the cause of religion?

A: Undoubtedly, sects do more harm than good in the cause of religion, for the very idea of a sect is something that causes division. The animating spirit of the sect is division.

However, a denomination is not necessarily a sect. The different denominations have arisen because different people saw some truths very clearly that others did not see, and around these people other people have gathered to enforce that particular aspect of truth. For example, the Congregationalists and the

Presbyterians arose in England and Scotland to stand for the truth of the liberty of the individual believer. Many other truths were associated with this truth in the development of these denominations. The Quakers arose to stand for the truth of the illumination and guidance of the Holy Spirit for the individual believer today. The Methodists arose to stand for the truth of a definite personal experience of regeneration and the necessity of a holy life. Afterward, other truths, such as the freedom of the will, became prominently associated with these truths in the teaching of the Methodist denomination. By standing strongly for some neglected truths that needed to be emphasized, the denominations have undoubtedly done good. In the present imperfect state of man, where no individual is large enough to take in the whole scope of God's truth, and where one man sees one line of truth strongly and another man another line of truth, denominations have been necessary. But it is fitting that denominational lines are now less defined and that each denomination is coming to understand and accept the truths for which other denominations have stood.

Q: What do you think of the institutional church? Is it not detrimental to the real work of the church as set forth in the New Testament?

A: I understand the term *institutional church* to mean a church that not only does the direct work of preaching the Gospel and building Christians up by teaching the Bible, but one that also looks after the physical and mental welfare of its members and congregation by various institutions. Such work is not necessarily detrimental to the real work of the church as set forth in the New Testament. It may be a valuable auxiliary, provided that the physical and intellectual are kept in thorough subordination to the spiritual.

The apostolic church was, in a measure, an institutional church. It looked out for the physical welfare of its members (Acts 6:1–5), all property was held in common (Acts 2:44–45; 4:34–35), and the Word of God increased and prospered under these circumstances (Acts 2:47; 4:4; 5:14; 6:7). Of course, the institutions were not many, nor were they very largely developed. In a similar way today, the church can have various institutions for looking after the physical and intellectual welfare of its members. If a church is located among the poor, it can offer financial counsel and assistance and can help people to heat their homes in the winter; it can provide libraries, educational classes, and so forth, accomplishing a vast amount of good, and making all this subservient to the preaching of the Gospel. All these things can be used as means of getting hold of men, women, and children and bringing them to a saving knowledge of Jesus Christ.

But there is always a danger in an institutional church. The danger is that the institutions will become the main thing and the Gospel will be put in a secondary place or will be lost sight of altogether. This has been the history of more than one institutional church in this country, and it is always a danger. In such a case, the institutional church becomes detrimental to the real work of the church as set forth in the New Testament. The first work of the church is seeking and saving the lost (Luke 19:10; Matt. 28:19–20). Its second work is the spiritual care of the congregation (Acts 20:28; 1 Pet. 5:2–4), and its third work is training the membership for intelligent service (Eph. 4:11–12). If the institutions connected with the church are allowed to put any one of these three things in the background, they do more harm than good. But if the institutions are carried on in the spirit of prayer and with the intention—never lost sight of for a moment—of winning men for Christ, and if everything is made subordinate to the preaching of the Gospel and the salvation of the lost and the edification of the saints, then the institutions may be very helpful.

Q: Is it ever right to ask unconverted though moral people to teach a Sunday school class or to do other definite Christian work in the church?

A: *Ever* is a pretty comprehensive word. The ideal way is to have only thoroughly regenerated and spiritually-minded people teach a Sunday school class or sing in a choir. The church with which I am connected takes the position that the very first condition of admission to membership in our choir is that the person applying must give good evidence of being born again. The second condition is that they have a good singing voice. But I can think of situations in which it would be warranted to have an unconverted person teach a Sunday school class. For example, suppose I were to go into a town to hold evangelistic meetings where there was no Sunday school and no religious work of any kind. If I could start a Sunday school there before I left, and get some moral person to teach the Bible—if there was no regenerated person available—I believe I would start the school and trust that the Spirit of God would use the Scripture as a blessing to both the teacher and the students. I would take the appointment of this person as a teacher as an opportunity to urge upon him the necessity of a personal acceptance of Christ.

I have held evangelistic meetings around the world, and the committees that organized the choirs for these meetings often received people who I do not believe were really converted. I have used the fact that they were in the choir as an opportunity of presenting the Gospel to them, and hundreds of people have thus been converted to God.

Q: What authority is there for or against women being prominent in the work of the church?

A: There is no authority given in the Bible for a woman to have the place of supremacy in the church. When she takes it, she steps out of her right place. She goes against the plain teaching of the Bible when she takes the place of the authoritative teacher in the church. *"And I do not permit a woman to teach or to have authority over a man, but to be in silence"* (1 Tim. 2:12 NKJV).

However, there is abundant authorization in the Bible for a woman being active and, in that sense, prominent in church work. Women were the first divinely commissioned preachers of the risen Christ. Jesus Christ Himself sent them to declare His resurrection to the men disciples (John 20:17–18; Matt. 28:5–10). Women were endowed by God with prophetic gifts (Acts 21:9). It is significant that in the very book in the Bible in which women are forbidden to do idle talking and ask questions in the church

(1 Cor. 14:33–35), there are directions as to how a woman should prophesy, that is, how she should speak in the power of the Spirit (1 Cor. 11:5). The apostle Paul spoke of the women who had labored with him in the Gospel (Phil. 4:3). There is clear indication that Priscilla was more gifted than her husband Aquila. She was associated with her husband in taking the preacher Apollos aside and expounding to him the way of God more accurately (Acts 18:24–26), and her name is mentioned first. (See NIV, NAS, and RV.)

Q: What is the scriptural way of raising money for church or other Christian uses?

A: The scriptural way of raising money is by the freewill offerings of saved people, each one setting aside on the first day of the week a definite proportion of his income (1 Cor. 16:2). Certainly, it is not the scriptural way of raising money to raise it by fairs, bazaars, or any other method that reduces the church of Christ to the level of vaudeville entertainment. These methods are unwise even from a business standpoint, and they are certainly dishonoring to Jesus Christ. The successful churches are those that step out in obedience to the Word of God and depend upon the freewill offerings of the people. They soon find that they have more money for their own work and more money for missions than those churches that stoop to dishonor their Lord by raising money in such a way that it makes the church a reproach even among people of the world.

Q: Would you ask an unsaved person to contribute money or goods for the support or benefit of church work?

A: No, I would not. God is not dependent upon His enemies to help Him carry on His work. God's work should be supported by the joyful freewill offerings of His own people, as explained in the previous answer. Furthermore, when unsaved people contribute to the support of God's work, it frequently acts as a salve to their consciences, and it makes them harder to reach. They say, "I am supporting the church," and many of them hope to get to heaven in that way.

Of course, if some unsaved person, of his own volition, should see fit to put money into the collection, or something of that kind, I would hesitate to insult him by refusing his money. However, when offerings are taken, I would let it be clearly understood that it is not the money but the souls of the unsaved that we are seeking, and that men should first give themselves to the Lord before they give their money.

Communion

Q: Should we invite to the Lord's Table all who believe themselves to be Christians, whether or not they have previously been received into the membership of the church?

A: Jesus Christ commands all believers, *"Do this in remembrance of Me"* (1 Cor. 11:24 NKJV). Therefore, all believers should have the privilege of doing this, whether or not they have previously been received into the membership of the church. But the importance and necessity of church membership should be urged upon all believers.

Confession of Sins

Q: Should we confess our sins to man or only to God?

A: First of all, we should confess them to God. David said in Psalm 32:5, *"I acknowledged my sin to You, and my iniquity I have not hidden. I said, 'I will confess my transgressions to the LORD,' and You forgave the iniquity of my sin"* (NKJV). In 1 John 1:9, we read: *"If we confess our sins* [and it clearly means, to God], *He is faithful and just to forgive us our sins and to cleanse us from all unrighteousness"* (NKJV).

However, if we have sinned against someone, we should confess our sin to the person against whom we have sinned. We should be reconciled to our brother who has something against us (Matt. 5:23–24). It is well also to confess our sins to one another so that we may pray for one another (James 5:16). There is not the slightest hint, however, that this means we should confess our sins to a priest any more than to any other brother. The verse says, *"Confess...to one another"* (v. 16 NKJV). There is not any more reason why we should confess our sins to a priest than that the priest should confess his sins to us.

If we have sinned publicly, we should make public confession of our sins. But there is nothing in the Bible to indicate that one should make a detailed public confession of all his transgressions, or even that he should confess to any man every sin that he has committed. Religious impostors often require this of their disciples, and, in this way, they gain control over their disciples and rule them by fear of exposure. I know of one religious impostor who gained control over his people in this way. He made them confess everything base and vile that they had ever done; then he terrorized them, got their money from them, and made slaves of them. There are some things that a man should keep to himself and God.

Conscience

Q: Is the conscience a sufficient guide for man?

A: No. Conscience, using the word in the sense of the moral intuition that every person possesses that right is right and wrong is wrong, and that each of us ought to commit to following wherever it leads us, is sufficient to lead us to an absolute surrender to do what is right, whatever it may be. However, then there comes the question of what is right. Conscience, in the sense of moral judgment as to what is right or wrong, is certainly not a sufficient guide for man. Many people conscientiously do things that are utterly wrong because their moral judgment has been improperly educated. Conscience needs to be enlightened by divine revelation and by the personal illumination of the Holy Spirit as to what is right.

If we surrender ourselves to doing what is right, wherever it leads us, and if we make an honest search for what is right and true, we will be led to see that Jesus Christ is the Son of God and a Teacher sent from God. (See Matthew 16:16; John 3:2; 7:16–17.) Then we will bring our moral judgment to Him for education. Having accepted Jesus Christ as the Son of God and a Teacher sent from God, we will logically be led by the study of His Word to accept the entire Bible as the Word of God, and we will consequently take it as our guide in conduct. Furthermore, we will be led to see that it is our privilege to be taught by the Holy Spirit and to be guided into right conduct by Him.

Consecration

Q: What is meant by "consecration"? How often should a person consecrate himself?

A: In today's usage (which, by the way, is not the way the Bible uses it), the word *consecration* means the surrendering of oneself and all that one has wholly to God. The word *sanctify,* as it is used in the Bible, has practically the same meaning when it is applied to sanctifying ourselves. It means to "set apart" for God.

Every Christian should consecrate himself to God once and for all. He should put into God's hands all that he is and all that he has, so that God may use him and everything that is his as He wills, send him where He wills, and do with him what He wills. Having thus consecrated himself, he should never take himself out of God's hands. However, many people do consecrate themselves to God and afterward go back on their consecration, as Samson did, and they are shorn of their strength, as Samson was. (See Judges 13:2–5; 16:1–19.) In such a case, a person should reconsecrate himself to God. Even when a person has not gone back on his consecration, it is a good thing to constantly re-acknowledge it so that one may keep it clearly in mind.

Furthermore, consecration gets a deeper significance the longer we live. At one time in our lives, we may wholly give ourselves up to God as far as we understand it at the time. However, as we study the Word and grow in grace, consecration will continually gain a deeper meaning. I believe I have been wholly God's for many years, but only yesterday I got a deeper understanding of what it means to be wholly God's than I have ever had before.

Conviction of Sin

Q: How is conviction of sin produced? In other words, what kind of preaching would you recommend in order to bring people to a realization of the awfulness of sin, and to bring upon them conviction of sin?

A: The law was given to bring men to a knowledge of sin (Romans 3:20), and I find that the preaching of the law does bring men to such a knowledge. I preach on the Ten Commandments, look-ing to the Holy Spirit to show men how they have not kept them. I also preach on Matthew 7:12, the so-called Golden Rule, to show people that they have not kept the Golden Rule and there-fore cannot be saved by it: *"Whatever you want men to do to you, do also to them"* (NKJV). In addition, I preach on Matthew 22:37–38. Through these verses, I seek to show people that they have not only sinned but they have also broken the first and greatest of God's commandments: *"'You shall love the LORD your God with all your heart, with all your soul, and with all your mind.' This is the first and great commandment"* (NKJV).

However, we read in John 16:8–9 that the sin of which the Holy Spirit convicts men is the sin of unbelief in Jesus Christ. Also, we see in Acts 2:1–37 that the sin of which the Holy Spirit convicted so many thousands on the Day of Pentecost was the sin of rejecting Jesus Christ. Working along these lines, I find that holding up before men the majesty and glory of Jesus Christ and the sacrifice He made for us, then driving home the awfulness of the sin of rejecting such a Savior, brings the deepest conviction of sin.

But in all our preaching, we must bear in mind that it is the Holy Spirit, not we ourselves, who convicts men of sin. He does it through the truth that we present, but we must realize our dependence upon Him and look to Him and count on Him to do the work. This is where many make their mistake. They try to convict men of sin instead of putting themselves in an attitude of complete dependence on the Holy Spirit so that He will convict men through them.

The Deity of Jesus Christ

Q: How would you prove that Jesus Christ is really the Son of God?

A: First, I would prove that He rose from the dead. Of this there is abundant proof. I have given it elsewhere and will not repeat it here.* The fact that Jesus Christ rose from the dead proves beyond a question that He is the Son of God.

When He was here on earth, He repeatedly declared that He was the Son of God—the Son of God in a unique sense, the Son of God in a sense in which no other man is the Son of God. In Mark 12:1–6, Jesus taught that while the prophets, even the greatest of them, were servants, He was a Son, an only Son. In John 5:22–23, He taught that all men should honor Him even as they honor the Father. In John 14:9, He went so far as to say, *"He who has seen Me has seen the Father"* (NKJV). Men hated Him for making this claim to be the Son of God; they put Him to death for making this claim (Matt. 26:63–66). However, before they put Him to death, He told them that God would set His

---

*See R. A. Torrey, *Powerful Faith* (New Kensington, PA: Whitaker House, 1996).

seal on the claim by raising Him from the dead. (See John 2:19.) It was a stupendous claim to make; it was an apparently absurd claim, but God did set His seal on it by raising Jesus from the dead. By doing this, God Himself has spoken more clearly than if He spoke from the open heavens today, "This Man is what He claims to be. He is My Son. All men should honor Him even as they honor the Father."

To summarize the first point, Jesus Christ proved Himself to be the Son of God by the claim He made to be the Son of God and by the way in which He substantiated that claim by His resurrection from the dead.

Second, He substantiated His claim by His character, by its beauty and strength and nobility. The character of Jesus Christ is nearly universally acknowledged. Jews nowadays acknowledge it. Even the most notorious infidels have admitted it. Robert Green Ingersoll once said, "I wish to say once and for all, to that great and serene Man I gladly pay the homage of my admiration and my tears." But here is this Man, whom all admit to be a good man, a man of honor and truth and nobility, claiming to be the Son of God. Certainly a Man of such character was what He claimed to be.

Third, He substantiated His claim by the miracles that He performed. Herculean efforts have been put forth to discredit the gospel accounts of Christ's miracles, but these efforts have all resulted in utter failure. He substantiated His claim by His influence on the history of the world. No argument is needed to prove that Christ's influence on the history of the world has done immeasurably more good than that of any other man who ever lived. It would be foolish to compare His influence on individual life, domestic life, social life, industrial life, and political life with that of any other man, or that of all men put together. Now, if Jesus Christ was not divine, as He claimed to be, He was a blasphemer and an impostor or else a lunatic. It is easy to see that His influence on history is not that of a lunatic, a blasphemer, or an impostor. Then, certainly, He must have been the Son of God as He claimed.

Fourth, I would prove that Jesus Christ is the Son of God by pointing to the fact that He possesses divine power today. It is not necessary to go back to the miracles that Christ performed when He was on earth to prove that He has divine power. He exercises that power today, and anyone can test it. There are two major ways in which His power is demonstrated today:

In the first place, He has power to forgive sins. Thousands can testify that they came to Christ burdened with a terrible sense of guilt and that He has actually given their guilty consciences peace, absolute peace.

Moreover, He has power today to set Satan's victims free. He sets the one chained by drink free from the power of drink, the one chained by drugs free from the power of drugs. You may say that various medical treatments also do this, but the cases are not parallel. These various treatments use drugs; Christ uses a mere word. Christ sets people free not only from vices but also from other sin. He makes the impure man pure. He makes the selfish man unselfish. He makes the devilish man Christ-like. He re-creates men and women. The divine influence that Jesus Christ is exerting today over the lives of countless men and women proves beyond a doubt that He is the Son of God. I know that Jesus Christ is divine because of the divine work that He, and He alone, has worked in my own life.

The Depravity of Man

Q: What do you mean by the doctrine of the total depravity of man, and how do you prove it?

A: The doctrine that man is totally depraved does not mean that he is totally corrupt. It means that the will of the unregenerate man is set upon pleasing self and is therefore totally wrong, for it should be set upon pleasing God. The will that is not absolutely surrendered to God is turned the wrong way. Yet while seeking to please himself, a man may do things that are morally attractive and beautiful. A man is not necessarily drawn to immoral and disgusting things. He may prefer things that are high and noble and true, yet he may not prefer them because they are what God wills but because they are the things that attract him. He is as truly depraved as the man who chooses the immoral things, but his tastes are not as corrupt as those of the man who chooses immoral things. What every unregenerate man needs is a total turning around of his will, so that he no longer seeks to please himself but surrenders himself in all things to do the things that please God and to do them because they please God.

The doctrine of total depravity may be proved first by the Scriptures. For example, consider these verses, as well as many other Scriptures: *"The carnal mind is enmity against God; for it is not subject to the law of God, nor indeed can be"* (Rom. 8:7 NKJV). *"Having their understanding darkened, being alienated from the life of God, because of the ignorance that is in them, because of the blindness of their heart"* (Eph. 4:18 NKJV). *"The heart is deceitful above all things, and desperately wicked"* (Jer. 17:9 NKJV).

The doctrine of the total depravity of man may also be proved by an appeal to facts. The picture of the unregenerate man given in the Scriptures at first sight seems to be too dark. However, as we come to know men better—especially as we come to know ourselves better, and above all as we come to know God better and see ourselves in the light of His holiness—this Bible doctrine is found to be absolutely accurate.

The Devil

Q: Do you believe in a real Devil—one that has the qualities of a person, such as a personality and a will? Or is he merely a metaphor for evil?

A: Most assuredly, I believe in a real Devil. I could not believe in the Bible without believing in a real Devil. In another book, I give conclusive proof that the Bible is the Word of God.* Therefore, I believe what it teaches about the existence of a Devil.

---

*See R. A. Torrey, *Powerful Faith* (New Kensington, PA: Whitaker House, 1996).

In the accounts of the temptation of our Lord, recorded in the gospels of Matthew and Luke, we are distinctly told that the devil (and the accounts clearly mean a personal Devil) was the author of the temptations that came to our Lord. (See Matthew 4:1–11; Luke 4:1–13.) These accounts have no meaning if we try to make the devil of these passages a mere metaphor for evil.

Furthermore, in the parable of the sower (Matt. 13:1–23), our Lord distinctly taught that there is a real Devil. The Devil does not appear in the parable, where he might be explained as being figurative, but rather in the interpretation of the parable: *"Then the wicked one comes"* (v. 19 NKJV). Now, in parables we have symbolic language, and in the interpretation of parables we have the literal facts for which the symbols stand. Therefore, we have a literal Devil in the interpretation of this parable. This is only one of the numerous instances in which Jesus taught the existence of a real Devil.

The apostle Paul taught the same. For example, in Ephesians 6:11–12, he wrote, *"Put on the whole armor of God, that you may be able to stand against the wiles of the devil. For we do not wrestle against flesh and blood, but against principalities, against powers, against the rulers of the darkness of this age, against spiritual hosts of wickedness in the heavenly places"* (NKJV).

No rational interpretation of the Bible can interpret the devil out of it. Any system of interpretation that does away with the devil would do away with any doctrine that a person does not wish to believe.

I also believe that there is a real Devil because my own experience and observation teach me the existence of an unseen, very subtle, very cunning spirit of evil, who has domination over men throughout human society. The more I come into contact with men, the more I study history, and the more men open their hearts to me, the more firmly convinced I become that there is a Devil such as the Bible teaches.

It is not pleasant to believe that there is a real Devil, but the question is not what is pleasant to believe, but what is true.

Q: Why did God create the devil, also called Satan?

A: God created Satan because God is love. God created him whom we now call Satan as a being of very exalted glory. In Ezekiel 28:12–15, we get a hint of what Satan was when he was originally created: *"You were the seal of perfection, full of wisdom and perfect in beauty. You were in Eden, the garden of God; every precious stone was your covering: the sardius, topaz, and diamond, beryl, onyx, and jasper, sapphire, turquoise, and emerald with gold. The workmanship of your timbrels and pipes was prepared for you on the day you were created. You were the anointed cherub who covers; I established you; you were on the holy mountain of God; you walked back and forth in the midst of fiery stones. You were perfect in your ways from the day you were created, till iniquity was found in you"* (NKJV).

Because he was a being of such exalted glory, he was a moral being, that is, a being with the power of choosing good or evil. He seems to have been the one who led the worship of the universe. But ambition entered his heart. He seems to have tried to direct to himself what properly belonged to God, and thus he fell. Falling from such a height, he fell to the deepest depths and became the appalling being that he now is. The Devil of Scripture is not a hideous-looking being with horns and hoofs, but a being of very high intelligence who has turned his mighty powers to wrong and has thus become the great enemy of God and man.

Q: Can God destroy Satan?

A: I do not know of anywhere in the Bible where it is taught that God can destroy Satan, but God certainly can destroy or annihilate any beings that He has created, if He sees fit. If He brought them into being, He can put them out of being; otherwise, God would not be omnipotent. But it is clear from Scripture that to destroy Satan is not God's will. Satan will exist and be *"tormented day and night forever and ever"* (Rev. 20:10 NKJV). If the question refers to Hebrews 2:14—*"through death He...destroy[ed] him who had the power of death, that is, the devil"* (NKJV)—the word *"destroy"* there means to "render powerless" or "bring to nothing," not "annihilate." (See NAS and RV.)

Q: Why does God not destroy Satan if He is omnipotent?

A: God does not destroy Satan because God has not yet worked out His purposes through him. Though Satan himself is evil, God accomplishes His purposes of good through him. The day will come when we will understand what these purposes are and will thank God even for Satan. God will make not only the wrath of man but also the wrath of Satan to praise Him. (See Psalm 76:10.) The *"messenger of Satan"* that was sent to *"buffet"* Paul (2 Cor. 12:7 NKJV) worked only good for Paul. He kept Paul from being *"exalted above measure"* (v. 7 NKJV).

Divorce

Q: Does the Bible permit a person, under any circumstances, to divorce his or her spouse and marry another while the divorced spouse is still living?

A: It is perfectly clear that the Bible does not permit divorce and remarriage on any grounds but one. It says, *"Whoever divorces his wife for any reason except sexual immorality causes her to commit adultery"* (Matt. 5:32 NKJV). Moreover, if the one who gets the divorce marries another, he or she also commits adultery (19:9). This much is as plain as day, namely, that there is only one scriptural basis for divorce and remarriage: impurity on the part of the other party.

Divorce and remarriage are, however, objected to by some who believe that remarriage even on this ground is not permitted by Scripture—that in Romans 7:2–3, it is stated without any exception that a *"woman who has a husband is bound by the law to her husband as long as he lives"* and that *"if, while her husband lives, she marries another man, she will be called an adulteress"* (NKJV). The answer to this objection seems evident. Paul in Romans 7 was not discussing the question of divorce but was simply using the matter of the marriage obligation as an illustration. Paul was making a point about death in this passage. It would have been entirely out of Paul's way for him to have gone into the matter of exceptions to the general law, as they had no bearing whatsoever on the question that he was discussing. The words of Christ clearly seem to imply that in this one case of infidelity, a man may divorce his wife and marry another, and be guiltless before God.

It would seem, however, that if a person has divorced an unfaithful partner, it would be better for the person to remain single, at least until the death of the offending party, and thus avoid *"trouble in this flesh"* (1 Cor. 7:28 NKJV). But if a person has divorced a spouse on the ground of adultery and has already married another, there is no scriptural reason why he or she should feel guilty.

Eternal Punishment

Q: Do you believe in the eternal punishment of the wicked? What proof is there of eternal punishment?

A: We know nothing positively and absolutely about the future except what God Himself has been pleased to reveal in His Word. Everything beyond this is pure speculation, and man's speculations on such a subject are practically valueless. God knows all about the future, and He has been pleased to reveal some things that He knows about the future. On such a subject as this, an ounce of God's revelation is worth tons of man's empty speculation. God has clearly revealed in the Bible the fact of eternal punishment for those who persist in sin and in the rejection of Jesus Christ, and this is conclusive proof of its reality. I have shown in another book that the Bible is unquestionably the Word of God.[*] The Bible tells us what God says, and the Bible distinctly teaches that there will be an eternity of punishment for those who persistently reject the redemption that is in Christ Jesus. Consider these verses: *"Depart from Me, you cursed, into the everlasting fire prepared for the devil and his angels:…these will go away into everlasting punishment, but the righteous into eternal life"* (Matt. 25:41, 46

---

[*]See R. A. Torrey, *Powerful Faith* (New Kensington, PA: Whitaker House, 1996).

NKJV). *"Then the beast was captured, and with him the false prophet who worked signs in his presence, by which he deceived those who received the mark of the beast and those who worshiped his image. These two were cast alive into the lake of fire burning with brimstone....The devil, who deceived them, was cast into the lake of fire and brimstone where the beast and the false prophet are. And they will be tormented day and night forever and ever....But the cowardly, unbelieving, abominable, murderers, sexually immoral, sorcerers, idolaters, and all liars shall have their part in the lake which burns with fire and brimstone, which is the second death"* (Rev. 19:20; 20:10; 21:8 NKJV).

The expression *"forever and ever,"* used here of the lake of fire prepared for the devil and his angels, to which the persistently wicked will also go, is used thirteen times in the book of Revelation. Nine times it refers to the duration of the existence or reign or glory of God and Christ, once to the duration of the blessed reign of the righteous, and in the three remaining instances to the duration of the torment of the devil, the Beast, the False Prophet, and the persistently wicked.

Q: Does the Bible teach that there will be eternal torment for all of the unsaved? If so, where?

A: The Bible teaches in 2 Thessalonians 1:7–9 that when the Lord Jesus is revealed from heaven, all those who do not know God and do not obey the Gospel of our Lord Jesus Christ will be *"punished with everlasting destruction from the presence of the Lord and from the glory of His power"* (v. 9 NKJV). The question then arises, what does *"destruction"* mean? The Bible itself defines the term. We are told in the eighth and eleventh verses of Revelation 17 that the Beast will go to *"perdition."* (See KJV, NKJV, RV.) The word rendered *"perdition,"* the same word that is elsewhere translated "destruction," is derived from the verb that is constantly translated "destroy." The word *"perdition"* should therefore be translated "destruction" in this passage in Revelation. So then, if we can find out what the Beast will go to, we will find out what *"perdition"* or "destruction" means. By turning to Revelation 19:20, we find that the Beast will be cast alive into *"the lake of fire burning with brimstone"* (NKJV). Turning again to Revelation 20:10, we find that at the end of a thousand years, after the Beast has been cast into the lake burning with brimstone, the devil will be cast into the lake burning with fire and brimstone, where the Beast and the False Prophet still are after the thousand years, and that they will be *"tormented day and night forever and ever"* (NKJV). So then, this is what "destruction" means in Bible usage: a share in the lake of fire. Whether this is taken literally or figuratively, it certainly means a condition of being in a place of conscious and unending torment.

Q: How could a loving God create some of His creatures for eternal punishment?

A: God did not create any of His creatures for eternal punishment. God created all people to love and obey Him and enjoy Him forever. But He also created them as a higher order of beings, with the capacity of choosing for themselves good or evil. Some chose evil. However, even then, God did not abandon them but made the greatest sacrifice in His power to save them from their own mad choice. He gave His Son to die for them so that repentance, forgiveness, life, and glory might be possible for them. If men see fit not only to choose evil but also, having chosen evil, to deliberately and persistently refuse the means of salvation that a loving God has provided for them at an immeasurable cost to Himself, then their eternal punishment is their own fault. To blame God for it is not only to be appallingly unjust but also unpardonably ungrateful and unreasonable.

Q: How can an infinitely holy and merciful God condemn creatures He loves to everlasting punishment?

A: It is not so much that God condemns anyone to everlasting punishment as that men and women condemn themselves to everlasting torment by refusing the mercy and grace of God. Many people not only choose sin but also choose to refuse the wonderfully gracious redemption from sin that God has provided. If people will not allow themselves to be saved from sin, they must necessarily continue in it; and if they continue in it, they must necessarily suffer torment as long as they continue in it. The time must come, sooner or later, when repentance becomes impossible, and so, of course, salvation becomes impossible. The everlasting torment that anyone may endure will be simply the inevitable result of his own deliberate and persistent choice of sin.

Q: Is it not unjust to punish a few years of sin with an eternity of torment?

A: The duration of the punishment of sin can never be determined by the time it takes to commit the sin. A man can kill another man in a few seconds, but a just penalty would be life-long imprisonment. Furthermore, sin involves separation from God, and separation from God is torment. The torment must continue as long as the separation from God exists, and the separation from God must exist until sin is repented of and the Savior is accepted. The time must come when repentance and the acceptance of the Savior become impossible; then one becomes eternally confirmed in his separation from God, and eternal torment must necessarily follow.

In addition, it is not a few years of sin that bring the eternity of punishment. A man may continue many years in sin and still escape eternal torment if he will only repent and accept Jesus Christ. It is the rejection of Jesus Christ that brings an eternity of torment. When we see sin in all its hideousness and enormity, the holiness of God in all its perfection, and the glory of Jesus Christ in all its infinity, nothing will satisfy the demand of our own moral intuitions except eternal punishment for those who persist in the choice of sin and in the rejection of the Son of God. This is especially so when we consider the fact that God, in His wonderful grace, gave Christ Jesus to die for our sins so that we might have salvation. Moreover, it is the fact that we dread suffering more than we hate sin and more than we love the glory of Jesus Christ that makes us reject the thought of eternal punishment for those who eternally choose sin, despise God's mercy, and spurn His Son.

Q: Would an earthly father send his child to everlasting suffering? And if he would not, can we believe that God is not as good as we are and that He would treat His children in a way that we would not treat ours?

A: First, this question takes it for granted that all men are God's children. The Bible teaches that this is not true. All men are God's creatures and were originally created in His likeness, and in this sense they are all His offspring (Acts 17:26–29). But men become God's children in the fullest sense by being born again of the Holy Spirit (John 3:3–6) through the personal acceptance of Jesus Christ as their Savior (John 1:12; Gal. 3:26).

Second, God is something besides the Father, even to believers. He is the moral Governor of this universe. As a righteous moral Governor of the universe, He must punish sin; consequently, if sin is eternally persisted in, He must eternally punish it. Even a wise earthly father would separate one of his own children who persisted in sin from contact with his other children. If a man had a dearly beloved son who was a moral monster, he certainly would not allow him to associate with his daughters. If a person whom you greatly loved committed a gross wrong against someone you loved more, and persisted in it eternally, would you not consent to his eternal punishment?

Third, it is never safe to measure what an infinitely holy God would do by what we would do. As we look about us in the world today, do we not see men and women suffering agonies that we would not allow our children to suffer if we could prevent it? Which of us could endure to see our children suffering some of the things that the men and women in the slums of the cities are suffering today? It may be difficult for us to explain why a God of love permits this to go on, but we know that it does go on. Moreover, what men and women suffer in this present life as a result of their disobedience to God and their persistence in sin and their rejection of Jesus Christ ought to be a hint of what people will suffer in the eternal world if they go on in sin as the result of their having rejected the Savior in this present life. It may sound good to say, "I believe in a God of love, and I do not believe that He will permit any of His creatures to go to an eternal hell." However, if we open our eyes to the facts as they exist everywhere around us, we will see how empty our speculations on this point are, for even now we see this same God of love permitting many of His creatures to endure terrible and ever increasing agonies in this present life.

Q: If anyone is lost eternally, has not Satan then gained the victory over Christ, and is he not stronger than Christ?

A: No, Satan has gained no victory. It is not Satan who determines that a person will persist in sin; it is the individual himself. If he persists in sin, Satan has gained no victory, and, on the other hand, Jesus Christ is not conquered. Jesus Christ will still be glorified, and God will be glorified. God's holiness is manifested and God Himself is glorified as truly in the punishment of the sinner as in the salvation of the believer. Righteous government here on earth is vindicated as truly when the offender is locked up in prison or executed as when the offender is brought to repentance.

Many seem to think that hell is a place ruled by Satan, but Satan does not rule there. Satan himself will be one of the prisoners, and the smoke of the torment of this persistent rebel against God will rise forever and ever as a testimony that God has conquered him.

Evil

Q: How can God permit evil to exist in the world?

A: When we enter the domain of asking how God can do this or that, we need to tread very softly, for God is a Being of infinite wisdom, and we know almost nothing. When we think about how vast God is and how infinitesimal we are, we do well to hesitate about questioning how God can do anything. An infinitely wise God may have a thousand good reasons for doing things, when we, in our almost utter ignorance, cannot see one good or even possible reason for them.

Having said this much, I may add that evil seems to be a necessary accompaniment of good. Moral good is the highest good, and freedom of choice is necessary for the attainment of moral good. In fact, no being can be good in the highest sense unless it is possible for him to do evil; but if it is possible for him to do evil, he may do it. God created all beings good, but the highest beings were created with the power of choice. They could choose disobedience to God if they desired. One of the very highest of such beings, he whom we now call Satan, chose evil. God also created man with the power of choice, and the first man chose evil, and the whole race followed him. Thus evil entered into the world as the outcome of God's having created man on the highest plane, that is, with the lofty power of choice.

God will permit evil to continue in the world until He has fully worked out His own benevolent plans. When we come to see no longer *"through a glass, darkly; but...face to face"* (1 Cor.13:12), we will undoubtedly rejoice that God did permit evil to exist in the world.

Faith

Q: What do you mean by "justification by faith"? Is faith the only means of salvation?

A: The Greek word that is translated "to justify" in the New Testament would, according to its word origin, mean "to make righteous." However, this meaning is extremely rare in Greek usage, if not altogether doubtful, and it certainly is not the New Testament usage of the word. In biblical usage, "to justify" does not signify "to make righteous" but "to reckon, declare, or show to be righteous." A person is justified before God when God reckons him righteous, that is, when God not only forgives his sins but also credits all "positive righteousness" to his account. This means that when God justifies us, He not only cleanses us from the sins that we have committed against Him (sins of commission) but also credits to our account all the good works that we should have done but failed to do (sins of omission).

There is one condition upon which men are justified before God: simple faith in Jesus Christ. (See Romans 3:26; 4:5; 5:1; Acts 13:39.) It is the atoning death of Jesus Christ on the cross in our place that secures justification for us. (See Romans 5:9; Galatians 3:13; 2 Corinthians 5:21.) His shed blood is the ground of our justification, and simple faith in Him makes that shed blood ours. Provision is made for our justification by the shedding of His blood; we are actually justified when we believe in Him who shed His blood. Faith is the only means of securing for ourselves the atoning power that there is in the blood of Jesus Christ. If a person will not believe, there is nothing he can do that will bring him justification.

If a person does believe, he is absolved from *"all things"* the moment he believes (Acts 13:38–39). Not only are all his sins put out of God's sight, but in God's reckoning, all of God's own righteousness in Jesus Christ is also credited to his account. When Jesus Christ died on the cross of Calvary, He took our place (Gal. 3:10, 13), and the moment we believe in Him, we step into His place and are just as pleasing to God as Jesus Christ Himself is.

Q: I would like to believe, but I cannot. Will God condemn me for something I cannot do?

A: No, God will not condemn you for something you cannot do, but you can believe. Anyone can believe. There is plenty of proof that the Bible is the Word of God and that Jesus Christ is the Son of God—proof enough to convince anyone who really wants to know and obey the truth.

In my book *Powerful Faith,*[*] I have given conclusive evidence that the Bible is God's Word and that Jesus Christ is God's Son. However, one does not need to read books like this to find this evidence. There is plenty of proof in the Bible itself. John said

---

*See R. A. Torrey, *Powerful Faith* (New Kensington, PA: Whitaker House, 1996).

in John 20:31, *"These are written* [the things contained in the gospel of John] *that you may believe that Jesus is the Christ, the Son of God, and that believing you may have life in His name"* (NKJV). We see in this verse that life comes through believing that Jesus is the Christ, the Son of God, and that believing that Jesus is the Christ, the Son of God, comes through studying what is written. If anyone will take the gospel of John and read it in the right way, he will know and believe before he finishes reading that Jesus is the Christ, the Son of God, and he will have life through believing it.

Now, what is the right way to read it?

♦ First of all, surrender your will to God. Jesus said, *"If anyone chooses to do God's will, he will find out whether my teaching comes from God or whether I speak on my own"* (John 7:17 NIV). One can read the gospel of John again and again and not come to believe that Jesus is the Christ, the Son of God, if he reads it with an unsurrendered will. However, if a person will first surrender his will to God to obey God, no matter what it may cost him, he cannot read the gospel of John through once without coming to see that Jesus is the Christ, the Son of the living God.

♦ Second, each time you read the Bible, look to God and ask Him to show you how much truth there is in the verses you are about to read. Then promise Him that you will commit to what He shows you is true. Do not read too many verses at once. Pay careful attention to what you read. Read with a real desire to learn the truth and to obey it. By the time you get through the gospel, you will find that you can believe. In fact, you will find that you do believe.

The reason people do not believe is that they are not living up to what they do believe, they have not surrendered their wills to God, or they do not study the evidence that is intended to produce belief. Men neglect their Bibles and read all kinds of trashy, unbelieving books and then keep saying, "I can't believe! I can't believe!" A man might just as well feed himself on poison instead of food and then complain that he is not healthy. There is abundant evidence that

Jesus Christ is the Son of God, and faith is a willingness to yield to sufficient evidence—it is a matter of the will. Unbelief is the refusal to yield to sufficient evidence. Unbelief is a matter for which every unbeliever is responsible.

God demands that we believe, that we yield our wills to the truth that He has abundantly revealed. Faith is the one thing that God demands of man, because it is the one thing above all else that we owe to God (John 6:29). Without the faith that is due to God, it is impossible to please Him (Hebrews 11:6).

Falling from Grace

Q: How do you harmonize the Calvinistic view of the perseverance of the saints with the Arminian belief that one may fall from grace?

A: If I understand the Calvinistic view, it does not teach the perseverance of the saints but the perseverance of the Savior. While it teaches that the saints are utterly unreliable and might fall away any day or any hour, it also teaches that the Savior is ever watchful and ever faithful. *"Therefore He is also able to save to the uttermost those who come to God through Him, since He always lives to make intercession for them"* (Heb. 7:25 NKJV). The Calvinist view teaches that the Savior has pledged that those who believe in Him will never perish (John 10:28). He has given His word that He and His Father will keep us to the end and that no man is able to snatch us out of the hand of Himself and the Father (vv. 28–29).

This does not mean that if a man is born again and then returns to live in sin that he will not be lost forever. It means that Jesus Christ will see to it that the one who is born again will not go back and live in sin. He may fall into sin—he may fall into gross sin—but Jesus Christ has undertaken his recovery. He will go after the lost sheep until He finds it (Luke 15:4). There is no warrant here for someone to continue in sin, saying, "I am a child of God and therefore cannot be lost." There is no comfort here whatsoever for such a person. If a person returns to living in sin and continues in sin, it is proof that he is not a child of God, is not saved, and never was regenerate. (See 1 John 2:19; 3:6, 9; 5:18.)

What the Arminians object to is not the doctrine of the faithfulness of the Savior—that He will prove true even though we prove faithless. What they object to is a doctrine such as "once in grace, always in grace" that enables a man to go on sinning and seeking to justify himself by saying, "I have been saved; therefore, I have been in grace and am still in grace."

On the one hand, we need to be on our guard against the doctrine that gives us comfort in continuance in sin. On the other hand, we need to be on our guard against a distrust of Jesus Christ that makes us fear that sometime we will prove unfaithful and Jesus Christ will desert us. The position we ought to hold is the one held by the apostle Paul. He asserted, on the one hand, *"I know whom I have believed and am persuaded that He is able to keep what I have committed to Him until that Day"* (2 Tim. 1:12 NKJV). On the other hand, he was led to discipline his body (figuratively, to give his body a black eye) lest, when he had preached to others, he himself should become disqualified (1 Cor. 9:27). (For a related topic, please refer to the section "The Unpardonable Sin" in this book.)

Fasting

Q: Should Christians fast?

A: Yes, Christians should do anything in their power that will bring blessing to themselves or others. Beyond a doubt, in many instances fasting brings blessings to the one who fasts as well as to others.

It is sometimes said that fasting belonged to the Jewish religion but not to the Christian. However, this contradicts the plain teaching of the Bible. In Acts 13:2, we are told that it was while they *"ministered to the Lord and fasted"* (NKJV) that the Holy Spirit spoke to the leaders of the church in Antioch. In the third verse, we are told that it was after they had *"fasted and prayed"* that they laid their hands on Saul and Barnabas and sent them off for the work to which Jesus had called them. In Acts 14:23, we are told that at the ordination of elders, they *"prayed with fasting."*

There is no virtue in a person's going without his necessary food. However, there is power in humbling ourselves before God by fasting because we have an acute awareness of our own unworthiness. There is power in a complete earnestness in seeking the face of God that leads us away from even our necessary food so that we may give ourselves up to prayer.

If there were more fasting and prayer and less feasting and frivolousness in the church of Jesus Christ today, we would see more revivals and more wonderful things worked for God.

Footwashing

Q: Why do Christians not generally wash each others' feet as commanded in John 13:3–17?

A: There is no commandment in this passage that every Christian should wash every other Christian's feet. Nor is there today any church in which every Christian washes every other Christian's feet. There is a command here that when some other Christian needs to have his feet washed (John 13:10), we should be ready to perform even so menial a service as this for him, and thus do as Jesus did to His disciples in their need.

There is not the slightest indication that Jesus was appointing a ceremony to be performed in the church. The disciples had come in from the road with their feet dusty. The passage implies that they had bathed earlier in the day (see verses 9–10), and therefore did not need a total cleansing, but because they were wearing open sandals, their feet had become dusty along the way and needed to be washed. Yet each one of them was too proud to wash the other disciples' feet. There was no servant present to do it, so Jesus, though He knew He had come from the Father and was going to the Father, and that the Father had given all things into His hands (v. 3), rose from the table and performed for them the menial service that was needed.

Jesus' action has no resemblance whatsoever to the mere performance of the ceremony of washing feet that do not need to be washed, solely for the sake of doing the same thing that Jesus did. The lesson of the passage is plain enough, namely, that we ought to have the kind of love for one another that makes us ready to perform the lowliest service for one another.

Forgiveness of Sins

Q: What does John 20:23 mean: *"If you forgive the sins of any, they are forgiven them; if you retain the sins of any, they are retained"* (NKJV)? Does this passage teach that the priest has power on earth to forgive sins?

A: The meaning of the verse is very clear if you notice exactly what is said and the exact context in which Jesus said it. In the preceding verse, Jesus had breathed on the disciples and said to them, *"Receive the Holy Spirit"* (v. 22 NKJV). Then He said to them, *"If you forgive the sins of any, they are forgiven them; if you retain the sins of any, they are retained"* (NKJV). In other words, Jesus taught that a disciple who had received the Holy Spirit would receive the power of spiritual discernment, through which he would know whether there had been true repentance or not, and whatever person's sins this Spirit-filled disciple pronounced were forgiven, were indeed forgiven.

The promise was not made to an official priest but to disciples who had been filled with the Holy Spirit. If a priest were filled with the Holy Spirit, he undoubtedly would receive this spiritual discernment. However, a man who is not a priest, except in the sense that all believers are priests (see Revelation 1:6), and who receives the Holy Spirit may have this spiritual discernment. There are times when any Spirit-filled person may know that a pretense of repentance that another person makes is not genuine; because of this, he may declare to that person that his sins are not forgiven, and indeed that person's sins are not forgiven. On other occasions, he may see that repentance and faith are genuine, and declare to the person that his sins are forgiven.

The apostle Peter, filled with the Holy Spirit, exercised this power in Acts 8:20–23. The apostle Paul, filled with the Holy Spirit, exercised it in Acts 13:9–11. Many humble believers have this Spirit-given discernment today. There is no mention whatsoever of priests in the passage, and there is absolutely nothing that can be built upon to prove that the priest as such has power on earth to forgive sins.

Giving

Q: Do you believe in tithing your income for religious purposes?

A: Yes, as the starting point in Christian giving.

Q: What is the biblical standard for a Christian in the matter of giving money for religious work?

A: The Christian is not under any particular law in the matter of giving. That is to say, there is no absolute law laid down in the Bible that a Christian should give just so much and no more. However, a Christian should consecrate all that he has to God. Every penny of his money should belong to Him. The money he spends on himself and his family should be spent for that purpose because he thinks God would be more honored if he spent it in that way than in some other way.

In the Old Testament, the Jew was under the law to give one-tenth of his income, and, over and above that, he was expected to give freewill offerings. This Jewish law should be a suggestion to us as to where we should begin our giving. We should begin by giving one-tenth to Christ. But a Christian should not stop with a tenth. He should seek guidance as to the use of every penny he has in addition to the tenth.

Many who follow the plan of giving one-tenth have found great blessing in it. In fact, after they have set apart one-tenth to the Lord, many people have experienced a prosperity in their businesses that they never knew before. Most Christians who do not systematically give a tenth believe that they are giving more than a tenth. However, when they start setting apart a tenth of their income for the Lord, they discover that in the past they actually had been giving less than a tenth but that now they are giving much more than they ever have.

The "rule of three" given by the apostle Paul to the Corinthian church in connection with the collection for the poor Christians in Jerusalem is a simple but effective guideline for giving. It is found in 1 Corinthians 16:2: "[1] *On the first day of every week,* [2] *each one of you should set aside a sum of money* [3] *in keeping with his income*" (NIV).

Q: Does Matthew 5:42, *"Give to him who asks you, and from him who wants to borrow from you do not turn away"* (NKJV), teach that a Christian should give to everyone who asks him for money if he has it in his pocket?

A: Matthew 5:42 undoubtedly teaches that the disciple of Jesus Christ should give to everyone who asks of him, but it does not teach that he should necessarily give money. When Peter and John were appealed to by the lame man at the Gate Beautiful, they gave to him, but they did not give him money. Instead, they gave him something better. (See Acts 3:2–8.) Paul distinctly said in 2 Thessalonians 3:10, *"If anyone will not work, neither shall he eat"* (NKJV). This does not mean that if a man is a tramp, we should not give to him when he asks, but it does mean that we should use discernment in what we give him.

Almost immediately following Matthew 5:42, Jesus tells us to be like our heavenly Father who *"makes His sun rise on the evil and on the good, and sends rain on the just and on the unjust"* (v. 45 NKJV). Our giving should be patterned after our heavenly Father's. He gives to everyone who asks, but He does not always give exactly what they ask for.

God

Q: Do the names *God*, *Lord*, and *Lord God* all mean the same person—God?

A: Yes, in the Old Testament they do. They are different names of the Deity that stand for different conceptions of Him. For example, the name *God* is the more general name of the Deity. The name LORD, printed in small capitals and the equivalent of "Jehovah," is the name of God used when referring to Him as the covenant God of Israel. The name *Lord* is generally used in reference to Jesus in the New Testament.

There is a school of critics who want us to think that the use of these different names of the Deity indicates a different authorship of the different portions of Scripture where the names are used. This, for a long time, was the favorite argument of the destructive critics. For example, they tried to prove that the Pentateuch (the first five books of the Old Testament) was a patchwork of portions written by different men, but this argument has been thoroughly discredited.

The names of God are very carefully used in the Bible and make an interesting and profitable study.

Q: How would you prove the existence of God to an inquirer?

A: It would depend somewhat upon the inquirer. If he was an earnest seeker after truth, I would pursue one line of reasoning. If he was a mere trifler, I would pursue another.

In general, I would ask a person what he did believe. I would ask him specifically, "Do you believe there is an absolute difference between right and wrong?" In 999 cases out of 1,000, he would answer, "Yes." Then I would say to him, "The way to get more spiritual light is to live up to the light you have; the way to get more truth is to live up to the truth you have. You say you believe there is an absolute difference between right and wrong. Will you live up to that? Will you commit yourself to following this belief wherever it leads you?"

Very likely, he would try to dodge the question, but I would hold him to it. If he finally said, "No," then I would say to him, "The trouble with you is not in regard to what you do not believe, but, in fact, it is that you do not live up to what you do believe." He would see this and be silenced.

If he said that he would commit himself to following it wherever it led him, I would next say, "Do you know for certain that there is not a God?" Of course, he would answer, "No." Then I would ask, "Do you know for certain that God does not answer prayer?" Very likely, he would answer, "I do not know for certain that He does not answer prayer, but I do not believe He does." I would answer, "I know that He does, but that will not do you any good. I will show you how to put this thing to the test. The scientific method is this: when you find a possible clue to knowledge, you follow it out to see what there is in it. Now here is a possible clue to knowledge. Will you adopt the scientific method and follow it out to see what there is in it? Will you pray this prayer, 'O God, if there is any God, show me if Jesus Christ is Your Son or not, and if You show me that He is, I promise to accept Him as my Savior and confess Him as such before the world'?"

Very likely, here he would try to dodge again, but I would hold him to it. If he would not agree to this, I would show him that he was not an honest seeker after truth. If he agreed to do it, I would take him another step. I would have him turn to John 20:31, *"These are written* [the words contained in the gospel of John] *that you may believe that Jesus is the Christ, the Son of God, and that believing you may have life in His name"* (NKJV). Then I would say, "Now, here John presents the evidence that Jesus is the Son of God. Will you take the evidence and read it? Will you read the gospel of John?" Very likely, he would reply, "I have read it already." I would answer, "Yes, but I want you to read it in a new way. Read it slowly and thoughtfully, paying attention to what you read. I do not ask you to believe it; I do not ask you to try to believe it. I simply ask you to read it honestly, with a willingness to believe it if it is the truth. Each time, before you read, offer this prayer: 'O God, if there is any God, show me what truth there is in these verses I am about to read. I promise to commit myself to whatever You show me to be true.'"

If he refused to do this, I would show him he was not an honest seeker after the truth, that his unbelief was not his misfortune but his fault. If he agreed to do it, I would go over the three things he had agreed to do, and then say to him, "When you get through the gospel of John, will you report to me the result?" If I did not do this, he very likely would go away and not do what he had promised. I have never had anyone report to me that he had actually done the things I had asked him to do who did not arrive at faith in God, as well as in Jesus Christ as His Son and the Bible as His Word. I have tried this method with all kinds and conditions of men.

I also use another approach with inquirers. Sometimes, I immediately begin by showing a person that there is a God from the evidences of design in nature. I take out my watch and say, "Do you think this watch had an intelligent maker?" The inquirer replies, "Yes." I ask, "Why do you think it had an intelligent maker? Did you see the watch being made?" He answers, "No." "Did you ever see a watch being made?" He replies, "No." "Then why do you think it had an intelligent maker?" He will answer, "The watch shows the marks of intelligent design, thus proving it had an intelligent maker." Then I say to him, "What about your own eye? Is it not as wonderful a mechanism as a watch? Did it not then have a Maker?"

Everywhere in nature, we find symmetry, order, beauty, law, and utility. In the minutest forms of being that are discernible by the most powerful microscope, we see the same symmetry, order, beauty, law, and utility that are observable in the larger objects with which we are familiar. All this goes to prove the existence of an intelligent Creator and Designer of the physical universe.

The evolutionary hypothesis, even if it were true, would not take away any of the force of the argument from design in nature. For if it were true that the universe as we see it today, with all its countless forms of beauty and utility, came into being by a process of development from some primordial protoplasm, the question would at once arise, Who put into the primordial protoplasm the power to develop into the universe as we see it today?

From nature, then, we learn the existence of an intelligent, powerful, and benevolent Creator. Of course, nature does not teach us some of the more profound truths about God.

Q: What reasons do we have for being sure that God is a personal God—that He is a being with a personality and takes an active interest in our lives?

A: There are many conclusive proofs of the existence of a personal God. First, there is the proof from the evidence of design in nature, as referred to in the previous answer.

Second, history also proves the existence of a personal God. If we look at only a little patch of history, it sometimes seems as though there was no intelligent and benevolent purpose behind it. However, if we look at history in a large way, following its course through the centuries, we soon discover that behind the conflicting passions and ambitions of men, there is some intelligent and benevolent and righteous Power restraining and constraining man and causing the wrath of men to praise Him (Psalm 76:10). We find in history that, as Matthew Arnold wrote, there is a "power, not ourselves, which makes for righteousness." From history we discover that there is a moral Governor of the universe. Everything in the universe is attuned to virtue. Everything in nature and history conspires to punish sin and reward virtue. This is a proof of the existence of a personal God.

Third, the history of Jesus of Nazareth, as recorded in the four Gospels, proves the existence of a personal God in a special way.

It is one of the first principles of science that every effect must have an adequate cause, and the only cause that is adequate to account for the character, conduct, and works of Jesus of Nazareth is a God such as the Bible reveals. The attempt has been made, over and over again, and is still being made, to discount the miraculous in the history of Jesus of Nazareth. Indeed, the attempt is being made to eliminate the miracles altogether from that story, but every attempt of this kind has resulted in total failure. The ablest effort of this kind was made many years ago by David Strauss in his *Leben Jesu,* and for a while it seemed to a great many people as if David Strauss had succeeded. His theories were almost universally accepted in the universities of Europe. But his book could not bear careful critical examination and after a while was totally discredited. Every other attempt of the same kind has met with similar failure.

For any honest student of the New Testament today, this much at least is settled: the story of Jesus of Nazareth as recorded in the four Gospels is at least substantially accurate history. (To my mind, far more than this is proven, but that is enough for our present purpose.) If this is true—and it cannot be honestly denied by anyone who goes into the evidence—then the existence of a personal God is proven. Only a personal God will account for the life, character, conduct, and miracles of Jesus of Nazareth, and, above all, for His resurrection from the dead.

But the supreme proof of the existence of a personal God is found in the experience of the individual believer in Jesus Christ. Every real Christian knows God through personal experience. I know God more surely than I know any human being. I once doubted the existence of a personal God. I did not deny His existence; I simply questioned it. I was not an atheist, but I was an agnostic. However, I determined that if there were a God, I would know it. I became convinced from the study of history of the probability of the existence of God, but to me at that time, it was only a theory. I made up my mind to put to the test of rigid, personal experiment the theory that there was a God, and that the God of the Bible was the true God. I risked everything that men hold dear on this theory. If there had been no God, or if the God of the Bible had not been the true God, I would have lost everything that men hold dear years ago. But I risked, and I won, and today I know that there is a God and that the God of the Bible is the true God. Every other person may also know this by doing what I did.

There was a time in my life when I was put into a place where I literally lived by prayer to the God of the Bible, in the condition so clearly stated in the Bible. Every penny for my expenses came in answer to prayer. This included living expenses for myself and my wife and four children, rent for our home and for the halls in which I held meetings, support for missionaries, and funds for anything else that was needed. I made the commitment that I would not go into debt a cent for anything. When I could not pay, I would not buy. I gave up my salary, ceased taking collections or offerings, and told no one but God of any need. This went on for days and weeks and months. Every former source of income was cut off, and yet the money came— sometimes in very ordinary ways, sometimes in apparently most extraordinary ways, but it always came. When I was through, I knew that there is a personal God and that the God of the Bible is the true God. To me, God is the one great Reality who gives reality to all other realities.

Q: What do you mean by saying that God is a person? Does God have a body, or is He merely an invisible Spirit?

A: When we say that God is a person, we do not mean that He has hands and feet and legs and eyes and a nose. These are marks of bodily existence, not of personality. When we say that God is a person, we mean that He is a Being who knows and feels and wills and is not merely a blind, unintelligent force. Jesus said in John 4:24, *"God is* [a] *Spirit, and those who worship Him must worship in spirit and truth"* (NKJV). In Colossians 1:15, we read that God is *"invisible"* or unseeable.

But while God in His eternal essence is unseeable, He does manifest Himself in visible form. For example, we read in the ninth and tenth verses of Exodus 24 that Moses, Aaron, Nadab, Abihu, and seventy of the elders saw the God of Israel. It is also clear from a study of the different passages in the Old Testament where *"the Angel of the LORD"* is mentioned that it was God Himself who manifested Himself in this being. (See, for example, Genesis 16:7; Exodus 3:2.)

We are taught in Philippians 2:6 that Christ Jesus existed originally (*"being originally,"* RV, margin) *"in the form of God."* The Greek word translated *"form"* in this verse means the outward form, by which one is visible to the eye. Beyond a doubt, the thought here is that Jesus Christ, in His original state, was seen by the angelic world in a form that was outwardly manifested as divine. We may safely conclude, from this and other passages of Scripture, that while God in His eternal essence is purely spiritual and invisible, He nevertheless manifests Himself in the angelic world and has manifested Himself from all eternity in an outward, visible form.

Q: What do you mean by "the Trinity"? How can God be one and three persons at the same time?

A: God cannot be one and three at the same time and in the same sense, and nowhere does the Bible teach that God is one and three in the same sense. Yet in what sense can He be one and three? A perfectly satisfactory answer to this question may be impossible from the very nature of the case. First, God is Spirit, and numbers belong primarily to the physical world. Difficulty inevitably arises when we attempt to describe the facts of spiritual being in the forms of physical expression. Second, God is infinite, and we are finite. Our attempts at a philosophical explanation of the triunity of God is an attempt to put the facts of infinite being into the forms of finite thought. Such an attempt, at the very best, can only be partially successful. The doctrine of the Trinity, which has been the accepted doctrine of the church through so many centuries, is the most successful attempt in that direction, but it may be questioned whether it is a full and final statement of the truth.

This much we know, that God is essentially one. We also know that there are three persons who possess the attributes of deity—the Father, the Son, and the Holy Spirit—who are called God and who are to be worshipped as God. There is only one God, but this one God makes Himself known to us as Father, Son, and Holy Spirit. Yet the Son and the Spirit are both subordinate to the Father. God the Father is God in the absolute and final sense—God in the source. The Son is God in the outflow. All the perfections of a fountain are in the river that flows forth from the fountain. Similarly, the Father has imparted to the Son all His own perfections, so that it may be said without qualification that *"he who has seen* [the Son] *has seen the Father"* (John 14:9 NKJV). Through all eternity, the Son has existed and has possessed all the perfections of the Father. While He possesses all the perfections of the Father, He is not the Father but is derived from the Father and is eternally subordinate to the Father. This seems to be as far as we can go in our understanding now. How much further we may go in that glad, coming day when we will no longer see *"through a glass, darkly; but...face to face"* (1 Corinthians 13:12), when we will no longer *"know in part"* (v. 12) but will know God as perfectly and as thoroughly as He now knows us, none of us can tell.

Q: If God is a God of mercy and love, and if He is the Director of the universe, why does He send earthquakes, tidal waves, and other phenomena when thousands of lives are lost almost instantly through them?

A: Because He sees fit to do so. If God saw fit, He would have a perfect right to plunge the whole earth beneath a flood and leave us all to perish instantly. All men have sinned. All men deserve the wrath of God. But God loves even a sinful and apostate race, and He has provided a way of pardon for all who will accept it—and not only a way of pardon but also a way by which we may become sons of God and heirs of God and joint heirs with Jesus Christ. (See John 1:12; Romans 8:14–17.) If anyone who accepts this way of pardon is swept away by an earthquake, tidal wave, or other disaster, he loses nothing. He departs to *"be with Christ, which is far better"* (Phil. 1:23 NKJV). If anyone does not accept this way of pardon, he is utterly wicked and ungrateful. His being swept away by an earthquake, tidal wave, or other phenomenon is far less than he deserves and far less than he will receive in the Judgment that awaits him in the world to come—not merely for his sins but also for the black ingratitude of his trampling underfoot the mercy of God that has been so marvelously manifested (Heb. 10:29).

In our day, men have largely forgotten that God is God, and they think that He is under an obligation to explain His dealings to us. God's ways are not our ways, and God's thoughts are not our thoughts. But as the heavens are higher than the earth, so are His ways higher than our ways, and His thoughts than our thoughts (Isa. 55:8–9). His judgments are unsearchable, and His ways are beyond finding out (Rom. 11:33). But when we reach the other side and no longer *see through a glass, darkly; but...face to face"* (1 Cor. 13:12), then we will understand that the providences of God that were the most difficult for us to comprehend in this present life were full of mercy and kindness to man. What we all need to learn now is that God, in His infinite wisdom, may have a thousand good reasons for doing something when we, in our finite ignorance, cannot see even one reason for it.

Q: If God exercises general governance and control over the entire universe, how do you explain the apparent dominance of sin?

A: It is only on this earth that sin is apparently dominant, and this earth is a very small portion of the universe. Furthermore, God's plans are eternal and will take eternity for their full working out. The apparent dominance of sin is only temporary. Through permitting it at the present time, God is working out His own plans of good. When these plans are worked out, we will see how the controlling power of God was all the time behind man's failures, rebellions, and sin. Indeed, we can see it to a large degree even at the present time.

Good Works

Q: May I merit heaven by my good works?

A: If your works are absolutely perfect, if you never break the law of God at any point from the hour of your birth until your death, if you do all that God requires of you and all that pleases Him, you can merit heaven by your good works. But this is something that no man except Jesus Christ has ever done or can ever do. *"There is no difference; for all have sinned and fall short of the glory of God"* (Rom. 3:22–23 NKJV). The moment any person breaks the law of God at any point, he can no longer merit heaven by his good works. The law demands perfect obedience (Gal. 3:10). Nothing but perfect obedience to the law of God will secure life or heaven. There is, therefore, no hope on the basis of our own works.

The moment a person has sinned at any point, his only hope is that he be justified freely through the grace of God in Jesus Christ (Rom. 3:24). But justification by free grace is offered to all who will accept Jesus Christ. All who believe are *"justified freely"*—that is, as a free gift—*"through the redemption that is in Christ Jesus"* (v. 24 NKJV). God set Him forth to be the *"propitiation* [atoning sacrifice] *by His blood, through faith"* (v. 25 NKJV). If you will study the whole passage, starting from the ninth verse of Romans 3 and reading through the eighth verse of Romans 4, you will see how impossible it is for anyone to merit heaven by his good works, and what God's method of justification is.

Guardian Angels

Q: Please explain Matthew 18:10: *"Take heed that you do not despise one of these little ones, for I say to you that in heaven their angels always see the face of My Father who is in heaven"* (NKJV). Does every child have a guardian angel?

A: This seems to be the plain teaching of the text. Some explain the text in another way. They say that the angels of the children that are spoken of here are the departed spirits of the children in the glory. However, there is not a hint anywhere in the Bible that the departed spirits of human beings are angels. All through the Bible, the clearest distinction is kept between angels and men. The old hymn, "I Want to Be an Angel," has no warrant whatsoever in Scripture.

The angels of the children that are spoken of here are the angels who watch over the children. It is the office of angels to minister on behalf of those who will be heirs of salvation (Heb. 1:14). According to the Bible, each child seems to have a guardian angel, and these angels occupy a position of special favor and opportunity before God. They stand in His very presence and always behold the face of the Father.

The Heathen

Q: How is God going to judge the heathen? Can the heathen be saved by following the best spiritual light they have?

A: God will judge the heathen in righteousness, according to the light they have had. Those who have sinned without knowing the law revealed to Moses will also perish without the law, and those who have sinned under the law will be judged by the law (Rom. 2:12).

The heathen are not without spiritual light. The fact that they do by nature the things required in the law shows that they have a law, though not the law revealed to Moses (Rom. 2:14–16). If any heathen were to perfectly live up to the light he has, he would undoubtedly be saved by doing so, but no heathen has ever done this. The twelfth through sixteenth verses of Romans 2 are often taken as teaching that the heathen are to be saved by the light of nature, However, anyone who will read the passage carefully in its context will see that Paul's whole purpose was not to show how the heathen are saved by keeping the law written in their hearts but to show that all are under condemnation—the Jew because he has not lived up to the law given by revelation, and the Gentile because he has not lived up to the law written in his heart. The conclusion of the matter is given in Romans 3:22–23: *"For there is no difference; for all have sinned and fall short of the glory of God"* (NKJV).

The verses that follow this passage point out the only way of salvation: free justification by God's grace through the redemption that is in Christ Jesus on the basis of His atoning death. Each person secures for himself this justification by faith in Christ (vv. 24–25). No one will be saved except through personal acceptance of Jesus Christ as his personal Savior. There is not a line of Scripture that holds out a ray of hope to anyone who dies without accepting Jesus Christ.

There are those who believe that people who die without hearing of Jesus Christ in this world will have an opportunity to hear of Him and to accept or reject Him in some future state. However, the Bible does not say so; this is pure speculation without a word of Scripture to support it. There are also those who believe that the heathen who would have accepted Christ if He had been presented to them will be treated as if He had been presented to them and they had accepted Him, but this is all pure speculation.

All that the Bible teaches is that no one can be saved without personal acceptance of Christ, and it is wisdom on our part to do everything in our power to see that the heathen have the opportunity to accept Christ in this present life. We do not have one word of Scripture to support us in the hope that if we neglect our duty here, the heathen will have an opportunity to accept Christ in some future age or state.

Heaven

Q: Is heaven a place or a state of the soul?

A: Jesus Christ plainly declared that heaven is a place. In John 14:2, He said, *"I go to prepare a place for you"* (NKJV). To make it even plainer, He added in the next verse that when the place is prepared, He will come again and receive us to Himself, so that *where* He is, we may be also (v. 3). Furthermore, we are distinctly told that when Jesus Himself left this earth, He went into heaven, from where He had come. (See, for example, John 13:3; Acts 1:9–11; Ephesians 1:20–21.)

The blessedness of heaven will not all be due to the character of the place. It will be even more blessed because of the state of mind that those who inhabit heaven will be in. Nevertheless, heaven is a place, a place more beautiful than any of us can imagine. All earthly comparisons necessarily fail. In our present state, every sense and faculty of perception is blunted by sin and by the disease that results from sin. In our redeemed bodies, every sense and faculty will be enlarged and will exist in perfection. There may be new senses, but what they may be, we cannot of course now imagine. The most beautiful sights that we have ever seen on earth are nothing compared with what will greet us in that fair *"city which has foundations"* (Heb. 11:10 NKJV). Heaven will be free from everything that curses or mars our lives here. There will be no menial, grinding toil, no sickness or pain, no death, no funerals, and no separations. (See Revelation 21:4; 1 Thessalonians 4:13–17.) Above all, there will be no sin. It will be a place of universal and perfect knowledge, universal and perfect love, and perpetual praise. (See 1 Corinthians 13:12; 1 John 3:2; 4:8; Revelation 7:9–12.) It will be a land of melody and song.

Q: What must one do to get to heaven?

A: To get to heaven, a person needs to accept Jesus Christ as his personal Savior, surrender to Him as his Lord and Master, and openly confess Him as such before the world. Jesus Christ said, *"I am the way, the truth, and the life. No one comes to the Father except through Me"* (John 14:6 NKJV). He also said, *"I am the door. If anyone enters by Me, he will be saved"* (John 10:9 NKJV). When a person receives Jesus, he immediately becomes a child of God, an heir of God, and a joint heir with Jesus Christ (John 1:12; Rom. 8:16–17).

Anyone can know whether or not he is already on the way to heaven by simply asking himself these questions: "Have I received Jesus Christ? Have I taken Him as my Sin-Bearer, the One who bore my sins in His own body on the cross? (See Isaiah 53:6; 1 Peter 2:24; Galatians 3:13.) Am I trusting God to forgive my sins because Jesus Christ bore them for me? Have I taken Jesus Christ as my Lord and Master? Have I surrendered my mind to Him so that it may be renewed by Him, and my life to Him so that He may guide me in everything? Am I confessing Him as my Savior and my Lord before the world as I have opportunity?"

If anyone can answer yes to these simple questions, he may know he is on the way to heaven. Of course, if one has really received Jesus as his Lord and Master, he will prove it by studying His Word day by day in order to know His will, and by doing His will as he finds it revealed in the Bible.

Q: Is the Bible an all-sufficient guide to heaven?

A: It is. It tells each one of us what sort of a place heaven is and just how to get there. There is not a thing a person needs to know about the road to heaven that is not plainly stated in the Bible. It is the only Book in the world that reveals Jesus Christ, and Jesus Christ Himself is the way to heaven (John 14:6).

Q: Will we recognize our loved ones in heaven?

A: Most assuredly, we will. The apostle Paul, in writing to the believers of Thessalonica, told them not to sorrow over their loved ones, from whom they would be separated for a time, as those who have no hope sorrow over the loss of their loved ones (1 Thess. 4:13). He went on to say that Jesus Himself is coming back again and that our loved ones who have fallen asleep in Jesus will be raised first. Then we who are alive will be transformed and caught up together with them to meet the Lord in the air (vv. 14–18). The whole reason for this exhortation was to let the believers know that when we are caught up together with our loved ones, we will be with them again. Furthermore, Moses and Elijah appeared to the three disciples who were with Christ on the Mount of Transfiguration, and were recognized by them. (See Matthew 17:1–4.) If we will recognize those whom we have never known in the flesh, how much more will we recognize our loved ones!

Q: Can a person be happy in heaven if he knows his loved ones are in hell?

A: Yes. A real Christian's supreme joy is in Jesus Christ (Matt. 10:37). The love that he has for even the dearest of his earthly loved ones is nothing compared with the love that he has for Jesus Christ, and Jesus Christ is in heaven. Jesus will satisfy every longing of the heart that really knows Him.

Furthermore, if any of our loved ones end up in hell, they will be there simply because they persistently rejected and trampled underfoot that One who is the supreme object of our love (Heb. 10:29). They will be with the devil and his angels because they chose to cast in their lot with them, and we will recognize the justice of it and the necessity of it. Many people will not allow themselves to believe in eternal punishment because they have unrepentant friends and loved ones. However, it is far better to recognize the facts, no matter how unwelcome they may be, and to try to save our loved ones from the doom to which they are certainly hurrying, than it is to quarrel with facts and seek to remove them by shutting our eyes to them. If we love Jesus Christ supremely, if we love Him as we should love Him, and if we realize His glory and His claims upon men as we should realize them, we will say, if the dearest friend we have on earth persists in trampling Christ underfoot, that he ought to be tormented forever. If, after men have sinned and merited God's terrible wrath, God still offers them mercy and makes the tremendous sacrifice of His Son to save them, and if, after all this, they still despise that mercy, trample God's Son underfoot, and are consigned to everlasting torment, anyone who sees as he ought to see will say, "Amen. True and righteous are Your judgments, O Lord!" (See Revelation 16:7.)

Hell

Q: Is hell a place or a state of the soul?

A: Hell, meaning the final abode of Satan and the unrepentant, is plainly declared in the Bible to be a place prepared for the devil and his angels. For a more thorough discussion of this topic and supporting Scripture passages, please refer to the following sections in this book: "The Devil," "Eternal Punishment," and "Heaven."

Q: Please explain Psalm 139:8: *"If I ascend into heaven, You are there; if I make my bed in hell, behold, You are there"* (NKJV). I cannot imagine God's presence in hell.

A: The word translated *"hell"* in this passage does not mean hell in the sense of the abode of the lost. It means the place where all the dead were before our Lord's ascension. (It is rendered as *"Sheol"* in the New American Standard Bible and the Revised Version. This is not a translation. It is the actual Hebrew word being used.) Both the righteous and unrighteous dead went to sheol—the righteous to that portion of sheol known as paradise, and the unrighteous to the place of suffering. Since God is everywhere, He must in some sense be present even in hell, but He certainly does not manifest His presence there as He does in heaven, or even as He does on earth.

The Holy Spirit

Q: Does the Holy Spirit live in and remain with the believer, or does He come and go?

A: I know of no place in the Bible where it is recorded that He comes and goes from the believer. It is true that the Spirit of the Lord departed from King Saul (1 Sam. 16:14), but we have no reason to believe that Saul was a true believer, a regenerate man. The Holy Spirit dwells in the believer, according to the teaching of Jesus Christ (John 14:17). The believer may grieve Him (Eph. 4:30), but the Bible does not say that the believer "grieves Him away," as it is sometimes quoted as saying. Indeed, it distinctly says that even though we grieve Him, we are *"sealed for the day of redemption"* (v. 30 NKJV). The believer, through sin or worldliness, may lose the consciousness of the indwelling presence of the Spirit of God. However, losing the consciousness of His presence and power is one thing; actually losing His presence is another. The Holy Spirit may withdraw into the innermost sanctuary of the believer's spirit, behind the believer's conscious awareness of His indwelling, but He is still there.

There is, however, a work of the Holy Spirit upon a person that is short of regeneration, as in conviction. In such a case, He may come and go.

Q: Please discuss waiting on God for power for service.

A: Our Lord Jesus distinctly taught in Acts 1:8 that there is a definite endowment of power from the Holy Spirit for those who seek it. The experience of thousands of ministers and other believers proves the same. This power is received under the following conditions:

 ♦ First, that we rest absolutely on the finished work of Christ as the only basis for our acceptance before God.

 ♦ Second, that we put out of our lives every known sin.

 ♦ Third, that we surrender absolutely to God for Him to use us as He wills.

 ♦ Fourth, that we openly confess our acceptance of Jesus Christ as our Savior and Lord before the world.

 ♦ Fifth, that we really desire this anointing.

 ♦ Sixth, that we definitely ask for it.

- Seventh, that we take by faith what we ask for. (See Mark 11:24; 1 John 5:14–15.)

There does not need to be a long time of waiting. God is ready to give the Holy Spirit at once (Luke 11:13). Of course, waiting on God is something that every believer should practice. Undoubtedly, God gives His Spirit when people individually or together spend a long time in prayer before Him, thus recognizing and acknowledging their dependence upon Him. However, the teaching that a person may have to wait a month or six months for "his Pentecost" has no foundation in the Bible.

Immortality

Q: How do you prove the immortality of the soul?

A: In the Bible, immortality as applied to man is used in reference to the body and not to the soul, but I suppose the question means: How do you prove that there is a future existence after death?

We prove it from the Bible. In another of my books, I have proven that the Bible is the Word of God and that all its teachings are absolutely reliable.* The Bible teaches beyond a doubt that all men will be raised from the dead—the righteous to the resurrection of life, and those who have done evil to the resurrection of judgment (John 5:28–29). It furthermore teaches what the exact state of those who accept Christ and of those who reject Christ will be in the future eternal existence. (See also the sections on "Eternal Punishment" and "Heaven" in this book.) Moreover, the resurrection of Jesus Christ is one of the best-proven facts of history and demonstrably proves that death is not the end of everything.

There are scientific and philosophical arguments for immortality, but if we leave out the arguments that are built on the resurrection of Jesus Christ, all that these other arguments prove

---

*See R. A. Torrey, *Powerful Faith* (New Kensington, PA: Whitaker House, 1996).

is the probability of life after death, the probability of a future existence. However, when we include the arguments based on the Bible—above all, the resurrection of Jesus Christ—our belief in a future existence is no longer based on a mere probability. It is removed from the domain of the merely probable into the domain of the absolutely certain and proven.

Q: Do the Scriptures teach conditional immortality?

A: The doctrine of conditional immortality is that man is naturally mortal and only gains immortality in Christ. There is an element of truth in the belief that man is naturally mortal. Since man began to exist at one point, he could, of course, cease to exist. But it is the plain teaching of Scripture that all the sons of Adam receive endless existence through Christ. In 1 Corinthians 15:22, we are told that *"as in Adam all die, even so in Christ all shall be made alive"* (NKJV). If we deal fairly with these words, one *"all"* is as comprehensive as the other. Everyone who loses existence in Adam, who returns to the dust (Gen. 3:19; 5:5), is raised from the dust in Christ. The whole race gets back in Christ what it lost in Adam.

But whether this existence, this immortality that we receive in Christ, will be a resurrection to life or a resurrection to judgment and everlasting shame and contempt (John 5:28–29; Dan. 12:2) depends entirely on what we do with the Christ in whom we receive it. Every man's endless existence becomes an existence of unspeakable blessedness if he accepts Christ, but that existence becomes an existence of unspeakable misery if he rejects Christ. It is *"the second death"* (Rev. 21:8 NKJV), a share with the devil and his angels in the lake of fire prepared for them (Matt. 25:41), a portion in the lake of fire where there is no rest, day or night, forever and ever (Rev. 20:10).

Infants

Q: Are those who die in infancy lost forever?

A: There is not a line of Scripture to indicate that they are. Jesus said, *"Let the little children come to Me, and do not forbid them; for of such is the kingdom of heaven"* (Matt. 19:14 NKJV). It is true that infants are born into this world as members of a fallen race under the condemnation of God, that Adam's sin is imputed to all his descendants, but the sins of the whole race were atoned for by the death of Jesus Christ on the cross. (See 1 Timothy 2:6; John 1:29; 1 Corinthians 15:22; 1 John 2:2.) This includes the children.

When a child reaches the age of accountability and commits sin, there must be a definite personal acceptance of Christ before he can be saved, but of course this does not apply to those who die in infancy. To them, Christ's *"one act of righteousness"* (Rom. 5:18 NIV)—His atoning death on the cross—brings the free gift of *"justification that brings life"* (v. 18 NIV). The time will come when these children will see Christ and believe in Him, and thus be saved in the fullest sense. They will never perish for Adam's sin. Jesus Christ bore the penalty of Adam's sin for them. No one is lost merely because of Adam's sin. There is absolutely no basis in Scripture for the doctrine of the damnation of infants.

Q: Is there any Scripture that demonstrates that the children of unbelieving parents will be saved if they die in infancy? If so, what does the latter part of 1 Corinthians 7:14 mean: *"The unbelieving husband is sanctified by the wife, and the unbelieving wife is sanctified by the husband; otherwise your children would be unclean, but now they are holy"* (NKJV)?

A: The latter part of this verse undoubtedly teaches that the children of believing parents stand in a different relation to God than the children of unbelieving parents. However, there is no teaching anywhere in the Bible that an infant who dies is eternally lost, as explained in the preceding answer.

Q: Where do those who die in their infancy go in the other world?

A: The Bible does not tell us specifically. It does, however, say that *"of such is the kingdom of heaven"* (Matt. 19:14 NKJV). There is absolutely no basis in Scripture for the doctrine that while infants do not go to the place of torment, they go to a place where there is not that fullness of blessedness that those who live to maturity and accept Jesus Christ enter into. We are not wise to go beyond what is written and make theories of our own regarding their future destiny, but certainly there is not the slightest ground for any anxiety regarding them.

Insurance

Q: Some people maintain that Christians should not insure their lives, property, etc., because by so doing they are distrusting God and His providential care. What does the Bible teach regarding this?

A: The Bible teaches that there is no conflict between trusting God and an intelligent and wise provision for the necessities of the future. For instance, we read in Proverbs 6:6–8: *"Go to the ant, you sluggard! Consider her ways and be wise, which, having no captain, overseer or ruler, provides her supplies in the summer, and gathers her food in the harvest"* (NKJV). Let's consider another biblical example. The apostle Paul had been imprisoned and was being taken on a ship to Rome by way of Crete. A great storm arose, and it looked as if everyone on the ship would be lost. But Paul prayed, and he received God's own assurance that both he and all those who were with him on the ship would be saved. He fully believed God that it would come out just as he had been told. Nevertheless, when the sailors tried to flee out of the ship, thus imperiling the vessel, Paul saw to it that they were not allowed to escape. (See Acts 27:21–36.) This was not an act of unbelief on Paul's part. He was simply cooperating with God in the fulfillment of His promise.

Now, as to whether it is an intelligent and wise provision for the future to insure one's life or to insure one's property, is another question that each one must decide prayerfully for himself. God promises wisdom to each one of us in the settling of such questions, if we look to Him for it and meet the conditions of answered prayer (James 1:5–8). But even if it proved to be an unwise expenditure of money to insure one's life or property, that still would not make it an act of distrust in God.

The Jews

Q: Is there any difference today in God's sight between Jews and Gentiles?

A: Most assuredly, there is. In 1 Corinthians 10:32, the apostle Paul divided men into three categories: the Jews, the Gentiles, and the church of God. Today, God has His plans for the Jew, His plans for the Gentile, and His plans for the church.

In the church, there is neither Jew nor Gentile (Gal. 3:28). When one accepts Jesus Christ as his Savior, surrenders to Him as his Lord and Master, and openly confesses Him as such before the world, he becomes part of the body of Christ, that is, part of the church. The relationship of the Jewish Christian to Christ is precisely the same as that of the Gentile Christian. The promises that belong to one belong to the other; the Scriptures that belong to one belong to the other. The method of dividing the Word that some employ, applying some of the promises to Jewish Christians and others to Gentile Christians, is not warranted by the Word. What belongs to any Christian belongs to all Christians, both Jewish and Gentile.

But outside of the church, there is Jew and Gentile, and God's plans are not precisely the same for both. The present dispensation is preeminently a Gentile dispensation. The Jew, for the time being, has been set aside, but his day is coming. (See, for example, Romans 11:1–32.)

Judgment

Q: Do the Scriptures teach that there will be one general judgment or several judgments?

A: The Scriptures plainly teach that there will be several judgments. There will be, first of all, the judgment of the believer when he is caught up to meet the Lord in the air. This will not be a judgment regarding his salvation—for that is settled the moment he accepts Christ (John 5:24)—but a judgment regarding his reward (1 Cor. 3:13–15; 2 Tim. 4:8). Then there will be the judgment of the nations living on this earth at the time the Lord comes to earth with His saints, described in Matthew 25:31–46. But those who do not have a part in the first resurrection will not be raised for their judgment for a thousand years (Rev. 20:4–5). At the end of the thousand years, the Millennium, the rest of the dead will be raised and will appear before God at the judgment of the Great White Throne (vv. 11–15).

Q: Does God soften the final judgment of those who sin ignorantly?

A: Certainly, God does not deal with those who sin ignorantly as He does with those who sin by deliberate and willful choice. (See 1 Timothy 1:13; compare Hebrews 10:26.) But every person on this earth has sinned knowingly (Rom. 3:10–12, 23), and therefore there is no hope for anyone outside the atoning work of Jesus Christ (vv. 24–26). Everyone who believes in Jesus Christ receives eternal life, and all who reject Him will not see life but will perish forever (John 3:36; 2 Thess. 1:7–10).

Man in God's Image

Q: What does Genesis 1:27 mean when it says that *"God created man in His own image"* (NKJV)?

A: We are told in Colossians 3:10 that the regenerated man is *"renewed in knowledge according to the image of Him who created him"* (NKJV). In Ephesians 4:24, we are told that it is in *"true righteousness and holiness"* that the *"new man"* (NKJV) is created in the image of God. It is evident, then, that the words *"image"* and *"likeness"* in Genesis 1:26–27 do not refer to visible or bodily likeness but to intellectual and moral likeness in *"knowledge"* and *"true righteousness and holiness."* However, we are taught in Philippians 2:6 that Christ Jesus existed originally (*"being originally,"* RV, margin) *"in the form of God"*—that is, in a visible form that was divine. Similarly, in our ultimate state of blessedness, we will be like Christ in our bodily appearance as well as intellectually and morally. (See 1 John 3:2; compare Matthew 13:43 with Matthew 17:2.)

Marriage

Q: Should a Christian ever marry an unbeliever?

A: Most assuredly not. To do so is to disobey the plainest directions of God's Word. God says in 2 Corinthians 6:14, *"Do not be unequally yoked together with unbelievers"* (NKJV). Undoubtedly, many do this through ignorance, but that does not make it right. When a woman and a man marry, they are yoked together in the most complete and intimate sense. By *"unbelievers"* in the above passage, God clearly does not merely mean outright "pagans," but all who have not definitely received Jesus Christ and surrendered their lives to Him.

More promising lives are shipwrecked by a marriage contrary to the Word of God than in almost any other way. Some women marry men for the purpose of converting them. Such marriages result in inevitable and unutterable misery. You cannot hope to convert another by disobeying God yourself.

Q: Do you believe in marriages between Catholics and Protestants?

A: While both Roman Catholics and Protestants may be real believers in the Lord Jesus Christ, the differences between them are so radical that a marriage between the two cannot but result in friction and misunderstanding. This will especially be true when children are born into the family and the question of rearing the children comes up. If the two parties in question cannot come to see eye to eye on the fundamental questions of difference between Catholics and Protestants before their marriage, then they had better not marry.

Q: Is the marriage of cousins sanctioned in the Bible?

A: There is no explicit commandment in the Bible that cousins should not marry, but it is a well-known fact that the marriage of near relatives is fraught with great physical dangers. If there is any hereditary taint in the family, it will be accentuated in the children of near relatives. For example, in countries where there has been constant intermarriage of relatives, many of the children are mentally disabled and have other genetic defects. Certainly, the Bible does not sanction two people entering into a marriage when the children would potentially be at such great risk.

Medicine

Q: James 5:14–15 says, *"Is anyone among you sick? Let him call for the elders of the church, and let them pray over him, anointing him with oil in the name of the Lord. And the prayer of faith will save the sick, and the Lord will raise him up"* (NKJV). Does this passage give grounds for believing that medical aid should have no place in the life of faith, or does the Lord expect us to use the means at hand, praying for His blessing upon such means?

A: This passage does not give grounds for believing that medical aid should never have any place in the life of faith. It tells us what we should do when we are sick, but it says nothing either for or against medicine. Undoubtedly, it is often the purpose of God to heal without any means except those mentioned in this passage, but it is also plainly taught in the Word of God that the use of medicinal means may be proper, as in 1 Timothy 5:23:

"No longer drink only water, but use a little wine for your stomach's sake and your frequent infirmities" (NKJV).

The Millennium

Q: What is the Millennium?

A: *Millennium* means one thousand years, and the Millennium is the thousand-year reign of Christ on earth after His second coming (Rev. 20:4, 6). There are many prophecies about Christ as an earthly King that have not yet been fulfilled but that will be fulfilled in His millennial reign on earth. He will occupy the throne of David. (See Jeremiah 23:5–6; Psalm 2:6; Zechariah 14:9.) This does not mean that He will sit on a throne in Jerusalem all the time. The king of a country occupies its throne, but he very seldom literally sits upon that throne. It may be that, much of the time, Christ will be with His bride in the New Jerusalem, and not in the old literal Jerusalem here on earth, but He will reign as King on earth for one thousand years.

Q: Will the Millennium be a period of soul-saving revival?

A: There seems to be reason to suppose that, in connection with the return of our Lord, the events that accompany it will result in many people coming to their senses and to an acceptance of Jesus Christ. Certainly, this is true of Israel. There is to be a national repentance, a national turning to Christ. Jesus, coming as a Deliverer, *"will turn away ungodliness from Jacob"* (Rom. 11:26 NKJV). God will pour out upon Israel *"the Spirit of grace and supplication"* (Zech. 12:10 NKJV). They will look upon the One whom they have pierced, and they will mourn over their sin. A fountain will be opened to them so that they may be cleansed from sin and uncleanness, and there will be a national turning to Jesus Christ. (See Zechariah 12:10–13:1.)

In connection with the conversion of Israel, there will also be a great turning of the Gentiles to Christ. *"Because of* [Israel's] *transgression, salvation has come to the Gentiles to make Israel envious. But if their transgression means riches for the world, and their loss means riches for the Gentiles, how much greater riches will their fullness bring!"* (Rom. 11:11–12 NIV).

Miracles

Q: How are miracles possible if the laws of nature are fixed?

A: God is the Author of the laws of nature. The laws of nature indicate God's customary ways of working. To what extent they are fixed, it is impossible to say. But even if they were absolutely fixed, that would not make miracles impossible. One of the most universally recognized laws of nature is the law of gravity. According to the law of gravity, a stone lying on the surface of the earth will be drawn toward the center of the earth. However, it is quite possible for a man to come along and, if he wills to do so, to lift that stone away from the earth. The law of gravity is not violated in the least, but a higher law, the law of the human will, steps in and produces an effect just the opposite of what the law of gravity by itself would have produced. If a human being can bring things to pass that the fixed law of nature would not have brought to pass, left to itself, how much more can a mighty God who is the Creator of all things do so!

This whole argument about miracles being impossible because of the fixed laws of nature appears wise to the shallow thinker, but when we look right at it, it is found to be supremely absurd. The real question is not whether miracles are possible, but rather if they have occurred and if they are well attested. Miracles are certainly well attested. The supreme miracle of all is the resurrection of Jesus Christ from the dead. A leading agnostic has said, "We do not need to discuss the other miracles. The whole question is, Did Jesus Christ rise from the dead? If He did, it is easy enough to believe the other miracles. If He did not, the miraculous must go." He has stated the case well. If Jesus Christ did rise from the dead, then the miraculous is proven. The argument for the resurrection of Jesus Christ from the dead is simply overwhelming. The resurrection of Jesus Christ from the dead is one of the best-proven facts of history.* Therefore, it is plain that miracles are not only possible but also historically certain.

Q: Has the age of miracles passed away? Why doesn't God work miracles today as in Christ's time?

A: There is no conclusive biblical proof that God does not work miracles today, nor is there any proof in history or experience. That physical miracles are not as frequent and abundant as they were when Jesus Christ Himself was on the earth is only to be expected. When Jesus was on the earth, He was God manifested in the flesh; but now He is with us in the Spirit, and the miracles that we should expect to see more abundantly in the present time are in the spiritual realm. Regeneration is a miracle. The raising of a spirit dead in trespasses and sins to life in Jesus Christ is a more wonderful miracle than the resurrection of the body. This miracle is constantly occurring. In fact, those who believe in Jesus Christ today are doing greater things in the spiritual realm than Jesus Christ accomplished while He was here on earth. This is only the fulfillment of Christ's own words (John 14:12).

We may expect that physical miracles will be more common again when Christ returns the second time to reign on earth.

Missions

Q: What part should support for missions have in the life of the church and the individual believer?

A: A very prominent part. Our Lord's last command to His disciples was, *"Go therefore and make disciples of all the nations"* (Matt. 28:19 NKJV). It was in connection with this work that He promised

---

*For a discussion of the evidence for the Resurrection, see R. A. Torrey, *Powerful Faith* (New Kensington, PA: Whitaker House, 1996).

His own personal fellowship. He said that when we do this, *"Lo, I am with you always, even to the end of the age"* (v. 20 NKJV). If, then, the individual believer wishes to have personal fellowship with Jesus Christ, he must go into all the world and *"make disciples of all the nations."* He may not be able to go personally, but in that case, he can go by his gifts and by his prayers. Any Christian who is not deeply interested in missions is not in fellowship with Jesus Christ.

Since a true church is a fellowship of obedient believers, what is true of each believer will be true of the church, with the added power and blessing that comes from cooperation.

The Old Testament Law

Q: Should Christians keep the Law of Moses? Is a Christian under law?

A: No. We are taught in Galatians 5:18, *"If you are led by the Spirit, you are not under the law"* (NKJV). But this does not mean for a moment that a Christian is to lead a lawless life. While we are not under the Law of Moses, we are under law to Christ; that is, we are under obligation to do, in all things, what pleases our new Husband, Christ. (See Romans 7:1–4.) Those who are led by the Spirit—who are the only ones who are not under law—will not do things that are forbidden by the Spirit in the Word of God.

There are many in our day who have gone into the most foolish extravagances in regard to not being under the law. They say that they are led by the Spirit and therefore are not under any obligation to obey the Word. They do things that they say the Spirit leads them to do that are directly contrary to the will of God as revealed in the Bible. Now, the Bible is the Holy Spirit's Book, and the Holy Spirit certainly does not lead a person to do things that are contrary to the Bible. Any spirit that leads men to do things that are contrary to the teachings of the Bible is certainly not the Holy Spirit. There are some Christians, for instance, who scoff at all obligation to keep the Lord's Day differently from other days, and who ridicule those who do set this day apart. These people are unscriptural and are doing much harm. While they claim to be in subjection to the Holy Spirit, they are really in subjection only to their own headstrong self-will and spiritual pride.

Original Sin

Q: What is original sin, and why is it just to hold us guilty of it?

A: The phrase *original sin* is used nowadays in a great variety of senses and is generally used inaccurately. Strictly speaking, original sin was the sin in which all other sins originated, that is, the sin of Adam and Eve in the Garden of Eden.

It is just to hold us guilty for this sin, first, because we were all in Adam when he committed the sin, and second, because Adam, who was the whole race as it existed at that time, sinned as our representative, and we sinned in him (Rom. 5:12; 1 Cor. 15:21–22). But when Jesus came as the Second Adam, He also was our Representative, the Representative of the whole race, the Son of Man. When He perfectly kept the law of God, He kept it as our Representative. By His atoning death, He cleared us from the guilt of the sin committed by Adam (Rom. 5:15–18). No one will be lost because of Adam's sin. If anyone is lost, it will simply be because he did not accept the Second Adam.

God's plan of holding us guilty because of Adam's sin is much more merciful than if each of us had had to stand for himself. If each of us had stood for himself, we would all have done just what Adam did. We would have sinned, and there would have been no hope. But because the first Adam stood as our representative, the Second Adam could also stand as our Representative. He did for us what not one of us would have done for ourselves. He perfectly kept the law of God, and, having perfectly kept it, He died for us who had broken it—not only broken it in Adam's sin but also broken it in our own personal transgression. There is a depth of mercy as well as wisdom in God's plan that will fill us with wonder and praise throughout all eternity!

Perfection

Q: Can a person live a faultless life?

A: No one lives a faultless life, and no one can live a faultless life unless he is perfect in knowledge. The sincerest men and women may make mistakes in moral judgment. We are constantly growing in our knowledge of God's will as we study His Word. If, at any point, we fall below God's highest will, our lives are not faultless.

However, while we cannot live a faultless life, we can live a *blameless* life; that is, we can live up to our highest understanding of God's will as revealed in His Word. We are not to blame for what we do not know, except when our lack of knowledge is the result of our own neglect. (See Colossians 1:21–23; 1 Thessalonians 2:10; 3:13; 5:23.) Every child of God should aim to lead a blameless life, but those who lead the most blameless lives are the most conscious of their deficiencies and know how far their lives are from being absolutely faultless.

Q: Is the doctrine of sinless perfection scriptural? How can the sixth and ninth verses of 1 John 3 and related passages in that epistle be adequately reconciled with the eighth and tenth verses of 1 John 1?

A: They can be adequately reconciled by noticing exactly what John said. In 1 John 3:6, he said, *"Whoever abides in* [Christ] *does not sin"* (NKJV). The phrase *"does not sin"* literally means "is not sinning," that is, is not practicing sin. The verb is in the present tense, which denotes continuous present action. John did not say that the believer never sins, but that he does not make a practice of sinning, does not continue sinning. This is the exact force of the language used here. The same thing may be said of 1 John 3:9. The literal translation of the words of this verse is, "Every one begotten out of God is not doing sin (that is, sin is not his practice), because His seed (that is, God's seed) abides in him, and he cannot be sinning (be making a practice of sin) because he is begotten out of God."

We should also bear in mind John's definition of sin in the fourth verse of the same chapter: *"Sin is lawlessness"* (NKJV). In John's usage here, sin is the conscious doing of what is known to be contrary to the will of God. Of course, one who is begotten of God may do that which is contrary to the will of God but which he does not know is contrary to the will of God; therefore, he does not sin in the strict sense in which *"sin"* is used here. Afterward, when he comes to know the will of God, he will see that it is wrong and will confess and forsake it. However, anyone who is begotten of God will not be making a practice of doing what is known to be contrary to the will of God.

Now, it is plain that there is no contradiction between what John actually said in the sixth and ninth verses of 1 John 3 and what John actually said in the eighth and tenth verses of 1 John 1. In the eighth verse, he said, *"If we say that we have no sin, we deceive ourselves"* (NKJV). This does not mean that anyone who says he is not sinning at the present moment, that he is not doing what he knows at the present moment is contrary to the will of God, is deceiving himself. There are certainly moments when we can say that we are not doing what we know is contrary to the will of God. But what John said is that if a man says he has no sins to be forgiven, no sins to be cleansed by the blood of Jesus (see 1 John 1:7–9), that is, that he has never sinned, he deceives himself, and the truth is not in him.

In the tenth verse, John added, *"If we say that we have not sinned,"* we not only deceive ourselves but *"we make [God] a liar, and His word is not in us"* (NKJV). A person may not be practicing sin at the present moment—and if a person is born of God, he will not be practicing sin at the present moment—but nevertheless, he has sinned in the past. If he says he has not, he makes God a liar, and God's Word is not in him. The reconciliation here, as in every other apparent contradiction in the Bible, is found by looking at exactly what the inspired authors said.

Prayer

Q: How do you know God answers prayer?

A: I know it, first of all, because the Bible says so, and I have conclusive proof that the Bible is the inerrant Word of God.* Whatever the Bible says is true, I know is true. The Bible abounds in statements that God answers prayer. For example, Jesus said in Matthew 7:11, *"If you then, being evil, know how to give good gifts to your children, how much more will your Father who is in heaven give good things to those who ask Him!"* (NKJV). He also said to His disciples who were united to Him by a living faith and obedient love, *"Whatever you ask in My name, that I will do, that the Father may be glorified in the Son. If you ask anything in My name, I will do it"* (John 14:13–14 NKJV).

However, I also know that God answers prayer because He has answered *mine.* Time and time again, throughout the years, I have asked God for things that He alone could give, for things that there was no probability whatsoever of my getting through human effort. I have told no one else of my need, and God has given me the very things for which I asked. There have been times in my life when I have asked God for specific things, and it has been so evident that if I received them, they must be from Him, that I have said to Him in asking for them, "If you will give me this thing, I will never doubt you again as long as I live"—and God has given me the very thing for which I asked. On one occasion, in answer to prayer, God gave six thousand dollars within two hours. On another occasion, when another person and I prayed for five thousand dollars for the Moody Bible Institute in Chicago, word was received by telegram that

---

*See R. A. Torrey, *Powerful Faith* (New Kensington, PA: Whitaker House, 1996).

five thousand dollars had been given to the Institute by a man whom I had never heard of and who lived about one thousand miles from the place where we had prayed. This man had never given a penny to the Moody Bible Institute before and has never given a penny since. I could relate many instances of this kind.

Now, it may be said that this kind of thing is merely a coincidence, but the "coincidence" has occurred so often and there has been such an evident connection between prayer (the cause) and the answer (the effect), that to say it is coincidence is to be unscientific.

The history of George Müller's orphan homes in Bristol, England, is, to a fair-minded investigator of facts, clear proof that God answers prayer. About two thousand children at these orphanages were housed, clothed, and fed over a long period of years in answer to prayer. No money was ever solicited, no debt was ever incurred, and no meal ever failed—even though, up to the very last moment, it often seemed as if it might fail. If anyone studies the facts in connection with George Müller's orphan homes and still doubts that God answers prayer, he is not only willfully obstinate in his unbelief but is also thoroughly unscientific in his treatment of demonstrated facts.

Q: When we pray, is this not asking God to change a law of nature that He established?

A: It is not. Even an earthly father can answer the prayers of his children without changing the laws of nature. Certainly, then, the heavenly Father, who made the laws, can answer prayer. God is not the servant of His own laws; His own laws are His servants. If it were necessary to change them in order to answer prayer, He could do that; however, it is not necessary. For a long time, I lived by prayer; everything I had came in answer to prayer. I know God answered my prayers, but I have no reason to suppose that He changed one single law of nature to do it. The laws of nature do not govern God. They are simply God's fixed way of acting, fixed by His own free choice. (For a related discussion, please refer to the section "Miracles" in this book.)

Q: Why should we tell God our needs when He knows them in advance?

A: We should tell God our needs because He has told us to do so (Phil. 4:6), and because in this way we are taught what we most need to know—our absolute dependence upon God. There are many things that even an earthly father would give his children if they asked for them, that he would not give them if they did not ask for them. It is for the good of the children that they be required to ask. I, for one, am very glad that there are some things that God has withheld from me until I have asked for them.

Q: To whom may I properly address prayer—to God the Father only? Is it right to pray to Jesus Christ and to the Holy Spirit?

A: The normal order of prayer is to the Father, through the Son, in the Spirit (Eph. 2:18). It is through Christ that we come to God (Heb. 7:25). God the Father is the ultimate person to whom we pray.

However, there is abundant precedent in the Scriptures for praying to Jesus Christ. In Acts 7:59, when Stephen was filled with the Spirit, we find him calling upon the Lord Jesus. In 2 Corinthians 12:8–9, Paul told us that he implored the Lord three times for a certain thing, and the context shows that the Lord he implored was Christ. In 2 Timothy 2:22, Christians are spoken of as *"those who call on the Lord"* (NKJV). and verse eight of 2 Timothy 4 shows that the Lord who was meant is the Lord Jesus. In 1 Corinthians 1:2, Christians are described as those who *"call on the name of Jesus Christ our Lord"* (NKJV). We are told in Romans 10:12–13 that *"the same Lord over all is rich to all who call upon Him"* (NKJV), and in verse nine, we are told that the Lord of whom Paul was speaking is the Lord Jesus.

Regarding praying to the Holy Spirit, there is only one instance recorded in the Bible in which a person directly addressed the Holy Spirit—when God commanded Ezekiel to prophesy to the *"breath"* to breathe on the dry bones so that they would live

(Ezek. 37:9). However, the Scriptures refer to our having communion with the Holy Spirit (2 Cor. 13:14). Furthermore, Jesus taught that, after His departure, another Comforter would come to take His place, and that this other Comforter is the Holy Spirit (John 14:16–17; 15:26). We are dependent upon the Holy Spirit for everything; therefore, we must look to Him— which implies prayer. Yet it is the Father and the Son who give the Holy Spirit (John 15:26; Acts 2:33), and it would seem that if we want the Holy Spirit, instead of praying directly to Him, we should pray to the Father or Son for Him.

Q: Why aren't all our prayers answered?

A: For various reasons. Some of our prayers are not answered because we ourselves are not right with God and in a position where God can wisely answer our prayers. (See 1 Pet. 3:7.)

Some of our prayers are not answered because they are not offered in the name of Jesus Christ. In other words, we need to depend on Christ's claims on God and not our own. We have no claims on God. If we approach Him on the basis of our own merit, we will get nothing.

Some of our prayers are not answered because they are not wise and therefore are not in accordance with the will of God (1 John 5:14–15).

Some of our prayers are not answered because we do not persist in prayer. (See Luke 11:5–10; 18:1–8.)

Finally, James 4:2–3 says, *"You do not have because you do not ask. You ask and do not receive, because you ask amiss"* (NKJV).

Q: If the Lord did not answer your prayers, what would you think was the matter? Would you think it was yourself?

A: Most assuredly, I would. I would get alone with God and ask Him to search me by His Spirit and His Word. If He brought anything to light that was displeasing to Him, I would confess it as a sin and forsake it. If He did not bring anything to light, I would continue praying, for I have learned that God does not always give us the best things the first time we ask for them. He tries and develops our faith and teaches us persistence by keeping us waiting. The longer I live, the more I feel that the teaching of Luke 18:1, *"Men always ought to pray and not lose heart"* (NKJV), is of the highest importance and should sink deeply into our hearts.

There was a time when God did not answer my prayers. I was living solely by faith at the time; that is, everything I got came in answer to prayer. However, the supplies stopped. I cried to God but got no answer. Then I looked up to God and asked Him to search my heart and bring to light anything in my life that displeased Him. He brought to light something that had often troubled me before but which I would not admit was sin. That night, I said, "O God, if this is wrong, I will give it up," but I got no answer. In the bottom of my heart, I knew it was wrong all the time. Then I said, "O God, this is wrong; it is sin. I will give it up," and the answer came. The fault was in me, not in God. There is nothing that God delights to do more than to answer prayer.

Q: How should I pray in order to get what I ask for?

A: You should follow these guidelines:

 ♦ First, you must be the kind of person that the Bible describes as the one whose prayers God answers. This is a person who believes in the Lord Jesus Christ with a living faith and shows the reality of his faith by living a life of daily obedience to His will. (See John 14:13–15; 15:7; 1 John 3:22.)

 ♦ Second, you must pray to the Father, through the Son, in the Spirit (Eph. 2:18). Much that is called prayer is not really prayer to God. There is no thought of God in the mind, no real approach to God in the heart. It is only on the ground of the shed blood of Jesus Christ that one can really approach God and be sure that his prayers are heard (Hebrews 10:19–20). It is only when we pray in the Holy Spirit, that is, under His guidance, that we pray in such a way that we may be sure that God will hear (Jude 20; Rom. 8:26–27).

♦ Third, you must pray according to the will of God (1 John 5:14–15). We may know the will of God by studying the Word, which is given to us to reveal God's will, and by the leading of the Spirit. Whenever you ask for anything that is promised in the Word of God, you may know that it is the will of God to give it, and He will give what you ask.

♦ Fourth, you must pray persistently (Luke 11:5–10; 18:1–8). Here is where many fail. They do not "pray through." They pray for a thing once or twice and then conclude it is not God's will to give it. God demands of us a persistent faith that will not take no for an answer. Many people pray and pray up to the very point of getting something, and then they fail because they do not pray through.

Predestination

Q: How do you reconcile man's freedom of choice with God's fore-knowledge and foreordination? Also, please explain the meaning of this verse: "[Jesus], *being delivered by the determined purpose and foreknowledge of God, you have taken by lawless hands, have crucified, and put to death*" (Acts 2:23 NKJV).

A: The above verse means that the actions of Judas and the rest who betrayed Jesus and put Him to death were taken into God's plan and were thus made a part of it. But it does not mean that these men were not perfectly free in their choice. They did not do as they did because God knew that they would do so, but the fact that they would do so was the basis upon which God knew it. Foreknowledge no more determines a man's actions than after-knowledge. Knowledge is determined by fact, not fact by knowledge.

Practically the same explanation applies to Romans 8:29: "*Whom He foreknew, He also predestined to be conformed to the image of His Son*" (NKJV).

Q: Please explain Acts 13:48: *"And as many as had been appointed to eternal life believed"* (NKJV). Are some born to be lost?

A: God knows from all eternity what each person will do—whether he will yield to the Spirit and accept Christ or whether he will resist the Spirit and refuse Christ. Those who will receive Him are ordained to eternal life. If any are lost, it is simply because they will not come to Christ and thus obtain life (John 5:40). *"Whoever desires"* may come (Rev. 22:17 NKJV), and all who do come will be received (John 6:37).

God does not ordain anyone to be lost against his own will. But in God's infinite wisdom and holiness, it is ordained that whoever deliberately and persistently rejects His glorious Son will be banished forever from His presence.

Prosperity of the Wicked

Q: How is it that a holy and just God allows the wicked to prosper while the good often suffer poverty?

A: What we call prosperity is often in reality a curse. On the other hand, poverty is often a great blessing. God allows the good to suffer poverty because that is what they need most, all things taken into consideration. One of the things that I often thank God for is that the large amount of money that I expected to inherit from my father never came to me and that, at one time, I was allowed to suffer extreme poverty. I have known what it means to be in a foreign country with a wife and child, in a strange city where the people spoke a strange language, and with my money all gone. I now thank God for it. It may have seemed hard at the time, but it brought great blessing. Poverty drives men nearer to God, makes them feel more deeply their dependence upon Him. It is not something to be dreaded but something to thank God for.

The psalmist was confronted with this same perplexity. He said in Psalm 73:3, *"I was envious of the boastful, when I saw the prosperity of the wicked"* (NKJV). In the twelfth and thirteenth verses, he added, *"Behold, these are the ungodly, who are always at ease; they increase in riches. Surely I have cleansed my heart in vain, and washed my hands in innocence"* (NKJV). But later on in the psalm, he told us that all his perplexity was solved when he went into the sanctuary of God—when he communed with God. The mystery was then explained to him. He understood the end of the wicked; he saw how their prosperity is just for a moment, how God has set them in slippery places, and how they are brought to desolation in a moment. On the other hand, he discovered of himself, and of the righteous in general, that even in their poverty they are continually with God. God upholds them. Down in this world of testing and trial, He guides us with His counsel, and when we come out of the fire purified, He afterward receives us into His glory (vv. 16–24).

Much of our difficulty comes from the fact that we forget that this world is not everything, that this brief world is simply a preparation for a future eternal world. We forget that happy is the man who has his bad things in this life but in the eternal life to come has his good things, and wretched indeed is the man who has his good things in this life and his bad things in that eternal world that is to come (Luke 16:25).

Purgatory

Q: Is the doctrine of purgatory scriptural?

A: The Scriptures do teach that there is an intermediate state after death, but this is not purgatory. Please refer to the following sections in this book: "Afterlife" and "Salvation after Death."

Religion

Q: What difference does it make what religion a person professes, provided he does the best he can?

A: It makes all the difference in the world. Christianity is true. Other religious are false, though they may have elements of truth in them. It does not make a lie any less a lie to believe it most sincerely. Indeed, the more sincerely and heartily a person believes a lie, the worse off he is. I may believe that poison is food, and believe it very sincerely, but if I take it, it will kill me just as quickly as it would if I had known it was poison. Consider another example. If I get on the wrong train, a train that is going in the opposite direction from my destination, it will not take me to my desired destination no matter how sincerely and earnestly I believe it is going there. It is the truth that sets men free when they believe it (John 8:32), and no amount of earnest faith in an error will set a person free. Indeed, the more earnestly a person believes an error, the more it will enslave him.

There is no more foolish idea in the world today than that it does not make any difference what a person believes, as long as he is sincere. What a person really believes determines what he is. If he believes error, he will be wrong, not only for the life that is to come but also for this present life, no matter how seriously or earnestly he believes it.

The Resurrection of the Body

Q: How is it possible that we will rise again with the same bodies we had on earth?

A: It is not possible. The Bible distinctly teaches that there will be a resurrection of the body. However, it does not teach that we will rise again with the same body we had on earth. It clearly teaches that we will not rise with the same body. In 1 Corinthians 15:37–38, we are told, *"And what you sow, you do not sow that body that shall be, but mere grain; perhaps wheat or some other grain. But God gives it a body as He pleases, and to each seed its own body"* (NKJV). In verse 42, we read, *"So also is the resurrection of the dead"* (NKJV). In other words—as the context clearly shows—just as grain that is sown rises up as a different kind of body, so it will be in the resurrection of the dead. The body that rises will not be the very body that was buried, though it will be the outcome of that body. It will not be composed of exactly the same material elements that were laid in the grave; nevertheless, it will be a body, a real body. As it says in 1 Corinthians 15:42–44, the bodies we now have will be *"sown in corruption"* but will be *"raised in incorruption."* They will be *"sown in dishonor"* but will be *"raised in glory."* They will be *"sown in weakness"* but will be *"raised in power."* They will be *"sown a natural body"* but will be *"raised a spiritual body. There is a natural body, and there is a spiritual body"* (NKJV).

Q: What kind of a body will we have in the resurrection?

A: It will not be flesh and blood (1 Cor. 15:50–53); on the other hand, it will not be pure spirit but will have flesh and bones (Luke 24:39). It will be incorruptible—not subject to decay, imperishable, glorious, powerful (1 Cor. 15:42–43). The days of weariness and weakness will be gone forever. The body will be able to accomplish everything the spirit purposes. It will be luminous, shining, dazzling, bright like the sun (see Matthew 13:43; Daniel 12:3; compare Matthew 17:2; Luke 9:29). Resurrection bodies will differ from one another. (See 1 Corinthians 15:41–42.) The resurrection body will be the consummation of our adoption, our placement as sons (Romans 8:23). In the resurrection body, it will be outwardly manifest that we are sons of God. Before His incarnation, Christ was *"in the form of God"* (Phil. 2:6 NKJV), that is, in the visible appearance of God. The word translated *"form"* means the external appearance— that with which something strikes the outward vision. In the resurrection, we also will be in the visible appearance of God. (See Colossians 3:4 RV; 1 John 3:2 RV.)

Rewards

Q: Is it scriptural for a Christian to work for reward?

A: It certainly is. The Bible constantly holds out rewards, both temporal and eternal, for faithful service. Our Lord Jesus Himself told us to store up treasures in heaven (Matt. 6:19–21). The Christian should serve not merely for the reward but also out of love for Jesus Christ. However, he has a right to expect a reward, and the reward is a great incentive to faithful service.

The Sabbath

Q: Why was the Jewish Sabbath, or the seventh day of the week that God commanded to be observed as the Sabbath day (Exod. 20:8–11), changed to the first day of the week—what we call the Lord's Day? Why is this day now observed as the Christian Sabbath?

A: Let me say, first of all, that there is no commandment in the Ten Commandments that says the Israelites were to keep the seventh day of the week. The words *of the week* were added by man to the commandment as given by God. What God really commanded through Moses was: *"Six days you shall labor and do all your work, but the seventh day is the Sabbath of the LORD your God"* (Exod. 20:9–10 NKJV). It does not say that the Sabbath is the seventh day of the week; it says that the Sabbath is the seventh day after six days of labor. Whether we keep the seventh day of the week or the first day of the week, we are keeping the fourth commandment to the very letter. If one is a Jew belonging to the "old creation," let him keep the seventh day of the week. But if he is a Christian and standing on resurrection ground, let him keep the first day of the week, Resurrection Day.

Second, the Jewish Sabbath was not changed to the Lord's Day. While both the Jewish Sabbath and the Lord's Day are a literal keeping of the fourth commandment, they are not the same day, and they do not stand for the same idea. One belongs to the old creation, the other to the new. (See 2 Corinthians 5:17; Galatians 6:15; Hebrews 9:11.) It has sometimes been said by certain Christians that there is no authority for the change and that the Roman Catholic Church or the pope made the change. This statement is absolutely untrue. History proves that Christians kept the first day of the week long before there was any Roman Catholic Church. We have indications that they kept it in New Testament times. It was on the first day of the week that the early disciples came together to break bread (Acts 20:7). It was on the first day of the week that believers put aside money for the needs of other Christians (1 Cor. 16:2). In the writings of the early church Fathers, long before the Roman Catholic Church had developed and, of course, long before there was any pope, we find it stated again and again that the first day of the week was the one that Christians observed.

The apostle Paul explicitly taught that a Christian should not allow himself to be judged in regard to the Jewish Sabbath, and that the Jewish Sabbath belongs with other Jewish observances concerning meat and drink, holy days, new moons, and so forth (Col. 2:16). These were the *"shadow of things to come,"* but the substance is in Christ (v. 17 NKJV).

Salvation after Death

Q: Luke 15:4 says, *"What man of you, having a hundred sheep, if he loses one of them, does not leave the ninety-nine in the wilderness, and go after the one which is lost until he finds it?"* (NKJV). Does this verse give clear proof that Christ is going to continue to seek and to save, after death, the lost who have had a good opportunity on earth to repent and come to Christ?

A: It certainly does not. All that is taught here is that the shepherd goes after the lost sheep until he finds it; but not all men are "sheep." The whole argument that seeks to prove that this verse teaches that all men will ultimately be found and saved proceeds upon the supposition that all men are sheep. But we are distinctly taught in the Word of God that this is not the case. There are sheep and there are goats. (See Matthew 25:31–46.) There are sheep and there are swine and dogs. (See 2 Peter 2:20–22.)

Undoubtedly, Jesus Christ will find every one of His sheep sooner or later. The Bible teaches that He will find them in this present life. But the Bible also teaches that some men are goats and will remain goats up to the Judgment Day. Christ will say to the goats, *"Depart from Me, you cursed, into the everlasting fire prepared for the devil and his angels"* (Matt. 25:41 NKJV). These are the words of Jesus Himself.

Q: First Peter 3:18–20 reads: *"For Christ also suffered once for sins, the just for the unjust, that He might bring us to God, being put to death in the flesh but made alive by the Spirit, by whom also He went and preached to the spirits in prison, who formerly were disobedient, when once the Divine longsuffering waited in the days of Noah, while the ark was being prepared"* (NKJV). Does this not teach that there is another opportunity to repent after death?

A: It certainly does not. It does teach that Christ, when He was put to death in the flesh (that is, in His body), was quickened in His spirit, and in His spirit went and preached to the *"spirits in prison."* But we are not told that the spirits in prison were men who had lived on the earth and died in their sin. There is reason to suppose that they were the angels who were disobedient in the time of Noah. (See verse 20; 2 Peter 2:4; Genesis 6:1–2; Jude 6–7.) But even supposing that they were the departed spirits of men who had died in sin, we are not told that Jesus preached the Gospel to them. The word translated *"preached"* in this passage does not mean "to preach the Gospel," but "to herald." There is another word often used in the New Testament that means "to preach the Gospel," and it is significant that this word is not used in this passage. Nor are we told that any of these *"spirits in prison"* to whom Christ preached repented, or even could repent. The passage simply teaches that the kingdom has been proclaimed in hell as well as in heaven.

Q: Is there any word of Scripture that gives us grounds to believe in repentance after death?

A: There is not.

Sanctification

Q: Some teach that a believer is sanctified instantaneously. Others declare that sanctification is a gradual process, perfected in heaven only. What does the Bible teach regarding this?

A: The Bible teaches that every believer is sanctified instantly, the moment he believes in Jesus Christ (1 Cor. 1:2; 6:11). The moment anyone becomes a member of the church of God by faith in Christ Jesus—in that moment—he is sanctified. *"Through the offering of the body of Jesus Christ once for all"* (Heb. 10:10 NKJV), we are cleansed forever from all the guilt of sin. We are *"perfected forever"* (v. 14 NKJV), as far as our standing before God is concerned. The sacrifice does not need to be repeated, as the Jewish sacrifices were. The work is done *"once for all."* Sin is put away forever (Heb. 9:25–28; see Galatians 3:13), and we are sanctified—"set apart"—forever as God's special and eternal possession. In this sense, every believer is instantly sanctified the moment he believes in Jesus.

However, there is still another sense in which every believer may be instantly sanctified. It is his privilege and his duty to present his whole body as a *"living sacrifice"* (Rom. 12:1 NKJV) to God.

Such an offering is well pleasing to God; when it is made, God sends down the fire of the Holy Spirit and takes to Himself what is thus presented. Then, instantly, the believer, so far as his will is concerned, is wholly God's, or perfectly sanctified.

But after he is perfectly sanctified in this sense, he may discover, and undoubtedly often will, as he studies the Word of God and as he is taught by the Holy Spirit, that there are individual acts and habits of his life, forms of feeling, speech, and action, that are not in conformity with this central purpose of his life. These should be confessed to God as sinful and should be renounced. In this way, these areas of his life will also be brought by the Holy Spirit into conformity with the will of God as revealed in His Word. But the victory in these newly discovered and unclaimed territories may also be instantaneous. There is no need for a prolonged battle. For example, if I were to discover in myself an irritability that was clearly displeasing to God, I could go to God at once and confess it and renounce it. In an instant, not by my own strength but by looking to Jesus and by surrendering this department of my life to the control of the Holy Spirit, I could overcome it and never have another failure in that way.

Yet, while there is this instantaneous sanctification that any child of God may claim at any moment, there is also a progressive work of sanctification—an increasing in love (1 Thess. 3:12; 4:9–10); an abounding more and more in a godly walk and in pleasing God (1 Thess. 4:1); a growing in the *"grace and knowledge of our Lord and Savior Jesus Christ"* (2 Pet. 3:18 NKJV); a being transformed into the image of our Lord Jesus Christ from glory to glory, each new gaze at Him making us more like Him (2 Cor. 3:18); and a growing up into Christ in all things until we mature into a full-grown man, *"to the measure of the stature of the fullness of Christ"* (Eph. 4:13 NKJV; see also verses 11–15).

Sanctification becomes complete in the fullest sense at the coming of our Lord and Savior Jesus Christ (1 Thess. 3:13; 5:23). It is not in this present life or at death, but at the coming of Christ, that we are entirely sanctified in this fullest sense.

The Second Coming of Jesus Christ

Q: Does the Bible teach that Jesus Christ is coming back to this earth personally and visibly?

A: It does. There is nothing more clearly taught in the Bible than that Jesus Christ is coming back to this earth personally, bodily, and visibly. In Acts 1:10–11, we read that two men in white apparel stood by the disciples as they gazed steadfastly into heaven at Jesus as He was being taken up before their eyes. These men in white apparel said to the disciples, *"This same Jesus, who was taken up from you into heaven, will so come in like manner as you saw Him go into heaven"* (v. 11 NKJV). Now, they had seen Him going into heaven personally, bodily, visibly, and they were told that He would come back just as He had gone.

An attempt has been made by those who deny the personal return of our Lord to say that *"in like manner"* means "with equal certainty," but the Greek words translated *"so...in like manner"* permit no such construction. They are never used in that way. Literally translated, they mean, "thus in the manner which," and are never used to describe anything but the manner, the precise manner, in which a thing is done. Jesus Christ is coming back exactly as the disciples saw Him going: personally, bodily, visibly.

The same truth is taught in John 14:3, 1 Thessalonians 4:16–17, and in many other passages. In Hebrews 9:28, we are told, *"So Christ was offered once to bear the sins of many. To those who eagerly wait for Him He will appear a second time, apart from sin, for salvation"* (NKJV). Translated literally, the word in this passage that is translated *"will appear"* would be "will be seen." It is a word used only to refer to seeing with the eye. In Revelation 1:7, we read, *"Behold, He is coming with clouds, and every eye will see Him, even they who pierced Him. And all the tribes of the earth will mourn because of Him"* (NKJV).

These very plain promises cannot, by any fair system of interpretation, be made to refer to the coming of Christ in the Holy Spirit, as some would say. The coming of the Holy Spirit is, in a very real sense, the coming of Christ. (See John 14:15–18, 21–23.)

However, it is not the Coming referred to in the above passages, and cannot be made such except by perverting the plain words of God. Nor is the Coming described in these passages the coming of Christ to receive the believer at the time of his death. The details given do not fit the death of the believer. Nor do these passages refer to the coming of Christ at the destruction of Jerusalem in A.D. 70. The destruction of Jerusalem was, in a sense, a precursor, prophecy, and type of the Judgment at the end of the age; therefore, in Matthew 24:3–31 and Mark 13:3–27, these two events are described in connection with one another. But God's judgment on Jerusalem was clearly not the event referred to in Acts 1 and the other passages given above. The second coming of Jesus Christ, which is so frequently mentioned in the New Testament, is the great hope of the church, and it is still mentioned as lying in the future. (See 1 Corinthians 11:26; John 21:22–23; Revelation 1:7; 22:20.)

Q: How is Jesus Christ coming again?

A: As I already mentioned, He is coming personally, visibly, and bodily. But in addition to this, He is coming very publicly (Matt. 24:26–27; Rev. 1:7). Every now and then, someone appears in some corner of the earth who is announced to be Christ in His second coming, but these obscure, "inner room" christs (see Matthew 24:26) are all frauds that have long since been predicted and discredited. Christ is *"coming on the clouds of heaven with power and great glory"* (v. 30 NKJV). He is coming in the glory of His Father with the holy angels. (See Matthew 16:27; Mark 8:38; 2 Thessalonians 1:7.) He is coming unannounced, without warning, unexpectedly, suddenly. (See Matthew 24:37–39; Luke 21:34–35; 1 Thessalonians 5:2–3; Revelation 16:15.)

Q: Do you believe that the second coming of Christ is near at hand? If so, why? What should we do to prepare for Him?

A: As far as I know, our Lord may return again any day. There is no event predicted in Scripture that must occur before Jesus comes to receive His own to Himself, although it seems as if there are some events that must occur before He comes to the earth with His saints. (See 2 Thessalonians 2:1–4, 8.) As far as we know, He may come for us believers at any moment, and He Himself has commanded us always to be ready because *"the Son of Man is coming at an hour you do not expect"* (Matt. 24:44 NKJV).

Furthermore, there seem to be indications that *"the coming of the Lord is at hand"* (James 5:8 NKJV). Second Timothy 3:1–5 gives a very accurate description of our own time. The increase of unbelief in the professing church and in the pulpit, the growing unrest in the social and political world, the apparently rapid development of the Antichrist—all these things seem to point to the near approach of our Lord. But we should bear in mind that earnest men of God and students of the Bible have often thought in times past that the coming of the Lord was very near. In a sense it was, and they were not mistaken. Those who thought it was so far away that they allowed it to have no effect on their lives were the ones who were really mistaken.

Today, men's hearts are *"failing them from fear and the expectation of those things which are coming on the earth"* (Luke 21:26 NKJV). But when the true believer and intelligent student of the Word sees these things begin to come to pass, he will not be discouraged. He will lift up his head and look up because he will know that his redemption is drawing near (v. 28). We should all be dressed and ready and have our lamps burning (Luke 12:35), and we should be like men who wait for their master to return from a wedding so that when He does come and knock, we may open to Him immediately (v. 36).

Q: What is the logical and adequate explanation of Matthew 16:28, where Jesus said, *"Assuredly, I say to you, there are some standing here who shall not taste death till they see the Son of Man coming in His kingdom"* (NKJV)?

A: The answer to this question is evident if one continues reading, ignoring the chapter division between the sixteenth and seventeenth chapters of Matthew. This division is not part of the original Scriptures but is an editor's addition, and sometimes these divisions are made in illogical ways. It is noticeably so in this case.

After quoting the words in question, Matthew goes on to describe the Transfiguration of Christ. In this Transfiguration, Jesus, the Son of Man, was seen *"coming in His kingdom."* He was manifested in the glory that is properly His. If things had taken their natural course, He would have been glorified then and there, without going through death. However, He turned His back on that glory and went down from the mountain to meet the awful tragedy of His death, the only way in which He could redeem men. It was of *"His decease* [that is, His atoning death]" (Luke 9:31 NKJV) that Moses and Elijah spoke with Him when they appeared with Him in the glory. This Transfiguration, seen by some who were standing with Him when He spoke the words found in Matthew 16:28, was the Son of Man seen coming in His kingdom.

Secret Societies

Q: Do you believe in secret societies? Do you think it is wise to publicly expose them through preaching?

A: I do not believe in secret societies, and I believe it is wise to show young Christians the danger of them. This ought to be done wisely. I do not believe in making a hobby of this sort of thing. I would not start by attacking lodges; the first thing I would do would be to get men and women converted to Jesus Christ.

Q: Should a Christian retain membership in a secret society?

A: No. I do not see how a Christian who intelligently studies his Bible can do so. The Bible tells us plainly, *"Do not be unequally yoked together with unbelievers. For what fellowship has righteousness with lawlessness? And what communion has light with darkness?"* (2 Cor. 6:14 NKJV). All secret societies of which I have any knowledge are made up, at least partly, of unbelievers—that is, of those who have not accepted Jesus Christ and surrendered their wills to God. In light of this express commandment in God's Word, I do not see how a Christian can retain membership in them. I am not saying that no members of secret societies are Christians, for I have known a great many excellent Christians who were members of secret societies. However, I cannot see how they can continue to be so. Many continue as members of the Masonic and similar orders simply because they are not acquainted with the teachings of the Word of God on the subject.

Furthermore, in the rituals of some secret societies, the Scriptures themselves are perverted. The name of Jesus Christ is cut out of passages in which it occurs in the Bible so as not to offend Jews and other non-Christians. How a Christian can retain membership in a society that thus deceitfully handles the Word of God, and, above all, cuts out the name of his Lord and Master, I cannot understand.

Still further, oaths of the most shocking nature are required in some secret societies, and there are ceremonies that are simply a caricature of biblical truths. For example, there is even a mock resurrection scene.

Moreover, Christianity seeks the light and not the darkness (Eph. 5:8, 11–12). Undoubtedly, many Christians go into the Masonic and other orders for the purpose of getting hold of the non-Christian members and winning them for Christ, but this is a mistaken policy. Experience proves that the secret society is more likely to swamp the spiritual life of the Christian than the Christian is to win his fellow Masons to Christ.

Soulwinning

Q: How may I gain a love for people and a concern for their salvation?

A: In the following way:

♦ First, by giving your whole self up—all your thoughts, feelings, ambitions, purposes—to the control of the Holy Spirit. The Holy Spirit loves people, and if you will give yourself up to His control, He will impart to you a love for people. The very first part of the description of the fruit of the Spirit is love (Gal. 5:22).

♦ Second, by dwelling on the actual condition of men who are outside of Christ, as revealed in the Word of God, and by studying what the Word of God says about their ultimate destiny. If you will reflect upon the hell that awaits lost souls, you will soon (if you are a Christian at all) have a passion for their salvation.

♦ Third, by observing Jesus Christ and dwelling on His conduct toward the lost.

Spiritualism

Q: Can a Christian be a Spiritualist?

A: An intelligent Christian cannot be a Spiritualist, for spiritualism is exposed and condemned in the most unmistakable terms in the Bible.

Spiritualism is not something modern. It is as old as the days of Moses. The mediums in those days had, or professed to have, familiar spirits who spoke through them. Consulting those who had familiar spirits was condemned by God through Moses in the strongest terms. For example, He said in Leviticus 19:31, *"Give no regard to mediums and familiar spirits; do not seek after them, to be defiled by them: I am the LORD your God"* (NKJV). In Leviticus 20:6, He said, *"And the person who turns to mediums and familiar spirits, to prostitute himself with them, I will set My face against that person and cut him off from his people"* (NKJV). Also, in Deuteronomy 18:10–12, He said, *"There shall not be found among you anyone who makes his son or his daughter pass through the fire, or one who practices witchcraft, or a soothsayer, or one who interprets omens, or a sorcerer, or one who conjures spells, or a medium, or a spiritist, or one who calls up the dead. For all who do these things are an abomination to the LORD, and because of these abominations the LORD your God drives them* [the Canaanites] *out from before you"* (NKJV).

One of the strongest charges brought against Manasseh, king of Judah, was that he was a Spiritualist, and thus provoked God to anger (2 Kings 21:1–2, 6). Saul lost his kingdom and his head for consulting a medium. We read in 1 Chronicles 10:13–14: *"So Saul died for his unfaithfulness which he had committed against the LORD, because he did not keep the word of the LORD, and also because he consulted a medium for guidance. But he did not inquire of the LORD; therefore He killed him, and turned the kingdom over to David the son of Jesse"* (NKJV).

Nearly all so-called modern spiritualism is a fraud. The tricks of the mediums have been exposed time and time again. Still, probably not all of it is fraud. While there is a natural explanation for most of the manifestations of modern spiritualism, and while most of these manifestations are done through deception, some of them do seem to have a supernatural origin. We must remember, however, that just because something is supernatural, this does not necessarily prove that it is right or true. According to the teaching of the Bible, there is a real, unseen world, a world of spirits, but some of the spirits are bad; they are emissaries and agents of the devil (Eph. 6:12; 2 Thess. 2:9–12). The fact that a person can do things and make revelations that we cannot explain by natural causes—things and revelations that seem to show he is particularly in contact with the supernatural world—does not prove that he is in league with God. Rather, it may prove that he is in league with the devil. It may be that spirits do manifest themselves, but it does not follow that they are the spirits of our departed friends or other good and wise people who have left this world. There is good reason to believe that these spirits who come to us pretending to be the spirits of our loved ones who have departed are demonic spirits.

A prominent medium, who was at the time operating in Chicago, once came to me and said, "Mr. Torrey, these things are not all sleight of hand and trickery. There are spirits, but they are demons. I was tormented all last night by the demons through whom I do my work." I asked him why he did not renounce the whole business. He replied that he was making a splendid living through it and knew of no other way in which he could do so well. A friend of mine who dabbled in spiritualism and developed unusual powers as a medium was afterward led to renounce the whole business. He went into it thinking it was all right, but he had not gone far before he found it was demonic. There have been many instances of the same thing.

Even if the spirits manifested are the spirits of our departed loved ones, we are commanded in the Bible not to seek knowledge in this way (Isa. 8:19–20). Whoever dabbles in spiritualism at all enters the devil's territory and disobeys the most explicit commandments of God.

The spiritual and moral influence of spiritualism is ruinous. Sooner or later, it leads to the renouncing of Jesus Christ and to all kinds of immorality. When we lose our loved ones, the temptation often becomes strong to seek communication with them, and well-meaning people are led into spiritualism in this way. But it is a snare of the devil and leads to the eternal ruin of the soul.

Trouble

Q: Does trouble come from God? Do you believe that God ever sends trouble to us purposely, or that it comes in the natural order of events?

A: What we call "the natural order of events" is God's ordering. God controls all things. Every detail of our history is in His hands, and what appears to us most natural and inevitable is just as much a part of His will as what we believe is a direct intervention on His part.

God undoubtedly permits trouble to come to us sometimes. He permits it to come when He sees that we need it. He would prevent its coming if He saw that we did not need it. If we would surrender our wills to God, we would not need trouble as a discipline or chastening, which we do need when our wills are not surrendered, and we would therefore escape a great amount of misfortune. If we would more quickly learn God's purposes in the troubles that come to us, we would more quickly be relieved of them. For example, undoubtedly, many people are sick who might be well if they would only learn the lesson that God is trying to teach them by the sickness and then look to Him for recovery. I have known people who were in trouble for months or years, and who suddenly were delivered from it when they learned to surrender their wills absolutely to God and to rejoice in His will—whatever it might be—and then looked to Him so that they might be delivered for His glory.

Satan, as a source of our troubles, is also under God's control. See, for example, the cases of Job (Job 1:12; 2:6) and Paul (2 Cor. 12:7–9).

The Unpardonable Sin

Q: What is the "unpardonable sin"? Can a person be saved who has committed it? What is the sin against the Holy Spirit?

A: The sin against the Holy Spirit, or, as it is usually called, the "unpardonable sin," is mentioned in Matthew 12:31–32. If you will look at these verses carefully, in context, you will see that it means blasphemy against the Spirit. That is, it is the deliberate attributing to the devil what is known to be the work of the Holy Spirit. The Pharisees knew in their innermost hearts that what Jesus was doing, He was doing by the power of the Spirit of God (see verse 28), but they were not willing to accept Jesus and His claims. In their opposition to Him, they deliberately attributed to the devil, *"Beelzebub"* (v. 24), what in their innermost hearts they knew to be the work of the Spirit of God.

If one commits this sin, he passes beyond the possibility of repentance. He becomes so hardened in sin that he will not come to Jesus. His eternal destiny is sealed.

The great majority of people who imagine they have committed this unpardonable sin really have not. If anyone has a desire to repent and turn to Christ, that in itself is proof that he has not committed it. We have Jesus' own word for it that whoever comes to Him, He will *"by no means cast out"* (John 6:37 NKJV).

Q: Some years ago, I was converted and led a happy Christian life for some time. Then I fell into sin. Now I am in despair, for I think that my case is the one described in Hebrews 6:4–6, and that it is impossible to renew me again to repentance. Is there any hope for me?

A: Yes, there is every hope for you if you will come to Jesus. He said in John 6:37, *"The one who comes to Me I will by no means cast out"* (NKJV). He did not say, "He who was never converted and who comes to Me, I will by no means cast out." He said, *"The one **who comes to Me** I will by no means cast out."* It is evident that you have a desire to come. It is as plain as day in God's Word that God desires you to come. (See Matthew 11:29–30; Revelation 22:17.) Therefore, just come, and you have Jesus' own word for it that He will receive you!

Hebrews 6:4–6 does not describe your situation at all. See how it reads: *"For it is impossible for those who were once enlightened, and have tasted the heavenly gift, and have become partakers of the Holy Spirit, and have tasted the good word of God and the powers of the age to come, if they fall away, to renew them again to repentance, since they crucify again for themselves the Son of God, and put Him to an open shame"* (NKJV).

The difficulty with the one described here is that it is impossible to renew him again to repentance, and that is the reason why he cannot be saved. But you show that you desire to repent. The words in Hebrews 6:4–6 were written to Jewish Christians who were suffering persecution and who were therefore in danger of apostatizing and renouncing Christ and going back to

Judaism. The Holy Spirit was warning them that if they did, after all the light they had had, there would no longer be hope for them because it would be impossible to renew them again to repentance. Later on in the chapter, the writer said that he did not expect any of them to do what is described (Heb. 6:9). The warning itself would help to keep them from doing it.

This passage in Hebrews 6, therefore, does not describe merely a backslider. It describes an apostate, one who not only falls into sin but who, after having been enlightened and having tasted the heavenly gift and having been made an actual partaker of the Holy Spirit, falls away, that is, apostatizes. The Greek word translated *"fall away"* in this passage is used in the Greek translation of the Old Testament (the Septuagint) to describe one who has apostatized from God and gone astray after idols. (See Ezekiel 14:13; 15:8.)

That a mere backslider may come back to God is abundantly proven from many Scriptures. (See Jeremiah 3:12–14; Hosea 14:1–4; Luke 15:11–24.) The apostle Peter himself, after having started to follow Christ, sinned most grievously, denying his Lord with oaths and curses, but his Lord received him back and gave him a greater fullness of blessing than he had ever known before. Anyone who has the desire to repent of sin and return to the Lord Jesus may know clearly from this fact that he is not the person described in Hebrews 6:4–6. I have met many people who were in hopeless despair because they thought their situation was described here. However, after being shown the truth of the Lord Jesus' willingness to receive them if they would come back to Him, they have come back and are now happy and useful Christians.

Q: What is meant by Hebrews 10:26: *"If we sin willfully after we have received the knowledge of the truth, there no longer remains a sacrifice for sins"* (NKJV)? Does it mean that if anyone sins knowingly after he has received the knowledge of the truth, there is no longer any hope of pardon or salvation for him?

A: No, it means nothing of the kind. The words translated *"sin willfully"* mean to sin willingly, voluntarily, of one's own accord.

Such sin is in contrast to the sins committed inconsiderately or from ignorance or weakness. One may sin *knowingly* without sinning *willfully*. He may know that what he is doing is wrong, and yet he does not do it voluntarily—he does not do it willingly, of his own accord—but because the temptation is too strong for him. The word translated *"willfully"* is the same word used in 1 Peter 5:2, where the contrast is drawn between the one who does his work by constraint and the one who does it out of his own glad choice. There are many who sin knowingly but who do not sin willfully in this sense.

If a person, after receiving the knowledge of the truth, deliberately and of his own choice chooses to sin rather than to obey God, there no longer remains a sacrifice for sins for him— only *"a certain fearful expectation of judgment, and fiery indignation"* (Hebrews 10:27 NKJV). Such a person will have no desire to repent.

If one has a desire to repent, this fact, in itself, proves that he has not sinned in this way. No one described in Hebrews 10:26 will be seeking light and desiring to come back to God. The very fact that a person asks such a question as this shows that he is not the person described in Hebrews 10:26.

Victory over Sin

Q: I was converted several years ago, but I am constantly giving way to temptation. I know that my sins are forgiven, but is there any way in which I can have daily victory over sin?

A: There is. The salvation that is offered to us in Jesus Christ is a threefold salvation:

♦ First, there is salvation from the guilt of sin. This we get through the atoning death of Christ on the cross. When Jesus Christ died on the cross of Calvary, He made a perfect atonement for our sins and put them away forever. (See Galatians 3:13; 2 Corinthians 5:21; Hebrews 10:12–14.) The very moment that we accept Him, we are saved from the guilt of sin. Every sin is blotted out. It is just as if we had never sinned. Our standing before God is perfect. We are justified in His sight. (See Acts 10:43; 13:38–39; 2 Corinthians 5:21.)

♦ Second, there is salvation from the power of sin. This we receive through the resurrection of Jesus Christ, who, having risen from the dead and ascended to the right hand of the Father, *"always lives to make intercession for* [us]" (Heb. 7:25 NKJV). He is *"able to save"* not merely from the uttermost but *"to the uttermost those who come to God through Him"* (v. 25 NKJV). By His resurrection power in our lives, He gives us victory over the power of temptation and sin day by day. Having been reconciled to God by His death, we are now saved day by day from the power of sin by His life, that is, by His resurrection life (Rom. 5:10).

Furthermore, the risen Christ imparts to us His Holy Spirit. What we cannot do in our own strength (namely, overcome sin) the Spirit of God whom the risen Christ gives to dwell in us accomplishes for us (Rom. 8:1–4). So then, the way to get daily victory over sin is to stop trying to fight sin with your own strength. Look up to the risen Christ, believing that He has all power in heaven and on earth and that He therefore has power to set you free from the power of sin. Just trust Him to do it.

Additionally, surrender your whole life to the control of the Holy Spirit. Ask Him to come in and take possession of all your desires, all your purposes, all your plans, all your thoughts. He will do it. He will bear His own fruit in your life—*"love, joy, peace, longsuffering, kindness, goodness, faithfulness, gentleness, self-control"* (Gal. 5:22–23 NKJV). If we *"walk in the Spirit"* (v. 16 NKJV), that is, submit our whole lives to His control, we will not *"fulfill the lust of the flesh"* (v. 16 NKJV).

♦ Third, there is salvation from the very presence of sin. This we will obtain through Christ's coming again. This we will enjoy when He does come again, and when we are made perfectly like Him because we see Him as He is (1 John 3:2).

"What Would Jesus Do?"

Q: Should the thought, "What would Jesus do?" be the standard for Christian conduct and practice today?

A: It certainly should, and it is the only standard. We read in 1 John 2:6, *"He who says he abides in Him ought himself also to walk just as He walked"* (NKJV). The standard of Christian living is not the Ten Commandments. It is not even the Golden Rule. It is Jesus Himself. Our Lord Jesus gave to His disciples a new law that includes the old but goes far beyond it. The new law is this: *"That you love one another; as I have loved you, that you also love one another"* (John 13:34 NKJV). If we study the life of Jesus and see what He did under the circumstances in which He lived when He was here on earth, then, under the Spirit's teaching, we can decide what He would do if He were in our circumstances today. The question for the Christian is never "What do other Christians do?" or "What do other Christians tell me to do?" but "What would Jesus want me to do, and what would Jesus Himself do?"

The World's Condition

Q: Is the world becoming better or worse?

A: If you use the word *world* in the biblical sense, that is, denoting the great body of mankind who reject Jesus Christ, then undoubtedly it is growing worse. The Bible says that *"the whole world* [that is, the whole mass of men excluding those who accept Jesus Christ, who are not of the world (see John 15:19)] *lies under the sway of the wicked one"* (1 John 5:19 NKJV). Therefore, the world cannot do anything but grow worse all the time it goes on rejecting Christ.

But if, by "the world," you mean the whole human race, there are two developments going on in it—a good development in those who have come out of the world and have accepted Jesus Christ (who are constantly growing better), and an evil development in those who reject Christ (who are constantly growing worse). In outward things, of course, the world is affected more or less by the believers who are in it, and this leads to many reforms. However, the Bible says that *"evil men and impostors will proceed from bad to worse, deceiving and being deceived"* (2 Tim. 3:13 NAS), and that *"in latter times some will depart from the faith, giving heed to deceiving spirits and doctrines of demons"* (1 Tim. 4:1 NKJV). Second Timothy 3:1–5 says, *"But know this, that in the last days perilous times will come: for men will be lovers of themselves, lovers of money, boasters, proud, blasphemers, disobedient to parents, unthankful, unholy, unloving, unforgiving, slanderers, without self-control, brutal, despisers of good, traitors, headstrong, haughty, lovers of pleasure rather than lovers of God, having a form of godliness but denying its power"* (NKJV). It will be difficult to find genuine faith on the earth when the Son of Man comes. (See Luke 18:8.)

Furthermore, the time is coming when the church will be taken out of the world, and then an awful state of things will go on in this earth, as described in the book of Revelation.

Again, there can be no question in the mind of anyone today that there has been a terrible moral decline in the past few years. This may be seen in the business world. Many of the leading businessmen, whom everyone has trusted, have been found guilty of a misapplication of funds that is so great it should have landed them in the penitentiary. This may also be seen in the terrible increase in immorality in all classes of society. Shameless adultery is on the increase. Divorces are multiplying; men are divorcing their wives and marrying other women with apparently no sense of shame. The increase of immorality among young men and women is appalling. Suicide is becoming alarmingly common. All this is undoubtedly due to the spread of skeptical and unbelieving views. Belief in a horrible future hell has declined enormously in the past few years. Even many ministers of the Gospel neither preach nor believe in a dreadful hell. Everywhere, people are questioning the authority and inerrancy of the Bible—in universities and theological seminaries and in supposedly orthodox pulpits. This appalling harvest of evil and sin is simply the result of the sowing of the seeds of skepticism and unbelief.

About the Author

Reuben Archer Torrey (1856–1928) was born in Hoboken, New Jersey, on January 28, 1856. He graduated from Yale University in 1875 and from Yale Divinity School in 1878.

Upon his graduation, Dr. Torrey became a Congregational minister. A few years later, he joined Dwight L. Moody in his evangelistic work in Chicago and became the pastor of the Chicago Avenue Church. He was selected by D. L. Moody to become the first dean of the Moody Bible Institute of Chicago. Under his direction, Moody Institute became a pattern for Bible institutes around the world.

Torrey is respected as one of the greatest evangelists of modern times. At the turn of the century, Torrey began his evangelistic tours and crusades. He spent the years of 1903–1905 in a worldwide revival campaign, along with the famous song leader Charles McCallon Alexander. Together they ministered in many parts of the world and reportedly brought nearly one hundred thousand souls to Jesus. Torrey continued worldwide crusades for the next fifteen years, eventually reaching Japan and China. During those same years, he served as Dean of the Bible Institute of Los Angeles and pastored the Church of the Open Door in that city.

Torrey longed for more Christian workers to take an active part in bringing the message of salvation through Christ to a lost and dying world. His straightforward style of evangelism has shown thousands of Christian workers how to become effective soulwinners.

Dr. Torrey died on October 26, 1928. He is well remembered today for his inspiring devotional books on the Christian life, which have been translated into many different languages. Woven throughout his many books, the evangelistic message that sent Torrey around the world still ministers to all whose hearts yearn to lead men, women, and children to salvation through Jesus Christ.